D1250191

Battling for Souls

Also by Alex Grobman

Denying History: Who Says the Holocaust Never Happened, and Why Do They Say It?

In Defense of the Survivors: The Letters and Documents of Oscar A. Mintzer, AJDC Legal Advisor, Germany, 1945-46

American Jewish Chaplains and the Survivors of European Jewry: 1944-1948

Genocide: Critical Issues of the Holocaust

Battling for Souls:

The Vaad Hatzala Rescue Committee in Post-Holocaust Europe

by

Alex Grobman

10104

KTAV PUBLISHING HOUSE, INC.
Jersey City, NJ

© Alex Grobman and Joseph Alpert

Grobman, Alex.

   Battling for souls: the Vaad Hatzala rescue
committee in post-Holocaust Europe / by
Alex Grobman.

      p. cm.
   Includes bibliographical references.
   ISBN 0-88125-843-1
   1. Vaad Hatzala (New York, N.Y.)--History. 2.
Baruch, Nathan. 3. Jews--Charities. 4. Holocaust
survivors--Social conditions. 5. Europe--Emigration
and immigration. 6. United States--Emigration and
immigration. 7. Reconstruction (1939-1951)--Reli-
gious aspects--Judaism. I. Title.
   D829.J4G76 2004
   940.53'187'0607471--dc22   2004007881

Published by KTAV

Picture taken at the hidden synagogue in the
Theresienstadt concentration camp.
The inscription reads:
"But despite all this we have not forgotten Your name.
We beg You not to forget us."
Photo courtesy of William Spivak, M.D.

Dedication

This book is dedicated to Rabbi Nathan Baruch and all those rabbis and lay leaders of the Vaad Hatzala who were their brothers' keepers. They worked long and hard to save lives, revitalize the *Yiddishkeit* and spirit of the *She'erith Hapleitah*, transcending ideology and organizational loyalty to rebuild religious communities and make them thrive.

This book is also dedicated to Rabbi Aharon Kotler, *z"tl*, the *rosh yeshiva* who inspired the Vaad and thousands of its supporters. He predicted that once it escaped the black abyss of Europe, the yeshiva movement would rebuild itself and flourish in America's freedom.

Table of Contents

Acknowledgments

Though there have been studies that have examined the role of American Jewish relief organizations in post-war Europe after the Holocaust, none has focused on the work of the Vaad Hatzala. Established in November 1939 by the Agudas Harabonim (Union of Orthodox Rabbis of the United States and Canada), the foremost American Orthodox rabbinical association, the Vaad sought to rescue rabbis, yeshiva students and, ultimately, any Jews they could in Poland and Lithuania. After the war, the Vaad sent representatives to Europe to assist in the spiritual rehabilitation of the *She'erith Hapleitah* (the surviving remnant).

This work concentrates on the activities of Rabbi Nathan Baruch, the director of the Vaad in the American Zone of Germany from September 1946 to mid-September 1948. Its focus is on the objectives of his mission, the challenges he encountered in Europe and the struggles within the American Jewish community that impeded his work. This is not a comprehensive study of Vaad activities in Europe, although Baruch directed the Vaad's European headquarters in Paris for some time.

The book begins with an overview of conditions in Germany after the war, a catalogue of challenges facing all areas of the post-war Jewish community, and a look at the organizations—including the American Army—providing relief and rehabilitation.

We endeavor to describe many things: Nathan Baruch's origins; the establishment of the Vaad Hatzala before and during the war years; the efforts to secure visas to the United States and find positions for rabbis and yeshiva students; the need to establish kosher kitchens and provide kosher food, *mikvehs* (ritual baths), *yeshivos* and educational facilities, ceremonial objects and programs to the survivors. We attempt to describe the great pressure Baruch had to endure in order to respond to a plethora of requests from the survivors and the Vaad office in New York. Finally, we describe the incongruous role of the Vaad as a publishing house of Jewish religious texts. All of these projects have one thing in common: Rabbi Nathan Baruch working as the emissary of the Vaad for the spiritual and religious revitalization of the *She'erith Hapleitah*.

In the course of writing this book, many institutions and individuals helped me, and I am most grateful to them. In addition to the use of Rabbi Nathan Baruch's personal papers and photographs, the following archives of the Jewish community were made available to me: The Vaad Hatzala, the Central Orthodox Committee (COC), Rescue Children Inc., and Maurice Enright at Yeshiva University; the Leo Schwarz Collection at YIVO; Abraham Hyman Archives; the Agudath Israel Archives in England and the United States, and the JDC Archives in New York and Israel.

There were many people who went above and beyond the call of duty to assist me in this work. They are Shulamith Z. Berger, Curator of Special Collections at Yeshiva University; Sarah Saiger of Yeshiva University Archives; Zalman Alpert, a research librarian at Yeshiva University; Rachel Keegan of the American Jewish Historical Society; Marek Web, head of the YIVO Archives and Yeshaya Metal of YIVO; Rabbi Moshe Kolodny, director of the Agudath Israel of America Archives; Amir Shaviv, executive vice president of the JDC, Sherry Hyman, director of the JDC Archives in New York and Shelly Helfand, archivist at the JDC Archives in New York; Dr. Sara Kadosh, director of the Archives at the American Jewish Joint Distribution Committee in Israel. I also would like to thank Shayna Malov who transcribed hours of taped interviews with Rabbi Nathan Baruch. Without their help this work would not have been possible.

I am extremely indebted to Rabbi Isaac and Mrs. Molly Fuhrman, my mentors during my youth, who inculcated me with spirituality that continues to sustain me in my work. Bud Levin has encouraged my research through the years and has acted as a beacon and a friend.

ii

I would also like to thank several other friends: Robert Felix, Aaron Rabin, Stanley Raskas and Arnold Yagoda. Throughout the months of my research and writing, they patiently listened to each new revelation and offered their insights and perspectives. I am also indebted to Joseph Alpert and George Klein for sharing their papers and experiences about their fathers, men who played vital roles in the Vaad. I also am grateful to Billy Spivak, Bennett Ruda, David Kranzler, the pioneer of research on Orthodox Jewry during the war, and Norman Sohn for their insights and Kenneth R. Tauber for sharing his father's papers with me. My wife, Marlene, has my heartfelt appreciation and gratitude for her support and for putting up with the tension engendered in the creation of a book. My sons Elon, Ranan, Ari, their wives Aviva, Karen, and Rochel and my grandchildren Tova, Tamar, Ephraim Elimelech, Chana, Binyamin, Akiva, Aliza, Nomi, Avigail, Bat-Sheva and Ayelet continue to be an inspiration and a source of strength.

My thanks to my dear friends and neighbors the Alperts: Gila, Joe, Ori, Elisa, Pirchi, Shoshana, Shiri, Chagit and Leeby, who were involved in countless discussions about the Vaad at their Shabbos table. They added another important dimension to my understanding of the subject. I also discussed many of these of issues with Rabbi Yale Butler, a veteran journalist, who participated in the only interview (July 20, 1979) about the Vaad Hatzala ever granted by Rabbi Simcha Wasserman, a Vaad emissary in Europe and America during and after the war. I would also like to thank my parents Reba and Frank (of Blessed Memory) Grobman and my in-laws, Belle and Joseph Weisblum. To expedite the publication of this work, I asked my talented friends and colleagues, Jeanette Friedman and Dr. Philip Sieradski of The Wordsmithy do the initial editing of the book as I was writing it, with special thanks to Jeanette for the finishing touches. Ethel Gottlieb's insight and editing skills were of great help in the final draft of the manuscript. Daniel Weiss' help with the bibliography was most appreciated. I thank them for their sage advice and care in preparing the manuscript for publication. Any omissions or errors are completely my responsibility.

Abbreviations

AJC	American Jewish Committee
AH	Abraham Hyman Archives
BMG	Holocaust Archives of Beth Medrash Gevoha
CCDP	Citizens Committee on Displaced Persons
CID	Criminal Investigation Division (USA)
COSAJOR	Comité Juive d'Action pour l'Assistance Sociale et la Reconstruction
COC	The Jewish Central Orthodox Committee
CRC	Central Relief Committee (Yeshiva University Archives)
DM	Deutsche Marks (German money)
DPs	Displaced Persons
DPC	United States Displaced Persons Commission
EUCOM	European Command (U.S.)
HIAS	The Hebrew Immigrant Aid Society
IGC	Intergovernmental Committee on Refugees
INS	United States Immigration and Naturalization Service
IRO	International Refugee Organization
JDC, AJDC	American Jewish Joint Distribution Committee
JWB	National Jewish Welfare Board
PCIRO	Preparatory Commission of International Refugee Organization
RNB FILE	Rabbi Nathan Baruch Files
SHAEF	Supreme Headquarters, Allied Expeditionary Force
UNNRA	United Nations Relief and Rehabilitation Administration
NRS	National Refugee Service
UJA	United Jewish Appeal
USFET	U.S. Forces in the European Theater
USNA	United Service for New Americans
WJC	World Jewish Congress
YIVO	YIVO Institute for Jewish Research
YUA	Yeshiva University Archives

Introduction:
Historical Background

Liberation

At the end of the World War II, there were between ten and eleven million displaced persons (DPs) in Germany and Austria. These millions of uprooted people were concentration camp inmates, slave laborers, prisoners of war, voluntary workers and foreign volunteers who had been taken to the Third Reich by the Nazis during the final months of the war.

The Allies anticipated that there would be millions of displaced persons, but were unsure how many to expect. Estimates ranged from nine to thirty million refugees, but in the end, after the majority of the DPs were repatriated, approximately 800,000 from Eastern Europe remained in the area.[1] Of these 800,000, there were approximately 200,000 Jews who had survived the concentration and extermination camps and the death marches. Many of them

1

returned to their hometowns in Hungary, Slovakia and Romania. A very small number remained in the DP camps in Germany and Austria after the summer of 1945. Survivors from Western Europe also returned to their homes, leaving about 55,000 Jews. The numbers in the DP camps increased when Jews hidden in Poland, Jewish deserters from Communist Polish armed forces, demobilized troops, and remnants of the Jewish partisans in Poland found their way into Western Germany.[2]

Most of the survivors from Poland and Lithuania and those who fled to Siberia and Central Asia were averse to returning to their former homes where their loved ones had been murdered. Those who did go back went to search for family and friends. Many went on foot and hitchhiked, wandering from one town to the next. Although they were aware that most of their family members were dead, they "clung to the slender hope" that perhaps somehow, somewhere, a family member had survived.[3]

Wherever the survivors went in Poland, they registered with local Jewish committees in major cities and in provincial regions. The walls in these "public service" offices were covered with handwritten names and addresses of survivors that friends and relatives could use to find each other and reconnect. Because Jews registered in many different places, we cannot know precisely how many lived in any one place at any given time.[4]

Another problem in determining the exact number of Jewish DPs is that there were between a few hundred to a few thousand Jews who decided to assume Polish identities after the war and severed their ties with the Jewish people. An additional several thousand Jewish children who had found refuge in convents, boarding schools and monasteries during the war years were purposely not returned to the Jewish people despite efforts to find them and/or ransom them.[5]

Some survivors went back to their former homes out of a "desire to settle in large groups of their own kind, partly out of concern for their physical safety, partly in response to their deep-seated need to live among their brethren."[6]

These groups were concentrated mainly in Lower Silesia,

where the former German inhabitants had been removed. Returning concentration camp inmates, including some Poles and those returning from the Soviet Union, eventually repopulated the area.[7]

Not all Jews who returned home were eager to rebuild their lives in Poland. Often, Jews were met with expressions of surprise by their former countrymen: "What, still alive?" or "What? Still so many Jews left?" Some Poles were convinced that they were seeing ghosts. Adding insult to injury, many Jews were harassed and some were arrested for having collaborated with the Nazis.[8]

It was a Nazi policy to permit non-Jewish locals to appropriate Jewish apartments and property during the war. This served two purposes: it was necessary in order to carry out the Nazi's dirty work and it was an incentive for Polish natives to help Germans carry out the Final Solution. Many Jews had their homes and possessions expropriated by former neighbors and friends with no possibility of restitution. Those who asked for the return of their property and possessions did so at great physical risk: Between November 1944 and the summer of 1947 as many as 1,000 Polish Jews were murdered. In 1946, there were pogroms in Lodz and Krakow.[9]

The event with the most significant impact on the Jews of Poland was the pogrom in Kielce on July 4, 1946.[10] Before the war, approximately 20,000 Jews lived in Kielce, constituting almost a third of its population. At the end of the war, only some 250 souls remained. Several factors made the Kielce pogrom particularly ominous. The pogrom lasted an entire day in a large urban center, and hundreds of Poles of all ages and economic backgrounds participated in it. Men in uniform lured the Jews out of their barricaded homes and handed them over to the mob. Forty-seven people were killed and more than fifty were injured.[11]

As a result, Polish Jews began a mass exodus to Western Europe. Almost all of the 176,000 Jews who returned to Poland after liberation from the Soviet Union fled to DP camps in the American Zones in Germany and Austria. By the middle of 1947, there were 250,000 Jews in Germany, Austria, and

3

Italy, mostly in DP camps. Fifty thousand were also billeted in France and in the Low Countries.[12]

In the American Zones, there were a number of official and unofficial organizations involved with relief and rehabilitation of Jewish DPs. These included:

• The United States Armed Forces;

• The United Nations Relief and Rehabilitation Administration (UNRRA), founded in 1943 by the UN to provide relief to people in areas stricken by war;

• The American Jewish Joint Distribution Committee (the Joint or JDC) established in November 1914, whose primary role was the rescue, relief and rehabilitation of world Jewry;

• The Hebrew Immigrant Aid Society (HIAS), established in 1881, an international migration and refugee resettlement agency that helped newly arrived Jews adjust to life in the United States;

• The World Jewish Congress (WJC), an international "voluntary association" of representative Jewish bodies, institutions, and communities organized to defend the interests of Jews and Jewish communities throughout the world;

• The Advisors on Jewish Affairs, a position created by the American Army in August 1945, to inform the Commanding General in the European Theater of any problems affecting the Jewish DPs;

• The Jewish Agency for Palestine;

• Organization for Rehabilitation through Training (ORT) that established rehabilitation and vocational training programs in the DP camps;

• The Vaad Hatzala, an organization founded in 1939 by the Orthodox rabbinate, was initially dedicated to the rescue of the *b'nei Torah*, the eminent rabbis and yeshiva students in Europe before, during and after the war.

Although not officially charged with aiding the DPs, the Jewish Brigade, composed of Jewish volunteers from Palestine who joined the British Army, did so anyway. Mostly, they assisted through *Brichah*, the illicit movement that smuggled Jews out of Europe and into Palestine. Established in

4

September 1944, the Brigade worked with survivors in Italy and later with those in Germany.[13]

Also among the unofficial personnel aiding the DPs, and among the first Jews to encounter Jewish survivors, were the American Jewish chaplains in the U.S. Armed Forces. They played a significant role in providing immediate relief and aid—most often as a spontaneous response to the suffering before their eyes.[14]

In addition to the larger relief organizations, there were a number of other groups catering to their own constituencies among the Jewish DPs. Included were: Agudath Israel, the Mizrachi Organization of America (religious Zionists), Young Israel, the Lubavitcher Hasidim and Rabbi Yekusiel Halberstam, the Klausenberger Rebbe. All were involved to some extent with the JDC and the Vaad Hatzala. (Those who became involved with the Vaad were mostly from Agudath Israel and a few from Mizrachi. They made up the core of the Vaad, though there were times when their religious and political differences impeded their ability to work together.)

Ezras Torah, a nonprofit Jewish relief organization established in 1915 by the Agudas Harabonim in the United States with the aid of the Mizrachi, also assisted the survivors. At the request of the Chofetz Chaim, Rabbi Yisrael Meir HaKohen and Rav Hayyim Ozer Grodzinski, Ezras Torah was created during World War I to help refugee rabbis, Torah scholars, their families and other starving and impoverished Jews. Under the leadership of Rabbi Yosef Eliyahu Henkin, considered to be among the most eminent *poskim* (Torah authorities), Ezras Torah sent money to Holocaust survivors and helped them once they reached the United States and the *Yishuv*.[15]

Agudath Israel (The Agudah)

Established in May 1912 at Kattowitz in Upper Silesia, the primary goal of the Agudath Israel (the Agudah) world movement was to ensure that *halacha* (Jewish law) guided every area of Jewish life and society. The leadership of the

Agudah felt that Jewish social and religious institutions, the religious way of life, the social values and moral conduct found in the Jewish communities of Eastern and Central Europe during the 19th century, were the absolute model for Jewish life that was to be emulated as Jews faced the 20th Century.

This association brought together German neo-Orthodoxy, Hungarian Orthodoxy and the Hasidic and Misnagdic communities of Poland and Lithuania. Agudath Israel was intended to be a corrective counterforce to the inroads made by the opponents of Hasidism, the Reform movement, assimilation, secular Zionism and the socialist Jewish Labor Bund. Branches of Agudath Israel were created throughout the Ashkenazi world. For the first time, Western European Jews of Germany, Holland, and Hungary joined with Eastern European Jewry of Poland, Lithuania and Latvia under a unified organization.

The Agudah also organized a young men's movement (Zeirei Agudath Israel), Pirchei for youngsters to age 13, and a women's movement (Neshei Agudath Israel and its youth movement B'nos). Agudath Israel was also the driving force behind the Bais Yaakov movement, founded by Sara Schenirer in Krakow, and was a key factor in ushering in a new era in Jewish life—one with religiously educated women.

The Council of Torah Sages, known as the Mo'etzes Gedolei haTorah, was created by the Agudah to offset the ideological intrusion of the German rabbinate that acknowledged secular learning as also important to Torah devotion. The council's decisions "were binding" and viewed "as the guiding force of the movement." Rabbi Hayyim Ozer Grodzinski, the leading rabbinical authority in Lithuania and of world Jewry, became chairman of the council[16] and, in 1939, with the creation of the Vaad, Rabbi Eliezer Silver established the American wing of the Agudah.

Beginning of the Vaad Hatzala

After the German invasion of Poland on September 1, 1939, and after the Soviets occupied eastern Poland later that month,[17] the Jewish community of Vilna, like so many others in the region, was inundated by an immense influx of Jewish refugees. Appeals for food, money and clothing quickly reached America.[18] By November 1939, Vilna had an estimated 37,000 to 57,000 refugees.

For the religiously observant, the existence of the major Polish *yeshivos* in the Kresy region of eastern Poland, now annexed by the Soviets, faced an even greater challenge. After living under the communist regime for a time following the end of World War I, a number of the *roshei yeshiva* (rabbinical leadership of the yeshiva) and many of their students knew that the Soviets would suppress Jewish life and institutions. The situation in areas occupied by the Germans was even n:ore precarious.[19]

On October 11, 1939, the Polish Jews learned that the Soviet Union and Lithuania had agreed that Vilna and its surrounding areas would be transferred to the neutral republic of Lithuania. Hundreds of yeshiva students, faculty and administrators from eastern Poland fled to the city, including those from the Bialystok, Slonim, Kaminetz, Mir, Kletzk, Radin and Grodno *yeshivos*. By late October, approximately 3,000 Torah scholars arrived in Vilna as refugees. Among the leading rabbis and *roshei yeshiva* were Rabbis Aharon Kotler (Kletzk), Boruch Ber Leibowitz (Kaminetz), Avraham Yaffen (Beis Yoseph of Bialystok), Elchonon Wasserman (Ohel Torah of Baranowich), Eliezer Yehuda Finkel (Mir), Shabsai Yogel (Slonim) and Yitzchak Ze'ev Soloveitchik (Brisk).[20]

As totalitarian communism loomed, the rabbis feared for the spiritual lives of their students and themselves and sought refuge from the impending danger. They had no idea of the life-threatening events that lay ahead. Under the direction of Rabbi Aryeh Leib Malin, a "shtarke" (strong-willed) member of the Mir yeshiva, Moshe Zupnick, a student from Frankfurt, Germany at the Yeshiva of Mir, and Nosson Gutwirth, a Dutch student at Telshe in Lithuania, acquired visas for the students and faculty of Mir so they could emigrate. Jan Zwartendyk, the honorary Dutch consul, and the Japanese Consul-General Sempo (Chiune) Sugihara in Kovno,

Lithuania, provided them with Dutch "exit visas," and together with Soviet exit visas granting them permission to travel to Odessa, they were able to find a safe haven in Shanghai, China for the duration of the war. For fourteen days, Zupnick went to the Consulate to help Sugihara stamp visas into the passports of some 2,400 members of the yeshiva.

In the discussions within Mir about how to respond to the threats of communism and the Nazis, Rabbi Malin strongly advocated finding asylum outside of Lithuania. He served "as chief of operations" in the yeshiva's unofficial quest to find refuge, and raised funds to secure the necessary travel documents. He declared that just as the *Kohanim* (the priests) had fought with their lives against the Greeks who sought to eradicate the Torah and deny belief in God, the Jews had to escape the communists.[21]

In response to the yeshiva refugee community in Vilna and other cities in Lithuania—and at the urging of Rabbi Grodzinski—Rabbi Eliezer Silver established the Orthodox Rabbis' Rescue Committee/Vaad Hatzala in November 1939, under the auspices of the Union of Orthodox Rabbis of the United States and Canada (Agudas Harabonim).

It was natural for the Vaad Hatzala to be under the auspices of the Union of Orthodox Rabbis, or Agudas Harabonim. Founded in New York on July 29, 1902, the Union was established to stem the tide of assimilation among new Jewish immigrants in the United States. The rabbis were deeply troubled that Sabbath observance was practically nonexistent, that laws of *kashrus* (keeping kosher) were being ignored, and rabbinical functions such as marriage and divorce were being conducted irresponsibly. Individual rabbis could not fight effectively to preserve *halacha* and tradition, but a united American rabbinate, including practically all the prominent rabbis from Eastern Europe living in America, made the Agudas Harabonim a potent force within the Orthodox community.[22]

Rabbi Eliezer Silver, who lived in Cincinnati, Ohio, became the first president of the Vaad Hatzala because he was a prominent Torah leader, a major spokesman for the American Orthodox Jewish community and a former student of Rabbi Grodzinski. Rabbi Avraham Kalmanowitz, *rosh yeshiva* of the Mir Yeshiva's American branch, joined Rabbi Silver as the initial impetus behind the Vaad. His involvement had a significant impact on the American Orthodox Jewish community and increased their support for the Vaad. In March 1941, the Agudah gained a considerable infusion of energy with the arrival of Rabbi Aharon Kotler. He held a "preeminent" position among the Orthodox rabbinate and was determined to build a Torah center in the United States to replace those bastions of Jewish study destroyed in Europe. Rabbi Kotler foresaw that the future of Torah study would be in America and devoted the rest of his life to building a network of educational institutions to ensure that goal. The Agudah also received additional support from K'hal Adath Jeshurun, the German Jewish community led by Rabbi Joseph Breuer in Washington Heights, New York and from a number of Hasidic rabbis.[23]

During the first two years of the Vaad's existence, it supplied relief to 2,400 rabbis and yeshiva students. This included almost all the people from the *yeshivos* of Mir, Kletzk, Radin, Kaminetz and Baranowich. From October 1940 to June 1941 the Vaad helped 650 of these rabbis and yeshiva students emigrate. A number went to the United States, some to Palestine (with visas obtained through the efforts of Chief Rabbi Isaac H. Herzog and Chief Rabbi of England Joseph H. Hertz), but the majority—about 500—went to Shanghai, where most stayed until the war ended. The Vaad also procured 80 Canadian visas for scholars in the fall of 1941, but only 29 managed to enter Canada.[24]

After December 7, 1941 when the United States entered World War II, the Vaad focused its relief efforts on the rabbis who had escaped to Shanghai and the several hundred rabbis and yeshiva students who were still in Soviet Central Asia. The group in the Soviet Union had been deported to Siberia by the Soviets before the Nazi invasion of Russia in June 1941, and was released as part of the Sikorski-Stalin Agreement of July 31, 1941. The Vaad sent both groups money and packages of food and clothing to enable them to continue their religious studies and Torah way of life, though they were precluded from doing so by the Soviet regime.[25]

When it became clear in 1942—from cables sent by Vaad representative Recha Sternuch and Gerhard Riegner of the World Jewish Congress in Switzerland—that the Nazis were systematically killing Eastern European Jewry, the Vaad embarked on a political campaign to rescue the Jewish leadership still under Nazi rule. In 1944, it expanded its activities to include all Jews regardless of religious persuasion. Through its branches in Sweden, Switzerland, Turkey and Tangier, the Vaad initiated relief and rescue operations and had an ongoing relationship with the Orthodox leadership of Hungary and Slovakia.[26]

As a result of negotiations begun by the Vaad between Heinrich Himmler, head of the Gestapo and the Waffen-SS, and former Swiss politician Jean-Marie Musy, 1,200 Jewish inmates of the Theresienstadt concentration camp in Czechoslovakia were sent to Switzerland in February 1945. Even though the war was almost over, a controversy erupted within the American Jewish community because the Vaad had transferred funds to Europe to ransom Jews. The Vaad was accused of being unpatriotic because what it had done ran counter to the "spirit, if not the letter" of American statutes. Throughout the war, the JDC and other Jewish organizations, for the public record, followed American regulations to the letter, and opposed any group that refused to do so.[27]

The Vaad aroused additional controversy over two other of its practices. Though the American Jewish community decided to combine its foreign and domestic fundraising campaigns under the auspices of the United Jewish Appeal, the Vaad insisted on conducting its own separate appeal for funds. This, coupled with the Vaad's decision to give priority to rabbis and yeshiva students, made it seem to some of the American Jewish community to be parochial and self-absorbed.[28]

Attempt to Unite Agudath Israel and Mizrachi

As well as being ideologically committed to the Agudah, Rabbi Eliezer Silver had been closely connected to it through his relationship with Rabbi Grodzinski. Yet he had also been involved with the Mizrachi in the United States, since most of the American rabbinate were in the Mizrachi movement. Rabbi Silver attended their conferences and raised funds for their institutions. He did so because the Agudah did not exist in America until 1939 (when he himself created it) and because he felt a kinship with his colleagues and friends in the Mizrachi movement. At one point he even referred to the organization as his "younger sister."[29]

In November 1933, Rabbi Silver proposed a merger between the Mizrachi and the Agudah at the convention of the Agudath Harabonim and the United Orthodox Rabbis of the United States and Canada, established in 1902. "Perhaps we can arrange for a central authority for all Orthodoxy. We must no longer suffer disunity," he proclaimed.[30]

Despite his efforts, Rabbi Silver did not succeed in bringing Agudah and Mizrachi together, but this did not deter him from trying again. After returning from Agudath Israel's third Great Assembly in Marienbad, Czechoslovakia in 1937, where he met the leading rabbis and scholars in the Council of Torah Sages, he sent a letter to his fellow rabbis urging that the Orthodox rabbinate in America begin assuming a key role in Agudath Israel.

"How much longer will we separate ourselves from these leaders of Torah?" he asked. "The time has come to overcome our hesitations, and to unite with the *gaeonim* [sic] (Torah giants) of the world."

More than 60 rabbis were willing to join Agudath Israel, but the Mizrachi vigorously opposed the idea as potentially divisive to its organization. Rabbi Silver responded that he merely wanted to bring together Jewish American and European scholars, but this did not persuade the Mizrachi.[31]

Why was Mizrachi—an abbreviation for *merkaz ruhani* (spiritual center)—concerned about the Agudah establishing an organization in the United States? In large part this was because of basic ideological differences between the two groups and a desire not to have to compete with Agudah for funds, membership, power and prestige. Founded in 1902, in Vilna, Lithuania—with the Mizrachi Organization of America coming into existence in 1911—the Mizrachi was the religious faction within the World Zionist Organization, a political organization that sought to establish a Jewish homeland in *Eretz Israel* (the Land of Israel). Seeking to achieve its goals by working within the Zionist movement, the Mizrachi believed in the return of Jews to *Eretz Israel*, but they also believed that the "Torah...must be the foundation of our regeneration in the land of our fathers."[32] This meant that the Torah, Jewish tradition, and observance of the commandments had to be at the spiritual center of the Zionist movement. They also believed in working with non-observant Jews to achieve this goal.

Rabbi Samuel Mohilever, one of the earliest proponents of religious Zionism, asserted that all the "Sons of Zion" had to work together "in complete harmony and fraternity, even if there be among them differences of opinion regarding religion." Mohilever was motivated by the 1881 pogroms in Russia that forced tens of thousands of Jews to flee to Galicia, Poland, then held by the Austrians. He posited that their attitude toward those who do not observe Jewish law should be as if a fire had broken out in their homes "imperiling our persons and property." If that happened, wouldn't someone who came to rescue them be greeted with "love, even if he were irreligious? Is this not the present plight?" he asked. "A great fire, a fearful conflagration, is raging in our midst, and we are all threatened. Our enemies have multiplied until they surpass many millions...If brethren put out their hands to us in aid, doing all in their power to deliver us from our dire straits, are there such among us as would dare spurn them?"[33]

In contrast, Agudath Israel, though not against the settling of *Eretz Israel* and development of the land when possible, had been established in part by groups who opposed all efforts to revive Jewish nationhood based on the peoplehood of Jews rather than by God. The *Gedolei Yisroel* (leading rabbinic authorities) recognized the potential threat of aligning themselves with the Zionists who wanted to establish a Jewish State on the basis of a Jewish people in a Jewish land without a solid commitment to observance of Torah and *mitzvos* (commandments). The idea of creating a Jewish state based solely on nationalism was contrary to their belief. Any involvement with the Zionist organization that claimed to be representative of Judaism posed a danger to the continuity of a Jewish tradition that had been passed down for centuries in a spirit of holiness and purity.

Many of the Torah sages of Eastern Europe also viewed Zionism as having a negative influence on their children. They disputed the Zionist contention that the Diaspora was a place religiously and socially harmful for Jews. The Agudah also resented the secular and nonreligious elements within the Zionist movement and opposed working with them. They were steadfast against the establishment of a secular Jewish society in the *Yishuv* (pre-state Israel). The secularist culture they saw developing in the settlements there— especially the secularist socialists—was considered by them as undermining and destroying the Torah way of life. Prior to World War II, Agudath Israel had already established itself in *Eretz Israel* to unite all the Jewish people "under the rule of Torah."[34]

Despite opposition from the Mizrachi, Rabbi Silver forged ahead to found Agudath Israel in America. With the influx of new arrivals from Europe, the Agudah had a natural constituency of Jews who wanted to continue their Torah way of life. He approached many of these new Americans to join the Agudah. He even asked the Lubavitcher Rebbe, Rabbi Joseph Isaac Schneersohn, who had arrived in the United States in March 1940, to join as well. The Rebbe told Rabbi Silver that he had been approached by the Mizrachi to join them, but had rejected this invitation outright. He agreed to work with Rabbi Silver and the Agudah, but would not become an official member of the organization.[35]

Eventually, the members and the leadership of the Mizrachi and the Agudah came together with the establishment of the Vaad Hatzala in 1939. With its main mission to save *b'nei Torah*, ideological differences were not supposed to intrude. Though the Agudath Harabonim acted to keep the various factions from using the Vaad to advance their own agendas, given the tensions and rivalry between the two groups and their supporters this was not always possible.

Two other Orthodox groups that were involved in postwar

relief work on behalf of their constituents were the Lubavitcher and the Klausenberger Hasidim. Lubavitch had a long-standing relationship with the JDC, so it was quite natural that it turned to that organization for assistance.[36] The Lubavitchers were never part of the Vaad because Lubavitch operated on its own within the Jewish community.

The Klausenberger Rebbe also did not align himself with the Vaad after the war. Like the Lubavitcher Hasidim, the Rebbe had established ties with the JDC and saw no reason to affiliate himself with the Vaad. Whether it was to ensure that his group received its fair share or whether he wanted to establish his own claim as representative of the fervently Orthodox, Rabbi Yekusiel Halberstam met with representatives of the JDC in New York in early 1947 where he complained that: "The real total material needs of his followers are not understood and are therefore not met by our [JDC] representatives in Germany." He wanted to "develop a long-range plan with the JDC which would maintain close cooperation with him in this country [the U.S.] and with his groups in Europe," where he "wanted greater control over the distribution of food and supplies earmarked for the ultra-orthodox. [sic]" For instance, he asked that his groups receive extra allocations of raisins, wine and flour so they could bake their own matzos for Passover by hand.[37]

Establishment of UNRRA

In the meantime, the military occupying forces had anticipated and developed plans to deal with DPs remaining in Central Europe at the end of the war. The subject was first raised at a cabinet meeting in the Roosevelt Administration as early as October 29, 1942, and continued to be discussed thereafter. On November 29, 1943, the representatives of forty-four allied governments met at the White House, and agreed to establish the United Nations Relief and Rehabilitation Administration (UNRRA), a relief organization that was to provide food, clothing, medical supplies and other forms of aid while the DPs awaited repatriation. Shortly after the creation of UNRRA, the military established a refugee section in the Government Affairs Branch of the Civil Affairs Division of the Supreme Headquarters of the Allied Expeditionary Forces in Europe (SHAEF). In January 1944, the refugee section was renamed the Displaced Persons Section.[38]

Once the military understood the extent of the problems the DPs faced, it expanded the DP Section. On May 1, 1944, UNRRA began to function as a separate branch of the Civilian Affairs Division, G-5, of the Army, serving as a subordinate administrative branch.[39]

In November 1944, SHAEF and UNRRA signed an agreement detailing the responsibilities each would assume with regard to the DPs. The American Army would provide food, clothing, and medical supplies and ensure the security of those living in the DP centers and camps. UNRRA would be responsible for the administration of the camps, provide supplementary supplies, recreational facilities, vocational guidance, self-help programs, as well as health and welfare services. UNRRA would also supply tobacco, toilet articles and other amenities. In an agreement signed on February 19, 1946, UNRRA agreed to further supervise educational programs for the DPs, establish a records office and tracing bureau and prepare statistics and research reports. The U.S. Army, however, was ultimately responsible for all movement of the DPs and "United Nations' citizens."[40]

UNRRA was hampered from functioning effectively because of a number of fundamental problems. UNRRA workers were chosen in haste and were not properly trained. Many were ex-soldiers who decided to remain in Germany—having nothing better to return to in the U.S. Many had German mistresses and "business connections" that afforded them good incomes. Many were incompetent, inefficient, unwilling or incapable of adapting to the fluid situation in Germany, and unable to communicate with the DPs because they did not possess the requisite language skills. Furthermore, UNRRA policies were confusing; its programs were not coordinated and were poorly administered. UNRRA's ability to function was further exacerbated by its poor relationship with the military.[41] Nevertheless, it is still important to note, that within UNRRA, as in the military, there were many dedicated individuals who did their best to help the DPs, despite the ineffectiveness of some of their programs.[42]

On October 1, 1945, several months after the war ended, the responsibility for the care of the DPs became the responsibility of the American, British and French commanding generals in each of their respective zones of occupation. The Russians were not involved because they refused to acknowledge that a DP problem existed in their zone. This was not the way it had been planned. To coordinate DP affairs and assist in the administrative transition, the Combined Displaced Persons Executive (CDPX) was established in July 1945. The CDPX represented the Americans, British and French, UNRRA and the Intergovernmental Committee on Refugees (IGC), an international organization founded in 1938 to assist refugees. After the CDPX was designated to cease functioning, UNRRA was supposed to assume its responsibilities, but the absence of enough personnel made it virtually impossible to do so.[43]

Because there were hundreds of thousands more DPs who stayed in Germany after the war than had been anticipated, centers that were designed to hold 2,000-3,000 people held more than 10,000. When the American Army asked for 450 UNRRA teams to accommodate these large numbers, UNRRA did not have enough personnel to send them. This placed the burden of responsibility on the military officers and soldiers in the field.

UNRRA teams were disproportionately understaffed. Teams that should have had thirteen people only had seven. In July 1945, the number increased to ten. At times, teams that were supposed to work with 2,000 DPs ended up with as many as four or five times that amount. Though Herbert H. Lehman, the former governor of New York and the Director-General of UNRRA, wanted 5,000-6,000 UNRRA workers in place by the summer of 1945, he ended up with only 2,656 by July.[44]

It is clear that "the problems encountered by the occupying troops in handling so many diverse groups and individuals found no parallel in previous military history. The logistics of processing, moving, feeding, clothing and communicating with these disparate groups boggled the mind."[45] Yet the military managed to repatriate almost 6,000,000 refugees between May and September 1945, while at the same time dismantling its own forces.[46]

The Jews, however, posed a number of problems for the Allies beyond those of the other DPs. This included their legal status; the need for kosher food for those who wanted to observe Jewish law after so many years of being unable to do so; their need for clothing, shelter, physical and spiritual rehabilitation, medical care and their desire to reestablish contact with families and friends. After years of systematic persecution and mass murder, it was understandable that the Jews would expect the Allies to provide them with special treatment. The need for separate camps was especially important to prevent them from sharing the same living space with their former tormentors.[47]

The Allies, however, were not prepared to treat the Jews any differently from other DPs. The British feared that the Jews would then exploit their special status to obtain visas to enter Palestine, which they bitterly opposed.[48] The Americans rejected the idea of special treatment because as one American War Department pamphlet written in 1944 stated, "such action will tend to perpetuate the distinction of Nazi racial theory."[49] Because fraternization rules prohibited contact with the survivors, unfortunately even some American Jewish soldiers shared this view.[50]

The JDC

When the first JDC representatives arrived in Germany in July 1945, three months after the Jews had been liberated, they found much chaos and little efficiency. Founded in 1914, the JDC's mission was to assist impoverished Jews in Palestine and Europe. In August of that year, Henry Morgenthau, Sr., then United States Ambassador to Turkey, sent a telegram to Jacob H. Schiff, head of Kuhn Loeb and Company, the most prominent Jewish banking house in

America, asking him to raise $50,000 to be sent to the Jews of Palestine who were being persecuted and starved by the hostile Turkish authorities.[51] At that time, the Jews of Palestine depended almost entirely on charity sent from abroad.[52]

Schiff brought the request to his friends at the American Jewish Committee (AJC), an organization founded in 1906 to protect Jewish civil and religious rights throughout the world and "to alleviate the consequences of persecution and to afford relief from calamities affecting Jews, wherever they occur."[53] The AJC "was *the* organized expression of the German-Jewish aristocracy of spirit, culture, and money."[54]

The leadership of German Jews in America was a very sophisticated, well-bred and intellectual group of people. Many were lawyers, doctors, bankers and merchants. They were patrons of the arts and sports. The Jewish religion, however, played an ever-decreasing role in their lives. They viewed assistance to their fellow Jews—whom they called their "co-religionists" and with whom they had practically nothing in common—as part of their heritage, "a kind of inherited trait." In their attempt to assimilate into American life, "they often rationalized their aid to Jews as part of their concern for humanity as a whole." The common past put a moral obligation on them to help Jews in backward Europe to reach the stage of equality—and therefore prosperity— that they themselves had attained. That, it was hoped, would be the end of the Jewish problem for Europe's Jews; it would also be the end of their own problem qua Jews. But, in the meantime, the obligation existed, and it had to be met honestly and openly.[55]

The response to Morgenthau's plea for help came from Schiff and the Zionist Provisional Committee, through Nathan Strauss, a leading Zionist. Appeals from European Jews followed, precipitating a number of relief drives by various religious and labor groups, the Zionists and B'nai B'rith. These spontaneous campaigns convinced the AJC that united action had to be taken because the Committee could not raise the funds by itself and it did not want to compete publicly with existing institutions. The solution was to establish "a neutral cooperative organization."[56]

On October 9, 1914, Louis Marshall, a prominent New York attorney and AJC president, invited thirty-nine representatives of national Jewish organizations to attend a meeting at Temple Emanu-El in New York City to plan a course of action. On October 24, this group established the American Jewish Relief Committee (AJRC) composed of 100 representatives of various organizations, but initially without the Orthodox group. On November 27, 1914, the Central Relief Committee (CRC) was founded by the Orthodox leadership to raise and distribute funds to their constituents. Not until the Orthodox and the People's Relief Committee, representing the labor groups, joined the AJRC in what became the JDC, did the AJRC accomplish any significant results.[57]

The American Jewish Committee did not control the AJRC, but "it was inevitable that the relief group's representatives on the JDC were among the most prominent of the Committee's executive."[58] Though all three groups— the CRC, JDC and the People's Relief Committee—had separate fundraising campaigns, their representatives sat on the JDC board together. Even so, more than two-thirds of the $38,000,000 the JDC raised between 1914 and 1920 came from German Jews. It was for this reason that the other groups deferred to the AJC representatives. [59]

Nevertheless, the creation of the JDC was a milestone for Eastern European Jewry because it meant that German Jews were no longer in total control of Jewish foreign policy. Both groups sat together in the New York *Kehillah* (community) that united synagogues, fraternal lodges, Jewish professional societies and federations, but with the creation of the JDC this was the first time that other members beside German Jews "were admitted as equals in an endeavor on behalf of the Jews of the world."[60]

With regard to Zionism, the membership of the JDC held divergent views. There were those like Judges Louis D. Brandeis and Julian Mack, who were staunch advocates of American Zionism during the Second World War. Others, such as Julius Rosenwald, the head of Sears Roebuck, viewed Zionism from a liberal German-Jewish perspective that saw Judaism as a religious doctrine and rejected the concept of a national Jewish identity.

The majority of the AJC members followed Marshall's lead by endorsing the development of Palestine, and accepted its significant spiritual role in Jewish history. Palestine was seen "as *a* place of refuge, not necessarily *the* place of refuge, for those Jews who wanted or were forced to go there."[61] They also worked hard to assist Jews to become equal citizens in the countries in which they lived, so that they would not have to seek refuge elsewhere. Nationalism, they hoped, would cease to be an ominous concept.[62]

As the primary American Jewish organization providing relief and rehabilitation to the Jews of Europe, the JDC came into conflict with other entities that it felt infringed on its territory, and perhaps hindered its work. The JDC and the World Jewish Congress (WJC), founded in 1936, for example, continually were at odds over who should administer aid to Jews. The differences were an outgrowth of their different world views. The WJC believed in the unity of the Jewish people throughout the world and sought to establish a political entity to represent world Jewry. The JDC rejected this view of nationalism and was disturbed that the WJC competed with it for funds.[63]

During and after the war, individual American Jewish chaplains had problems with the JDC. Most critical of the JDC was Chaplain Abraham Klausner, a Reform rabbi who played a key role in assisting the DPs. The chaplains were among the first to enter the camps in Germany after the war, and provided invaluable assistance to the survivors.[64] When one chaplain asked the JDC to empower them in a "semiofficial capacity until their representatives arrived," he was ignored. Given their experiences with the survivors and the military, and their ability to communicate and empathize with the DPs, the JDC could have used them, especially since it had difficulty in recruiting competent personnel to go to Europe. Permission wasn't granted except in one or two cases, and then only for a relatively short period of time.[65]

For Klausner the reason for this was clear: "Moses Leavitt and Dr. Joseph Schwartz, the professional leadership of the JDC, resented the chaplains. They saw themselves as experts, and the chaplains as irritants..." At various times they could have "made use of the chaplains, but instead fought them again and again."[66]

In a March 1947 report, Klausner said the JDC had grown in size, but "continues in its disorganization and consequently its limited effectiveness." After nine months, Leo W. Schwarz, the JDC Director of Germany, returned to the U.S—the third director in twenty months to do so. The continuous turnover in JDC personnel and constant "case after case of dissatisfaction and bickering and reassignment" meant that representatives stayed short periods.[67]

Schwarz's resignation letter proves Klausner's assessment was correct: "From the beginning I found no policy, no guidance, no decisions and no organization. I accepted this challenge...but the unwillingness of responsible personnel on all echelons of the organization to face realities in terms of handling unsuitable personnel and establishing administrative practices, complicated and nullified my efforts...If my major energies had not perforce been diverted in trying to convert an unoriented [sic], undisciplined staff into the semblance of a professional organization, and trying to clear the administrative lines [with the European headquarters in Paris], this objective might have been achieved in four months rather than in eight months; and as a consequence, we would have been in an even stronger position to cope with the increasingly complex problems of this operation." Schwarz "could no longer continue to carry on under the present conditions."[68]

The JDC had a serious ongoing problem with the Vaad Hatzala, as well. For example, during the war, the JDC and the Vaad differed on rescue priorities; attitude toward the government of the United States; American policy with regard to Germany on how to deal with American laws that hindered potential rescue opportunities; types of rescue activities, and whether the need for communal unity should preclude unilateral action by individual organizations.[69] After the war, these differences were further compounded.

In addition, the independent fundraising campaigns conducted by the Vaad in America during and after the war were seen by the JDC and the Council of Jewish Federations and Welfare Funds (CJFWF) as especially divisive. They repeatedly tried to stop the Vaad from obtaining funds from Jewish Federations and other communal institutions.[70] The JDC did not take a public stand against the Vaad, but the JDC and the CJFWF's official attitude was that "...in order to avoid a multiplicity of fundraising drives, contributions for programs and projects subventioned by the major overseas organizations should be centralized through one agency."[71] This was not to be.

As matters stood, however, no other organization could compete with the JDC in terms of numbers of personnel it had in Europe, its funding or the extent of its achievements. A list of employees of the voluntary agencies working in Germany in January 1948—representative of the numbers of previous years as well—showed that the JDC had 266 representatives during that month, the Jewish Agency for Palestine 92, HIAS 34, while the Vaad had only 12.[72] Between 1945 and 1950, the JDC's budget exceeded $200 million, providing "cash relief" to between 180,000 and 200,000 Jews. In 1945, the JDC fed 200,000 Jewish DPs, 349,000 in 1946 and 411,800 in 1947. More than 154 million pounds of food, 750,000 pairs of new shoes, 500,000 coats, 300,000 dresses, 250,000 new suits, and 2,000,000 pieces of underwear were sent to Europe between 1946 and 1950. JDC medical clinics treated 2.5 million cases and 42 million hot meals were distributed through its kitchens and canteens.[73]

The JDC spent money to help establish schools; provide aid to vocational training centers; cultural and sports activities; print books; furnish school supplies and religious articles for observant Jews, and help pay for the transportation of DPs to immigrate to the United States, Palestine and other countries. The JDC ended its work in the DP camps after Foehrenwald closed in 1957.

The Vaad Hatzala

Given the JDC's enormous resources, large numbers of personnel and the backing of the American Jewish community, why would any other organization feel the need to work with the survivors, even in the area of spiritual rehabilitation? The answer lies in the special mission each group determined to be its priority and the perceived lack of importance relegated to spiritual and religious issues by the JDC. This was especially so for the Vaad Hatzala, which regarded the *b'nei Torah* as the cornerstones for the reestablishment of Torah Judaism throughout the world. Because this was the *raison d'etre* of the Vaad, and because of the JDC's secularist approach to rescue and rehabilitation, the Vaad challenged the JDC on its lack of activities with regard to Orthodox Jewry.

Any study of the Vaad Hatzala must take account of the number of Orthodox Jews in Europe before the war. In Western Europe, the majority of the Jews were not Orthodox. In France they constituted about twenty-five percent of the population, while in Germany they were between fifteen and twenty percent. In Eastern Europe, Orthodox Jews were the majority of the older generation and most likely about a third of the younger generation. In the small towns, villages and *shtetls*, it is estimated that four out of every five Jews were Orthodox, in some areas, "more than nine in ten. The more rural the Jews, the larger percentage of the dead and the greater the number of Orthodox Jews."[74] An entirely accurate estimate of how many Orthodox Jews were killed is impossible, but they were clearly the majority, somewhere between 50-70 percent.[75]

It is equally unclear how many Orthodox Jews survived. One study showed that fifty-five percent of the survivors could be classified as observant before the war, but that this number decreased to thirty-four percent "just after the Holocaust," whether the survivors were in DP camps, shelters or in Palestine. This increased the number of non-observant to sixty-six percent. As of 1980, when the

23

survey was done, the number of observant increased to forty-three percent and the non-observant decreased to fifty-seven percent.[76]

Significantly, a large number of Jews who were categorized as non-observant before the Holocaust acknowledged having kept at least a few religious observances, including conducting a Passover *seder* and lighting candles on Hanukkah. Many indicated observing some religious practices, such as briefly attending synagogue or a modified fasting on Yom Kippur. Still others recited the *Kaddish* (mourner's prayer) on the anniversary of a loved one's death. Even taking into account that the "ethnic factor played a part in determining religious practices" in Europe and the Diaspora, "whatever else may be said concerning the Jews of Europe before the catastrophe, one generalization applies: They constituted a religiously observant community."[77]

Typically, Rabbi Dovid Lifshitz, the Suvalker Rav and *rosh yeshiva* of RIETS (Rabbi Isaac Elchanan Theological Seminary of New York), saw the rehabilitation of the DPs as an essential process in rebuilding the Jewish nation. As such, American Jews were obligated to help the DPs establish synagogues, Talmud Torahs, *yeshivos*, old age homes, *mikvehs* (ritual baths) and hospitals. Rabbis and teachers had to be secured and sent to Europe to staff these institutions.

In addition to education and ritual fulfillment, social services had to be incorporated as well. For example, an approach to saving women *agunahs* (widows) and male *agunim* (widowers) also had to be found. Since these people did not know whether their spouses had been killed by the Germans or were still alive, until a rabbinical court could ascertain the status of a husband or wife, Jewish law forbade them to remarry.

The challenges were many, but by providing aid in these areas, American Jews could "breathe new life, encouragement and renewed vigor to communities almost entirely destroyed."[78]

The precarious nature of the task of rekindling the embers of religious life terribly burned by the Nazi conflagration was evident in an incident at the Feldafing DP camp shortly after war's end. "Some of us were sure that Jewish life had reached its end," the Klausenberger Rebbe had said, yet a number of young men who had attached themselves to the Rebbe helped him find a suitable place to pray. Some people were opposed to establishing a synagogue lest a new oppressor rise up against them. When the group set up wedding canopies, a few people threw stones at them. Yet within a short period of time, there were synagogues everywhere and weddings were conducted according to Jewish law.[79] Stanley Abramovitz, a religious JDC worker from England, also reported helping the Rebbe establish a *mikveh* and a kosher kitchen at the camp.[80]

For these reasons, the leadership of the Vaad Hatzala felt it had to do all it could to provide immediate spiritual and religious help to the survivors. They understood that this was a period of transition for survivors, when decisions would be made about future connections to the Jewish people and their faith. The Orthodox leadership understood that after years of being unable to practice their religion, many Jews would be eager again to eat kosher food, put on *tefillin* (phylacteries), learn Jewish sacred texts, and observe the laws of Jewish family purity that entailed going to the *mikveh*. These things could not be postponed, but were vital to their successful reconnection to their pasts and essential to their rehabilitation.

After Rabbi Alexander S. Rosenberg, JDC's Religious Advisor in the United States Zone of Germany, arrived in Germany in September 1945, he helped the DPs to build a *mikveh*, and secured *taleisim, tefillin*, prayer books and religious texts for them. When Rabbi Rosenberg was about to leave Europe, Rabbi Mozes Ruttner, Chief Rabbi of the DP Center at Weilheim/Oberbayern, complained to the JDC in New York that Rabbi Rosenberg's departure: "would be an unspeakable crime against the helpless remnants [of our people], and above all would cause irreparable harm to their dormant spiritual and cultural values, but particularly against our youth, who more than ever needs such a noble and unselfish example as the revered person of Rabbi Rosenberg, so that they may find themselves and confirm their faith in the eternal value of our people, our culture, and our religion...

"Demoralization is spreading rapidly...Rabbi Rosenberg knows how to seize this evil by its roots and tries to stem the tide of demoralization by the strengthening of the faith in God...Keep our beloved Rabbi Rosenberg, so that our poor children should have hope for a Jewish future...No other one has recognized the need for practical action as clearly as he, or understand [sic] to place action first...." [81]

In light of the specificity of its mission, the purpose of this book is to examine the activities of the Vaad Hatzala in Germany in the immediate post-war period, the struggles it faced in trying to accomplish its goals—especially those of Rabbi Nathan Baruch, its on-site representative—and the challenges it encountered from the American establishment, the Jewish community and the Orthodox community in particular.

Chapter 1

Nathan Baruch:
Background, Mentors and
Initial Vaad Hatzala Involvement

Nathan Baruch was born in Dubiecko, Poland in 1924 and came to the United States with his parents and eight siblings when he was five years old. The family lived on the Lower East Side of Manhattan, in an area teeming with Jewish immigrants. After graduating from the high school of Mesivta Torah Vodaath, he entered the yeshiva's *smicha* (rabbinical ordination) program. To supplement his income during the summer months, Baruch found teaching jobs or a position as a part time rabbi. For several summers he worked in Spring Valley, 30 miles from Manhattan, where he officiated at a little *shul* (synagogue). After receiving *smicha*, Baruch became a fund-raiser for Torah Vodaath.

During his years at the yeshiva, Baruch met and became involved with a number of the leading rabbis of the period, including Rabbi Avraham Kalmanowitz. In his youth, Rabbi Kalmanowitz had been a student of Rabbi Hayyim Ozer Grodzinski, one of the foremost European rabbinical leaders.[1] Rabbi Kalmanowitz often told Baruch how he helped Rabbi Grodzinski, who had been instrumental in establishing the Va'ad ha-Yeshivos (The Union of *Yeshivos*) that provided financial and moral support to students and *yeshivos* in Europe.

In 1926, Rabbi Kalmanowitz was elected president of the Mir Yeshiva in Europe. Three years later, he became the rabbi of Tykocin, where he established another yeshiva. Then Hitler invaded Poland on September 1, 1939 and Rabbi Kalmanowitz immigrated to the United States (1940).

A driven man, Rabbi Kalmanowitz always seemed breathless and pressed for time because he was consumed by the plight of the Jews of Europe. His briefcase always bulged with copies of letters and telegrams sent to government officials pleading for help in rescuing yeshiva students who were being murdered or left stranded and starving in the Soviet Union. The rabbi would go anywhere and meet anyone who could help Jews in distress.[2]

Typical of his dedication was his response to the arrival in September 1943 of Shlomo Mikhoels, the actor and manager of the Moscow Jewish Theater, and Itzik Feffer, the Yiddish poet, both members of a Soviet-sponsored Anti-Fascist Committee, who were in America to enlist the financial support of American Jews in the fight against the Nazis[3] (even though the Soviets had originally allied themselves with Hitler). With the assistance of Yiddish writer Sholem Asch, one of the most popular Yiddish novelists in the Jewish world and a darling of the Left, Rabbi Kalmanowitz hoped to meet Mikhoels and Feffer to ask that they intervene with the Soviet authorities on behalf of these yeshiva students.

Asch spent the summer in Saratoga Springs, New York where Rabbis Kalmanowitz and Baruch went to see him. When Rabbi Kalmanowitz told Asch, "*Zey farbrennen Yidn*" ("they are burning Jews"), Asch revealed that he knew about the killings from anti-Nazi underground groups in Europe and from sources in France and other countries. He accused *The New York Times* and other publications in the west of refusing to publish this information without "sufficient proof," making it extremely difficult for the general public to accept the truth. To emphasize the need for immediate action, Rabbi Kalmanowitz told Asch a well-known story from the Book of Kings (Kings II, 6:30):

> There once was a wicked king in Israel. When he was told his subjects were dying of starvation, he bared his chest and screamed. Our sages considered this king an evil man, but he still reacted with pain to the terrible news about his people. You can imagine what our sages would say about a man who knows what is happening to his fellow Jews and does nothing to help them.

Asch appeared so shaken by the power and force of this presentation that he pleaded, "*Rebbe, Rebbe, hut rachmones*" (Rabbi, Rabbi, have pity on me!). He suggested that the rabbi contact him through Alfred Knopf, his publisher in New York City, and he would arrange a meeting with Mikhoels and Feffer. Baruch took the telephone number, but despite repeated efforts, they never succeeded in making contact.[4]

Rabbi Aharon Kotler (Rav Aharon)

Baruch ascribes the greatest influence on his life to Rabbi Aharon Kotler, one of the great rabbinic scholars of the time. Thanks to a special "above quota emergency visa" granted to him, Rav Aharon escaped from Europe by traveling across the Soviet Union and the Black Sea to Kobe, Japan. He arrived in San Francisco on April 13, 1941 and took a train to Pennsylvania Station in New York City. Along the way, he stopped in Chicago and Cincinnati.[5] Thousands of students, laymen and prominent rabbis descended on Pennsylvania Station in midtown Manhattan to greet him.

Rabbi Hayyim Ozer Grodzinski
Courtesy of Beth Medrash Govoha,
Lakewood, NJ

Rabbi Avraham Kalmanowitz
Courtesy Orthodox Jewish Archives, Agudath Israel of America

Rav Aharon was a diminutive figure who radiated great strength of spirit. Although it pained him to leave many of his students and the yeshiva behind, he thought he could do more for them from the United States.[6]

Rabbi Meir Karelitz, the elder brother of the Chazon Ish, another of the great European rabbis with a large following, offered Rav Aharon a certificate to immigrate to *Eretz Israel* (The Land of Israel) after Poland ceded eastern Poland to the Soviets on September 27, 1939. But when the Soviet Union and Lithuania agreed that Lithuania would become a neutral republic, Rav Aharon insisted on staying in Lithuania as long as yeshiva students were unable to leave.[7] In a letter written on March 3, 1940 to the Jewish Agency for Palestine, he pleaded for 240 certificates to be issued for his students, his brother-in-law and Rav Menachem Shach.[8]

In a letter to Rabbi Eliezer Silver on July 7, 1940, Rav Aharon asked for his help in transferring the *yeshivos* to America. Such a rescue operation, he said would be "akin to the action of Rabbi Johanan ben Zakkai" who was smuggled out of Jerusalem during the siege of the city in 70 B.C.E. to establish a yeshiva in Yavneh, thus ensuring the future of the Jewish people. In making this request, Rav Aharon insisted that "for the sake and benefit of all *yeshivos,*" that all of them be considered as one entity. No distinctions should be made between them, "for the merit of all the *yeshivos* is greater than the merit of any individual one." He was confident that Rabbi Silver would rally the support of influential Jews, such as Governor Herbert H. Lehman of New York and others including "pious" non-Jews.[9]

And so Rav Aharon continued his campaign to rescue his students. It was only when he was in danger of being arrested by the Soviet authorities and was convinced by his friends in the U.S. and Lithuania that he could do more in the U.S. to help secure visas for his students, that he agreed to escape via Russia.[10] Rav Aharon sailed from Russia via Shanghai, landed in San Francisco, and took a train to New York.

At Penn Station, Rav Aharon looked at the masses before him and described how he and his students took leave of each other. He cried out to those who came to greet him: "Remember your great and sacred obligation during this

Rabbi Aharon Kotler
Courtesy of Beth Medrash Govoha, Lakewood, NJ

terrible period. Once, when the curtain covering the Holy Ark was stabbed, blood started flowing. Now the Ark itself and Torah scrolls and those who study Torah are bleeding...If, God forbid, our spiritual treasure over there will be destroyed, it will affect our own lives because we will miss these wells from which all the Jews, including those in America, have drawn. We cannot postpone the work. Every minute is valuable. Who knows what will happen in the future? The *Sefer Torah* (Torah scroll) is bleeding and it is up to you, leaders of Israel, to do everything possible to save the yeshiva students. Despite all the gratitude we owe the Agudas Harabonim, almost nothing has been done. We still have not fulfilled our obligation. Time is short and we must act immediately. Everyone must volunteer for this holy task...Only you, the Jews of America, are able to help them. Do it now! Save them!"

He exhorted those who welcomed him to help transplant the *yeshivos* of Europe to America. To those who were convinced that Torah could not take root in this *treife medinah* (non-kosher land), he proclaimed, "There is a future for Torah in America."[11]

Baruch met Rav Aharon in Spring Valley when he was working as a part-time rabbi at a local *shul*. Baruch visited him almost daily and observed how the rabbi "held court" for the important Torah scholars who came to see him. Rav Aharon sat with a map of Europe in front of him and told his guests about the destruction of Europe. Restless and deeply bothered, with force and fervor, he continually thundered, "We must save the Jews"—*"Mir darfen rateven Yidn."*

Because he spoke in a staccato cadence, the Rav was not always easy to understand, but his indomitable spirit inspired all those in his presence. He tried to make people realize that the European world of Torah as they had known it was being systematically destroyed. He explained how the famous *yeshivos* of Kletzk, Radin, Telshe, Kaminetz and Slobodka had disappeared into the abyss. Saving European Jewry was Rav Aharon's deep concern. He carried the burden like a sack of rocks. American Jews could only imagine what was happening overseas. He was an eyewitness to it.[12]

Shortly after he arrived in New York, Rav Aharon attended a meeting of the Agudas Harabonim and declared, "I am the father of sons who are wandering aimlessly from one place of exile to another, totally abandoned, forsaken. It is my responsibility and yours to save them. I cannot even describe the bitterness and pain we felt upon my departure. Our one consolation is the hope that I will be able to find some help."[13]

Because of his spirit and erudition, no one was given more respect by rabbis and laymen than Rav Aharon. Baruch marveled at seeing Rabbi Kotler walk into a room and watch outstanding luminaries rise in his honor; such was the degree of respect and recognition of his greatness.

Baruch developed a relationship with Rav Aharon and kept in touch with him. Because he maintained contact with a network of rabbis he knew from his childhood, he was permitted to attend some meetings of the Agudas Harabonim, the leaders of the Vaad Hatzala. Though he would never claim to be one of them in terms of scholarship, reputation and stature, he nevertheless endeavored to make himself useful.[14]

Rabbi Eliezer Silver

Rabbi Eliezer Silver was an Orthodox leader who also exerted a strong influence on Baruch during his formative years. They had met when Rabbi Silver gave a rabbinic discourse at Torah Vodaath. Trained in Europe, Rabbi Silver had also studied under Rabbi Hayyim Ozer Grodzinski and Rabbi Hayyim Soloveitchik. He was unusual in that he had immigrated to the United States in 1907, and had served as a pulpit rabbi in Harrisburg, Pennsylvania, then in Springfield, Massachusetts, and finally in Cincinnati, Ohio from 1931 until his death in 1968.[15]

As with Rabbi Kotler, Baruch developed a relationship with Rabbi Silver, another strong figure in the pantheon of the contemporary rabbinate.[16]

Sooner than expected, Baruch saw Rabbi Silver after their meeting at Torah Vodaath. On October 6, 1943, a few days before Yom Kippur, 400 Orthodox rabbis, almost all of whom

Rabbi Eliezer Silver
Courtesy of Beth Medrash Govoha, Lakewood, NJ

were members of the Agudas Harabonim, traveled to Washington, D.C. to rally Congressional pressure on the White House to create a separate agency to save the Jews of Europe.

At one point, Jewish politicians had tried to convince the rabbis not to march. Their strategy backfired when a Democratic Congressman from New York, Sol Bloom, chairman of the House Foreign Affairs Committee from 1939-1945, declared "it would be undignified for these un-American looking rabbis to appear in the nation's capitol." When they heard that, the rabbis were more determined than ever to carry out their unprecedented action.[17]

March on Washington

The march on Washington had been conceived by Peter Bergson (Hillel Kook), head of the Emergency Committee to Save the Jewish People of Europe. Bergson, a nephew of Rabbi Abraham Isaac Kook, the Chief Rabbi of Palestine before the creation of Israel, arrived in New York in July 1940 to represent the Irgun Tzvai Leumi (National Military Organization of the Revisionist Zionists), the militant anti-British underground organization most active from 1944-48. He came to recruit men and materiel for a Jewish Army from Palestine to fight against the Nazis and to raise funds to smuggle Jews out of Europe to Palestine.

Since the failure of the Bermuda Conference (April 19-30, 1943), a public relations effort to find a palliative solution to the refugee crisis, rescue emerged as a major item on the Orthodox Jewish agenda, while most American Jewish organizations had already given up on the idea. Though the conference itself had been convened by the United States and Great Britain to address the problem of wartime refugees, it was essentially a charade designed to appease those petitioning them for action.

Choosing Bermuda as the site for the conference allowed the American and British delegations to control access to the location and to information. Furthermore, the conference was doomed from the start once it became clear that the

Peter Bergson (Hillel Kook)
Photo courtesy of
David Wyman & Raphael Medoff
A Race Against Death: Peter Bergson, America and the Holocaust
(The New Press, 2002)

leadership of Britain and the United States would not change their immigration policies. Britain would not rescind its "White Paper" of 1939 limiting the number of Jews allowed to immigrate to Palestine to 75,000 over a five-year period; the United States and Britain refused to let any more refugees immigrate to their countries.

Also, the American State Department refused to focus on the destruction of the Jews and instead framed the refugee problem in universal terms. By creating the term "political refugee," they obscured the antisemitic nature of Nazi policy. Furthermore, representatives from the JDC, the Vaad, the WJC and other Jewish groups representing Jewish refugees were deliberately barred from the discussion.

After the failure of the Bermuda Conference, Bergson's group held an Emergency Conference in New York in July 1943. Working with Harold Ickes, Sr., Secretary of the Interior, New York City Mayor Fiorello LaGuardia, newspaper publishers William Allen White and Randolph Hearst, the committee developed a number of rescue proposals and discussed ways to convince the American government to implement them. It was decided to establish the Emergency Committee to Save the Jewish People of Europe, which superseded the work of the Committee for a Jewish Army. The Emergency Committee increased the Army Committee's rescue agenda by holding mass meetings, placing full-page advertisements in newspapers, gaining editorial support in newspapers and lobbying in Washington.[18]

As part of his campaign to publicize the plight of European Jewry and to move the Roosevelt administration to action, Bergson decided to organize a March on Washington.[19]

When the Zionists heard about the proposed march, they were disturbed because Bergson had usurped their program and they feared his potentially provoking antisemitism with his brash tactics. But just as the Agudah did not seek ideological conformity from its allies, neither did the Bergson group. Both groups saw the rescue mission as a priority and were determined to work together.[20]

Bergson enlisted the rabbis and the American Jewish Legion

Upon arrival of the rabbis in Washington, D.C. Dr. J.H. Gordon, National Commander of the Jewish Legion of Veterans (left) leads the honor guard from Union Square Station in the nation's capital. In the foreground (l-r) Rabbis Eliezer Silver, Israel Rosenberg and Bernard Levinthal (Rabbi Nathan Baruch in front on left).
Photo courtesy of the *Congressional Record*,
Oct. 6, 1943

of Veterans for the march. He had expected all segments of the American clergy to participate, but no Protestants, Catholics, Baptists or members of any Christian denomination joined them. Only other Jewish organizations—the Union of Orthodox Rabbis of the United States and Canada, the Union of Hasidic Rabbis and a commander of the Jewish Legion—participated. The Rabbinical Council of America, representing modern Orthodox rabbis, sent Rabbi David Silver, the son of Rabbi Eliezer Silver.[21]

When he first heard about the march, Baruch asked Rabbi Shraga Feivel Mendlowitz, *menahel* (principal) of Torah Vodaath, if students could participate and Rabbi Mendlowitz gave his permission. He added, however, that the yeshiva had no funds to pay for buses to transport any students wishing to attend. Undaunted, Baruch contacted Rabbi Silver through the Agudas Harabonim, and arranged to accompany him to Washington.[22]

Dressed in long, dark rabbinic garb, the 400 rabbis walked from Union Station to the Capitol Building. There, on the vast and imposing marble staircase, Rabbis Silver, Israel Rosenberg and Bernard Louis Levinthal led a recitation of *Psalms*. Bergson made the introductions to Vice President Henry Wallace and a number of Congressmen.[23]

While the Orthodox rabbis were calling for rescue, establishment Zionists, led by Reform Rabbis Stephen S. Wise, Abba Hillel Silver and Israel Goldstein, continued to protest against the 1939 British "White Paper." When the systematic destruction of Jews became known in 1942, the Bergson group put the creation of a Jewish State on hold, since it knew it would be impolitic for congressman to attack British allies in the midst of the war. Throughout 1943, rescue became the main issue. But some of these Zionists viewed the Bergson group as the enemy because it had a revisionist agenda, which was to establish a Jewish army to fight the Nazis, rescue Jews, and only then concentrate on creating a Jewish State in Palestine.[24]

These same Zionists also feared that Bergson's rival organization—by already getting credit, media coverage, building extensive relationships on Capitol Hill and recruiting pro-Israel celebrities—threatened to divert badly needed funds and members from their own organizations. Attempts to work with Bergson failed when the establishment Zionists insisted that the Bergson group submit its proposals to them for approval. Unity, they believed, could not be attained as long as Bergson's organization retained its autonomy.

As a response to Bergson's decision to follow his own course, the Zionist establishment marginalized his group and defamed him. Bergson supporters and sponsors received frequent letters, telephone calls and personal visits from members of the Zionist establishment to convince them to withdraw their backing from him.[25]

After mid-May 1944, the attacks increased when Bergson launched the Hebrew Committee of National Liberation and the American League for a Free Palestine. The Zionists tried to stop it. They even attempted to have the departments of State and Justice draft Bergson into the American armed forces or deport him to Palestine—where he would have been arrested. The British Embassy, the American Jewish Committee and Congressman Sol Bloom all worked toward getting Bergson deported. Despite his stomach ulcers, Bergson was almost drafted, and during much of 1944 and 1945, the Justice Department tried to expel him. Only strong intervention by his friends in Congress prevented it.[26]

Congressman Emanuel Celler, who fought against U.S. immigration quotas, noted that Bloom "always wanted to curry favor" with the State Department. He enjoyed going to state dinners and "the diplomacy" the State Department provided for him. Bloom became "more or less a sycophant" of State. He was "a weakling," and when it came to rescuing the Jews, "he didn't help."[27]

On October 6, when the rabbis were marching in Washington, D.C., Nahum Goldmann and Rabbi Stephen Wise of the World Jewish Congress met with Breckinridge Long, the Assistant Secretary of State, and "excoriated" Bergson's group as a "body composed of a lot of persons, many of whom were not Jews," and all of whom failed to "represent the thinking of most Jews in this country." [28]

At the Lincoln Memorial, the rabbis—who had declared a

fast for the day—prayed for the success and well-being of the Allied armed forces, for a swift victory and for the welfare of the Jews still alive in Europe. Then they walked to the White House and prayed outside the gates.

Though they had expected to meet with the President, they were told that he was unavailable, attending to important matters of state. Later they learned President Roosevelt was at Bolling Field for a minor ceremony inducting 40 Yugoslavs into the U.S. Air Corps and dedicating four new bombers for their use. After the ceremony, Roosevelt left for his home in Hyde Park, New York for a five-day weekend.

The purpose of Roosevelt's visit to the Air Force was to avoid meeting with the rabbis. At the urging of some Jewish leaders, Judge Samuel Rosenman, a frequent advisor to the President on Jewish affairs, tried to stop the march altogether.[29] A White House staffer who was in the West Wing that day heard Rosenman inform the president that "the group behind this petition was not representative of the most thoughtful elements in Jewry." Rosenman admitted to having failed to "keep the horde from storming Washington."[30]

In the absence of the President, the Vice-President accepted a Rescue Memorandum from Rabbi Silver on behalf of the Agudas Harabonim. The petition stated:

> In view of this tragic emergency, it is a holy obligation to take drastic steps to save the Jewish people. America was asked:
>
> 1. To adopt immediate and practical measures of rescue and to use all possible means to end the murders committed by Nazi criminals.
> 2. To warn Germany and all that every atrocity and crime perpetrated against their Jewish residents, whether by governments or private individuals, will be held against them and that, likewise, every act of kindness toward their unfortunates will not pass unnoticed.
> 3. To send ships with food and medical

On the steps of the Capitol, the rabbis are welcomed by
Vice President Henry Wallace and Senate leaders.
Photo courtesy of the *Congressional Record*,
Oct. 6, 1943

supplies to the Jews starving in ghettos, under the supervision of a neutral commission or through the International Red Cross.

4. To influence and persuade neutral countries to allow the Jewish refugees who flee from the Nazi sword to seek security within their borders and to guarantee to these countries the means for the temporary maintenance of these refugees.

5. To open the gates of the United Nations to provide havens therein, and to facilitate the entry into our land, the United States of America, of those who can escape the Nazi terror.

6. To open the doors of Palestine immediately to these refugees.

7. To create a special intergovernmental agency to save the remnant of Israel in Europe with powers and means to act at once on a large scale.[31]

Rav Aharon was probably the only major Orthodox rabbinic figure who did not attend the march. For him, dealing with the plight of the Jews in the public forum was inappropriate, because he believed the nations of the world reveled in the Jews' tragedies. In his estimation, the most appropriate form of activism was for the American Jewish community to aim its anger and frustration at its elected officials. He believed that only quiet diplomacy, conducted behind closed doors, could succeed. Furthermore, he feared his participation might overshadow the presence of the other rabbis, and he did not want this to happen.[32]

Although Rav Aharon did not participate in the march, he did influence the Rescue Memorandum. He recommended that:

• "First and foremost, our anger and frustration must be expressed in a strong and strident voice...We must make people hear about the unprecedented levels of cruelty, cruelty of a kind that never existed before in all the generations of

The "Rabbis' Petition" is read by Rabbi Eliezer Silver to
Vice President Henry Wallace and Senate leaders.
Photo courtesy of the *Congressional Record*,
Oct. 6, 1943

Rabbi Wolf Gold reads the "Rabbis' Petition" on the
steps of the Lincoln Memorial.
Photo courtesy of the *Congressional Record*,
Oct. 6, 1943

Photo courtesy of Mir Yeshiva Archives.

The Melitzer Grand Rabbi leads the group in
"Kel Mole Rachamim," a memorial prayer for the
victims of the Holocaust.
Photo courtesy of the *Congressional Record*,
Oct. 6, 1943

Rabbi Avraham Kalmanowitz (left)
Photo courtesy of the *Congressional Record*,
Oct., 6, 1943

mankind. Those who hear of these atrocities will be in a state of shock and disbelief about the German plan to systematically annihilate an entire nation—millions of men, women, children, pregnant women, newborn children and the elderly—by the most gruesome torture in special slaughterhouses.

• The Senate and the Congress should make their opposition loud and clear to all those associated with the Final Solution, including those who have the power to stop or prevent such actions, but who instead stand silently by. The perpetrators should be told that ultimately they will be taken to account for their actions.

• The Senate and the Congress, from their podiums, must warn all the nations who may be party to this mass murder of Jewry that such participation will ultimately serve to create a rift between them and the countries who seek peace for generations to come.

• Furthermore, a plea must be made in the Congress and the Senate and to all those who are in any way connected to the German people, to prevent and desist from the spilling of blood—which for all eternity will not be atoned.

• It also behooves everyone to request that the Senate and the Congress sponsor resolutions in the U.S. government and with the allied nations to immediately adopt all necessary measures to stop the mass murder, to save the remnants of Israel and to assist in their rescue as much as possible."[33]

Response to Rabbis March in the Press

For days before and after the march, the march was covered on the front pages of three Yiddish newspapers— the *Forward*, the *Jewish Morning Journal* and *Der Tog* (*The Day*)—all sent reporters to accompany the rabbis to Washington.

Samuel Margoshes, the editor of *Der Tog*, noted that the enormous attention the rabbis received in Washington was important because "tens of thousands of bystanders... got to know, possibly for the first time, that millions of Jews were being killed in Nazi-held Europe and that millions more

Rabbi Aharon Kotler
Courtesy of Torah Schools for Israel-Chinuch Atzmai

were in jeopardy. Also, that the Jews of America, profoundly agitated by what [was] happening to their kin, were appealing to the Government and people of the United States for help in saving their brethren from imminent doom." Margoshes was particularly pleased that the procession of Orthodox rabbis in their traditional garb and black hats had evinced such "interest, wonderment" and "respect." There "was something of the quality of a religious procession that characterized the Rabbinical Pilgrimage and compelled the respect of every passerby."[34]

The *Times-Herald,* a secular newspaper, noted that a spokesman for the group expressed disappointment that a meeting with the President did not materialize, and that there was "considerable resentment," among the rabbis who assumed they would be meeting with the President. "Some delegates speculated that the failure of the President to receive their representatives may have been dictated by the presence in Washington of representatives of the government of Iraq...." The paper observed that, "Jewish organizations have long blamed the British government's desire to conciliate Arabs, who claim the Palestine area, for the inability of Jewry to fully realize their dream of a homeland there."[35]

The delegation accepted the President's absence with the apologies offered by Marvin H. McIntyre, the presidential secretary, who greeted them at the White House. One of the rabbis said: "...If the matters engaging the President were not of 'the weightiest nature,' he would seek to have the entire delegation go on record as protesting the Chief Executive's denial of a personal interview."[36]

Several Yiddish newspaper editors offered their own speculation about the delegation's failure to meet the President. Writing in The *Jewish Daily Forward,* the largest New York Yiddish daily and the voice of the Jewish labor movement, the respected journalist known as Zivyon understood the reluctance of Roosevelt to meet with the group: "One has to have consideration for the President. It seems that he is tired of receiving delegations when he is unable to promise more than he has already promised."[37]

Others opined that other ethnic groups would not have

been "snub[bed]." Margoshes of *Der Tog* noted that while the rabbis were disappointed at not having met with the President, "they were free from blame. The fault was not theirs that they were snubbed as undoubtedly no other religious representatives of their rank and standing would be if they made their pilgrimage to the White House. Somebody has failed us, and it was not the rabbis."[38]

Another columnist from *Der Tog* doubted "whether the President would have acted in this manner with regard to the several hundred Protestant or Catholic spiritual leaders and whether he would not find a few minutes to receive them." He did not blame the President because "the blame probably was to be found elsewhere."[39]

The editorial in the Labor Zionist weekly *Yiddisher Kempfer* declared that Roosevelt would have acted differently if 500 Catholic spiritual leaders came to the White House. "The Catholics are a great power, an increasing power—a power in the political life of the country, a world power—the President would have something to tell them."[40]

In summary, the American Jewish establishment and the Zionists attacked the march—even though no one else brought the issue of the destruction of the Jews of Europe to the forefront. It was the only public demonstration by American Jews in Washington, D.C., throughout the war against the Holocaust. Without such prodding the government might never have acted. John Pehle, who served as the first director of the War Refugee Board, agreed. He said: "Only when the matter (of rescue) was brought to the President forcefully did Roosevelt act."[41]

In November, after intensive months of lobbying by the Emergency Committee, Congress introduced a rescue resolution urging President Roosevelt to create a separate government rescue agency independent of the U.S. State Department. By the end of 1943, there was considerable support for the resolution.[42]

In the meantime, without any connection to the Emergency Committee, Treasury Department officials had discovered that the State Department had purposely failed to pursue possibilities to rescue Jews and had thwarted rescue attempts by American Jewish organizations. The State Department also decreased immigration to less than 10 percent of the allowable quotas. The American Legation in Switzerland obstructed information to the U.S. about the destruction of the Jews of Europe at the request of mid-level State Department officials. When this was discovered 11 weeks later by a high official, the channel was re-opened.[43]

On January 13, 1944 the staff of Henry Morgenthau Jr., Secretary of the Treasury, gave him an 18-page memorandum documenting the State Department's deliberate obstruction of the rescue of the Jews of Europe. Three days later, Morgenthau took a shortened version of the document entitled "Report to the Secretary on the Acquiescence of This Government in the Murder of the Jews" to a meeting with President Roosevelt. He urged the president to establish a rescue agency immediately to preclude the Senate from debating the rescue resolution, which would reveal the duplicitous behavior of the State Department. To avoid a potential crisis and scandal, Roosevelt established the War Refugee Board by executive order.[44] As a result, the board worked with American Jewish organizations, diplomats from neutral countries, and resistance groups in Europe to save 200,000 Jews.[45]

Not long after the march, Nahum Goldmann, chairman of the executive of the World Jewish Congress, and Isaiah Berlin, the noted Oxford philosopher, political scientist and Zionist, met at the British embassy to discuss what had happened. Judge Rosenman told Goldmann that Roosevelt was so "displeased by the March of the Rabbis instigated by the notorious Bergson," that he used language that "would have pleased Hitler himself." Given Goldmann's noted tendency for hyperbole, this has to be taken with some caution, but it is clear that Roosevelt was quite disturbed by the march.[46]

Roosevelt was not alone in deploring the march. As late as 1972, Berlin gave a lecture at The Hebrew University of Jerusalem wherein he described the march as "notorious" and an example of "excess of zeal or disregard for the truth or...breaking the rules of politically decent conduct." Berlin softened his criticism somewhat in 1984 by conceding that he may have been wrong to accept "the official Zionist view of Bergson's activities." [47]

This internecine warfare did not go unnoticed. An early War Refugee Board memorandum warned, "One of the problems is to get all the groups, particularly the Jewish groups, to work together and to stop fighting among themselves."[48]

For the young Baruch, the march was his first initiation into the world of Vaad Hatzala politics.

Chapter 2

American Policy and the Vaad Hatzala

When it came to the fate of European Jewry, American Jews could not agree on the nature of the threat or policy to confront it. Because they constantly jockeyed for political power amongst themselves and were continually fighting with each other, they could not even send a message in a single voice to their own elected officials. Even in 1943, when the trains were transporting large numbers of Jews to the extermination camps, all the efforts to create unity inside the American Jewish community failed.[1]

During the war years, the primary focus of the Vaad was to provide relief to the yeshiva world. Even before the destruction of European Jewry was exposed, the Vaad did everything within its limited powers to remove Jews from danger and find them a safe haven. Ideological differences between different groups were immaterial to them. The leadership of the Vaad worked with anyone who wanted to save Jews.

Many American Jewish organizations reacted to the Holocaust by planning for the reconstruction of Jewish life in Europe after the war; [2] while others tried to establish a Jewish State in Palestine. The Vaad's mission was to rescue Jews as dictated by Jewish law ["Do not stand idly by while your brother's blood is shed" (*Leviticus* 19:16)]. The Vaad never gave up.

Despite its efforts on behalf of Orthodox Jewry, not all groups within the American Orthodox community actively worked with the Vaad. The Vaad represented a large segment of that community, but not all of it, even though its leaders were the foremost Orthodox rabbis and lay leaders in America.

Aside from the divisiveness between the Orthodox, their secular counterparts had their own problems as illustrated by "The Above Quota Emergency Visitors' Visas" issued to the European intellectual elite and political refugees. Initiated by the Jewish Labor Committee with the help of the American Federation of Labor, pressure was placed on the Roosevelt Administration to provide sanctuary in the United States to qualified, endangered European refugees. Included in this group, were Jewish and non-Jewish artists, writers and union leaders, among them: Marc Chagall, Hannah Arendt, Jacques Lipchitz, Thomas Mann, Lion Feuchtwanger and Franz Werfel. Ostensibly, Roosevelt granted the visas on an emergency basis to visitors who came for the 1939-1940 World's Fair in New York. More than 2,500 visas were issued on that occasion, and the Jewish Labor Committee received half of them. [3]

Initially, the program involved Varian Fry, a New York editor of the Foreign Policy Association's *Headline Books*. He went to Marseilles, France after the Nazis invaded to locate people and help them escape. The Emergency Rescue Committee, a group of Americans whose "sole purpose" was "to bring the political and intellectual refugees out of France before the Gestapo [or some other group] got to them," recruited Fry. By the time the Vichy government expelled Fry as an "undesirable alien" in September 1941, he had helped almost 2,000 people immigrate to the United States. [4]

But having your name on a list did not automatically guarantee you a visa. Each individual had to have intrinsic value to the world and the United States. Each applicant had to produce a three-page brief enumerating the benefit of that individual—an onerous clerical task considering that thousands of applicants were involved.

As other organizations realized the importance of this special visa program, they asked that their own lists be considered. The World Jewish Congress submitted the names of approximately 100 major Zionist leaders it wanted to bring to the United States. The American Jewish Congress and dozens of other Jewish and non-Jewish organizations also prepared lists of specific people they wanted to rescue.

The Agudah and Vaad Hatzala represented the Orthodox community. Sometimes their work overlapped; at other times they coordinated their efforts—as when they lobbied in Washington, D.C. In this case they wanted to secure above quota visas for approximately 2,600 to 2,800 Torah scholars from 30 *yeshivos*, the elite of the Polish yeshiva world.[5]

But when they approached Rabbi Stephen Wise, then president of the Zionist Organization of America and the World Jewish Congress, and other American Jewish leaders with their list, they were turned away. Wise and his associates deemed it prudent for the Agudah and the Vaad not to pressure the Roosevelt Administration for more than 500 applications, though there was, ostensibly, no limit on the number of people eligible under the program.

When rejecting the Agudah and Vaad proposal, Wise declared that "there were political and social and other implications" for not obtaining visas for such large numbers of people to immigrate to the United States. In particular, he saw the problem from a "public-relations angle," because it meant trying to "transplant close to thirty such institutions in the United States, involving 3,000 to 4,000 persons."[6]

Moses A. Leavitt, secretary of the JDC, explained that Wise believed perhaps "three to five hundred [Jews] might be absorbed," but "did not feel it was feasible to think in terms of resettling a large number in this country." Furthermore, Wise advised the Agudah and the Vaad to refrain from applying "pressure on the [Roosevelt] Administration in connection with the issuance of visas."[7]

Why this negative response? One reason was that rescue "posed tremendous technical and financial problems" for the American Jewish community.[8] While there were obstacles to rescue, Wise did not use these arguments to justify his refusal. Others suggest that, "The Zionist movement, the Joint, in fact all the Jewish agencies," except for the Vaad, "were not prepared to deal with this case due to anxiety lest it increase the anti-Semitism then widespread in the United States."[9]

And this was basically the case. Wise and other American Jewish leaders specifically feared "being identified by Americans with these most Orthodox" Jews because of the "widespread notion that such outwardly different Jews would increase American antisemitism—and, that antisemitism itself was fostered by the 'unassimilable' ethnic Jew, who retained his different Old World mode of dress and culture."[10]

Many secular Jews worried that these highly visible Jews would prevent them from joining exclusive clubs and schools. The German-Jewish establishment, in particular, looked down on Eastern European Jews and longed "for full acceptance as equals in American society." They feared being identified with Russian Jews who they viewed as un-American, "alien" and ill mannered. This simply reflected the attitude of the white Anglo-Saxon community hostile to the hordes of Irish, Catholic, Italian and especially Eastern European Jewish immigrants.[11]

It is also important to recognize the extent of antisemitism in the United States during the '30s and '40s, and the relationship between Rabbi Wise and President Roosevelt. American-Jewish fear of antisemitism was so pervasive throughout the 1930s that very few American Jews objected to the restrictive quota system. Jewish statements differed from other Americans only "in the regretful tone in which some of them were cast."[12]

In addition, given the history of Jewish involvement in socialist and communist ideology, some members of Congress and the American public believed that Jews coming from Eastern Europe were radicals, perhaps even communists. By allowing these refugees into the country, they feared the

U. S. would be infiltrated by a "fifth column." When dealing with national security, American-Jewish leaders were wary of having their patriotism and loyalty impugned. They were afraid of being accused of caring more for Jews than the good of the country.[13]

Some American officials "advised" American Jews to "decide whether they were more interested in protecting the nearly five million American Jews from the intensified anti-Semitism that would result from an 'influx' of refugees, or in aiding a very small number of German Jews to come."[14]

In fact, as early as June 5, 1934, Colonel Daniel W. MacCormack, then-United States Commissioner of Immigration, suggested to Judge Julian Mack—a respected jurist, Zionist leader and chairman of the board of trustees of the Jewish Institute of Religion—that Jewish leaders limit the number of Jewish refugees immigrating to the U.S. to prevent antisemitism in America from rearing its ugly head.[15]

Judge Mack shared this conversation with Irving Lehman, a judge in the New York Court of Appeals and president of the National Jewish Welfare Board. Lehman said he was "disturbed, not by the supposed danger, but by the fact that Colonel MacCormack believes it exists and the reasons he has given for his belief." Furthermore, Lehman felt that "undoubtedly, with hardly any exceptions, even liberals have come to feel that our restrictionist policy has been beneficial during this Depression, and would deprecate any change in that policy." This was especially true in labor circles, "and it would be hopeless to combat these views at the time. Any attempt to open wide the doors would be doomed to failure."[16]

The executive vice-chairman of the JDC, Joseph C. Hyman, told the National Conference of Jewish Social Welfare in May 1940 that American Jews would be influenced "by the policies, by the attitudes, by the approaches of the whole American people and the Government."[17]

On September 17, 1940, Rabbi Wise wrote a confidential letter to Otto Nathan, a confidant and an economic advisor in the former Weimar Republic. In it Wise declared: "With regard to the political refugees, we are in the midst of an unmanageable quandary." He and other Jewish leaders presented the State

Department with lists of people they wanted to be admitted to the United States, and then they heard that the American consuls "do nothing" about these requests. A few Jews managed to "slip through," but Wise feared that the consuls were under instruction from the State Department "to do nothing," which, if true, "would be infamous beyond words."

Wise assumed that friends of the President in the State Department feared that "any large admission of radicals to the United States might be used effectively against him in the [election] campaign. Cruel as I may seem, as I have said to you before, his re-election is much more important for everything that is worthwhile and that counts than the admission of a few people, however imminent be their peril."[18]

The Vaad and Rabbi Wise eventually compromised on the requests for visas for 500 rabbis and yeshiva students with the understanding that their admittance to the United States was ultimately in the hands of the American consuls in Europe.[19]

The Above Quota Emergency Visitors' Visas program provided a unique opportunity. The Jewish Labor Committee, the World Jewish Congress, the American Jewish Committee and other Jewish organizations saw it as a duty and responsibility to save whomever they could within the parameters established by the American government. The Jews simply tried to use the opportunity to benefit their brethren in Europe. The United States, not any of the Jewish and non-Jewish organizations, determined the elitist nature of this program.

What is clear from this episode is that before the Nazi death machine began in earnest, the American Jewish community had conflicting priorities with regard to rescuing some Jews. Wise believed that keeping President Roosevelt in office was more important than rescuing Jews, because it would be best for the country and ultimately the Jewish people. For Wise and many American Jews, Roosevelt's New Deal represented a messianic era.[20]

A day after Roosevelt's inauguration in 1933, Rabbi William F. Rosenbloom of New York's Temple Israel explained to his congregation that the election had been a watershed in

American history. "No president, not excepting Washington, Lincoln, and Wilson, has assumed the office with so universal and genuine hope on the part of the people that he will prove to be a Messiah, the Messiah of America's tomorrow."[21]

Most Jews viewed Roosevelt in this light because they were influenced by his "concern for the common man and the poor; his optimism for the future, his hatred of all forms of exploitation, and his ever-insisting pleas for education...[which] indicated his conviction that democracy and humanism could not function without knowledge."[22] In other words, the New Deal promised to transform America into "an ideal, just, and egalitarian society."[23] Rituals, liturgy and communal organizations were outmoded and no longer relevant. In its place, politics became the American Jews' de facto religion. "Having lost the faith that there is a God, but not wanting to give up 'Messianism,' they go into politics."[24]

Rabbi Wise saw "this secular religion of liberalism" as "the culmination of Judaism's highest ideals."[25] A well-known Yiddish idiom of the period illustrated the adoration Jews held for Roosevelt: "*Die velt, yene velt, und Roosevelt*" ["This world, the other World to Come and Roosevelt"]. For many it came to mean "What's good for Roosevelt is good for the Jews."[26]

This faith and adoration for Roosevelt came at a price. Many Jews were so caught up in being part of the "popular struggle for national redemption," that they did not view the Nazis as a "threat particularly to the Jews, but to the world." Therefore, the issue had "to be treated not parochially but at the root, by striking at all gross social and economic inequality."[27]

Morris B. Abram, who served on the staff of U.S. Supreme Court Justice Robert H. Jackson at the Nuremberg Trials and in various high-level government positions under five presidents—from John F. Kennedy to George Herbert Walker Bush—recalled that Jews were quite hesitant about asking for "things to be done for ourselves."[28] As a young man he was much more prepared to work on behalf of blacks, for the oppressed and to fight for general religious tolerance than he was to fight for Jewish causes. He believed he was not much different from the "great masses of Jewish people who had voices, and ability and who had consciences. But we directed them in other channels."[29]

The political and secular considerations of Rabbi Wise and other American Jews did not influence Vaad Hatzala policy. Following the mandate of Jewish law, members of the Vaad were bound to rescue the spiritual leaders, teachers and students who ensured the continuity of the Jewish people—even if it meant violating the law. It was first and foremost a matter of *pikuach nefesh* (a matter of life and death). They followed the Talmud in these matters. When Jerusalem lay under siege before the destruction of the Second Temple, Rabbi Johanan ben Zakkai urged that he be given the academy of Yavneh and its wise men so he could rebuild Jewish life (see Talmud in Tractate *Gittin* (56a-b). Ben Zakkai understood that the future of the Jewish people would be endangered if this leadership disappeared. After the destruction, the Jews were without a Temple or State. To secure their future, they organized a Jewish community "firmly anchored in a life governed by the Torah and its commandments." It was "these [Torah] values" that "were the foundation and support of the nation's life and aspirations throughout its long existence as a people without a country." Thus, the rabbis ensured that the "religious and cultural unity of the entire nation was preserved."[30]

The Vaad and members of the Orthodox Jewish community saw parallels in the history of Ben Zakkai and the threat facing the Jewish community in Europe. Members of the Union of Orthodox Rabbis of the United States and Canada had close ties to the refugee rabbis in Vilna. Some of them met when the European leaders visited the United States to raise funds and recruit students. Others had studied in Europe or were former students. Many had longstanding and deep relationships, and sought counsel from their mentors long after they returned to the United States. The importance of these religious leaders could not be underestimated. Rabbi Jacob Levinson, one of the leaders of the Vaad, wrote: "The pipeline of influence stretches across the ocean from Europe to the American Jews. All of the true Torah and rabbis that we have amassed in this country came to us from there. The *roshei yeshiva* and Torah luminaries who are spreading the light of the Torah in America are products of the *yeshivos* of Poland and Lithuania." The fact that most of the American Jewish community and its leaders were not especially observant or very knowledgeable only increased concerns about the future if the European Jewish scholars were lost in the flames.[31]

Few other American Jewish organizations appreciated the urgency of saving the spiritual leadership of the Jewish people. Their priority remained the rescue of labor and Zionist leaders, artists, writers and other intellectuals. If the Vaad had not attempted to rescue the rabbis, no other organization would have tried to do so. The American Jewish community mandated that the JDC save the "masses" of the Jewish people. The members of the Vaad understood this, but they had to ensure that as long as the rabbis were at risk, their interests would also be addressed.

Because there were no choices, the Vaad used whatever methods it had at its disposal. *Halacha* mandates that Jews observe the laws in the countries in which they reside, but the saving of human life supersedes these laws. The JDC overtly followed American laws to preserve its status as a nonpolitical American social agency, but the Vaad's *only* objective was to save Jews. The differences in these approaches, outlook and priorities made the Vaad's ability to work with other Jewish organizations problematic.

The disparity in approach was apparent in the administration of a food package program for the Jews in the ghettos in Occupied Poland in 1940-1941. Letters arrived from starving Polish Jews begging American Jews to send them food. The JDC, other Jewish and non-Jewish organizations, and individuals with friends and families in Poland responded by sending packages on a regular basis. The Agudah sent packages to rabbis, scholars and other Orthodox Jews, and the program was so successful, they sent packages to Europe for $5.25 each without regard to the religious affiliation or political persuasion of the recipients. Approximately 2,000 to 4,000 food packages were sent to Poland every month, and each recipient signed a return receipt to verify delivery. During Passover 1941, the JDC asked the Agudah to help them send matzohs to Poland because their system was so efficient.[32]

In mid-1941, the U.S. State Department pressured Jewish organizations and individuals to stop sending food to Poland to prevent the Germans from benefiting from these shipments. From 1936 on, the Joint Boycott Council, established by the American Jewish Congress and the Jewish Labor Committee, worked to ban German goods from the U.S. and prevent material from being sent to Germany and its occupied territories. The goal was to bring the German economy to its knees or to inflict severe economic damage. When the British ambassador called the State Department to ask that the package program be terminated immediately, the Council applied pressure on the Jewish community to end the practice.[33]

Except for Agudath Israel and the Vaad, every American Jewish organization complied with this request. The Agudah opposed the "Jewish Boycott" on the grounds that it might harm fellow Jews. Providing food to the starving Jews of Poland was "far more important..." they believed, than the dictates of the Boycott Council.[34]

The Agudah had little support for its position outside the Orthodox community. Editorials in the Jewish press criticized its stance, but when the Agudah asked that an impartial board resolve the conflict, the Council refused to participate. The Agudah demanded proof that the Nazis were stealing the packages and asked how feeding starving Jews helped them in their war effort. At the same time, the Agudah wondered why the British did not object to boatloads of American grain being sent to civilian populations in occupied Yugoslavia and Greece.[35]

Dr. Joseph Tenenbaum, Chairman of the Boycott Council and president of the Federation of Polish Jews, became so angry at the Agudath Israel's refusal to comply with the boycott that he picketed their offices for weeks beginning on July 15, 1941. He wrote, "Many are of the opinion that England cannot decide what is good for the interest of the Jewish people and what is not. To which we reply that this question is not only to the interest of the Jewish people but to the world at large, with which the interest of the Jewish people must be in accord." Everything that is against the interests of the British is "against the interest of the Jews." Tenenbaum was particularly concerned that the Jews do nothing to "awaken those slightly stilled cries that we are only for ourselves."[36] Letters smuggled to the United States, he said, revealed that these $5 packages caused problems for the recipients since they had to pay $5 to have the packages delivered. Many packages arrived with only part of their original contents and some never arrived at all. Especially galling for Tenenbaum was that private American companies felt justified sending packages to Nazi-occupied countries because the Agudah did.

The dispute with the Boycott Council soon descended to personal attacks. The Council "deplored" that the Agudah, "a sickly weed transplanted from foreign soil to the liberal American environment, should continue to poison the atmosphere without regard for the consequences to the entire Jewish people."[37] The rabbinic scholars who had recently come to the United States were called "Jewish-Polish refugees, recent arrivals in this land of freedom and opportunity, who, though they speak of Torah and prayer with pious glances, yet [to them] a dollar is a dollar."[38] The Union of Orthodox Rabbis countered throughout this controversy that, "it sees no crime in the work of saving Jewish lives from hunger."[39]

For Tenenbaum, ending the boycott became an issue of self-sacrifice, selfishness and universal ideals: "There are times when bringing sacrifices are more important than even our own lives. Now we are living in a period such as that. Are the Jewish people different from other nations? Is the Jewish Sacrifice to be of lesser importance than the Gentile Sacrifice?"[40]

Not long before the United States entered World War II on December 7, 1941, the Agudah stopped sending packages to the Jews in Poland. A report by the Boycott Council had spurred Lord Halifax, the British ambassador to the United States, to intervene by implicitly threatening to arrest Jewish refugees in Britain. The Agudah had no choice but to stop.[41]

Lack of Unity In The American Jewish Community

The enormity of the problems at home and in Europe was not enough to motivate American Jews (or European Jews, for that matter) to set aside their disagreements and work together. Cooperation was a utopian dream. "Not only was there no one to order the Jews to unify, but in America there was not even a memory of a unity which might be recouped. Not even in the darkest moments in the ghettoes of Europe where Jews had been entombed could unity be achieved." Only in the minds of antisemites are Jews "imagined to be a unified conspiracy to dominate the world." Even the term "American Jewish community," when used to describe the Jewish community of the '30s, was misleading. No single American Jewish community existed, though there were a number of separate communities, "each with its own ideology and agenda, which lived in, at best, an uneasy, and, at worst, an uncivil relationship with each other." All in all, German and Eastern European Jews in the United States did not share many of the same values. Moreover, no organization existed, nor was there a single leadership, to compel its will on the community.[42]

In March 1943, eight of the leading American Jewish organizations—four Zionist and four non-Zionist—established the Joint Emergency Committee on European Jewish Affairs (JEC) to focus on Jewish rescue. When members of the JEC wanted to hold public demonstrations to protest Roosevelt's failure to rescue the Jews of Europe, Wise suggested that a delegation from the JEC meet with government officials privately. Wise lamented to Dr. Nahum Goldmann, representative of the Jewish Agency for Palestine in the West, that he had to "protect President Roosevelt from the wild men of the [JEC] committee," by which he meant members of the Jewish Labor Committee and the Orthodox groups.[43]

Regrettably, the JEC was dissolved in a few months because Wise would not allow any "broad-based rescue institution not under his control" to exist. Any organization that might generate adverse publicity to pressure the President could ultimately threaten Wise's dream of a "more equitable society." Rescue issues were relegated to groups where Wise could better control the outcome. When the atrocity stories detailing the murder of 2,000,000 Jews could no longer be denied, Wise meekly asked Roosevelt for a meeting with delegates from Jewish organizations: "I do not wish to add an atom to the awful burden which you are bearing with magic and, as I believe, heaven-inspired strength at this time." Should the President not be able to find time to meet, Wise indicated that, "It would be gravely misunderstood if, despite your overwhelming preoccupation, you did not make it possible to receive our delegation and to utter what I am sure will be your heartening and consoling reply."[44] Despite the potential for eliciting from Roosevelt some action on behalf of European Jewry, "the Holocaust continued, and the opportunities for rescue present in the campaign bargaining of the elections of 1943 and 1944 went ignored."[45]

Among those who benefited from the disunity within the American Jewish community and the indifference of the Roosevelt Administration was Breckinridge Long, Assistant Secretary of State for Special Problems from 1940 to 1944. During his tenure at State, Long was well-known in the department and among Jews as the "individual most identified with restrictive and antisemitic views."[46] He worked hard to thwart Jewish immigration to America by erecting "paper walls,"[47] a series of regulations and obstacles that were practically insurmountable, thereby compounding the difficulties already inherent in the immigration process.

On June 26, 1940, Long informed Assistant Secretary of State Adolf A. Beryl and James Dunn, State Department Advisor on Political Relations: "We can delay and effectively stop for a temporary period of indefinite length the number of immigrants into the United States. We could do this by simply advising our Consul to put every obstacle in the way and to resort to various administrative advices [sic] which would postpone the granting of visas." As a result, only in the year 1939 were the relevant quotas filled.[48]

After convincing Roosevelt in 1941 that the refugees posed a security risk to the U.S., the number of visas decreased even more.[49] The word "refugee" implied "alien" to the bureaucrat and "secret agent" to the military, justifying a policy of keeping Jews, even special refugees, from entering the country.[50] Between 1931-1944 the total number of regular quota immigrants admitted to the U.S. was 377,597—the immigration law permitted 2,154,306.[51]

Long soon learned that the lack of common cause among American Jews would be an asset in his work. On January 11, 1944, shortly before he left his job at State, he wrote in his diary, "The Jewish organizations are all divided amid controversies. There is no cohesion, nor any sympathetic collaboration—rather rivalry, jealousy and antagonism."[52]

Undaunted (Preparations for Europe)

Against this background of turmoil, Baruch would visit the office of the Vaad whenever he could. A day after the war ended, he overheard the members talking about a movement to rebuild the body and spirit of the remnants of European Jewry. Preparations were being made to send *shlichim* (emissaries) to Europe to assist the local surviving Orthodox leadership. Among those leaving were Rabbi Isaac Lewin, professor of Jewish history at Yeshiva University, and the son of the Rzesower Rav, Rabbi Aaron Lewin; Rabbi Sol Rosenberg, a Mizrachi leader from Connecticut; Rabbi Sholom Pinchas Wohlgelernter from Seattle, a scholar with exceptional leadership skills and also a member of Mizrachi; Rabbi Mordechai (Motche) Londinski, the son of a *rosh yeshiva* in Radin; Rabbi Samuel Chill, the rabbi at Brooklyn's Kingsway Jewish Center and Rabbi Shmuel Schechter of the Mir Yeshiva, a very forceful, personable rabbi and scholar who was active in Yeshiva Rabbi Chaim Berlin.[53]

A number of laymen in the Vaad were involved in the process of selecting these men and developing the post-war program. One was Irving Bunim, a key leader and builder of the Young Israel movement. In 1935, when Rav Aharon came to the United States to lecture and meet with the American Orthodox Jewish community, he befriended Bunim, a noted philanthropist, businessman and activist. In 1940, when the rabbi fled to neutral Lithuania to escape the Nazis, Bunim alerted American Jews of the crisis[54] and had Young Israel fund the rabbi's escape to America. Subsequently, he became the rabbi's right hand man. He was the key layman to deal with *rabbanim, roshei yeshivos* and others during the war years and after.

Another leader was Stephen Klein, CEO and founder of Barton's Bonbonniere, a chocolate factory in Brooklyn (the first *Shabbos*-observant retail chain store in America— that grew into the leading maker of kosher candy.) Klein was the chairman of the Vaad Hatzala immigration committee, a former refugee who fled Vienna after the Anschluss in March, 1938. Klein, who was close with Rav Aharon, was a founder of Chinuch Atzmai, an independent Torah school network in Israel in 1953.

Baruch wanted to go to Europe as a Vaad emissary, but many of the rabbis objected because they felt he was too young. Baruch, however, had advocates in Rabbis Silver and Kalmanowitz and others with whom he had developed relationships during the war.

Among the influential non-rabbis who supported his efforts was William I. Alpert, a well-known philanthropist, communal leader and Vaad benefactor. Years earlier, Alpert's son, Charles, had contracted scarlet fever. Having missed a great deal of school, Alpert sought a way for his son to make up his lost school work. When Alpert called Torah Vodaath and asked them for a tutor, they sent Baruch, who became a lifelong friend of the family. Alpert used his influence as a supporter of the Vaad to secure Baruch's assignment as director of the Vaad's office in Germany. Alpert also provided Baruch's airfare and additional funds to facilitate his work, funds which were to be used to help individuals.

Those finally selected to go overseas met with Rabbi Schechter and Stephen Klein, who instructed them how to perform their overseas duties. Their training was cursory at best. When Baruch and Shmuel Schechter heard that Rabbi Motche Londinski was going to Poland, Baruch asked if he feared being posted in this most antisemitic of countries. Londinski told them he bought little American flags to sew onto his uniform. Baruch observed: "We were such amateurs. We weren't trained, we didn't have academic degrees, but we did have heartfelt dedication."[55]

They knew they had a special function to perform. Rav Aharon had said, "An emissary...needs to be entirely clean and free of motives." There was no room for feelings of personal accomplishment, selfishness or self-aggrandizement. The only purpose was to focus on their holy work. They had to have the proper motivation and care deeply about the plight of each Jew.[56] They also knew what the rabbinic sages had said: "There is nothing dearer before God than an emissary who is sent to perform a mitzvah, and gives his entire soul on behalf of it so that he may be successful in his mission."[57]

Despite their impatience to leave for Europe, there were delays. Washington had to clear their trip to Germany via the Joint Chiefs of Staff, which was responsible for background checks. The emissaries also needed the proper documents assigning them to UNRRA. People became frustrated. With families, obligations and duties being put on hold so they could help their fellow Jews, the delays were wasting their available time. This could ultimately prevent them from not only doing their jobs, but actually from even getting to Europe.

Irving Bunim
Photo courtesy of Torah Schools for Israel-Chinuch Atzmai

Stephen Klein
Photo courtesy of Torah Schools for Israel-Chinuch Atzmai

William I. Alpert
Photo courtesy of Alpert family

Chapter 3

Establishing Vaad Hatzala Headquarters in Munich

At the end of the war in May 1945, the Allies divided Germany into four zones: American, Soviet, British and French. The American Zone included the southern states of Bavaria, Hesse and North Wurttemberg-Baden; the Soviets controlled Eastern Germany; Bremen and Bremerhaven were in the British Zone, and the French occupied the Saar Valley, South Wurttemberg and the Rhineland. A portion of Berlin was under the joint authority of the Four Powers.[1] The Four Powers also occupied Austria, but it was treated as a separate entity.[2]

By June 1945, the American Army and the Military Government (MG) were established in Frankfurt, operating as United States Forces, European Theater (USFET). Though there was a general demobilization, the Third and Seventh

Armies still remained in the country as occupiers, with the Military Government in charge of the German European Theater.[3]

Unfortunately, most members of the MG did not speak German, had little or no knowledge of German politics, culture or economics and relied on "unreliable interpreters." There was also a good deal of tension between the MG and the soldiers. As one general opined: "When fighting troops take an area, they consider they own it." There was also a lack of coordination between Army units and each level of command made its own policy.[4] This was especially problematic for Jews because of all the DPs, they presented the Allied armies with the greatest problems.

After the war, the Jews comprised 10 to 20 percent of the displaced persons. The military, because of its inexperience and failure to recognize the realities of the situation, assumed that like the other refugees the Jews would be eager to return to their former homes. But the Allies had failed to address the legal status of the Jewish refugees, their need for kosher food, clothing, shelter and rehabilitation, as well as their desire to re-establish contact with whatever family and friends they could find. Pressured for such special consideration, the American military, acting as an ad hoc relief agency, resented being asked to provide Jews with such preferred treatment or to recognize them as a separate and unique entity.

Nevertheless, though the soldiers viewed the Jews as a burden, they knew if they mishandled the survivors their actions could adversely affect their careers. And so, since many of the officers were combat soldiers uncomfortable in their roles as civilian administrators, they were eager to preserve the status quo, punch their overseas tickets and return home with their careers unscathed. Problems developed, however, when they were rotated home and were replaced with men in positions of leadership who didn't have firsthand knowledge of the atrocities perpetrated against the Jews. As a result, these men had a callous efficiency in the performance of their duties, hardly what was required in dealing with those who had suffered so greatly. Still, many

American officers and soldiers deeply moved by the Jewish plight, extended themselves to assist however they could.[5]

Reports from American Jewish chaplains, American Jewish soldiers, survivors and members of the American press persuaded the American government to investigate the army's treatment of Jews. As a result, in August 1945, the Office of Advisor on Jewish Affairs was created to keep the Commanding General in the European Theater of Operations (ETO) informed of problems facing Jewish DPs. The office, which remained in operation until December 1949, served as an advocate for the needs of the Jewish survivors.

In August 1945, Chaplain Judah Nadich became Consultant on Jewish problems to General Dwight D. Eisenhower. In October 1945, Judge Simon S. Rifkind, the first Advisor on Jewish Affairs, replaced Nadich. Rabbi Philip S. Bernstein, Judge Louis E. Levinthal, Professor William Haber, Harry Greenstein and Major Abraham S. Hyman followed. Each served a term as Jewish advisor before returning to the States. The various Jewish organizations communicated with the Military Government in the American Zone through them.[6]

As more and more survivors emerged from the carnage of the Holocaust, the American Zone became a magnet for these refugees because those in charge were willing to provide assistance. The American Army was there to protect and occupy Germany, but it was also there to help rebuild the Germany economy. One third of German wealth had been destroyed during the war, including "nearly one-fifth of all productive buildings and machines, two-fifths of the transportation facilities, and over one-seventh of all houses. In the American Zone cities, "only 60.5 percent of the homes were usable, of which 4.5 percent" were being used by the troops and DPs. Of the 870,000 buildings still standing in the cities, 320,000 were in need of major repairs.[7]

DP camps, where people could be temporarily housed, were established throughout the German countryside. But they were soon filled with hundreds of thousands of people of different nationalities, none too eager to return to their former countries. The interned Jews refused to be repatriated since they had no families or homes to which to return. Many Ukrainians, Poles and Slovaks also did not want to go back to their countries of origin, even though they still had homes and families. Though they were given every means and encouragement to do so, they did not want to return because most of them had been collaborators and were wanted by the Russians or their own governments for working with the Nazis.

Official Recognition of Vaad Mission

On May 1, 1946, UNNRA Central Headquarters for Germany informed the Vaad that the U.S. Immigration Service and State Department had approved its application "to facilitate immigration to the United States from Germany of displaced persons in the U.S. Zone of occupation in Germany."[8] The Vaad also received permission to work "for the relief and rehabilitation of European Jewry in Germany...."

But the President's War Relief Control Board wanted assurances that Vaad activities justified the organization's registration as a war relief agency because "organizations primarily engaged in the reestablishment of religious life and institutions" did not qualify as relief agencies. Given the board's doubts about "the propriety" of the Vaad's "application," the Vaad did not register as a war relief agency as long as it confined its work to religious activities.[9] Nonreligious equipment and supplies were sent through UNNRA to ensure proper reporting. The Vaad shipped regular relief and religious supplies on its own by securing export licenses from the New York City Office of the Foreign Economic Administration.[10]

Under the terms of the agreement, the Vaad would provide educational training, relief, rehabilitation and religious supplies. This included the establishment of *yeshivos* and seminaries to attract former yeshiva students and young men who wanted to become rabbis, *shochtim* (ritual slaughterers of animals according to Jewish Law), *mohalim* (individuals who perform circumcisions), cantors and scribes.

Bais Yaakov schools for Jewish girls would be established as seminaries to train future teachers. Specialized training in Jewish family purity laws would also be provided since most young women did not have mothers to teach them these laws. Adult education programs, religious *kibbutzim* (collectives), children's homes and cooking schools for girls were also to be organized and supplied with books and materials.

Additionally, the Vaad was expected to provide clothing, import kosher food from the United States and Europe, and establish kosher kitchens and *mikvehs*.[11] By helping the survivors observe *Shabbos* and *kashrus*, the Vaad hoped to reconnect them to Judaism, as well as provide them with direction and stability.[12]

The Vaad's mission was to help the Jewish DPs leave Germany by assisting them to prepare emigration documents, finding institutions to sponsor them, and providing the government with assurances that the refugees would not become financial burdens. It further agreed to assist the DPs until they were self-sufficient. UNRRA was assured that the Vaad would work under its supervision and coordinate its activities. The Vaad also agreed to assume full responsibility for salaries, uniforms and field equipment and to reimburse the agency for any expenses it incurred.[13]

Dr. Samuel Schmidt from Cincinnati, the European director of the Vaad, and a personal friend of Rabbi Eliezer Silver, opened the European office of the Vaad in Paris in 1945. A seasoned public health expert, with a degree from Massachusetts Institute of Technology in public health and biology, Schmidt had served with the Zionist Medical Unit in Palestine in 1918 and as a member of the JDC relief unit in Poland in December 1919. From 1920-1923, he directed the JDC's public health work in Poland. In 1927, he became the editor of *Every Friday*, Cincinnati's English-language Jewish weekly. Born in Kovno, Lithuania, Schmidt spoke a fluent Yiddish.

In February 1940, Rabbi Silver and the Vaad Hatzala had sent Schmidt to Vilna to meet with the great Torah leaders, including Rabbi Hayyim Ozer Grodzinski, to determine the best course of action for relief and rescue and perhaps bring the *yeshivos* to America or *Eretz Israel.* Rabbi Grodzinski implored the Vaad and the American rabbis to redouble their efforts. At the *yeshivos* of Mir, Slobodka, and Kletzk, Schmidt distributed funds given to him by Rabbi Silver. The meeting with Rabbi Grodzinski inspired Schmidt to become an observant Jew.[14]

After the Germans surrendered on May 8, 1945, Schmidt, at the urging of Rabbis Kotler and Silver, contacted his volunteers—including Rabbis Isaac Lewin, Solomon P. Wohlgelernter, Samuel Chill, Shmuel Schechter, Mordechai (Motche) Londinski, Solomon Rosenberg and Zerah Warhaftig, a leader in the Mizrachi and a scholar from Lithuania—to join him in spreading out across Europe as Vaad representatives.

Schmidt established the Vaad's European headquarters and stayed for a few months before going back to the U.S. He returned in October 1946 for eight more months.[15] Rabbi Londinski covered all of Poland with Rabbi Wohlgelernter and shuttled from country to country. Rabbis Lewin and Rosenberg also "floated." The only two resident Vaad representatives in all of Europe were Rabbi Schechter in Frankfurt and, eventually, Baruch in Munich.[16]

While Baruch waited in Paris from late August and early September 1946 for a "call forward" from the Military Government to allow him to enter Germany, he spent his time working with Vaad representatives. Some of them, he complained, were running around without much direction and accomplishing little. He was also disturbed by the people from the States who came for short visits—ostensibly to study the needs of the survivors. One of these "sightseers" (as Baruch called them) went to Prague and Poland, where he found a relative and returned to the U.S without doing much else.

"It is a shame and disgrace to send a visiting fireman like that into Germany," he wrote to William I. Alpert. "Don't we owe the Jews in Germany more than just sending in a delegate of the V.H. [Vaad Hatzala], [take a] look at them and then [fly] off."

Someone needed to straighten out the New York Vaad office, and Baruch wanted Alpert to assume that role. "There

Dr. Samuel Schmidt
Photo courtesy of Rabbi Nathan Baruch

is no question or doubt that there is still a world of work and relief to be dispensed...with the Joint and all other organizations. The V.H. did and still can do...European Jewry a tremendous service," if the Vaad would organize its operation, and enable representatives to work together in a coherent manner, Baruch added.[17] Though Alpert would continue to fund Baruch and the Vaad, his wife's chronic illness and his devotion to her welfare precluded active participation in any organization.

With Rabbi Londinski, Baruch raised a few hundred dollars from people in Paris to clothe 90 young Polish Jewish orphans who were "sitting and learning" day and night while "waiting torn and shattered" in Prague until they could enter France or Belgium. (The French Government had agreed to bring 500 yeshiva students and their teachers to France and 250 into Belgium, where they would be housed in homes acquired by the Vaad.) With their "tattered clothes," they were "a pitiful sight." On one of Londinski's visits to Prague, an 8-year-old pleaded with him for clothing. Crying to Baruch, the child told him how everyone had promised him a coat and shoes, but no one had given him anything. Baruch took $180.00 from Alpert's stipend to clothe 10 of these children. (A cap, coat and a pair of shoes cost $18.00.) [18]

Baruch had "a world of faith and confidence" in Londinski who was "simple, upright and straight," and Londinski had asked him to stay in Paris, but Baruch had committed to going to Germany. There he would be responsible for transferring all the yeshiva students from Germany to France. After he heard from Rabbi Wohlgelernter that the religious *kibbutzim* in Germany were "neglected" and in "desperate need" of someone to help them, he was eager to leave for Germany.[19]

Arrival in Munich

When Baruch arrived in Munich on September 11, 1946, he felt as if he had been dropped into a no-man's land. He reported to UNRRA headquarters and introduced himself to the local officials who assigned him to live with a group of non-Jewish men in a house they had requisitioned. Since they were all single men, they lived in dormitory-style accommodations.[20]

From the moment it first opened its doors in Munich in late August 1946, people waited impatiently for the Vaad Hatzala office to begin its work. Rabbi Rosenberg had been in the Munich office at some point, but Baruch never found out when or why he "very hastily departed."[21]

When Baruch walked into the small, cramped Munich office in September, he was confronted with a huge stack of letters waiting to be mailed. Under the German postal system, it could take months for a letter to be delivered. The U.S. military postal service was more reliable, but DPs were forbidden to use it. To circumvent the red tape, the DPs brought their mail to the Vaad office to use its APO address and post their letters. With no one in charge of the office that service stopped, and the incoming mail had piled up. Emissaries from America passed through Munich, but no permanent director was in charge until Baruch arrived. There were now thousands of letters on his desk. He had the letters put into envelopes and relabeled with his personal APO address. It would be the first of many things Baruch had to do that were of dubious legality, but it made a huge difference in the lives of the DPs.

The Vaad Hatzala had only two other people beside Baruch on site, both survivors: Rabbi Aviezer Burstin and Jacob Deutscher. Rabbi Burstin, a student from the Chachmei Lublin Yeshiva, had just married and was out of the office when Baruch arrived. Upon his return, Baruch facetiously asked him where he had been. Burstin looked at him over his little spectacles and said, "*Mir hoben fahr eich lenger gevahrt*" (We waited longer for you). "He was a very sharp fellow and looked at me as if to say, 'And who are you?' But we hit it off and began working together very amicably."[22]

When people discovered that an American representative had arrived, they flocked to the Vaad's little office. There were lines and clusters of people in front of the building, but nowhere for people to sit while they waited to see Vaad staff. Other relief agencies in the building did not like people waiting

Rabbi Nathan Baruch

Photo courtesy of Rabbi Nathan Baruch

in the street all day and complained, but there was nothing Baruch could do. The Vaad would not turn people away. Traditional Jews were more comfortable with other Orthodox people and the Vaad was a focal point for their needs.[23]

Soon his office was choked with "all sorts of requests," as Baruch informed William Alpert. Stephen Klein had insisted that Baruch focus on immigration and concentrate on specific cases, but Baruch did not have the heart to tell the survivors he could not help them. "Stephen Klein...and the rest must realize...that we can not tell these people...that we are only interested in immigration." From the time he arrived in Paris, Baruch realized that he could not remain "a party man," associated with solely the Agudah or the Mizrachi. "I belong to no party, just to serve these children and these people."[24]

An incident at the Neu Freimann DP Camp outside Munich during his first *Shabbos* in Germany, solidified this view. That Saturday afternoon a group of 50 Russian Jewish children from the Mizrachi, ages 6 to 16, walked a mile and a half with their leaders to Neu Freimann to *daven Mincha* (say afternoon prayers) and eat *seudah shleshis* (the third meal on *Shabbos*). When they had arrived from Russia, "they actually came naked."

Even after they received some clothes in Berlin, "the lucky ones wear a jacket, shirt and pants, no underwear and without coats." A number had no shoes. Twelve members of the group were left behind at Funk Caserne, the camp that processed applicants wanting to settle outside Germany, because they had no shoes. Baruch complained how "It was most aggravating to sit...and listen to the three Mizrachi leaders address them about 'If God wills it' and all that, especially" since "it was so much political talk to such poor little souls who went through so many years of agony and suffering. Some of them so young they don't even remember or know what it means to laugh or play." Yet he was overwhelmed with the children's "spirit" ...their zeal and hope and sureness of finally getting to *Eretz Yisrael*. Baruch wished that "their leaders and liberators would only forget party lines, and concentrate to do the utmost for them according to the spirit of the Torah."[25]

Rabbi Aviezer Burstin
Photo courtesy of Rabbi Nathan Baruch

Jacob Deutscher
Photo courtesy of Rabbi Nathan Baruch

After *Shabbos*, the children put on a presentation of Hebrew songs. When Baruch asked their leader to take the children back to the camp because it was a cold night, he refused. Given what they experienced in Russia, he assured Baruch they could endure any kind of weather until they were taken back to the camp. None of the boys had *tzitzis* (a fringed religious garment), although each wanted his own. *Tefillin* were available, but they had to wait their turn to use them.[26]

Baruch asked Alpert to send children's clothing, cigarettes and especially nylon stockings from Vaad supporter Nathan Hausman. Cigarettes and nylons "are the key to everything here. Without them you can not get anything done, with UNRRA people...and with the secretaries of the Consulate," Baruch said. Everything had to be wrapped in old clothing to hide it from Post Office workers who stole whatever they could.[27]

Because Baruch anticipated the arrival of supplies for the DPs, he looked for a warehouse in which to store them. Since there was no space in Munich, he investigated the facilities at the closed Munich airport. While searching through some deserted hangers, he found a huge supply of "bloomed" hard chocolate, abandoned by the Red Cross, but still edible. He also found many cases of Turkish figs. Commandeering some trucks, he brought them to the Vaad office, distributed the chocolate to the delighted DPs, and soaked and cooked the figs before distributing them. He also received permission to use the deserted hangars as storage facilities.[28]

On November 3, 1946, Baruch wrote to Irving Bunim to explain what he had seen: "I am very sorry to say that everyone back home seems to have a distorted concept of what is being done here, and what is necessary to be done. Of course, we formed our ideas only from what we heard, or from eyewitness reports of delegates who were here." Those who come for only a few days cannot appreciate "the needs, hopes and wishes of our people in such a short time."[29]

Baruch reported that, "Crowds broke their way through the line to see me, as they knew from previous experience that our people drop in for a few days and then disappear. More came daily. I would not exaggerate if I would say there were about a hundred a day. I needed to assure them that I would remain in Germany and would receive every one of them and at least listen to their requests. But I knew it would take some time to organize the Vaad office. The conditions I found there were quite disturbing. The few people...working for us felt no responsibility whatsoever, as they had no one to report to."[30]

One incident illustrated the chaotic state of affairs in Munich. Isaac and Recha Sternbuch, the Vaad Hatzala representatives in Montreux, Switzerland, sent 400 cases of figs to Munich and for some inexplicable reason 200 of them were given to the JDC. After the remaining cases were brought to the Vaad offices at UNNRA Emigration Headquarters, the UNNRA director complained that they had been stored without her consent and that the offices could not be used as a warehouse. To make matters even worse, a pungent odor permeated the entire building. As a result of the slipshod handling of the figs, the other volunteer agencies in the building regarded the Vaad as irresponsible.

Baruch was also mortified about the Vaad's reputation when he conferred with UNNRA officials and was "embarrassed to learn the names [of his] predecessors in the Munich area and...the impression they had left." After outlining his plans, "they said it was all very well, but they were fed up with talk because Vaad Hatzala people had a tendency to appear and disappear and all that remained were promises." Struck by the obvious failure of the Vaad's previous representatives, Baruch resolved, "My only alternative was to prove myself in actual work."[31]

For several weeks before his arrival, 38 cases of clothes from the U. S. were waiting to be picked up from the train station for distribution to the DPs. After he obtained the warehouse at the Munich airport, he had metal doors and shelves installed, secured a truck to transport the clothes and put a DP in charge of the facility. An additional 10 cases of clothing were also found that had been on the site for some time. When he asked UNRRA for a truck, the director of the local UNNRA team said that the clothes and other supplies had to be distributed through normal channels, but earmarked for the Orthodox. The distribution was to be recorded and made available for inspection by the Vaad at any time.[32]

Whenever he went to the warehouse to observe how they were sorting the clothes, Baruch "felt ashamed" and shocked by "what American Jews had the nerve and audacity to send to these people. Every conceivable rag you could think of, items that dated back from one to 50 years, every piece of old, torn, discarded junk was sent here. What did the people back home think of their brethren? To see the Jews of Europe being treated in this way was most aggravating and shameful."[33]

Thankfully, not all the clothing was in such poor condition. Lester Udell, a clothier in New York who was close to Rav Aharon, and later became a member of the board of Directors of Lakewood Yeshiva, sent men's winter coats in time for the season. And another shipment of good clothing came from Hapoel Hamizrachi Overseas Relief Committee.[34]

With weather forecasters predicting that the winter of 1946/47 would be extremely cold, Baruch asked Bunim for winter clothes for the tens of thousands of Polish and Russian Jews in the American Zone with barely any clothing. At Landshut, a town near Munich, he said that the Army had a transit camp for newly arrived Jews where they were kept under UNNRA's jurisdiction until they could be transferred to more permanent housing: "Five thousand Jews were housed in Army tents and slept on Army cots or [on] the bare ground. Hundreds of children walked around barefoot on wet ground, wearing only pants and shirts." When Baruch visited the camp, hundreds of people flocked around him, "mothers with babies in their arms, little Jewish orphans standing and looking at the representative of the Vaad Hatzala. It does not take long—after a few days or weeks—before the left-wing and secular organizations begin to raid these camps and take them under their wings."[35]

Baruch was quite concerned about the youth who "were particularly vulnerable to the secular Zionists and others who tried to entice them into joining their clubs and social groups. After years of living in concentration camps without any religious educational training and having had the most minimal, if any, opportunity to observe Judaism during this time, they were probably indifferent or maybe even antagonistic toward Jewish religious life. Some might have even forgotten about their religious experiences prior to the war altogether. Others might be questioning the existence of God. Under the poor and demoralizing conditions in which the Jews were forced to live after being liberated, it is understandable how these young people could be tempted to abandon their traditions. 'Is that what we want to happen to the remainder of our people?' I asked. 'Must we forsake them?' We have an opportunity to help save these souls. I visited a number of religious homes where they were struggling so hard against the irreligious forces who control all of the committees...and who are trying to completely destroy anything that resembles true Judaism."[36]

Each day he met with delegations from all over Germany who represented *yeshivos*, Talmud Torahs, *kibbutzim*, children's homes and kosher kitchens that were in dire need of clothing, food and relief. No one left empty-handed. When he arrived in Munich he found 70 cases of margarine, about 50 cases of fish, figs, and 25 cases of raisins, some potato flour and candles. "Every bit means so much to them," he said, "as UNRRA is cutting their rations to meet with the new requirements and the up-building of the German economy. The JDC has tremendous warehouses and stockpiles of supplies, but who gets it I am still trying to find out. What I did find out is that our religious people did not receive anything from them. The little that is extended is most encouraging to them, as they come from as far as four hundred to five hundred...kilometers, and many of these people and camps are really in bad shape.'"[37]

As Vaad supplies dwindled, he appealed to everyone connected to the organization not to abandon these people again. He struggled "so hard to build up the name of the Vaad and did not want it to be shamed by our lack of response..." To expedite the supply of food, he suggested that it be sent from

London, and asked for chocolate bars, since UNNRA said it would stop supplying them to the children.[38]

Every day people asked Baruch for German Marks. With little in the way of money coming from the Vaad offices in the U.S., he used the special funds specifically designated for individuals given to him by William Alpert and Benjamin Leichtung, another philanthropist. Those funds were very limited and Baruch desperately wanted to find a way to continue helping the survivors. His predecessors had made unrealistic commitments and the DPs expected Baruch to fulfill them. Furthermore, he was having a difficult time raising the money to continue paying for office staff and other incidentals.[39]

In the meantime, in addition to his money problems, Baruch was constantly at odds with the Vaad, especially vis-à-vis the Vaad's focus on emigration. Faced with recalcitrant consuls still working under Long's "paper wall" ideology, Baruch sought to impress upon his stateside brethren the need to lobby Washington on behalf of the survivors.

"With regard to emigration ('Vaad Hatzala's baby')," Baruch pointed out the need to appreciate "what was realistic and what was not. Members of the Vaad were under the impression that when their representative came to Europe for a quick tour lasting a couple of weeks or so and managed to process a few immigration cases, that he saved the lives of some Jews. 'And who are we to judge the value of one Jew's life?' we ask. Everyone in the Vaad in America then proclaims, 'that the entire trip was worthwhile.' But this is a distorted view of the process because this is not how it works."

Even assuming that he spoke to the prospective immigrant, mentioned his name to the American Consul, and informed the Vaad office in New York about the case, this "did not constitute saving their lives...Emigration was a long, tiring, tedious and dragged out process. Prospective immigrants had to go through certain prescribed procedures. And even when they were eligible to receive visas, there was no guarantee they would be granted any. Everything depended upon which quota they came under and the number of visas allotted. The consuls, in turn, received their directives from Washington. No matter what we attempted to do here, no matter how many conferences we had with the members of the consulate in Germany, policy was made there. And that is why we had to focus our energies on Washington."[40]

Baruch also believed the Vaad had erred in not having its own agency in Germany to register the people when the process began. In the Vaad's absence, the rabbis, their families and yeshiva students registered with the JDC, UNNRA teams, or HIAS, and the cases "were neglected. There was no one to push them through the various steps to UNNRA and from UNNRA to the Consulate and then from the Consulate to the CIC [Consul in Charge]. From there it was up to the Consul to take action." Precious months were lost as the cases "were mislaid and held up."[41]

Baruch began taking case histories to gain some control of the process. He could not understand why some individuals who had registered months earlier had already departed for the U.S. while others were still waiting and had not yet even been called to the CIC. When Baruch asked the Consul about this anomaly, he "answered jokingly, that is how [Abe] Grossman, who headed the HIAS there, made his bread and butter. Grossman was at the Consulate all the time to see to it that HIAS cases were taken step-by-step through the process, while all that time our cases were lying in other people's hands and nothing was being done about them." In other words, all of the Vaad's cases in the Munich area were "...botched up. One is worse than the other." Baruch would have done much better "if he could only start each case anew."[42] Baruch also received requests from rabbis to intervene on behalf of Jews who were jailed for some alleged illegal activity.[43]

"All in all," he concluded, "it is very encouraging when you visit the religious camps and *kibbutzim* to see how proudly they maintain their religious life, kosher kitchens, *mikvehs*, Talmud Torahs—how faithfully they cling to teachings of the Torah. They remain undaunted, though they see the freer [non-observant] camps receiving better care...But they are satisfied with their way of life, if at least we would show an interest in them and in their cause...[A]gain I state, they ask so little from us." He hoped that his report had "provided a clearer picture of the situation...and that something concrete would be done to rectify our past errors."[44]

A little more than a month later, Bunim warned Baruch about the American Jewish merchants who visited Germany for a brief period and then returned to the U. S. with reports about the Vaad. A number described how our representatives "live in luxury...in contrast to the miseries of the people there..." One individual told Bunim "that our people in Europe live like bureaucrats and have lost every sense of human compassion with the individual who comes to see them." Bunim could understand "how anyone would act with thousands of people clamoring for his attention, but we must at all times be mindful that the basic cause of our mission is mercy and kindness and each individual counts."[45] He demanded "the cause of such complaints be eliminated forthwith."[46]

This was the first and last time Baruch received any communication of this nature from the Vaad. Whatever real or imagined problems existed prior to his arrival, they were no longer an issue.

To appreciate the financial constraints under which Baruch labored as he began his work in Germany, one only had to read Irving Bunim's report on Vaad activities. It showed that from January 1, 1946 to September 1946 the Vaad had a gross income of $1,243,000—$52,850 of this sum was earmarked by relatives for transportation, while $103,000 was loaned by the directors of Vaad Hatzala. This left an income of $1,087,286 of which $671,320 was divided up: 38 percent for child reclamation, relief and rehabilitation; 17 percent to support the *yeshivos* and to establish new ones; 10 percent for emergencies; 8 percent for transportation and relocation, and 2 percent for administration. In addition, the Vaad sent $98,000 to the Jews in Shanghai to sustain 600 people. Immigration and transportation: $55,000. To Poland, $44,000; relief supplies and clothing, $34,000; special for children's homes, $37,000.[47]

The JDC

Lack of funds was only one of the obstacles Baruch faced. The JDC was among his most difficult adversaries. The JDC had come to Germany in July 1945. By the end of November, it had between 50 and 60 JDC representatives working in the larger DP camps in the American Zone.[48] Like the other relief organizations, it was woefully unprepared for what it faced.

In March 1946, Chaplain Oscar M. Lifschutz, an Orthodox rabbi and Assistant Chaplain for United States Forces Austria (USFA), asked the Agudath Israel of Great Britain for "religious aid," because the JDC was "primarily concerned with food and clothing." Lifschutz was "concerned" about providing fundamental religious items "that were completely lacking."[49]

Rabbi Lifschutz had tapped into one of several "parallel supply channels" which appeared several months after liberation to provide aid to observant Jews. Those associated with Agudath Israel obtained supplies from the American Agudath Israel, the JDC and the Vaad. The Klausenberger Rebbe received supplies from his sources in America and from the JDC. Lubavitcher Hasidim in Pocking were supplied by the Lubavitchers in America, by the JDC and the Vaad.[50] Groups affiliated with the Mizrachi were furnished with supplies from the JDC and the Vaad.

Thus, "The JDC served as a common denominator supplying the physical and spiritual needs of all Jewish DPs in Germany regardless of affiliation. Out of necessity... a working relationship was maintained between the JDC and the various sectarian groups that were on the receiving end of its multifaceted distributions. [But] no such cooperation could exist...between the JDC and the Vaad, its parallel and rival sectarian American counterpart, nor among the various Orthodox groups in Germany intent upon achieving post-war religious control over various aspects of the lives of observant DPs."[51]

Baruch believed that the JDC wanted the Vaad to fail because it alone wanted to care for all the survivors, including those of the Orthodox and yeshiva world. Yet when it came to providing kosher food, he was disturbed with the JDC's inability to provide it. He concluded that the JDC viewed it as too expensive and too difficult to procure. Non-kosher UNNRA rations would have to suffice for many Jews. And this became the crux of one of Baruch's confrontations with the JDC: One of the Vaad's main priorities was to obtain kosher food.

The apparent lack of sensitivity to the needs of observant Jews was visible in a number of other areas. JDC-funded recreation and entertainment events, such as soccer games, were scheduled on the Sabbath. When Samuel Schmidt worked for the JDC, he always worried about the concerns of Orthodox Jews. He believed that such thoughtfulness and solicitude would exist in Europe, but it never did. He might have assumed that Joseph Schwartz, who chaired the European executive council of the JDC, would have been especially sympathetic. Schwartz received *smicha* from Yeshiva University's rabbinical seminary and was a member of a very prominent Orthodox family in Baltimore, Maryland. Yet Baruch constantly argued with the JDC representatives about scheduling these activities on *Shabbos*.[52]

Another wedge preventing cooperation was educational systems. Given the JDC's secular educational philosophy, the JDC still believed it could oversee the religious education of Orthodox Jews. According to Dr. Koppel S. Pinson, JDC educational director in Germany and Austria, the JDC believed that "Jewish life is a pluralistic one and that each group in Jewish life is worthy of help and encouragement. Such a philosophy does not mean passive disinterestedness in educational or cultural ideas; it should mean a positive approach to Jewish life and active encouragement of all sizable groups, religious or nonreligious, orthodox, conservative or reform, Zionist, non-Zionist and anti-Zionist, Hebraist or Yiddish, Polish, German or Greek Jews, all of them are entitled to our help in working out their programs of educational and cultural work."[53]

In pursing this policy of "active tolerance," Pinson believed the JDC should be "an active force in making Jewish life richer, broader and more tolerant." The JDC was the only Jewish relief agency in Europe that believed it had a "special responsibility of being the guardian of tolerance for all groups and special protector of minority groups."[54]

Pinson felt the JDC had to play this role because "there are many evidences in the Jewish community of Germany and Austria of undue pressure being exercised by either majorities upon minorities or organized minorities upon unorganized majorities." From this he concluded that, "Totalitarianism has left its impression upon Jews."

JDC personnel were thus obligated to ensure that such pressure was reduced to a minimum. Failure to do so would mean that they were betraying the trust placed in them by the American Jewish community. Pinson warned that they be careful not to impose their own educational philosophy and familiarize themselves with the "different types of legitimate cultural needs."[55]

Recognizing that one of "the main criticisms leveled against the JDC has been the cultural gap existing between our workers and the DPs," and realizing that they could not "become steeped in Yiddish and Hebrew culture overnight," JDC personnel could compensate for their "lack of familiarity with warm sympathy and interest for their cultural values and accepting them on par with our own."[56]

In delineating the purposes of this educational program, Pinson suggested that one of the reasons for the program was "to provide a complement to the deep Jewish consciousness, which up till now is based almost entirely upon martyrdom and suffering and thus [is] most of the time hysterical in character, with deeper knowledge of Jewish culture, thus giving a healthier foundation to their Jewish consciousness."[57]

Pinson indicated that JDC workers should "modify the now dominant spirit in these children's schools which keeps harping on the gruesome experience of the past years, on ideas of revenge, on fanatical contempt for the rest of the world and an unrealistic feeling of complete self-sufficiency against the rest of the world." He acknowledged that there was time for "these children to be children" and saw no reason why the process should not begin even in this "temporary and unsettled state."[58]

Pinson recognized that Orthodox Jews would require a house of study (*beis medrash)*, for those who wished to pursue "rabbinical studies," because "rabbinical students" conduct their studies in a collective fashion.[59]

Under the heading of relations with other voluntary agencies, Pinson listed the Jewish Agency for Palestine, the British Council for Jewish Relief Abroad and ORT. The relationship with these groups was cordial and Pinson expected it would continue. The Vaad Hatzala was not included in this group, in part because spiritual and religious rehabilitation was not mentioned anywhere in the directive. When Pinson discussed the destruction of the "Jewish intelligentsia," he indicated, "that every poet, painter, musician, scholar or scientist salvaged from the wrecks of European Jewry is a treasure that must be carefully protected to a position where they can begin once again to release their creative energies for the good of the Jewish people and mankind."[60] It was telling that he never mentioned the great Jewish thinkers or Torah scholars.

In the "Report of Education Survey-American Zone Third Army Area Germany" of December 26, 1945-January 5, 1946, M. Jacob (Jack) Joslow, who was a high school principal until he joined the JDC in 1945 to organize educational activities for the Jews of Europe, wrote that: "The fact that they are alive is an indication that they possessed either a cunning or a special ability useful to the Hitler war machine. The intelligent members of the Jewish European race for the most part have been 'exterminated' leaving as remnants of six million only those who were 'hardened' to the type of treatment they endured."[61]

To evaluate the existing educational programs and determine what was needed with regard to materials and organization, Joslow personally visited camps and communities and held conferences where he met with officials, camp members, and with the cultural committees in every camp he visited. Except for acknowledging plans for establishing *yeshivos* in the DP camps in Landsberg and Feldafing "for those so inclined," the report focused on the need for vocational training, English and Hebrew

97

language instruction, kindergartens and nurseries, plays in Yiddish and Hebrew and theatrical kits for the various dramatic groups, teacher training, libraries, Yiddish and English films, educational slides and film strips, sports and other recreational equipment and securing teaching personnel. Joslow's report included an extensive list of items, including religious texts, *tefillin, taleisim* (prayer shawls) and other items for traditional Jews. Jacob L. Trobe, who in mid-September 1946 became the JDC director for Germany, submitted the report to JDC headquarters in New York.[62]

The failure to mention spiritual rehabilitation in either Pinson's directive or Joslow's statement revealed the basic flaw in those sent to help DPs. Many JDC personnel couldn't connect with the survivors because they did not speak their languages; they knew little of European and Jewish culture, and did not empathize with their religious beliefs. Some also patronized the survivors.

In a very real sense, it was difficult, if not impossible, for outside individuals or groups to cooperate with the JDC, because the JDC viewed these efforts as an intrusion on its turf. For the Vaad this was not new, for since its inception in November 1939, the Vaad had been in an ongoing fight with the JDC.

Chapter 4

A Call for Unity and a Mission to Europe

Given the tremendous needs of the survivors not being met and the absence of a concentrated effort by the American Orthodox community to help observant European Jewry, the Vaad insisted there be unity among the Orthodox Jews or the mission of saving the Torah community in Europe would be doomed. At a meeting in New York on March 6, 1946, Irving Bunim warned that the Vaad could not tolerate other Orthodox organizations conducting independent fundraising campaigns and duplicating the Vaad's work. He suggested the election of an executive board from all segments of the Orthodox community. Without this cooperation, he felt the JDC would become responsible for the fate of Orthodox Jews in Europe—an unacceptable condition, given the JDC's lack of understanding of the religious and spiritual needs of observant Jews.[1]

Rabbi Jacob Rosenheim, president of the World

Organization of Agudath Israel, asked that older organizations be permitted to continue their work while cooperating with the Vaad. He felt it was unrealistic for the Vaad to be the umbrella fund-raiser for relief work. He cited a request from 500 Agudah-affiliated Jews in the Landsberg DP camp. The Agudah felt obligated to respond *directly* because their members had made the request to them, and it was paramount that the Agudah "retain its identity and prestige." The Vaad also could not ask the Agudah to refrain from touting its own accomplishments. These "function[s] belong to [the Agudah] and they have the right to publicize it." Rosenheim claimed the same was true regarding the packages the Agudah sent overseas.[2]

Leon Gellman, the head of Mizrachi, defended the JDC, and indicated that the Vaad had come under significant criticism in Europe. But since every Orthodox Jew in Europe was either affiliated with Mizrachi or Agudah, he agreed that the Vaad, under the leadership of the Union of Orthodox Rabbis, should be the only organization to help religious Jews in Europe. He concurred that only one agency should raise funds. As such, Mizrachi would not conduct its own campaign unless the Agudath Harabonim left the Vaad.[3]

Rabbi Hoffman of the Hungarian Federation disagreed. Not all Orthodox European Jews were partisan. He challenged the notion that the Vaad was capable of taking care of all the religious Jews in Europe. He believed the JDC did good work, but they did not understand the needs of the Orthodox "as well as we do." That's why the Hungarian Federation cooperated with the Joint to care for Orthodox Jews.[4] Hoffman also opposed the single-agency fundraising campaign, because the Hungarian Federation could raise more money among its own people than the Vaad could by approaching the same individuals. When asked why the $50,000 raised by the Hungarians was channeled through the JDC rather than the Vaad, Hoffman answered that it was because the JDC had trucks bringing medical supplies to the people in Hungary. The Vaad was not yet in that league.[5]

Bunim said he understood the criticism and replied, that "an organization as small as ours...would fall short" of people's expectations. "The Joint with its $10 million program" is criticized for its shortcomings so "we…must expect" that "with only a million dollar budget" we would be criticized as well. But when individuals "in the audience direct criticism against the Vaad Hatzala, they are directing it at themselves, since they are the Vaad Hatzala."[6]

Rabbi Benjamin Hendles, executive director of the Agudah, suggested that a committee composed of one representative each from Mizrachi, Agudah Youth (Zeirei), Poale Mizrachi, Agudath Israel of America, Young Israel and the Hungarian Federation be formed to discuss this issue and that it be chaired by Rabbi Israel Rosenberg.[7]

In a follow-up meeting, Rabbi Rosenheim informed Bunim that the Agudah would not put "its longstanding activities for relief and immigration into a new organization." To show its good will, however, the Agudah would not hold mass meetings, Agudah speakers would cooperate with the Vaad and no campaigns would be run when the Vaad conducted its annual fundraising activities.[8]

In return, Rabbi Rosenheim wanted a guarantee that when delegations were sent to Washington or elsewhere, they would include at least one member of the Agudah and Mizrachi. When necessary, the Agudah would explain the relationship between the Agudah and the Vaad to prevent the "erroneous impression" that the Agudah had abdicated its position in favor of the Vaad Hatzala. "On the basis of such legal agreements, unity and active cooperation should and could be achieved," declared Rabbi Rosenheim.[9]

While Vaad activities continued in Europe, Bunim tried to find a way to resolve differences back home. In a letter to Rabbi Rosenheim on July 2, 1946, he made it clear that the problems facing the Jews were not about the Agudah or the Mizrachi. Poles were murdering Jews in post-war Europe and the British were preventing Jews from entering Palestine. "Unless something is done immediately by you and your colleagues in the Agudah, as well as by the leaders in the Mizrachi and others, the result will be tragic," he warned. "And the price will be paid not by those who are responsible for the results, here, but by our unfortunate brethren who have every right and reason to demand from us more than help and deeper sympathy and understanding." He ended by pleading for his colleagues to "resume your active participation in the Vaad Hatzala."[10]

The Sternbuchs in Switzerland heard about the organizational disunity in America and wondered whether the Vaad would be dissolved in the near future. Bunim assured them that the Vaad was not being "liquidated" because the Jews in Europe were looking to the Vaad "to be rescued and rehabilitated...We have no intentions of selling these people 'down the river.'"[11]

In August, Bunim informed the Agudah that some of their people were endangering the Vaad's work in Poland by selling passports. The French government detected one irregular visa that could have jeopardized all the Vaad's activities in France.

In another instance, an Agudah advertisement appeared in a local paper soliciting funds and named Jews taken out of Poland by Recha Sternbuch. The Agudah claimed credit for this, but Bunim believed the Vaad was entitled to the money raised by this "false advertising." He said that unless the organizations work together in the U. S. "on a satisfactory basis" he would instruct Vaad representatives not to honor any requests from the Agudah or their agents.[12]

Bunim remembered the days when the Agudah would put everything aside to go to Washington in the interests of the Vaad. He remembered when "the word of Rabbi Kotler and other great men meant so much to them, and [he did] not like that to sink into the callousness of political machinery."[13]

Bunim's criticism intensified in November when he could not explain why dissension continued among all segments of the Orthodox community.[14] The constant bickering took its toll on him and he lashed out at those criticizing the Vaad.[15] Vaad work, he declared, came before wedding anniversaries, wives' birthdays or visits from friends. "We never got a call to go to Washington that we did not go [sic]. We have been on trips constantly, flying all over the country, carrying the word of V[aad] H[atzala]. We paid our bills—we owe you nothing."[16]

Rabbi Silver and Rabbi Israel Rosenberg, chairman of the presidium of the Agudath Harabonim, were determined to find a solution to the bickering. In late November 1946, after returning from a fact-finding trip to Europe,[17] Rabbi Silver and Rabbi Rosenberg decided to institute sweeping changes to enable the Agudath Harabonim to take control of the organization, partly because the Vaad had gone beyond its original mandate. While they had no problem with laymen raising funds and helping lobby Washington, the major administrative fundraising and decision-making positions were to be filled by rabbis only.

Rabbi Silver wanted the immigration offices of the two groups combined because he believed the Agudath Harabonim would "gain quick access" to the American consuls and the State Department. At that point, Rabbi Silver was president of both the Agudah and the Vaad, and did not anticipate any objections to appointing a committee to lobby Washington for visas.[18]

Rabbi Silver also asked for an accounting of the monies received and the activities for Rescue Children, Inc. a national foster-child and adoption program that provided aid to thousands of orphans in Vaad Hatzalah homes.[19] The mission of Rescue Children, according to their Certificate of Incorporation, was nothing less than to save thousands of surviving Jewish children in Europe. They would: "a) Establish Orthodox Jewish children's centers in Europe to provide adequate housing and shelter, food and clothing, medical and dental care, secular and religious education for Jewish War orphans in Europe; b) Voluntarily assist and aid in the continued maintenance and care of children's centers already in existence in Europe; c) Voluntarily assist in location of relatives of European war orphans with a view of reuniting them with members of their own families; d) Spend net funds... for sole benefit of European War orphans, [and] e) Solicit, collect and otherwise raise funds for carrying out charitable and philanthropic purposes."[20]

Rabbi Silver also wanted the rabbis in Europe, especially those from Poland who wanted to settle in *Eretz Israel* to be able to do so. He was disturbed that some Vaad funds were used to help those leaving for America instead of maintaining Jews left in Europe. Many people he met thought that the Vaad Hatzala had "died" and "gone out of business." Others, including Torah scholars, had complaints against the Vaad.[21]

Bunim bristled at the demand of Rabbi Silver, Rabbi Rosenberg and the Agudath Harabonim for rabbinical control of all decision-making. He said laymen had become involved in the Vaad at the invitation of the rabbis and took direction from them. If their assistance was no longer needed, they would withdraw. Rabbi Silver countered that the reorganization was not intended to estrange the laymen, but to bring them closer together. He did not say how this might be accomplished.

Bunim said the Vaad's mission had changed from solely helping the *b'nei Torah*. Donors wanted the funds they provided to bring their relatives out of Europe. Though these people were not rabbis or students (three quarters of Vaad funds were spent on rabbis and yeshiva students) the Vaad was forced to comply, recognizing that if it did not help them, the Vaad's income would be reduced to about half of what it collected annually.[22]

Bunim agreed that the Vaad had to stop fighting with the JDC, but he had serious reservations. Rabbi Silver wanted an agreement with the JDC to clarify areas of responsibility and avoid duplication. Bunim stressed the fact that the JDC provided only $200,000 for religious relief work. American Jews raised millions a year for the JDC, but only $200,000 would be allotted for rehabilitation. And if the Vaad accepted this offer, it would be obligated to cease all independent fundraising.[23]

Rabbi Silver criticized the Vaad representatives in Europe who preceded Nathan Baruch. He maintained that they had done nothing and should not remain there. He was especially critical of one representative who created a major problem ("spoiled everything") by promising sums that could not possibly be raised. Rabbis would still be encouraged to go to Europe on behalf of the Vaad, but no laymen would be of use unless they went with "hundreds of thousands of dollars."[24]

Rav Aharon said that the Vaad still had lots to do, but

Rabbi Eliezer Silver (left) on fact-finding mission
with Isaac Sternbuch.

At Prague railroad station with Recha Sternbuch.

Photos from *Ish Ha'Halacha v'haMasheh* (1946)

that the burden rested on the shoulders of just a few people. This was not because they wanted the responsibility, but because no one else would assume it. Those who came to meetings every six months to complain were urged to volunteer their time more frequently. While there were valid complaints about the work of the Vaad representatives in Europe, Rav Aharon asserted they were doing a good job helping Jews leave Europe through the *Brichah,* and that its presence was important. Rather than cut Vaad activities for lack of money, he urged that more funds be raised. And he felt strongly that the Jewish orphans should not be left in the hands of the JDC.[25]

Stephen Klein's Mission to Europe

In the midst of this discord, Stephen Klein went on a fact-finding mission to Europe, at his own expense, on behalf of the Vaad Hatzala. He was there from October 26, 1946 and visited England, France, Belgium, Switzerland and Germany before returning to the U. S. on February 3, 1947. Before he left the States, he shipped clothing, shoes, underwear, candles and religious books to the Vaad Hatzala Committee in Paris[26] through American Aid To France, Inc., which sent relief supplies to France for free for the Vaad and other relief organizations—as long as each shipment weighed 200 or more pounds.[27] Klein brought chocolates from his own factory, a luxury in post-war Europe, and used them to thank officials who helped him.[28]

Before Klein left, Irving Bunim arranged a "little social send-off party" on September 23 to let Vaad supporters know that Klein's mission was to strengthen the Vaad and expand its activities.[29] Together with Rabbi Simcha Wasserman, who had a yeshiva in Paris, and Rabbi Motche Londinski, he established committees to oversee Vaad operations. Each committee had to have at least one member from the Agudah, one from Mizrachi, one nonpartisan member and the local rabbi. When there was more than one rabbi in the community, the rabbinical council would assign one or more of their colleagues to serve on the committee.[30]

The money Klein brought with him, and the funds he received while he was there, were given to the local communities who controlled their distribution. Half was to be used to educate the children. The other half was to help rabbis function as the heads of their communities— and maintain kosher kitchens, *mikvehs*, Talmud Torahs and other institutions.[31]

The other priority was to assist Jews fleeing from Poland, Russia and Slovakia. The Vaad wanted to reorganize committees in Lodz, review the status of the committee in Katowice and assist yeshiva students and rabbis to emigrate as soon as possible. Until the children could leave Poland, the Vaad wanted to provide religious education and relief for them. And everywhere he went, Klein was asked to find a way to use the nonquota visas to get rabbis and yeshiva students to the U.S.[32]

Scholars in France were housed in inappropriate and "unsuitable" accommodations, so Klein found them places to stay until final arrangements could be made for their departure to the U.S. or *Eretz Israel*. If the JDC offered him appropriate solutions to these problems, Klein would consider its offer.[33]

After six weeks in Europe, Klein wrote to his friend Benjamin Pechman that he was working an average of 18 to 20 hours a day. To save time, he worked during the day and traveled by train or car at night. He visited embassies and consulates to determine how to facilitate the immigration process. "You cannot imagine the sort of condition[s] that these unfortunate people are in, especially those that have arrived in Germany during the last few months. They are mainly [O]rthodox Jews. I cannot understand how I can remain sane after seeing all the terrible tragedy that is happening to our people. How big the *Zores* [suffering] Israel is [sic] cannot possibly be described on paper."[34]

If Pechman could understand how a person worries about not earning a good living for his family, then he could "...imagine what it is like to worry about tens of thousands of people who are looking to you as a Messiach [Messiah], and you are only able to give them so little. Not once have I cried for the pain I have seen among our people."[35] People who once

107

Stephen Klein with DP children.
Photo courtesy of Yeshiva University Archives.

had large families and were quite comfortable economically "are today happy if they are able to get the delicacy of a piece of potato or soup, such as we couldn't eat or even stand the smell of it, being served in tin cans."[36]

Klein had not written to anyone previously because he felt there was no point in "talking about it for nobody does anything, so it is much better to save the words,"[37] but he could no longer keep silent.

With Vaad funds, Klein was able to open 20 kosher kitchens with food he purchased in Switzerland and France. He lauded Recha and Isaac Sternbuch for providing food on a steady basis to the Jews in Germany. They worked with "inhuman strength and long hours...."[38] "With the little [money] he received, [Isaac] Sternbuch performed miracles."[39]

Although they were friends, Klein had never previously asked Pechman for help, but after seeing the desperate situation of the survivors, he requested that he send food packages, each weighing up to 70 pounds, to Vaad offices in Munich and Frankfurt. He asked that each package should contain flour, vegetable fats, oil in cans, condensed milk, coffee, cocoa, tinned fruit, raisins for making wine, cigarettes, tuna fish, a *Chumash* (Bible) with Rashi commentary, *tzitsis* (fringed garments for men) and a *Nusach Sephard Siddur* (prayer book).[40]

In December 1946, Klein sent a number of telegrams to prominent Orthodox Jews in the U.S. asking for their immediate help. In separate telegrams to Arthur Belfer and Emanuel and Josef Berger he wrote: "Some of European Famous Leading Balabatim [successful businessmen] Who Lived Siberia During War Are Now In Danger In Their Lives [sic] In Poland. Need 1000 Dollars From You Immediately To Rescue Them...Remember Our Tragedy of 1943 Too Little Too Late."[41]

To Joseph Shapiro he wrote: "Group of Nine Mothers and Four Fathers Who Survived Siberia For Four Years Have Now Opportunity Of Taking Their Children Out Of *Goyish* Homes Where There [sic] Lived For Five Years. Special Emissary Available To Do The Job. Need 1500 dollars...."[42]

In separate telegrams sent to William Alpert and Jack and Israel Kestenbaum, he wrote: "8 Great Scholars With Tuberculosis Must Leave France For Switzerland At Once. Winter Here Hard Brutal. Safe [sic] Them From Death After All They Have Been Through. Deposit 1000 Dollars With [Irving] Bunim For Stephen Klein Account Apply Hotel Moderne Paris."[43]

To Vaad Hatzala New York he wrote: "Mrs. [Recha] Sternbuch Returned From Poland. There Are Possibilities To Rescue 1000 Outstanding Families. Polish Government Gave Definite Promise To Give Passports. I Could Get Belgian and French Visas But Cannot Start That Movement Until At Least 50000 Dollars For transportation Only Are Secured...Other telegrams were sent to Max Eisenberg, Abraham Mazer and Leon Fruchthandler."[44]

Immigration and Visas

The Hotel Moderne housed the Vaad offices in Paris. There they worked on immigration and transportation with a staff of five, three women and two men. Rabbi Wasserman temporarily ran the office. A man from a local yeshiva was also at the office to lobby for the needs of his institution. During a four-week span, 40 people were sent from Paris to the U.S., and the Vaad paid most of the costs. At first, Klein secured 500 French visas for Polish Jews,[45] and ultimately obtained more than 1060 visas—allowing the Vaad to legally bring people out of Poland.[46]

Because the American Consul was short of staff, he allowed the Vaad to process its visas at the Vaad office. Applicants visited the Consulate to receive medical examinations and have their fingerprints taken. Before Klein arrived in Paris, only eight visas were issued. After his arrival, he expected the number would increase to 50 per week.[47]

Klein also met with the Polish Consul to obtain the documents for American visa applications. When a group of students did not have valid passports, Klein secured them, enabling the Consul to issue visas. To expedite the visa procedure, Klein also arranged for a member of the Consul staff to be assigned to the Vaad Hatzala.[48]

It wasn't long before Klein ran into the roadblocks erected by the State Department to keep Jews out of the United States. Visa applications had to state where the people had been during the past 10 years. As Klein noted, this was "a little difficult because they were in four or five countries...and if...[the American Consul] had to ask each Consulate in each of these countries if the people applied for visas or [if he had to ask for] any other information...it would take a lot of time and lot of expense, since all these cables had to be paid for by the Vaad Hatzala." Klein suggested that State Department officials be assured that the Vaad knew these people personally and that they were morally upstanding individuals. Klein hoped that Bunim would be able to obtain a "general ruling" for Vaad Hatzala cases so that this obstacle would be eliminated. In the meantime, Klein worked with yeshiva students and rabbis who were in one or two countries during the war, and so was able to get visas quickly. Among other things, applicants had to offer officials proof of future employment in America.[49]

Bunim and other members of the Vaad met with officials from the State Department on November 16, 1946. They were promised that the American Consul in France would receive a cable informing them that the Department had investigated the authenticity of the employment contracts from synagogues and *yeshivos*, as well as the rabbinical status of the applicants and were satisfied with the documents. They would ask the Consul to authorize visas, unless he found evidence to the contrary. Bunim asked Klein for a list of the rabbis who had difficulty in obtaining visas, so the State Department could refer these cases to the Consul for clarification.[50]

Bunim and his group also met with Ugo Carusi, the Commissioner of Immigration, and his advisor about student visas. For 24 years there had been a rule in force: A temporary visitor or student had to provide documentation where he would go after completing his studies or at the end of his visit. Carusi and members of his staff were satisfied with the

Vaad's guarantee, but the legal department said that the American Consul would have to follow the regulations unless the ruling could be changed or amended. A meeting with the Attorney General and the State Department needed to be arranged and this required time. The Vaad was also told that if an individual had a Polish passport for only a short time, they would recommend that the Consul provide the person with a temporary visa for the U.S. for as long as the passport was valid. The Polish Consul would then extend the passport in the U.S.[51]

In the meantime, American consuls in Germany were giving visas to rabbis, but not to students. Bunim suggested that Klein approach the Inter-Governmental Committee on Refugees (IGC) to obtain its support so that stateless students and their wives could enter Germany or some other country once their visas expired in the U.S. Bunim urged him to get documents from the consulates of Morocco, Luxembourg, Costa Rica or other South American countries because the State Department did not care where Jews went after their American visas expired.[52] Klein turned to the IGC, established in 1938 to find homes for refugees, because its post-war responsibilities included coordinating DP affairs and easing administrative transitions.[53]

When Klein went to London to meet with the IGC, he found that they only wanted the JDC and the Jewish Agency for Palestine to represent the Jews in Europe. Klein explained that the Vaad had a different mission than other relief organizations and questioned whether the IGC had the authority to make such arrangements. When he informed them that he did not want to go to Washington to discuss the exclusion of the Vaad, he sensed that they were very concerned that he "might complain to the Five Powers, especially Washington."[54]

In response to a claim by the JDC that the Vaad was duplicating its work, Klein observed that "it is not we who are duplicating, but it is Joint who is trying to imitate and duplicate us."[55] At another point he remarked that, "It is unbelievable how little relief work is done by the JDC in Europe, especially in Germany. They depend entirely on UNRRA and the Military."[56]

Klein realized the only way to overcome the slow process of getting people out of Germany was to increase the number of Jews coming to the U.S. on a non-quota basis. He made some initial attempts to so, but he turned the work over to Rabbi Sol Rosenberg before leaving the country.[57]

Finding transportation for DPs immigrating to the U.S. also consumed a great deal of Klein's time. U.S. Lines and the Chief Consul in Germany promised him some ships from Bremen that would stop in Le Havre, France to pick up yeshiva students. To ensure that other additional avenues of transportation would be available, Klein urged Pincus Schoen, executive director of the Vaad in New York, to arrange reservations for sick DPs on the Queen Elizabeth from Southampton, England to the U.S.[58] Klein also tried to gain permission from the Palestine Colonial Minister for students from Germany and France to study in Palestine. The American Embassy's Special Emissary for the Middle East was close to Klein and worked hard to convince the minister to implement this policy.[59]

Financial Assistance

Wherever Klein went in Europe people asked him for financial help. The JDC supplied the yeshiva in Paris with a home, and gave each student 125 francs a day for food. The Vaad Hatzala provided an extra 200 francs per day for their other needs, which was still not enough. Klein also found a group of 35 rabbis with their families—about 200 altogether—mostly from Poland, Galicia and Hungary who wanted $3,000 a month. He gave them $1,700, which included $1,000 from the Vaad, $500 from his own funds and $200 from a Rabbi Abramsky of London. The JDC provided each with 180 francs per day and 90 francs per day, per child. Klein asked the Vaad board to allocate money for them, and suggested they leave France as soon as possible. Since there was no hope of going to Palestine at that point, they wanted to go the U.S. He urged that they write to the Agudath Harabonim and the Vaad for additional help.[60]

113

Pockets of Orthodox Jews living in very bad financial straits were found in St. Germain, Henneville and other areas. The JDC was able to provide them with only 125 francs per day. Klein gave them some money, but he was quite limited in what he could offer. He felt that they, too, had to immigrate.[61]

Klein also found five children's homes under the auspices of the Vaad: Aix-les-Bains had 450 children including two *yeshivos*; at Strasbourg and Schirmeck there were 250 children; at Barbizon there were 40 children and 75 at Fublaines.[62] All the homes were maintained and supported by Rescue Children Inc., which paid an average of 5,000 francs per child each month. It also paid for their clothing and other necessities, and salaries for the teachers and administrators. Jewish education at the homes was inadequate because they lacked teachers and the strong leadership needed to develop a curriculum and administration. The homes were run along political party lines, which only exacerbated the problems.

Since the Vaad was responsible for the education of these children, Klein warned that a proper educational infrastructure was needed or the children would be lost to Torah-true Judaism. A knowledgeable educator, familiar with European educational systems and culture, he wrote, should be sent from the U.S. to prepare the children for life in Palestine, where most of them wanted to go.[63]

Irving Bunim shared this information with Rabbi Kotler. Rav Aharon participated in Vaad meetings, including those with State Department officials in Washington, D.C.[64]

During his two trips to Germany, Klein visited the Vaad offices in Frankfurt and Munich, the *yeshivos* in Windsheim, Zeilsheim, Bergen-Belsen in the British Zone and a yeshiva in Ulm.

"Nobody can imagine in how wonderful spirits these *yeshivos* are [sic]," he reported, especially at the yeshiva in Zeilsheim where at least 200 boys had been brought from Poland by Recha Sternbuch. The school was run along religious party lines, but since the children were very young Klein was not concerned about their indoctrination. He gave the *yeshivos* some money, but they needed a regular subsidy of $2 per yeshiva student a week. Allocating $750 per week, Klein believed, would meet the needs of the *yeshivos* at that point.[65]

Visit to Germany

On his first visit to Germany, Klein saw an immediate need to establish *yeshivos katanos* (elementary schools) in camps with large numbers of Orthodox Jews, especially those with Polish DPs. Klein asked Rabbis Baruch and Schechter to open *yeshivos* in the camps, which they did with funds he provided. Altogether, the Vaad established almost 20 *yeshivos*. Each yeshiva had a board of education under the leadership of a rabbi or under the man with the most knowledge of Judaism in the camp.[66]

The Vaad subsidized large numbers of kosher kitchens in the camps, as well as *mikvehs* and Agudah and Mizrachi *kibbutzim*. The Vaad supported two *mohalim*, who were called to various camps almost every day to perform circumcisions. He noted that during the previous year 20,000 children had been born.[67]

In the meantime, the Vaad offices developed a reputation throughout Germany as a place where DPs could obtain religious items. Camp committees constantly visited Vaad offices to collect these religious objects and discuss other religious needs. Klein concluded that if the Vaad Hatzala did not exist, there would be a need for such an organization. He was proud that the Vaad was "practically the only [O]rthodox organization recognized by almost every government in Europe." It was the only Orthodox institution with official status in Germany and Austria. But at the same time, he was heartbroken because so much more "could be accomplished if [O]rthodoxy were united," especially considering "the amount that we have accomplished with so little" thus far. This was the time when the Agudah, Mizrachi, Hungarian Jews, Bobover Hasidim and the Klausenberger Rebbe "should get together and form a strong fund to give the people the help" they need.[68]

(l-r) Rabbi Aharon Kotler, Rabbi Eliezer Silver and Rabbi
Avraham Kalmanowitz.
Photo courtesy of Mir Yeshiva Archives.

Dean Samuel L. Sar of Yeshiva University, who would later play a role in the rescue and rehabilitation activities for the DPs, was also critical of what appeared to be parochial interests and concerns.[69] Finally, Klein hoped that another layperson would follow his lead and come to Europe to continue the work he started.[70]

Klein was especially disturbed to hear from people who had recently come to Europe from the U.S. that "not everything is going smoothly" at the Vaad headquarters in New York. He hoped the rumors were "not true," since he had been "killing" himself "to do everything in the world possible to get visas from various countries, only to find that there was no harmony in New York."[71]

Throughout Klein's stay in Europe, Schoen sent him requests to transfer funds and to aid specific individuals. Schoen also wired instructions from the Federal Reserve Bank on how to transfer Swiss francs to Switzerland and provided him with documents necessary to facilitate the immigration of people being detained by the French relief organization.[72]

Rabbi Jacob Karlinsky, executive secretary of the Vaad in New York, asked him to secure the release of a 10-year-old Jewish girl being cared for by a Polish Christian family by having Recha Sternbuch bring the child from Poland to France or Germany.[73] He also advised Klein that the Vaad had secured documents to bring approximately 600 Jews that the Vaad had supported since 1940 from Shanghai to the U.S. Two hundred fifty were already in the U. S., and the rest were to arrive on the next two ships from Shanghai.[74]

Before Klein left Europe, Schoen asked him for "documentary proof" that the Vaad was assisting Mizrachi in Germany and other parts of Europe. The Mizrachi alleged that its institutions were not receiving their fair share of aid and as a result the Vaad was having "extreme difficulties with them."[75] Klein investigated and found that "most of the money" was being distributed to the Mizrachi and Agudah.[76]

In turn, Klein asked Schoen to send him *siddurim, tefillin, Chumashim, mezuzos* and other religious items that were desperately needed.[77] He cabled Herbert Tenzer (Klein's partner and later a Congressman from New York) to send

$1,600 for Rescue Children, Inc., $10,000 to Isaac Sternbuch and $4,000 for the *yeshivos* in Paris.[78]

Klein also received a number of letters from Irving Bunim asking him for help.[79] In December 1946, a delegation of American Jews attended a Zionist convention in Basel, Switzerland. Many were from Mizrachi. Klein thought it would be a good opportunity for them to come to Paris to see the work the Vaad was doing, especially since some members of the group were "not too friendly" to the Vaad.[80] Pincus Schoen concurred and suggested that the delegates visit Vaad Hatzala homes in Switzerland and meet with key Vaad representatives in Europe.[81]

In mid-December 1946, Bunim informed Klein that Rabbi Eliezer Silver was demanding that Rabbis Schechter, Londinski and Rosenberg return to the U.S. immediately. Perhaps this was an attempt to exercise greater control of events by Rabbi Silver, who was a main fund-raiser for the Vaad and under extreme pressure to raise the monies so desperately needed. Silver's dedication and commitment were such that when he could not secure funds for a particular cause, he would borrow money from his bank and use his life insurance as collateral.

By ordering the three rabbis back home, Rabbi Silver may have reasoned that Vaad expenses would be decreased and thus the demands upon him lessened. Bunim said that, "it took a lot of...diplomacy" to convince Rabbi Silver to take a more moderate stance, which meant delaying their departure for at least a month.[82]

In subsequent correspondence, Bunim informed Klein that Rabbi Silver had mentioned nothing further about the return of the rabbis, so that the matter would be allowed to die. Bunim informed him that Samuel Schmidt would be going to Europe at the "request and insistence of Rabbi Silver,"[83] and that several meetings had been arranged with the Agudah, Zeirei Agudah and World Agudah in the hopes of coming to an understanding with them about the Vaad. In addition, Rabbis Pinchas Teitz, Joseph Baumel and Bezalel Cohen of the Mizrachi made an appeal for the Vaad in the name of all the organizations.[84]

Klein urged Bunim to be careful that Rabbi Silver did not make "any agreement with the JDC about changing the role of the Vaad." Klein believed that Rabbi Silver could not make any changes concerning the Vaad by limiting its role or through an agreement with the JDC without their consent. "I do not think he can do it without you and me," Klein told Bunim, but he was wrong. He asked Bunim to avoid meeting with the JDC "under any circumstances" and should not ask them for any funds. He stopped the yeshiva students from requesting transportation from the JDC, and purposely avoided meeting any of their staff, except for a low level official. He asked that Bunim do his "utmost to keep Vaad Hatzala alive, as it is important for my work with the Inter-Governmental Committee." Rav Aharon had insisted that Bunim do all he could to maintain the viability of the Vaad.[85]

Baruch was so impressed with Klein's accomplishments, that in late January 1947 he wrote to William Alpert that Klein "did a fine job and accomplished a great deal while in Europe, worked real hard, never sparing himself. He certainly went all out in his work, which was indeed appreciated by all of us."[86]

Klein's Return to the U.S.

Back in New York, Klein continued his work on immigration and other areas. He sent funds to Europe,[87] worked out fundraising campaign strategy with Irving Bunim[88] and concentrated on public relations and publicity.[89]

Klein talked about the Vaad's work in Europe on WEVD, a Jewish radio program in New York, and urged the audience to provide help to their fellow Jews. He described how the Jews in Europe received dry rations of 1200 calories a day and asked the audience to compare this amount with the number of calories they consumed daily. He asked that 11 pound packages be sent to supplement this meager daily ration. The packages were to be sent to a relative in the camps. If people had no one in particular to send a package to, the Vaad office in New York would provide a name and an address. He stressed that there was no need to be

**Rabbi Nathan Baruch indicating areas supported
by the Vaad in Germany**
Photo courtesy of Rabbi Nathan Baruch

concerned about sending things that could not be used. Everything, especially canned food, was in demand. They needed prunes, raisins, chocolate, fats, sugar and fruits. If the recipients could not use the items, they could be exchanged. Throughout Germany there were exchange centers with a point system for different items. For instance, a pound of coffee was worth 80 points, a pound of Spry (a shortening) was worth 40 points, and a single pack of cigarettes, among the most desirable items, was worth 45 points. Money had little value in Germany. Food, cigarettes and clothing had greater value because they could be bartered.[90]

Klein also described how in Germany a woman walked a great distance to see him while carrying a child on her back because the child had no shoes to wear. "It's all very nice for the Vaad to make schools, but how is my child going to school if he has no shoes?" she asked. They found a pair of shoes for the child.[91]

Large numbers of marriages were also taking place, Klein reported, sometimes as many as five a week. The Vaad gave many newlyweds a dowry of $25 and two bed sheets. "There is probably no greater present you can give anyone in Europe...than a bed sheet," he observed.[92]

Lack of Unity

It wasn't long before the political factionalism that pervaded the American Jewish community became trench warfare. On February 5, 1947, the Mizrachi Organization of America announced that it took umbrage at certain Vaad activities and was leaving any previously acknowledged alliance. Mizrachi explained its decision to leave the Vaad Hatzala and embark on its own campaign for the "rescue of Orthodox Jewry in Europe" in a letter to "Esteemed Rabbis and Scholars Everywhere" signed by Leon Gelman, its president, and Rabbi Mordecai Kirschblum, its executive director.

"With great sorrow, we were forced to take this drastic step in order to redress the oppression and injustice perpetrated against thousands of our unfortunate colleagues in several European countries by the local representatives of the Va'ad ha-Hatzalah through terrible deprivation and mean spiritedness, which neither Torah values nor human logic can tolerate," they declared.[93]

When they first heard about these financial "deprivations," more than two years before, they made several appeals to the leadership of the Vaad in the U.S. Promises that Vaad representatives in Europe who "were responsible for this terrible chaos" would be removed were not kept. At the 22nd Zionist Congress in Basel in December 1946, there were more than 100 delegates and representatives from the *She'erith Hapleitah*. According to Gellman and Kirschblum, "there was a great lament and bitter outcry on the part of our brothers-colleagues who endure famine and want and who have not benefited at all from the monies" collected by the Vaad.[94]

At their request, the Mizrachi decided to publicize these alleged grievances and "declare that the Mizrachi movement no longer takes responsibility for actions of the Vaad Hatzala in Europe."[95] In addition, they asked that everyone "set aside a suitable amount from the funds for the Va'ad ha-Hatzalah [sic] that are raised in your city for our drive, whose purpose is sacred: to rescue and succor our Orthodox brethren, survivors of the *hurban* (the Holocaust)."[96]

Irving Bunim responded to these attacks in a letter to Rabbis Bezalel Cohen and Mordecai Kirschblum on March 11, 1947. The Mizrachi alleged that two years earlier the Vaad had discriminated against its membership over the issue of kosher wine. Bunim asserted that the Vaad had not been a party to the slight and that this could be easily verified. Yet even if "such a terrible calamity to be charged against the Vaad Hatzala...[could be proven]...does this mean that we should now, two years later, interrupt the activities of rescue, mercy and relief?"[97]

Why was it necessary, he asked, for the Mizrachi to air its grievances with the Vaad in the American press, especially in *The New York Times?* Why did the readers of the *Times* need to know "that religious Jews discriminate against other religious Jews and favor the Agudah? Is that good Jewish policy, is that *tznius* [modesty], is that Zionist propaganda on a page in *The New York Times* dedicated to Zionist news? Will that help the position of the Jewish Agency [for Palestine] with Britain? Will that create better relations with the *goyim* [non-Jews] in America towards the Jews, or what other noble thought was behind it?"[98]

Bunim also questioned why the Mizrachi had to inform the Jewish Federations about the alleged discrimination against them by the Vaad. Mizrachi had no intention of obtaining money from the Federations, since they received funds from the United Jewish Appeal. "Is this an action intended only against Torah-true Jews in their battle for recognition in America?" he asked.[99]

Bunim reminded Rabbis Cohen and Kirschblum that the three of them had been appointed at the meeting of the Agudas Harabonim to an interim committee on February 20, 1947 and had agreed that an armistice would prevail until the negotiations had been concluded between the Vaad and the Mizrachi. Yet two days later Rabbi Kirschblum called to demand that Mizrachi get 33.3 cents of every dollar raised by the Vaad, that the funds be paid to the Mizrachi office in New York and that Mizrachi was free to spend these funds on European relief in any way it should decide.[100]

The three of them held a meeting during which Bunim suggested that the Vaad dedicate 50 percent of its budget to the activities of the Mizrachi according to a formula established by a delegation to be sent from the States to Europe. When Bunim presented this proposal, they "were quite agreeable, in fact [they] took copies of the agreement" to discuss at their next meeting.[101]

"How on earth," he asked, "did you allow your organization to come out with an open declaration of secession and war against the Vaad Hatzala, at a time when the Vaad Hatzala had neither accepted or rejected your 'unusual demand' of 33 1/3 percent, and when your organization neither accepted nor rejected my counter proposal of 50 percent."[102]

One of the benefits the Vaad enjoyed was that the European governments recognized its organization, because the British did not object to its nonpolitical activities—the British knew the

Vaad had no hidden political agenda since they were not Zionists. When the Mizrachi or any other political organization became involved in relief work, this aroused the suspicions of Britain and her allies. He urged that the obligations the Mizrachi had to the survivors "should outweigh any other considerations" that it had at this point.[103]

Bunim wondered how the Mizrachi, which was supposed to protect Zionism and religion, was able to make peace with the Conservative and Reform rabbinate, and Poale Zion (Workers of Zion) or Socialist Zionism and "all the assimilationists," yet declare "war against the Agudas Harabonim and the *Roshei Yeshivahs*?" To put it succinctly, the Mizrachi had "slighted and disdained Rabbi Israel Rosenberg, the President of Agudas Harobonim and declared war on Rabbi Kotler and Rabbi [Reuven] Grozovsky [formerly of Kaminetz]!" Bunim believed that "the Jewish world will never understand how you have chosen your friends and what made you create your enemies!"[104]

Bunim concluded by appealing to the conscience of Rabbis Cohen and Kirschblum. "In the name of God, revolt against such injustice and go out to the public, to the Jews at large, with a clear conscience and clean hands, and say, 'Let us Unite—At least Now!'"[105]

On April 15, Bunim chaired a meeting of the Finance Committee of the Vaad and reported on the status of the ongoing negotiations between the Vaad and the Mizrachi. The latest condition for Mizrachi's re-entry into the Vaad alliance was that Rabbi Israel Rosenberg assume the chairmanship of the Vaad and that two co-chairmen serve with him. Stephen Klein, who was at the meeting, discussed the possibility with Rabbi Rosenberg and hoped to hear his response within the next day or so. Bunim asked for a meeting on April 23 to resolve the issue.[106]

Bunim was particularly concerned that unity be preserved so as not to endanger the Vaad's immigration activities in Washington, D.C., where the organization was respected and well-received. "If the Vaad breaks down, it will mean that many of our brethren will remain stranded for many years in the European '*Gehanna*' [Hell]."[107]

On May 6, 1947, the committee appointed by the Agudas Harabonim to negotiate peace between Mizrachi and the Vaad Hatzala held its final meeting. The group concluded that the reorganized Vaad would be headed by three members of the Agudas Harabonim, consisting of Rabbi Israel Rosenberg—who would be chairman of the presidium—and Rabbis Eliezer Silver and Jacob Levinson. The Executive members of the Vaad would have eight nonpartisan laymen and organizational representation from the Agudas Harabonim, Histadruth Harabonim, Mizrachi, Hapoel Hamizrachi and Agudath Israel Youth.[108] The Agudath Harabonim would be permitted to appoint as many members as necessary to the executive committee, including heads of *yeshivos*. The number of members-at-large was eight, including Stephen Klein, Irving Bunim, Menashe Stein, Shabse Frankel, David Meckler, Abraham Cohen and Mendel Stavisky.[109]

A special department for *kibbutzim* was to be established as well with members of the Mizrachi acting as the chairman and treasurer. A member of the Agudah would serve as co-treasurer if and when the Agudah decided to forgo its own campaign. The *kibbutzim* would receive 33.3 percent of the income the Vaad collected. It was also decided that after the new administration took over, an executive director and assistants would be appointed.[110] On May 8, a meeting of the old executive committee and the new executive committee was held. It was understood that the agreement would be submitted to the Agudas Harabonim for ratification,[111] but internecine politics would continue to mitigate against positive resolution.

Chapter 5

Pasing: Trials and Tribulations

After a few months in Munich, the Army and UNRRA moved their operations to Pasing, a suburb 15 miles from Munich. Munich had limited living and working facilities, while Pasing offered freestanding houses where UNRRA established offices for the voluntary relief agencies. Baruch was given two buildings, one at 12 Bachmeier Strasse for Vaad headquarters; the other became his living quarters.

Once established, Baruch recruited a staff. He hired Joseph Geselewitsch, a non-observant Jew from Lithuania, who spoke English and served as his driver. Geselewitsch organized a warehouse, engaged German chauffeurs, and managed to keep the Vaad's vehicles running by obtaining rationed gasoline. Many Vaad programs depended on transportation, because Baruch and his team went from one camp committee and institution in the American Zone to another to maintain relations with them.

In Munich, Baruch met Gertrude Bartel, a non-Jewish DP, who worked for the American Consul. She was fluent in German, English and Italian and was also an excellent typist. Additionally, Bartel understood the methods used by the Consulate to deny American visas to the survivors. Baruch offered her a substantial increase in salary to come work for him. However, her departure from the American Consul's office caused problems for Baruch. When he complained about the delays in the immigration process, the Consul insinuated that if Baruch had not taken his best secretary, the office would be functioning more efficiently.

Two other non-Jewish members of the staff, Vera Owen and Patricia Quaint, had previously worked for UNNRA. When members of the New York staff questioned his employment of non-Jews, he countered that these women were skilled and highly motivated workers who spoke several languages. Since they were paid only $10-$15 a week, where else would he find more competent and dedicated workers?[1]

The dearth of Jewish personnel bothered Baruch very much. He wrote to Rabbis Mendlowitz, Silver and Kotler to send young men to work with the DPs. When Rav Aharon suggested someone to come for just a few months, Baruch explained that it wouldn't work because more time was needed to become familiar with the situation in Germany. If the Vaad put a team in every camp like the JDC did, Baruch believed the entire structure of the survivor communities and the situation in *Eretz Israel* would be very different.

This was a time of transition. For some survivors, returning to religious life was an automatic response—no reflection was needed. Others felt they owed it to their dead families to continue where they had left off before the war. Jewish religious life provided some stability in what was otherwise a disrupted world. Many, however, had undergone significant changes. Baruch frequently heard survivors question God, "My parents were so pious, why did this happen to them?" For these people return to their Jewish roots was problematic. Baruch felt that if there were role models committed to Torah, those who offered some direction to a Torah way of life, then perhaps more survivors would have become more observant. For want of those few role models, many survivors were lost.

Matters became even more difficult for Baruch after Rabbi Schechter received word that his wife was not well, forcing him to go back to America. With his departure, Baruch also became responsible for the Frankfurt office.

In the meantime, Rabbi Burstin, Baruch's main assistant, proved himself to be an able administrator and innovative thinker. Together they planned ways to help the DPs, but they were continually fighting an uphill battle since there were so many survivors that needed their help.[2]

After the war, the best estimate of the number of Jews left in Europe was about 250,000. In the American Zone, excluding the American enclave of Berlin where there were about 6,000 Jews, there were 126,563 Jews on December 31, 1946; 123,778 on June 1,1947, and 30,408 on June 30, 1949. By June 30, 1950 the number had dwindled to 10,909. Approximately 30,000 to 40,000 Jewish DPs lived in the cities and towns. In May 1947, when the Jewish DP population was at its highest level, "there were 60 assembly centers, 14 children's homes, 38 *hachsharot* (training centers to prepare people to live in Palestine), 17 hospitals, a convalescent home, three rest centers, three sanitariums, one transit camp, one staging area and 139 community groups in the U.S. zone, and two assembly centers in the U.S. enclave in Berlin."[3]

Requests for Assistance

Baruch arrived at his office between 5 and 6 A.M. every morning to respond to the hundreds of letters he received inquiring about the welfare of relatives and requesting assistance. Although the Vaad's mission was to help the *b'nei Torah* and not compete with the JDC, all manner of people lined up in front of the Vaad's office in Pasing. No one was turned away.

Vaad headquarters at
12 Bachmeier Strasse in Pasing.
Photo courtesy of Rabbi Nathan Baruch

Special requests came from the Vaad staff in New York, Irving Bunim, Stephen Klein, rabbis and *roshei yeshivos*. Baruch was at a loss to understand if those involved in the Vaad had any notion of the true situation in Germany or fathomed the pressure their demands placed on him. Most requests were sent by mail, but Baruch received a fair number of telegrams from people who expected him to drop everything to attend to their latest crisis of the moment. The Vaad and the Agudath Harabonim compounded the problem by continuing to send people from America with special letters of introduction. Implied was an obligation for Baruch to take care of them, disrupting his work and putting their concerns above others.[4]

Baruch was even asked to locate an American soldier missing in Germany. A father pleaded with Pincus Schoen to find his son whom he thought might be suffering from amnesia. The father received permission to enter France but not Germany. Schoen asked Baruch to disseminate a flyer about the soldier through Army channels, the radio, in various towns throughout the country, and in any other way he "deemed advisable." Schoen realized his request did not fall "within the province of our work," but we are "*Bnei Rachmanim* [compassionate people], and the least we can do..." is to help in this way.[5]

After people started coming to the Vaad's office, they contacted their relatives in the U.S. to send parcels to the Vaad's APO address. Baruch thought it would be a harmless procedure. At the same time, they gave him letters for the New York Vaad office to forward to their relatives under separate cover. He urged the Vaad to send the letters out immediately, as these people anxiously awaited replies. Baruch also suggested the Vaad accept mail from within the United States to send to the Vaad office in Germany. This would render an important service and generate a significant amount of publicity for the Vaad.

Unfortunately, Baruch failed to gauge the possible success of his requests. Soon hundreds of parcels arrived at his office, all addressed to him but including a letter indicating to whom the package should be forwarded. The volume was such that he had to assign Jacob Deutscher to keep records. Deutscher became the distributor of the mail and parcels—parcels that were not inspected because they arrived through the military APO. Within a short time, the mail service evolved into a terrible and time-consuming burden. Baruch was not equipped to handle the volume of daily mail, so there were complaints. Because only official Vaad representatives could pick up the mail—after all they were mailed to Nathan Baruch—there was an unrealistic expectation that it was the Vaad's responsibility to ensure that the packages arrived in pristine condition, untouched by thieving hands. When packages got lost, Baruch was branded the culprit, and unpleasantness resulted.

Many people also offered Baruch gifts for the work he was performing on their behalf, usually items from their packages. Baruch took nothing to avoid any semblance of corruption. Nevertheless, there were people who complained that Baruch and his associates were not overseeing the shipments properly.[6]

Additional requests involved providing money and packages to people in the DP camps.[7] When Rabbi Tuvia (Tobias) Gefen from Atlanta, Georgia asked Baruch to send packages to his relatives, or when others urged him to find someone after all other attempts had failed, he felt obligated to respond. Requests were also made to confirm relatives' physical conditions or to check if packages had been picked up. Sometimes Baruch served as a bank until the New York office could reimburse him.[8]

In some cases, people deposited money with the Vaad office in New York and Baruch was expected to distribute it to their relatives on a regular basis. For example, a man in Cleveland, Ohio gave the Vaad funds to support his nephew for half a year. The nephew informed the uncle that only one payment had been made, so the uncle complained to the Vaad. Schoen asked Baruch to transfer the boy to Paris to facilitate his immigration to the United States. "This you must do without fail so please give it priority," Schoen pleaded.[9]

Baruch, in turn, pleaded with the New York office to refuse

Distributing packages at Vaad headquarters.
Photos courtesy of Rabbi Nathan Baruch

such requests, but Schoen continued to insist that donors and others had no other place to go. A letter from Schoen illustrates this: "Although you have already warned me and requested me not to do this, I must ask you to make available...."[10] Baruch was asked to transfer people from one camp to another so they could be sent to France and from there to Palestine, the U.S. or some other country.[11] Queries about the status of particular cases were made almost daily, along with requests to intervene on behalf of prospective immigrants.[12] After the Vaad secured employment contracts for individuals, Schoen contacted Baruch's office to help with the necessary immigration papers.[13]

Samuel Schmidt empathized with Baruch's predicament, but asked for his help anyway: "In one of your recent letters you remind me to cut out individual requests. Believe me Nat, I am fed up with them and refuse to take on any new ones. That is why I suggested that you make direct arrangement[s] with Rabbi Karlinsky." Since Rabbi Karlinsky was flooded with requests, Schmidt proposed that the Vaad in New York establish a special department for "*Hamlazoth* [recommendations]" to assist individuals through a "separate fund" with no connection to the Vaad's general operating budget. In this way, there would be a steady stream of money to pay for obligations incurred on behalf of individuals. Until then, Schmidt said, there were three cases giving him "no end of trouble." He asked Baruch to "please see that these cases are cleared up." If Baruch had no Vaad money, Schmidt indicated he would be personally responsible for any expenses incurred.[14]

Rescue Children, Inc.

On May 20, 1946, the Vaad announced it had established a National Foster Child Adoption program to provide a year's maintenance for more than 2,000 orphans and other children in Vaad Hatzalah homes and schools throughout Europe. Rescue Children Inc., under the chairmanship of Herbert Tenzer, raised the funds for orphans rescued by the Vaad. It cost $365 per year to adopt a child. Adoption meant paying for food, clothing, medical and dental care, religious and secular education, developing personal contact with the children and sending food packages, gifts, photographs and other amenities.

Through this program, the Vaad felt that it might give the children a feeling of "belonging" to someone somewhere. The Vaad also sought to reunite families, and more than 400 children were "found" after American rabbis placed an advertisement in their local newspapers.[15]

Board members of the Vaad who were also members of the Executive Committee of the Rescue Children, Inc. included Stephen Klein, Irving Bunim, Herman Hollander, Nathan Hausman, Charles Ullman, Jacques Weill, Maurice Enright and Moe Rosenberg. Rabbi William Z. Novick served as executive director. Centers were established in France, Belgium, Sweden and Germany. The JDC worked closely with the organization to register the children with the Chief Rabbi's Council in France and to arrange for many to be sent to Palestine.[16]

Periodically, Baruch had to clarify the status of an "adopted" child. In one case, the "parents" asked for the correct spelling and pronunciation of his and the child's name because they had been given conflicting names and addresses. Without an address, they sent the child's package to Baruch and assumed he would deliver it. They even sent along a pound of coffee for him. Since the girl was only 5 years old, they asked him to write a letter about her and enclose a picture. They also wanted to know the conditions under which she was living, how many children were in the home and what else she might need.[17]

At times, Baruch corresponded with "adopted parents" and passed on children's letters to them. In one case, salesmen from the Saffer-Simon Company in Newark, New Jersey, distributors of Schraft's Chocolates, adopted a child with whom they had an ongoing correspondence. Again, Baruch was the go-between for the "parents" and the children.[18] On other occasions, he drew outlines of the children's feet for shoe sizes, provided their clothing sizes and ensured that the children sent their "parents" thank-you notes.[19]

Visits to the Camps

Once established in Pasing, Baruch visited the camps to meet the DPs and determine their needs. He managed to check out every Jewish camp and community in the American Zone and others, as well. Such was his dedication that whenever he spent a night or a *Shabbos* in a camp, he never used the special guesthouse reserved for relief agency personnel, preferring to stay with the survivors to gain some understanding of the problems and issues they faced. Though the Vaad actively tried to get the Jews out of Germany, as of September 1948 thousands were still living in camps and temporary communities.[20]

Regardless of what the press or visitors from the U.S. reported, on his visits Baruch discovered that conditions in the camps were deplorable. Six, eight or even ten people shared a room originally meant to accommodate two. Most camps were former Wehrmacht barracks, and the best buildings were reserved by the administration as staff billets. There were only three camps where the DPs lived in houses. These private homes, originally built to accommodate one family, were shared by six or seven.[21] Camps with water and toilet facilities were shared by 50 to 200 families. The furniture in the rooms usually consisted of a bare table, several wooden chairs and improvised double-decker beds with no sheets.[22]

Food was served from two large kitchens, one kosher and the other non-kosher. Each individual or head of the family came to the kitchens with pots or other containers to carry the daily rations from UNNRA and its successor, the IRO. Each person received 85 grams of butter, 190 grams of sugar, 250 grams of black bread and 250 grams of meat per week and one piece of soap per month. These were the conditions Jews lived in nearly three years after their liberation.[23]

The DP camp in Pocking, a former German stable, was one of the worst camps Baruch visited. Several hundred Lubavitcher men, women and children who had spent the war hiding in the Soviet Union were living there. After the war, Rabbi Plotkin, their leader, former head of the Lubavitcher

Hasidim in Russia, secured the requisite documents to get them out. When they arrived in the American Zone of Germany, the Americans and UNRRA tried to find places for them to live, but the group insisted on remaining together. With no other facilities available to house such a large group, they went to Pocking.

During the bitter cold winter of 1947, Baruch spent a *Shabbos* with these families from the Tomchei Temimim Yeshiva—approximately 5,000 to 10,000 Jews living in temporary barracks with no water, toilets or heating facilities.

When Baruch told the Vaad that he tried to help them, they were surprised his help was accepted. The American Lubavitch organization prided itself on being independent of other Jewish organizations, including the Vaad. Yet the Vaad leadership encouraged Baruch's work with the Lubavitchers—they were, after all, *b'nei Torah*, and therefore a focus of the Vaad's mission.

When Rabbi Plotkin became sick, Baruch took him to the Bogenhausen Hospital in Munich. Though it was a German Catholic facility, Baruch arranged for the rabbi to receive kosher food and treatment by a Dr. Pesachowitz, Chairman of the Health Committee of the Central Committee of Liberated Jews in Bavaria.

During the year, Baruch often visited Pocking to give the Lubavitchers coats and other supplies. No matter how harsh the weather or how difficult the circumstances, they did not complain.[24]

In a letter to *Hapardes*, a monthly journal for rabbis, Rabbis Simonowitz and Shlomo Matusov of Tomchei Temimim Yeshiva, thanked Baruch and the Vaad for the monthly support they received. This assistance, provided in a gracious manner, was especially important "inasmuch" as the yeshiva was "unable to rely on the support of the Joint Committee," which, despite the best of intentions, could not supply all of their needs.[25]

Baruch's camp and community visits, as well as his other excursions, were generally not without problems. On his first Rosh Hashanah in Europe in late September 1946, he and Rabbi Schechter went to Zeilsheim, the very large DP camp with a yeshiva organized by Rabbi Gershon Liebman of the Shearith Beth Joseph Yeshiva.

For Yom Kippur, Baruch went to Windsheim, where there were many survivors from the Slobodka, Kletzk, Telshe and Radin *yeshivos*. En route, *erev yom tov* (the evening before the holiday), he and Rabbi Schechter were on a secondary road full of bomb craters, detours and obstacles, when two Germans driving a large truck saw Schechter with his flowing rabbinic beard and forced them off the road. The Germans drove away laughing. Hours later, an American truck pulled their jeep out of the ditch.[26]

Just before Succos (the feast of Tabernacles), Rabbi Londinski suggested they visit the Sternbuchs in Montreux, Switzerland to celebrate the holiday and unwind. Though they had passports, Baruch insisted on getting Military Travel Orders because they allowed the bearer unrestricted travel to various zones and other countries—even those behind the Iron Curtain—under the full protection of the U.S. Army and government.

At the Military Travel Office, Baruch met Vickie Brown, a secretary from England. To induce her to expedite their travel orders, he promised to bring her back whatever she wanted from Switzerland. He brought her back a special lining for a coat she was having made, and so she remained grateful to him for the rest of her stay in Germany. Through her good graces, Baruch obtained blank and signed military travel orders he used to get people out of the country.[27]

On their way to a DP camp one winter night in 1947, Rabbis Burstin and Baruch sat in the back seat of their car when their driver fell asleep at the wheel and crashed into a tree. Rabbi Burstin and the driver passed out and Baruch bled profusely from the injuries he sustained. In the midst of this chaos, Baruch realized that his portfolio, filled with valuable documents, including Deutsch Marks, American dollars and scrip—usable only on the black market—was still in his car. He also had unauthorized documents: blank military travel orders he had acquired from Vickie Brown, a serious violation of military occupation law.

Despite the cold and his injuries, Baruch set out to search for assistance. Finding a cabin in the blustery freezing cold, he dragged his companions to the door and managed to persuade the occupant to contact military personnel for help. When the American military brought the three of them to an American field hospital, the MPs discovered Baruch's portfolio and reported him to CID (the Criminal Investigation Division).

While Baruch waited for the anesthesia to wear off from his emergency surgery, two CID officers interrogated him. They greeted him with "Hello *landsman* [Yiddish for countryman]. Just relax." When asked why he was in possession of illegal items, he explained that they were important to his mission in Germany. The CID men took his statement and left.

When Baruch returned to his office, he contacted Carl Atkins, a troubleshooter for UNRRA. Atkins arranged an appointment for him with Major General Frank W. Milburn, the Commanding General of the First Military District to whom the CID interrogators had sent their report. Baruch told the General why he was in Germany, and candidly admitted that his methods were unorthodox, but that it was all for a good cause—to help the DPs. Atkins vouched for Baruch's integrity and assured the General that Baruch's activities were not for personal gain.

General Milburn closed the case and told Baruch, "Please stay out of trouble." But Baruch couldn't make such a promise because of the exigencies of his work. Milburn turned out to be a very considerate individual. Had it been imposed, the penalty for Baruch's multiple illegal acts was immediate expulsion from Germany.[28]

Baruch's encounter with General Milburn turned out to be fortuitous. One day, Rabbi Plotkin urgently requested that Baruch meet him at the Munich Bahnhof, the main train station. Baruch immediately packed a bag. At the station he found the entire Lubavitcher group from Pocking—with all their worldly possessions gathered in broken valises and cartons tied with string—waiting for the Orient Express. He was shocked to learn that they had tickets to Paris, and could not imagine how they had obtained the documents on their own. It turned out that they had pawned their jewelry and other valuables to pay the necessary bribes to flee Germany.

Baruch explained to them that when trains stopped in Munich only certain car doors opened. Military police accompanying the train would ask the rabbi why so many people were boarding with him. The rabbi's planned response was that when they originally came through Germany on their way to Paris, a number of their group had taken ill and had to disembark. Now that they had recovered, they were all going to Paris.

When the train arrived, the group hastily boarded just as the captain of the military police asked Baruch what was happening. All of them managed to get on the train, squeezing into the aisles with their bundles and packages. As the whistle blew and the train started moving, Baruch took the captain aside and told him that if he had any questions, he should check his credentials with the provost marshal in Munich, Brigadier General Dalby. "And," he continued, trying to quell the captain's agitation at this mass exodus of people, "they have the documents for France." The captain was suspicious and said that this was all very irregular. How did all of these people arrive in Munich at the same time? What were they all doing there?

When the train arrived in Stuttgart, another group of Lubavitcher Hasidim from Czechoslovakia boarded the train. Sheer bedlam ensued—there were too many people and not enough cars. But somehow everyone managed to get on board, much to the chagrin of the disgruntled Army captain.

As the train reached the French Zone in Germany, the group encountered another problem. Though the French were very liberal in admitting people to France, the French Zone of Germany was sacrosanct, because the French enjoyed being an occupying power. Everyone had to have a visa to enter and depart French territory. Many of the Lubavitcher did not have the proper documents. The French inspectors were annoyed and angry with the group and their crying babies, and would not let them continue to France.

The matter was out of American jurisdiction now and in

the hands of the French. Baruch, with his broken high school French, tried to convince French officials to let the train go, but did not succeed. The French decided to uncouple several cars so the rest of the train could continue, and leave the Lubavitcher group behind. Eventually, after much discussion and cajoling, the French allowed the Lubavitchers to proceed to Paris.

The issue of travel orders came up again when Jacob Griffel came to see Baruch and ask for his help. Griffel was the representative of the Agudath Israel and the Vaad in Istanbul, and had helped Jews in the Balkans immigrate to Palestine. In mid-1945, the Rabbinical Rescue Committee in Palestine asked him to continue his work in post-war Germany.[29]

At Feldafing, Griffel visited the Klausenberger Rebbe. (The Rebbe had spent two years in Auschwitz; his wife and 10 children perished in the Holocaust.) From there he went to Munich, where a group of Holocaust survivors asked him for help. At first, he thought they wanted money and visas to go to Palestine, but all they wanted was his assistance in organizing a *minyan* for *Shabbos*. Many did not remember their Hebrew or never had the opportunity to learn the language. Some had to cover their heads with handkerchiefs because they did not have hats or caps. The fervor and emotional level of praying with people whose spiritual growth had been stunted by the war could not adequately be described, but clearly the flame had not been extinguished.[30]

Baruch had first met Griffel in Paris in late 1946 at a meeting chaired by Rabbi Isaac Herzog, the future Chief Rabbi of Israel. The conference had been called to discuss the placement of orphans and to rescue those children still in hiding or in the hands of non-Jews. But things soon devolved into a heated debate as representatives of the different organizations sought credit for their rescue efforts. Griffel entreated the group not to waste its energy on where the orphans should be placed. Other children were still in monasteries or with Catholic families and he had to urge the organizers to concentrate on finding and rescuing them.

One night, as Baruch was in his office in Pasing with

Rabbi Burstin, Griffel appeared dressed like a diplomat in a black homburg and frock coat. He quickly explained that he was on a mission to Romania, a country then under Communist control. He told Baruch that his Romanian contacts wanted immediate help to smuggle out a group of orphans, but that he could not obtain a visa because during one of his previous trips he had been detained when he tried to rescue another group of Jewish children. For that imprisonment, getting a visa through legitimate channels was now impossible. For this reason, he had come to Baruch because the Orient Express was soon leaving from Munich and he needed his help to obtain an American military travel order.

Once this would not have been a problem for Baruch, as he had kept a supply of blank orders in reserve for just such an emergency. But because of his previous encounter with the CID, he no longer kept any unauthorized travel orders on hand. Recognizing the urgency of the situation, however, Baruch sought out Vickie Brown in the middle of the night and managed to convince her to prepare the necessary travel documents. As a result of Baruch's efforts, Griffel was able to get 500 orphans out of Romania.[31]

Antisemitism

Throughout his stay, Baruch encountered the same difficulties as the occupying American forces. Each camp had extraterritorial status that precluded Germans from entering, but wherever there was a camp there were those who sought to cause trouble. Often they petitioned the military authorities to take action against the DPs or incited the DPs themselves.

As the Americans reduced their troop strength in Germany this situation grew worse. Some Germans displayed their antisemitism openly, directing their hostility toward the Jewish DPs, blaming them for shortages of food, housing, fuel and clothing. The Jews were vilified for "controlling the black market and causing problems that impeded the restoration of Germany."[33] Jews were also resented because they were given special privileges for housing and food. As the resentment increased, Jews were abused in public, had stones thrown through their windows, and to add insult to injury, were serenaded with antisemitic songs. Jews from Eastern Europe were particularly vulnerable to physical attacks, because the Nazi stereotype labeled them as "sub-humans."

A minority of the German population supported these acts and the German authorities officially denounced them. A number of non-Jewish Germans who suffered under the Nazis expressed their solidarity with the Jews, but most Germans and officials reacted with "total insensitivity and indifference." This insensitivity was so ingrained that when Jewish officials in Dusseldorf reopened their community institutions after the war, a municipal official presented them with a writ of attachment to collect property taxes from 1938-1945. Significantly, the writ was passed through several bureaucratic levels before it was personally delivered to the Jewish community leaders in 1946.[34]

When members of the Committee for Social Policy of the Bavarian Parliament discussed DPs in 1947, they did so in terms generally reserved for criminals. In debates describing the DP camp at Kaltherberge, the Committee referred to the DP centers as "hideouts for unsavory elements not accessible to any German authorities" and suggested the time had come for "law and order [to] be created there."[35]

In a closed session of the ruling conservative Christian Social Union (CSU), also in 1947, Bavarian Agricultural Minister Josef Baumgartner said: "Without the Jews and particularly the Jewish businessmen in the U.S.A. and the rest of the world, we will never manage: We need them for the resumption of our old trade relations!"

With regard to the *Ostjüden* (Jews from the East) living in Germany, he said he had little use for them. After attending the Jewish Congress meeting in Bad Reichenhall, he noted that, "The one pleasing thing about the meeting for me was the resolution that was unanimously adopted: [Jews] Out of Germany." His colleagues laughed.[36]

At the same time, the desecration of Jewish cemeteries reached epidemic proportions. Many of the top military leaders in Germany recognized this as a "brazen challenge to the authority of the United States Occupation Forces." Unofficially, some considered the desecrations "as a trial balloon launched by the Germans to see how far they can go without inviting reprisals on the part of the Army."[37]

At one point, William Haber, Advisor on Jewish Affairs to the Theater Commander of the U.S. Forces in Europe from January 1948 to January 1949, urged General Lucius Clay, Military Governor of Germany, to issue a public statement "denouncing the wanton destruction of these cemeteries."[38] He asked the General to confer with the heads of the German states to explain the need for German authorities to stop the desecration, to require that they repair the damage, and that guards be posted at the sites. Until the German authorities demonstrated a willingness to apprehend offenders and punish them, the Military Government would continue to investigate and try the offenders.[39]

Antisemitism continued to be an issue during the entire DP period. In December 1948, Haber concluded, "[I]t is almost hopeless to expect much progress in this field for the foreseeable future."[40] From his own discussions with Germans of different economic strata, including professionals and trade unionists, he learned that "the anti-Jewish psychosis is so thoroughly imbedded in the German mind that it will take generations of reeducation to make much headway with this problem."[41]

Most people he spoke to believed that antisemitism "is now more deep-seated than in Hitler's day and that it has spread to the working class, which was relatively cooler than most German groups" to Hitler's antisemitism. This could be attributed to the lack of progress in establishing democratic institutions and popular support for democratic ideals. "All the bombs that fell on the Germans have not shaken them out of their dreams and those dreams have not included devotion to democratic ideals. Little is to be gained by investing money and effort in fighting anti-semitism [sic] in Germany."[42]

Haber saw no point in staying in Germany. Labor leaders made it clear that there was no room for Jews in the

German economy and that "most people are agreed ...when the American forces leave Germany, overt acts would be directed against Jews."[43]

Because of the continuing tension between the Germans, Army personnel and the DPs, there were often confrontations. One incident created an international furor.

In May 1947, a harried and distraught Rabbi Yossel Friedenson, a survivor of Auschwitz-Birkenau and five other camps, banged on Baruch's door in Pasing. Somehow he had managed to get from Munich to Pasing in the middle of the night to ask for help on a matter of great importance. He excitedly told a story about a group of rabbis, members of Agudath Israel, who were arrested and being detained by the Army. Some of them had been shot at; some of them had been injured.

According to Rabbi Friedenson, the group came from different camps to discuss religious matters. Those who were *shochtim*, those who ritually slaughter kosher meat, came to discuss where they would go to work. Meeting in the backroom of a German guesthouse that had a bar in the front, the rabbis were in the midst of their discussions when a couple of drunken GIs entered the premises. Though the bar was off-limits to military personnel, they barged in and subsequently abused and beat the rabbis. Somebody called the MPs, and when they arrived with guns drawn, the soldiers screamed that the Jews—most of them bearded—were making anti-American comments and that they had indignantly decided to break up the meeting.[44]

The rabbis became frightened and some tried to flee through a window. Shots were fired and Friedenson didn't know exactly what happened. Twelve Jews were taken to the hospital. Among the injured were 70-year-old Rabbi Israel Goldberg and Rabbi Isaac Zemba. Rabbi Eliezer Weinberger of the Ulm DP camp had broken his legs as he and Rabbi Moshe Blau of Bad Reichenhall jumped out of a window. Friedenson got away and drove to Pasing.

Rabbis Friedenson, Burstin and Baruch immediately drove to Munich. At MP headquarters they learned that all the rabbis at the meeting had been arrested for disturbing the peace. The MP captain had already written a report based on the testimonies of the inebriated soldiers. No statement was taken from the rabbis because they didn't speak English. Baruch asked the captain to show him the report he was submitting to Brigadier General Dalby, commander of the Munich area. The "witnesses" had painted a very self-serving picture.

At General Dalby's office, Baruch explained to the General what had happened: that the GIs had been drunk and were incited by their *freulein* girlfriends of the evening. Dalby accepted Baruch's explanation and had charges filed against the GIs. A subsequent news article reported that "Military authorities concede that...[the complainants] were under the influence of alcohol when the incident occurred." General Dalby denied, however, that there had been any excessive mistreatment of the DPs, although he did confirm that all the rabbis had been forced to line up with their hands in the air and were struck with truncheons by the military police if they lowered them. He expressed regret about the incident, but explained that it had occurred spontaneously and as a result of an alleged provocation and misunderstanding. [45]

As a result of the incident, Baruch made friends with Dalby who agreed to help him whenever he could. The general further promised to use the case to teach troops how to behave with DPs. In the meantime, the news had gotten back to New York and the Agudah sent a protest to Washington. Baruch felt that this wasn't wise, but the Agudah insisted on protesting to the War Department. Eventually, the matter quietly died. [46]

Control of the Camps

Another ongoing problem involved German police trying to control the DP camps. The DPs were outraged when German police entered the camps in "hot pursuit" of suspects who allegedly violated regulations outside camp environs.

The Military Government and the German administration saw the raids as a "sure way" of responding to black market activity throughout Germany. Yet occupation guidelines placed the camps outside the jurisdiction of the German police. Unarmed German police could only enter a Jewish camp if accompanied by American military personnel and then only to identify DPs who had allegedly committed offenses. On February 18, 1947, the Bavarian Deputy Minister-President declared that if German police did not gain total access to the camps, they could not enforce German laws. In the previous three months, he said, they were forced to stop at camp gates 520 times.[47]

A substantial number of Army officers, especially in the American Military Government, agreed with him. As of June 1948, a large number of Jews were living outside the camps. Since they had adjusted to German rule, the Americans felt those in the camps should be subject to the same German regulations. Haber argued that there was a significant difference between DPs who lived outside, where they interacted with the German police on an individual basis, and those who lived in the camps, where DP antipathy to Germans was more pronounced.[48]

The Advisors on Jewish Affairs thwarted attempts to change the status quo by convincing the Civil Affairs Division that it would be imprudent to do so until the magnitude of the problem had been reduced.[49] General Clay supported this view. Even when Germany became a western state, the American military would still continue caring for the DPs.[50]

Clay insisted he would not surrender sovereignty of the camps to the Germans, a position established by his predecessor, General Joseph T. McNarney. (McNarney served as Commander-in-Chief, U.S. Forces of Occupation in Germany, from November 1945 until March 1947). A combat general, McNarney had witnessed the atrocities, havoc and destruction wrought by the Nazis. He and his men hated the Germans, but soon these men were rotated home; their replacements had little or no idea what the Jews had experienced.

Initially, American troops "considered all Germans as 'Krauts.'" Then they discovered that former Nazi officials knew how "to address an officer" and could assist them in finding good accommodations, cheap liquor, and loose women. "And so the local U.S. Army colonel's secretary was a former SS girl, and an ex-SS trooper in the district got rich on illegal sales and purchases, made possible by helping Americans in black market deals." Americans responsible for hiring construction crews chose German POWS instead of Jewish DPs or other POWs because the Germans were viewed as being more "industrious, obedient and well-behaved." As additional American soldiers arrived in Germany from 1946 onward, the more difficult it became for them to accept "the image of a bloodthirsty Nazi with the neat, clean, orderly world they found among Germans."

That the Jews were far less appealing is not surprising. Though concern for the DPs and their plight existed at the higher levels of the military establishment, at the operational levels, American and British soldiers fraternized with the Germans, resulting in the Germans gradually conditioning "the military officers and military government to regard the DPs as inferior and undeserving people."[51]

As time went on, the Civil Affairs Division requested that revisions be made in the laws governing the camps to permit pretrial incarceration of DPs in German jails and to allow "pinpoint searches." These were search-and-seizure operations targeted against named individuals in which no more than 50 German police could participate when accompanied by an equal number of U.S. military personnel. Haber approved this change, but protested against German police conducting the searches.[52]

In a statement on July 27, 1947, made before the House Subcommittee on Immigration and Naturalization, Lieutenant Colonel Jerry M. Sage, Chief of the Field Contact Section at the Headquarters of European Command in Frankfurt, observed "some exaggerated reports of DP misbehavior" because the "DPs have always been a good source of news." Incidents involving DPs which are "handled by our military agencies, attracts more attention than a similar incident involving Germans, which is handled by German police."[53]

General Lucius Clay, Commander-in-Chief,
U.S. Forces of Occupation in Germany
Photo courtesy of Rabbi Nathan Baruch

Sage's office was responsible for maintaining law and order among all the DPs, and keeping the records of incidents involving them. He personally assisted in arresting and prosecuting some of the DPs. While there were some who violated the law, Sage found that information from the German Bureau of Criminal Identification and Statistics noted that "non-Germans have committed proportionately less [crimes] than the Germans."[54]

The Advisors on Jewish Affairs protested the raids, which they saw as a form of retribution and inconsistent with American justice, but were ignored. When the camps were raided, it reminded inmates of their experiences under the Nazis. This exacerbated community relations, and made it seem as if the Americans supported antisemitism.

When the Americans launched a "search-and-seizure" raid, U.S. Military Police generally entered at dawn, roused the people from their beds and ordered them outside. Sometimes they surrounded the camp with tanks and half-tracks. Some DPs felt sorry for the soldiers who were placed in such a humiliating position. At no time, however, did the raids ever uncover large-scale black market activities. The soldiers did sometimes find food that had been acquired by bartering items received from the Army and Jewish relief organizations, food the DPs obtained to supplement what their diet lacked: proteins, fats, fresh fruit and vegetables. Most of what the Army confiscated was procured in the legitimate market. When the DPs could prove their case, the soldiers returned the items to their owners—unless they kept them for themselves.[55]

A raid at the Zeilsheim camp on March 24, 1948 was typical. The MPs ostensibly came to look for caches of dynamite, but no explosives were found. Of the half dozen people arrested for alleged possession of black market items, only three were brought to trial—two were acquitted and one received a minor sentence. The Provost Marshal who conducted the raid told Haber that he thought the mass raids were not "worth a damn."[56]

Standard Operating Procedure (SOP) Number 96 was another point of contention. Promulgated by the military in

April 1948, it gave the Germans full benefit of Anglo-American safeguards in search-and-seizure operations. Mass raids on Germans were strictly prohibited and German homes could be searched only with a warrant issued with probable cause. DPs were excluded from this directive. A significant number of people involved directly and indirectly in law enforcement personally resented the DPs being relegated to second-class status. They cited the directive as an example of the convoluted thinking on the part of some members of the occupation forces charged with implementing occupation policy.[57]

On December 9, 1949, the raids on Jewish and non-Jewish camps were terminated when the Army finally realized they were worthless exercises in law enforcement.[58]

Black Market

Why did the Army pursue such a vigorous search-and-seizure policy against the Jewish DPs? Abraham Hyman, Assistant Advisor on Jewish Affairs and later the last Jewish advisor, believed the Army "was obsessed with ...its primary mission in Germany," to help "in Germany's economic recovery." By disregarding the harm the black market caused the German economy and by using "the camps as the base of their operations, the Jews gave the impression that they dominated the black market..." Jews were "probably not more numerous than their non-Jewish counterparts...[but] they were more brazen...Having been stripped of their possessions and left orphaned by the Germans, they felt no obligation to consider the harm the black market might be causing the German economy." In a certain sense, Hyman believed the Jews helped bring this situation upon themselves.[59]

What was the nature of black market activities? The value of the German currency was approximately 300 Deutsche Marks to the American dollar—good enough only to buy designated rations supplied to the Germans or a few other available commodities. The American Army paid indigenous personnel with almost worthless Marks but compensated them further with PX privileges. There they found American cigarettes. Europeans were addicted to tobacco: It was a common sight to see Germans picking up discarded American cigarette butts in the streets of Munich. Holocaust survivors were no exception. Burstin recounted how he would give up his meager slice of bread in the concentration camps for a cigarette or part of a cigarette.

Cigarettes were plentiful in Germany. The Americans brought in shiploads that were available in PXs to authorized personnel—soldiers, officers, members of those organizations attached to and recognized by UNRRA and the American Army. Those who were authorized had the privilege of purchasing cigarettes, coffee and other commodities in the PX—precious items that made their way unto the black market.[60]

As of mid-1948, the number of people involved in the black-market was estimated "at a minimum of 30%." This did not include those in the "gray market or the basic food market. The luxury market, as contrasted to the basic food market, range[d] from single dealings in American PX items to carloads of cigarettes. The earnings in this market likewise range[d] from a few American dollars per year to 60 or 70 thousand dollars a year."[61]

Typically, Germans blamed the Jews for the entire black market. For many Jews, the black market was the primary place to barter for food, clothing and whatever else they could not find from other sources. Yet, in reality, American soldiers were the most blatant participants in the black market.

Most of this corruption was caused by "cigarette power." "A pack of 20 cigarettes would sell for $15...At the Post Exchange (PX) a carton [of 10 packs] cost 70 cents, and GIs were allowed to purchase one carton a week. A soldier who did not smoke could buy his carton, sell it and take a $149.30 profit."[62] Soldiers "in Berlin in one month, October 1945, sent home $84 million more dollars than they earned."[63] Officers were "usually the biggest operators in the markets, leaving the work on their desks to make deals in the street."

The Army did not respond quickly to the problem perhaps because "the practice was so prevalent and involved so many high ranking officers, it was difficult to know where and how to start a stiff program of correction." Because black market activities among the Americans were so ubiquitous, many Germans came to view them as "fundamentally dishonest and weak."[64]

Eventually, the Army could not ignore the problem because it represented a breakdown in discipline. General McNarney initiated a crackdown in April 1946.

Baruch, as well, used cigarettes as a source of cash for his Vaad activities. In a June 10, 1947 letter, Baruch informed Schoen that his food supplies had dwindled until they were almost gone. But since the demand for food was increasing, Baruch contacted Stephen Klein to help relieve the "endless pressure"[65] through supplies of cigarettes.

Using cigarettes as currency involved a great deal of paperwork. As Baruch reported: "I first had to submit an application stating how many cigarettes would be imported, where they would be coming from, whether I was purchasing them or [if they] were a gift and what purpose they [would] be used for in the American Zone. Before submitting the request, I had to prepare a full detailed report in triplicate to the International Refugee Organization on how the previous shipment had been distributed. Once I received a new shipment, a similar report would have to be submitted in triplicate on a monthly basis."[66]

The Vaad's Lack of Funds

Because the Vaad had a singularly tight budget, Baruch received food and financial assistance directly from Stephen Klein, Pincus Schoen and Irving Bunim.[67] Another special donor was William Alpert, who focused on helping individuals. Baruch used the funds Alpert gave him to help rabbis when they got married. Alpert resolutely avoided recognition for his work, but when he died, his casket was placed in the *beis medrash* (study hall) of yeshiva Mesivta Tifereth Jerusalem. This extremely rare honor, accorded to only two other lay leaders, indicated the high esteem, respect and gratitude that Rabbi Moshe Feinstein, the *rosh yeshiva*, had toward this man.[68]

As Passover neared, Agudas Harabonim initiated a fundraising campaign with the following appeal: "You would not believe it, but twenty-two months after liberation there are still thousands of Jews for whom this will be their first Passover in many years. This year, no one must be forgotten. We call upon you as a Jew to say to your starving, homeless co-religionists in Europe's camps, 'Let us all who are hungry enter and eat.' Ten dollars enables a Jew to celebrate Passover. This year a Passover food package is not only a religious necessity, but a necessity for life itself."[69]

Irving Bunim asked that 70 percent of the shipment for Passover 1947 be sent to Baruch for distribution, and that they also do what they could for the Jews in Austria and Italy. Furthermore, it was suggested that *sedorim* should be arranged under the auspices of the Vaad and Vaad personnel should invite reporters from *The New York Times* and the Associated Press because the *sedorim* made for a good human-interest story.[70]

Gertrude Gould, who worked in publicity and public relations, urged Vaad personnel to take pictures of the packages as they were distributed to the DPs and any other Vaad activities that took place.[71] One of the pictures was published in the *Morning Journal* on Passover eve. Other pictures were sent out with general releases to the non-Jewish and Anglo-Jewish press.

Baruch tried to have a photographer with him whenever the Vaad opened a school, a kosher kitchen or other institution. There were never enough funds to maintain these facilities—eventually their funding was taken over by the JDC—but the Vaad deserved some credit for having started the projects. Pictures were used in the *Vaad Hatzala Bulletin* distributed to Vaad supporters. To document the Vaad's activities, Rabbi Burstin even published an extensive picture book that proved to be a very effective vehicle to promote the Vaad to military personnel, politicians and lay people throughout the world.[72]

Gould also asked Baruch to approach top-ranking Army officers to write letters extolling the work of the Vaad and requesting it to extend its activities.[73] It was a very clever suggestion, but the military did not allow personnel to write fundraising letters.

Securing funds from the relief agencies became even more difficult after July 1, 1947 when the International Refugee Organization (IRO)—also known as the Preparatory Commission of the International Refugee Organization (PCIRO)—assumed responsibility for the refugees and DPs.[74] The agency immediately cut costs to conform to its very limited budget.[75] Daniel Adelson, Baruch's supervisor at the IRO, informed him that only 50 percent of UNRRA's former personnel would remain, which meant losing personnel and funding for Vaad programs. Baruch urged Adelson to maintain his current subsidies because the Vaad alone was rehabilitating the Jewish spirit and soul.[76]

The Vaad could not be content with just 30 to 40 percent of the survivors observing *kashrus* or being considered Orthodox. When Adelson suggested that the Vaad's budget be based on the amount expended in the United States, Baruch objected. That formula, he said, failed to take into account the incalculable losses sustained in Europe, which had been the world's major center of Jewish learning. The greatest rabbinical minds and *yeshivos* were based there. Many seminal works on Jewish law had been written there. Furthermore, a much larger percentage of Jews in Europe were observant and involved in religious studies than the Jews in the United States. When the very foundation of Judaism had been practically annihilated, the Vaad could not make its plans on the percentages and the figures of the Jewish religious and educational needs in America.[77] This became an ongoing battle with Adelson.

Unorthodox Methods

Throughout his stay in Europe, Baruch attempted to maintain good relationships with UNRRA, and later with the IRO. His failure to submit monthly activity reports,[78] and the Vaad's unorthodox methods of operation made it difficult. After he hired Vera Owen and Patricia Quait without prior clearance from the PCIRO, Baruch was informed that he had done so illegally. He managed to retain their services, but these activities were minor compared to the tactical errors he made.[79]

In early 1947, the Vaad helped establish a religious children's center in Bad Nauheim under the auspices of Agudath Israel. Rabbi Samuel Schechter, then the Vaad representative in Frankfurt, met with the UNNRA director of Bad Nauheim and obtained an uninhabitable, derelict building. He reached an agreement to acquire the property from the Town Committee with the help of Rabbi Solomon Rosenberg, then the Religious Director of the JDC. At considerable cost, the Vaad renovated the structure to make it suitable for housing children.[80]

A few months after the home was established, Baruch met with members of the UNRRA staff who wanted the construction stopped. They also wanted the children returned to their former residences or to the children's centers until it was known how the home would function and what further physical modifications were needed. A May 27th meeting was scheduled to review the plans.[81]

In the interim, UNNRA officials decided that the home should be under UNNRA supervision. On May 16th, J.M. Gadras, UNNRA's Chief Field Operations Officer in Frankfurt, sent Baruch a directive stating that UNNRA did not recognize the Vaad's claim to the Children's Home. In the meantime, the U.S. Army assigned the home to UNNRA as a DP Assembly Center so that the agency had "direct operation, control and maintenance" of the institution. The directive also noted that as a voluntary agency, the Vaad had to report its activities to UNNRA officials and to work under their "general supervision and co-ordination."[82]

Gadras was upset that the children had been sent to Bad Nauheim without UNNRA or Army approval—a clear violation of UNRRA directives. UNNRA planned to operate the home as a convalescent center because the children had never been taken care of "properly and decently" under Vaad supervision. Moreover, Gadras considered it "unfair from the Welfare [sic] standpoint to use children as an instrument of a policy."[83]

155

Beth Josef Yeshiva in Zeilsheim
Photo courtesy of Rabbi Nathan Baruch

Bais Yaakov Girls' School, Grade 3, Wasserburg
Photo courtesy of Rabbi Nathan Baruch

Bais Yaakov School, Camp Ulm

Given the important and dominant role occupied by Jewish women in Jewish life, the Vaad established Beth Jacob Girls' Schools where girls of all ages received religious training. They were taught Jewish history and given a basic knowledge of *Kashruth*, *Shabbos*, and in more advanced classes, family purity laws. The Vaad maintained 14 Bais Yaakov Girls' Schools in the American Zone and one in the British Zone. In the British Zone, girls were trained to become instructors.

Photo courtesy of Rabbi Nathan Baruch

157

Following Gadras' letter, Baruch received a very harsh rebuke from W.S. Boe, Chief Voluntary Services Agencies Liaison Officer, stating: "We cannot emphasize too strongly the serious nature of this report and what seems to us the most unfortunate part you played in the matter. We must, moreover, bring to your attention the fact that any reoccurrences of a like nature will result in more drastic action by this Division." Boe also asked for a full report of Vaad activities in connection with this entire episode.[84]

Baruch subsequently learned that the JDC wanted to sponsor this home as a children's rest center. This led to other unpleasant incidents. The director of the home was threatened with expulsion from his community. Members of the Agudath Israel Kibbutz, who had used the home as a vocational training center, were also threatened. Some of the children were blamed for damaging the toilets, walls and pipes in the center. They were treated as if they were criminals, although there was no proof they were responsible for the damage. While the children were still in the home, German workmen were already renovating the premises for the new occupants.[85]

The entire experience embarrassed the Vaad because it was blamed for something it did not do. Baruch protested that whenever the Vaad tried to introduce religious life to Jews, it encountered intense opposition. It was especially regrettable that the opposition had come from UNNRA.[86]

This was not to be the last time that Baruch ran afoul of a relief agency. In April 1948, he received a letter from Robert J. Corkery, PCIRO Chief of the Department of Repatriation and Resettlement, informing him that 30 Jews were smuggled out in the luggage car of a Vaad transport on March 23, 1948. "Owing to the lack of security or other check at the border and because of the insistence of the escort, the illegal emigrants were allowed to cross the border against the wishes of the PCIRO escort officer."[87] To preclude this from happening again, all future Vaad transports organized under the auspices of PCIRO were to be under the command of the PCIRO escort.[88]

Another incident occurred while Baruch was in the United States to attend a Vaad dinner.[89] On September 16, 1948,

Vaad book prepared by Rabbi Aviezer Burstin to
promote the Vaad Hatzala's activities
Courtesy of Rabbi Nathan Baruch

The Hebrew school of the Vaad Hatzala in Gebrica
Photo courtesy of Rabbi Nathan Baruch

Windsheim Rabbinical Seminary
Photo courtesy of Rabbi Nathan Baruch

Vaad Children's Home in Bad Nauheim
Photo courtesy of Rabbi Nathan Baruch

Student at a Vaad yeshiva in Lyon
Photo courtesy of Rabbi Nathan Baruch

Baruch received a letter from the PCIRO requesting he contact the PCIRO Field Supervisor at Ulm immediately.[90] According to an earlier letter of August 24, the living conditions of the children at the rabbinical school in Heidenheim were the "subject of grave concern." The children allegedly were "living in rooms devoid of fresh air and seldom get out into the fresh air." As a result they were "pale and thin." Because they observed Jewish dietary laws, they did not eat "much of the food...they get in rations." All efforts by the officers of the Jewish Agency for Palestine to allow the children to "work under healthier conditions have failed." The PCIRO representative was also disturbed that he had "never seen nor heard of a Vaad Hatzala officer ever contacted this office on the questions of the Rabbinical School [sic]."[91]

In Baruch's absence, Vera Owen responded to this letter and arranged for Rabbi Burstin to inspect the school.[92] After his visit, Rabbi Burstin countered that the Vaad had attempted "to procure sufficient room for the religious schools in all the camps, but unfortunately, so far, we have not been successful in persuading the camp commanders to put adequate accommodations at the disposal of these religious schools."

Burstin also noted that the rabbinical school received monthly support from the Vaad through the *Vaad Hayeshivoth*, an organization that supervised all the *yeshivos* in Germany. At least once a week, a member of the organization visited all the *yeshivos* in the U.S. Zone.

After a telephone discussion with the PCIRO, Burstin was informed that the problems had been taken care of and that a letter would follow to confirm this. The PCIRO also suggested that a Vaad representative visit the installation more often.[93]

Another of Baruch's difficulties was purely of a social nature. When he visited DP camps, either at night or Friday afternoon just before *Shabbos*, he was expected to stop at the UNRRA house to present himself as a visitor. Baruch never had time for that nicety of protocol. He was also expected to have a drink with the staff, but always arrived in a hurry and left in a hurry. For this he received a significant amount of correspondence notifying him that he was in violation of protocol.[94]

Yeshivos and DP Courts

As of October 20, 1947 the Vaad maintained 14 *yeshivos* in the American Zone and one in the British Zone at Bergen-Belsen. Though many immigrated to the United States or France, the number of students in the *yeshivos* did not decrease because other students immediately replaced those who left.[95]

At each institution the rabbis and advanced scholars were responsible for the day-to-day operations of their *yeshivos*. They also chose a dean. The Vaad's role was to provide supplementary food and clothing.

The Vaad was especially concerned about helping these rabbis and scholars maintain the respect, dignity and esteem they deserved. Maintenance of these programs was costly, but the investment ultimately affected the lives of many Jews in the American Zone. Individuals could once again turn to rabbis and scholars for guidance, counsel and direction. With rabbis in recognized positions in the camps and communities, disputes and misunderstandings involving observant and non-observant Jews were brought to rabbinical courts [*Batei Din*] to be arbitrated and settled. This united the elements of the community and encouraged their acceptance of rabbis as leaders.

There was also a court system in effect similar to the ones in the pre-war ghettos. Jews needed a judicial system to resolve civil disputes among camp residents, to try those who had committed offenses such as assault, theft, excess use of electricity, violation of sanitary conditions, or defamation, as well as dealing with accusations against residents who had served as *kapos* (Jewish guards) in the concentration camps or as ghetto police. The Jews could have taken their civil cases to the German civil courts, but that was not a realistic alternative.

When criminal and civil offenses were committed in the DP camps, in theory the Jews had access to the Military

Yeshiva in Lublin
Photo courtesy of Rabbi Nathan Baruch

Kibbutz Victory
Photo courtesy of Rabbi Nathan Baruch

Zev Jabotinsky Boys School
Photo courtesy of Rabbi Nathan Baruch

Government, but using it would have violated a basic Jewish tenet of not informing on your fellow Jews to non-Jewish authorities. Courts were empowered by DP committees to impose fines and detention. In cases where imprisonment was warranted, the guilty party was confined to a detention room in the camp.[96]

No court in Germany became involved in issues regarding people who had served as *kapos* or ghetto police. But the camp courts had to deal with it because the people who had abused their fellow Jews were potential targets for assault or worse. In the beginning, the courts dealt exclusively with these people and then branched out to other more mundane offenders. Had the courts not intervened, "street justice" would have prevailed. Some former collaborators did not wait to be brought to trial and petitioned the court to find them innocent so as to preclude their being taken into custody. Those who were found guilty received punishment ranging from a few months confinement to incarceration for the entire period in which the camps were in existence. In some cases, the sentences were published in DP newspapers throughout the zone. "Courts of Honor" as they were called, also existed in Bergen-Belsen in the British Zone and in Rome.[97] (The courts, which functioned openly, were in violation of U.S. Military Government directives, but UNRRA camp directors "presumably, with the knowledge of the military authorities," allowed them to operate throughout the DP period.) [98]

The local Orthodox rabbis also served as Vaad field representatives in each camp and community. Through these representatives, the Vaad was directly linked to the spiritual and material needs of the people.

There were 59 Talmud Torahs (Hebrew schools) established and maintained by the Vaad. The majority had an ongoing relationship with the Vaad scholars and helped them develop programs. The total number of students in the Talmud Torahs was 3,116.[99]

Halachic Issues

The rabbis who had survived the war immediately

166

Rabbis Burstin and Baruch visit one of the yeshivas
supported by the Vaad
Photo courtesy of Rabbi Nathan Baruch

Rabbis Burstin and Baruch with child DPs
Photo courtesy of Rabbi Nathan Baruch

convened in Munich in August 1946, at a conference chaired by Rabbi Shmuel Abba Snieg of Kovno, a former chaplain in the Lithuanian army. Rav Snieg became chief rabbi of the Rabbinical Council in the American Zone, involved in organizing religious institutions. Because this was one of Baruch's main venues, he kept in constant touch with him. When there were questions of Jewish law, Rav Snieg would bring them to the appropriate *Gedolim* for resolution.

At that Munich conference, the rabbis established a council to ensure that major decisions affecting the community—a*gunos* (female) and *agunim* (male) ("chained" spouses), marriages, divorces (*gets*), kosher meat, family purity and *Eretz Israel*—would be decided by the leading rabbinical scholars. This umbrella organization had an executive committee of eleven distinguished rabbis and a committee of Torah scholars to oversee all matters concerning the Jewish lives of the survivors. The Klausenberger Rebbe was asked to serve as the Congress's honorary president.

Another committee, headed by five rabbis, was created by the Council to resolve the *agunah* issue. It was comprised of Rabbi Pinchas Herzog in Pocking; Rabbi David Horowitz in Landsberg; Rabbi Yehudah Gottlieb in Feldafing; Rabbi Meyer Gruenwald in Munich, and Rabbi Mordechai Shlapersavski, also in Feldafing. They decided that only a rabbi who functioned as part of a three man rabbinical board, or a rabbi appointed by the committee for *Agunos*, was allowed to hear evidence. Furthermore, no individual, except a rabbi or a suitably appointed representative, was permitted to arrange a marriage.

Marriages had to be registered with a rabbi at least 15 days before the wedding, and both parties had to present a Jewish family purity certificate to prove they had gone to the *mikveh*. A bride could obtain her health certificate only by being examined by a female doctor. Also, the Orthodox camp committees were obligated to arrange for each groom to have a *kittel*, a white robe to wear over his suit at the marriage ceremony. Rabbi D. Shapiro in Furth and Rabbi Gottlieb in Feldafing handled all matters of *gittin* (divorce). Those matters relating to marital infidelity, chained spouse issues, infertility, domestic violence and other issues were arranged in accordance with specifications set by the *Agunah* Committee.

Rabbi Meyer Gruenwald, who was Rav Snieg's assistant, was appointed the *mashgiach*, the religious supervisor, of the *shochtim* (ritual slaughterers). The Council decided meat would be ritually slaughtered in Munich, Regensburg, Stuttgart and Frankfurt. Every ritual slaughtering involved at least two *shochtim* who had to show their special ritual slaughterer's knives to each other or have a rabbi present. Any *shochet* who ignored this edict was relieved of his position. A *kashrus* committee was organized comprised of Rabbis Snieg, Yom Tov Lipa Goldin, Shlomo Yom Tov Polack, Chaim Yaacov Rosner and Meyer Gruenwald. The Vaad also appointed two people to travel to all of the DP camps to oversee *kashrus* and all matters related to it.

The rabbis set aside a week to publicize the observance of *Shabbos*, and all the rabbis were required to lobby for observance of *Shabbos* wherever there were Jews. For example, they asked the sports committee of the Central Committee of Liberated Jews in the U.S. Zone of Germany not to hold sports events on *Shabbos*. They also spoke to the representatives of the *kibbutzim* to request that their members observe *Shabbos*. Rabbi Snieg had written a book on Jewish family purity that had a deep impact on those who read it, so it was reissued in three languages—Yiddish, Polish and Hungarian.

At the Congress, the rabbis reproached the Central Committee for failing to include Orthodox involvement in anything related to *aliyah* and absorption. They informed them that since the Congress of Rabbis was preeminent in the Jewish religious life of the survivors, it reserved the right to send representatives to take part in Central Committee deliberations about *aliyah* and absorption. If they wouldn't be heard in committee, they could certainly air their grievances in the free media.

Rabbi Shmuel Abba Snieg of Kovno, chief rabbi of the
Rabbinical Council in the American Zone
Photo courtesy of Rabbi Nathan Baruch

Chapter 6

Kosher Food and Kosher Kitchens

When Rabbi Alexander S. Rosenberg arrived in Germany in September 1945, he reported that "there was no organized effort to have kosher meat."[1] Just before his arrival, the JDC received letters from the Synagogue Council of America and the National Council of Young Israel [2] asking for a response to a cable from an American Jew in Europe alleging that the JDC had made "no provision for urgently needed religious requisites and kosher food for liberated Jews in Germany." The author sent the cable to "protest [the] inefficiency and apparent callous disregard...." [3]

Given all that the JDC had done from its inception to promote and support the religious life of the Jews in Europe, the JDC leadership was "surprised" and disturbed by these accusations. In a letter to the Synagogue Council of America, Joseph C. Hyman, Executive Vice-Chairman of the JDC,

171

assured the Council that "the JDC has never purchased one ounce of non-kosher food for distribution ...in overseas countries. We have consistently adhered to the policy of purchasing the type of food about which there can be no question as to *kashruth*...."[4]

The JDC further pointed out that it had agreed to act as an intermediary on behalf of individuals in South Africa, Palestine, South America and elsewhere who wished to send food packages to their relatives in Belgium, France, Holland and Luxemburg, for which they were willing to pay. The JDC acted as the agent in placing the orders and paying for them. A local commercial firm was engaged to assemble the packages. Before the JDC approved of the contents, they consulted Rabbi Dr. Leo Jung, a leading American Orthodox rabbi, who chaired the JDC's cultural-religious committee, and with a representative of the Union of Orthodox Rabbis to make sure that the dried salami and the cheese were kosher. They even went so far as to ask if these commodities could be included in the same package, despite the fact that they were packed separately in a hermetically sealed wrapper and covered with corrugated paper. The JDC also sent prayer books, Bibles, *tefillin*, Torah scrolls and other religious articles needed to observe Judaism. Some of the supplies were sent from Switzerland, and they were collecting and purchasing additional supplies for immediate shipment to the Jews in Germany.[5]

In a letter to the National Council on September 6, 1945, the JDC said it had already begun shipping kosher food to Europe from England and Argentina, including meat, even though it was rationed.[6] Efforts to supply meat were hindered by the need to produce a shipping permit and to demonstrate that the organization had the means to transport the items at a time when there was a very limited number of refrigerated boats.[7]

Rather than wait for someone to provide kosher meat for them, some survivors arranged for *shochtim* at the DP camps at Landsberg and Feldafing to slaughter live cattle purchased from the Germans. But for all practical purposes there were hardly any ordained *shochtim*. Even a ritual knife could not be found. In addition, the *shochtim* killed the animals either in the camp kitchens or in the barracks under the most "appalling sanitary conditions." At some of the other camps, such as Zeilsheim, with a population of 7,000, they did without meat altogether.[8]

At Zeilsheim, Rabbi Rosenberg did the initial slaughtering himself "to induce" the camp committee to establish a kosher kitchen. He later brought *shochtim* to continue the work. Here, too, the cows were purchased from the Germans and killed under primitive conditions. This process continued until the end of October 1945, when Rabbi Rosenberg made arrangements with slaughterhouses in Frankfurt and Landsberg where Jews could bring the cattle to be killed. At Feldafing and Foehrenwald, the slaughtering continued again under appalling conditions.

In November, Brigadier General Stanley R. Mickelson, chief of the United States Army's Displaced Persons Division in Germany, informed Rabbi Rosenberg that *shechitah* would have to stop to protect the German stock. Since there was no kosher canned meat available, Rabbi Rosenberg immediately submitted a memorandum to Judge Simon Rifkind, a federal judge who came to Germany on October 20, 1945 to serve as Advisor on Jewish Affairs, and alerted him to the possibility of losing access to kosher meat.[9]

Rabbi Rosenberg also spoke to Jacob Trobe, the director of JDC operations in Germany, who asked the JDC in New York to send kosher canned meat. On December 20, 1945, Trobe informed General Michelson that the JDC was going to send 200,000 pounds of kosher meat to the Jews in Germany. He also notified the Army that based on past experiences, the process of purchasing, securing export licenses, shipping, obtaining port clearance, and distribution could take as long as three months. Orthodox Jews would remain dependent upon the system they were using until the meat arrived.[10]

Rabbi Rosenberg continued "to hammer away" at Rifkind and Trobe to allow the *shechitah* to continue. The local rabbis in the Third Army Area sent their demands to General Walter J. Muller, United States Military Governor in Bavaria, and General Lucian K. Truscott, the commander of the Third

Army (who replaced General George Patton). Visitors to the camps from the American Jewish Conference and the American Jewish Committee protested to General Truscott to no avail. For the next three to four months, the religious Jews either did not eat meat or obtained the animals through the black market and killed them at "great risk."[11]

On December 18, 1945, three rabbis came to Rabbi Rosenberg and asked him to lead a delegation to Generals Frederick E. Morgan and Walter Bedell Smith to plead their case for kosher meat. Morgan was head of UNNRA operations in Germany and Smith was General Eisenhower's chief of staff. Trobe refused to allow Rabbi Rosenberg to see either of them because he knew that the Army would not budge on this issue. According to Trobe, the blame for this intransigence lay with Rabbi Joseph Shubow, an American chaplain stationed in Berlin. Shubow, a Reform rabbi, "volunteered the information to [Army] Headquarters that it was not fair to discriminate in favor of a small group of DPs when all American soldiers are forced to eat canned meat."[12]

Rabbi Rosenberg persisted and Rifkind finally agreed to a meeting with General Smith. In a report on his hour-and-a-half meeting on December 20, 1945, Rabbi Rosenberg wrote that at one point he and Smith almost came to "an unfriendly breach, when I sternly told him that I was amazed at the indifference with which he had stated that they [the DPs] will have meat in three months," when the kosher canned meat ordered by the JDC would arrive, "and that nobody cared what they will have in the meantime." He "snapped back also sternly that the American public would be even more amazed if they would find out that a small group of Jews is being discriminated in favor against the American Army."[13]

Rabbi Rosenberg asked whether the opinion of Rabbi Shubow had influenced him. Smith "retorted" that Rifkind had concurred with this view and they would not have paid attention to Shubow's opinion alone. After further discussion, Smith agreed to allow ritual slaughtering if the rabbis guaranteed that the privilege would not be abused.

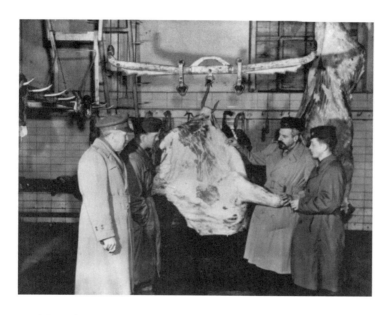

Rabbi Alexander S. Rosenberg (second from right)
reviewing the preparation of kosher meat.
Photo courtesy of JDC Archives, New York

Smith accepted their guarantees. He also agreed that in the few remaining days before he left Germany he would try to convince the staff to let them be.[14]

Before leaving, Rabbi Rosenberg turned to Rabbi David Horowitz of the Landsberg DP camp to ask that he offer a blessing in Hebrew for Smith on the eve of his departure from Germany. Rabbi Horowitz, who had sat through the meeting without uttering a word, hesitated since such blessings were reserved only for kings. Rabbi Rosenberg suggested that Rabbi Horowitz recite the "priestly blessing" without mentioning the name of God. He then turned to the General to request permission for Rabbi Horowitz to bless him. Smith replied, "Ask him to include me in his daily prayers." Smith rose from his chair and walked over to the rabbi who offered his hand. Rabbi Horowitz recited the "priestly blessing" in Hebrew. With that they left the General.[15] Smith never told Rabbis Rosenberg or Horowitz that his mother was Jewish, and that he had been raised as a Protestant.[16]

Rabbi Rosenberg was then able to arrange for *shechitah* in Munich, Frankfurt, Nuremberg, Regensburg, Stuttgart and Eshwege. Whether Jews received kosher meat outside the camps depended on the agreements local Jewish committees could work out with the Germans. Rabbi Rosenberg also took a fully equipped Nazi-owned restaurant in Munich and turned it into a kosher restaurant. The operation was established on a 30-day trial basis and its future was conditional on the arrival of canned meat from the JDC.[17]

Rabbi Rosenberg urged Judge Rifkind and Herbert Katzki, the JDC director in Germany in 1945, to make a forceful case to allow them to perform *shechitah*. Katzki succeeded and Truscott's headquarters agreed that the directive remain in force. At least 12,000 people were eating kosher food instead of the 4,800 envisaged in the directive.[18]

At the end of July 1946, 90 percent of the Jews fleeing to Germany from Russia wanted kosher meat. Rabbi Rosenberg asked Leo W. Schwarz, director of the JDC in Germany from 1946 to 1947, to provide these people with the basics that would allow them to maintain their religious way of life. "There is no reason why these religious people should be penalized for their principles and forced to subsist on salmon and bread for days," he wrote.[19] The Jews eating kosher food in the camps paid a high a price for doing so. They had to "turn in their ration of canned fish, canned meat and canned cheese, which robs them not only of calories but also of the variety of food. As a result, many prefer not to accept kosher meat in order not to lose this food, and suffer in their conscience; a situation arises where the camp management has not enough of the other supplies to turn in and the camp goes without meat often for weeks."[20]

Obtaining kosher fats was another problem. When the American Red Cross stopped supplying margarine, lard and non-kosher German-made margarine was sent to the camps in Germany, Austria and Italy. Rabbi Rosenberg proposed that the military immediately release American margarine, which was kosher and available in American military stores. He also asked for the release of German vegetable oil to replace non-kosher fat, and for a German factory to manufacture vegetable margarine under rabbinical supervision. Employing a German factory would assist the economy and assure a constant supply. The Germans could be compensated with non-kosher fats from the Americans. Unlike lard or animal oils, the margarine was used as a spread for bread, as a butter substitute. Rabbi Rosenberg thought this policy could be implemented immediately. He argued that, "There was no reason why people should unnecessarily suffer two or three weeks, and sometimes longer, before they can have their proper meals, since it is only a matter of proper organization. The needs of the religious people should not be taken any more lightly than the needs of the general population," he argued.[21]

Rabbi Rosenberg also sought help from Chaplain Emanuel Rackman, an American Orthodox rabbi and an aide to the Advisor on Jewish Affairs. Rabbi Rackman brought the matter to the attention of Jack Whiting, the zone director of UNNRA. Whiting did not think the request for "an enormous increase" in kosher rations was unreasonable and told Rabbi Rackman that he would cooperate to the fullest.[22]

Just before Passover 1947, in speaking with some of the 1,450 Jews in the Monchenberg DP camp, Chaplain

Abraham Klausner, heard complaints about the lack of food for Passover.[23]

"The non-observant Jew can manage, they argued, but the observant Jew can not even use the oleomargarine that the AJDC sent to the camps. The label, they noted, clearly indicated it contains two items, one to make it *milchig* (dairy)—and who eats *milchig* on Passover?—and one to bar it from Passover use." When Chaplain Klausner asked what they wanted instead, they said potatoes. He then arranged for five tons of potatoes to be delivered to the camps at a cost of 22,000 RM or $100.00.[24]

Rabbi Klausner intervened regularly to provide appropriate food for *sedarim* (Passover meals), even to Merxhausen, a hospital with 160 Jews suffering from tuberculosis. A number of days before the holiday, the patients sent a representative to the JDC with a request that "at least do not forget us on Passover." The JDC turned to Rabbi Klausner for help. Later he reported "At Merxhausen, on Passover evening there was truly a *Seder* with all good things to eat. There was joy and there was singing—all this at the cost of 23,500 RM, or if you will, at seventy cents per person."[25]

At Camp Rochelle, one of the newer camps established in Kassel, Rabbi Klausner was asked to provide potatoes. He asked the National Jewish Welfare Board (JWB) to reimburse him so he could continue to help the DPs. Since the JWB was responsible for the chaplains, and not for providing aid to the DPs, Rabbi Klausner realized they might be reluctant to give him the money. They could legitimately say, "Klausner, all these things are good, but there are institutions and responsibilities...." To that he would respond, "We can not feed our people the sins of institutions!"[26]

On July 7, 1947, Rabbi Joshua Aronson, Chief Rabbi of the U.S. Zone in Austria, sent a letter to the JDC in New York from the Union of Rabbis of Austria to ask that only kosher food be distributed to the DPs. "All Jews want to eat kosher" he said, but the "fact that the 'Joint' distributes *trepho* [sic] meat...is too great a temptation for them after years of torture and hunger...."

The rabbis were also upset that although prior to Passover they succeeded in having all the kitchens for the DPs in Austria *kashered* (made kosher) for the holiday, the JDC brought in non-kosher chickens from Hungary. The chickens were very fat, and because many people had not eaten chickens since the beginning of the war, they ate them. All their hard work to *kasher* the kitchens was in vain. "It is the task of all of us to make all efforts...to bring our poor brethren back to normal life.... One of the most experienced ways to do this is [through] the observance of Jewish religious law. It is the guarantee for the revival of national Jewish life." The rabbis appealed to their "Jewish hearts and conscience" to order only kosher meat for the DPs.[27]

In Italy, Jews, including many who ate non-kosher food during the war, wanted kosher food for their first Passover after liberation. The survivors asked Jacob Griffel to have it delivered, but officials of the JDC refused, and claimed it would cost too much. Only those who had requested food earlier would be given it now. In protest, the Jews threatened to set the kitchen on fire if they did not get what they wanted.[28]

In an attempt to convince the JDC to provide kosher food, Griffel wrote a long letter to Brooklyn-based, Rabbi Joseph Schneerson, the then-Lubavitcher Rebbe. Though partially paralyzed and in poor health, the Rebbe succeeded in making kosher food available through the JDC. A few days after he received Griffel's letter, a call came from the American Embassy to those who ran the camp instructing them to "supply kosher to anyone who wants it, whether he asked for it before or not." Griffel never learned how Rabbi Schneerson managed to make this happen.[29]

After receiving Griffel's letter, the Rebbe sent a letter to the JDC on June 2, 1947, in which he said he had received reports about canned meat products being distributed by the JDC to the DPs that "included *Terefah* foods." Many DPs were not satisfied with the level of *kashrus* of some of the food and abstained from eating it. The Rebbe found it hard to believe that the JDC would be guilty "either knowingly or inadvertently" of supplying non-kosher food to the DPs. But because of the "seriousness of the matter," he asked that it be investigated immediately, and if true, that it be corrected "without delay," and that it not happen again.[30] On June 30, 1947, M. Jacob Joslow responded that the JDC makes every effort to provide kosher food to the DPs and that the Rebbe's letter would be brought to the attention of JDC European headquarters.[31]

On October 24, 1947, the Agudath Israel in Milan, Italy sent a letter to the JDC director in Rome complaining about the non-kosher fats and meats being sent to the camps by the IRO. The Agudah asked the JDC to intervene with the IRO before the kosher kitchens in the camps have to be closed. The Jews in Italy would "prefer to suffer hunger" than to go against "their traditions."[32]

Another source of kosher food came from Dublin, Ireland and was known as the Irish Meat Project. One million pounds of meat was offered by the Irish government for the DPs, with the JDC assuming all the costs for preparing and shipping it to Europe. It was part of ten million pounds of meat donated by the Irish Free State for general relief purposes in Europe. The project was planned to start in July 1947 and employ Lubavitch *shochtim* and *mashgichim* from Germany and Austria under the direction of Robert Briscoe, an Irish-Jewish member of the *Eire Dail* (parliament). However, it was delayed until the JDC could obtain 300 tons of tin-plate in the United States to pack the meat in the cans.

In April 1947, Briscoe arrived in Paris to inform the JDC that no *shochtim* acceptable to Chief Rabbi Herzog could be found in London or Ireland, and hoped to recruit workers to be taken back to Dublin. When this plan failed, the Lubavitch were engaged for three months.[33]

To make sure kosher food was provided on a regular basis, Rabbi Nathan Baruch assisted in establishing kosher kitchens in DP camps throughout the American Zone of Germany. If a DP camp had a kitchen, camp personnel could improvise, but if this was not possible, he tried to arrange for a kosher kitchen to be built. Whenever the Vaad established a kitchen, it made each opening a special event. In October 1947, when it opened a kosher kitchen for the

Frankfurt community and for the hundreds of transients that passed through the city each week, Baruch invited many dignitaries to participate. General Thomas L. Harrold, Chief of the DP Operations, EUCOM (European Command), delivered very warm greetings to the assembly. Major Abraham Hyman and Chaplain William Dalin of Judge Louis E. Levinthal's Office of the Advisor on Jewish Affairs were also present. (The Judge was in Austria.) There were also representatives from the JDC, HIAS, the IRO and a Mr. Werber, the president of the Frankfurt Jewish Committee.

The following week, Baruch hosted another group of dignitaries including Judge Levinthal and his wife; General Harrold and his staff; Colonel G. R. Scithers, Liaison Officer for the Central Committee for the Liberated Jews of Germany; Rabbi Michael Munk of Berlin and David Trager, president of the Central Committee. Unfortunately the Vaad did not have enough funds to maintain these facilities, and eventually they had to be funded by the JDC. The Vaad, however, was a driving force and they deserve some credit for their establishment.[34]

Dr. Philipp Auerbach, a survivor of Auschwitz, Gross-Rosen and Buchenwald, made it easier for Baruch to establish kosher kitchens. As chairman of the Association of Jewish Communities in Bavaria, he was put in charge of the Jewish DPs in the British Zone of Occupation, and in 1946 became state commissar for the racial, religious and politically persecuted in Bavaria.[35] Through him, Baruch was given big pots, pans and utensils that were requisitioned from German factories. Of course, Auerbach was not supposed to do this. All such items were supposed to be shipped from America, but the JDC was not sending all the necessary supplies and equipment.

Baruch received these supplies because of his close friendship with Auerbach, who was headquartered in Munich. Auerbach was a typical German who took his position very seriously. Baruch was very nice to him and kept him fully supplied with cigars. Mrs. Auerbach liked cigarettes and Baruch gave them his tobacco rations. Baruch also provided Mrs. Auerbach with items from the PX, endearing him to her

Distributing Passover supplies in Pasing
Photos courtesy of Rabbi Nathan Baruch

husband even more. As a result, Auerbach provided Baruch with requisition orders whenever Baruch needed them.

The first Passover Baruch was in Germany Auerbach requisitioned truckloads of dishes and glassware to distribute for the holiday. He also procured material from clothing factories—rolls of silk and woolens. As a result, whenever a couple got married, Baruch was able to give them things they needed, including fabric for a suit and a dress, which could be inexpensively produced by German tailors and seamstresses.

Whatever Rabbi Baruch did to show his appreciation to Auerbach—cigarettes or other PX items—it was miniscule in comparison to what he received in return. But Auerbach had a tendency to criticize the German administration on German radio on a regular basis, and it got him into trouble.[36]

His undoing came in 1952, after Baruch had already returned to America. "In that year [Auerbach] was accused of accepting bribes, blackmail, misusing his office and illegally using the title of Doctor. As a consequence of these serious accusations and of his precarious health, Auerbach committed suicide on 16th August 1952."[37]

All in all, providing kosher food, especially meat, to the DPs was a complex and emotional issue. There was a dearth of trained *shochtim* and proper facilities were almost nonexistent. In addition, many JDC personnel in Europe failed to understand or appreciate the importance kosher food played in the survivors' spiritual rehabilitation.

Rabbi Rosenberg had learned firsthand how vital it was to so many survivors and that the DPs needed religious advocates to help them. Unfortunately, the JDC did not have many in Europe or the U.S.

In any event, the establishment of kosher kitchens in the DP camps made it easier to provide kosher food on a regular basis. Rabbi Baruch and the Vaad worked hard to set up or build as many kosher kitchens as possible, as well as to provide kosher food. Needless to say, doing so was a challenge—emotionally, financially and logistically.

Colonel G. R. Scithers, Liaison Officer for the Central
Committee for the Liberated Jews of Germany
Photo courtesy of Rabbi Nathan Baruch

Dr. Philipp Auerbach (left) chairman of the Association of
Jewish Communities in Bavaria and in charge of the
Jewish DPs in the British Zone of Occupation

Photos courtesy of Rabbi Nathan Baruch

Vaad kosher
kitchens
Photos courtesy of
Rabbi Nathan Baruch.

Chapter 7

A Publishing Empire

Observant Jewish survivors needed religious articles, but these items were scarce. Beginning in the late 1930s, the Nazis began confiscating Jewish books and artifacts in Germany. During the war, the Nazis extended the operation, using German military forces, other Nazi agencies and individuals to seize Jewish books, archives and ritual objects wherever they went—from "occupied Ukraine to the French-Spanish border, and from Greece to the British Isle of Man."[1] Rabbinical and communal libraries from Italy, an Axis power, were also looted.[2] Books were stolen from the Ecole Rabbinique, the Israelitische Gemeinde Bibliotek and the Verein fur Jüdische Geschichte und Literatur of Nuremberg, the Bibliotheca Polska, Alliance Israélite Universelle, and the Rothschild libraries.[3]

In January 1940, Hitler ordered the Nazi Party and State offices to assist Alfred Rosenberg, the official National Socialist ideologue, to steal these books and artifacts for a future library that would be part of the Hohe Schule, the educational and research institute of the Party, planned to be built in Chiemsee in Bavaria. A small fraction of the looted material was kept for research purposes. Most of the ceremonial objects were melted down and the books were either burned or made into pulp.[4]

At the end of the war, the Allies found huge amounts of books randomly strewn in "makeshift depots." They also found books and ceremonial objects scattered throughout Bavaria and other places, particularly in the Rothschild Library in Frankfurt-am-Main and the towns of Hungen and Hirzenhain in Hesse.[5]

In late June 1946, Koppel Pinson, educational director of the JDC, found the remnants of the collection of books and objects stolen by Julius Streicher and the Streicher-Verlag in Nuremberg. Streicher, the editor and publisher of *Der Stürmer*, the virulently antisemitic German newspaper, had personally appropriated a large number of Torah scrolls, silver ornamental pieces, paintings, photographs and approximately 10,000 books, most of which were rabbinical expositions. The collection had been built around the former Nuremberg libraries of the Israelitische Gemeinde Bibliotek and the Verein fur Jüdische Geschichte und Literatur.

A large number of the books were old and valuable; many were standard texts and more recent editions. Pinson thought the *Der Stürmer* staff used them for references to Jews and Judaism. For example, the *Shulchan Aruch* (lit. Set Table), a book of Jewish religious law written by Rabbi Joseph Karo of Safed in the 1560s, and subsequent commentaries, were marked extremely important. A small book on Kabbalah by Karo was marked "a confession by the author of the *Shulchan Aruch*, most important," as if to suggest the work revealed the innermost secret beliefs of this "infamous" author. Other notations on the books indicated they had been "quoted or used" by other antisemitic authors.

Officers of the International Military Tribunal took the most valuable items to the Nuremberg Trials for use as evidence, except for the *Mahzor Nurnberg* and the Rashi manuscript housed in the Germanisches Museum and the municipal library. They were still packed away along with all the other valuable items in the museum before the war. Only a small portion of the Gemeinde archive remained, since the Gestapo had destroyed most of it.

Aside from the books taken from Nuremberg, there were several thousand volumes from other Jewish communities in Germany and Eastern Europe that came from special agents of *Der Stürmer* in different parts of Europe, or were duplicates from either the Alfred Rosenberg library in Frankfurt or the Heinrich Himmler library in Berlin.

American Army Chaplain Isaiah Rackovsky, an Orthodox rabbi, formerly chief Jewish chaplain in Frankfurt, had informed Pinson about the collection and introduced him to a Mr. Kolb, who had been a member of the executive committee of the Jewish community in Nuremberg before the war. After being liberated, Kolb returned to Nuremberg where he assumed control of the Jewish cultural treasures that had not been taken by the American Military Government. Kolb agreed to give Pinson the entire collection if he would ship it to the United States.[6]

On March 2, 1946 the American military established the Offenbach Archival Depot (OAD) in conjunction with Monuments, Fine Arts and Archives Wiesbaden, to house, protect and restore this enormous collection. Housed in a vast five-story warehouse across the river from Frankfurt that had belonged to the I.G. Farben company, the OAD "processed—received and/or shipped—over 1.8 million items contained in 2,351 crates, stacks, packages, and piles" by March 25, 1946. By August 1947, 2,000,000 books and "identifiable materials" were returned and distributed to the survivors. Rabbi Baruch secured some important *seforim* (religious texts) belonging to Rabbi Avram Ziemba of Poland from the OAD after hearing about them from two of Rabbi Ziemba's nephews. Arrangements were eventually made with the American Army to have them transferred to Israel.[7]

The JDC received 24,000 volumes on loan to distribute to the Jews in the DP camps in Europe. But these "supplies" from the JDC in Europe and the United States were insufficient to meet all the needs of the observant survivors. As of December 1946, the JDC provided 35,000 prayer books as well as a number of other religious items, but the observant DPs were still in need of additional religious texts.[8]

Rabbi Abraham Kalmanowitz understood this necessity from the first days of the American occupation of Germany. During the winter of 1945-1946, the Army, together with UNRRA, began to respond to requests for religious texts by a number of DP rabbis who were in contact with Rabbi Kalmanowitz. In February 1946, Rabbi Alexander Rosenberg reported to JDC headquarters in New York: "Three tractates of the Talmud, a prayer book, a *Haggadah*, a [B]ook of Esther, and a guide to religious marriage are either in process of publication [by the JDC] or are already published."[9]

In November 1947, Rabbi Kalmanowitz approached General John H. Hilldring, Assistant Secretary of State for Occupied Areas, to help him publish "200,000 Bibles and Prayer Books in the U.S. Zone of Germany for use of Jewish children in Western Europe." In 1945, when Hilldring was the director of the Civilian Affairs Department (CAD) of the War Department, the rabbi asked him to send religious articles to the Jewish DPs in Germany. A call by Hilldring to his friend General Lucius Clay ended three months of exhausting and fruitless attempts by Rabbi Kalmanowitz to convince the Army Service Forces to send these items.

When Rabbi Kalmanowitz asked Hilldring to help him again, Hilldring wrote a note to Clay reminding him that they had helped the rabbi in 1945. Hilldring noted that he was a "patient and appreciative old patriarch...I can think of no assistance I gave anyone in Washington...that gave me more satisfaction than the very little help I gave the old Rabbi...."[10]

Rabbi Kalmanowitz now needed a permit for paper, priority for using electricity, an export license, and a permit to send his personal representatives to the U.S. Zone of Germany to supervise the printing and distribution of the copies of the Bibles and prayer books. This time, Clay rejected his request because there was an acute shortage of paper in late 1947, and only vital government documents could be published.[11]

In the meantime, at the urging of Rabbi Burstin, Baruch had also begun exploring ways to publish religious texts (*seforim*) himself. The need to print the Talmud—the oral tradition—became especially important for the students who were being taught in the *yeshivos* and for individuals who wanted to study with a *chevrusa*, a study partner. Rabbi Burstin, who was from Lublin, Poland, wanted the Talmud so Jews could begin studying the *Daf Yomi* (Daily Folio Page of the Talmud) again.

At the Congress of the Agudath Israel in Europe in 1923, Rabbi Meir Shapira of Lublin proposed that Jews throughout the world study the same page of the Talmud (*Daf Yomi*) simultaneously—as a sign of a unifying commitment to Judaism and Jewish learning. In this way, observant Jewish males could complete the study of the Talmud every seven and-a-half years and mark it with a formal celebration commemorating the end of the learning cycle and the beginning of the new one. The proposal was accepted and a special calendar was created. Jews everywhere began to study the *Daf.* Rabbi Shapira participated in the first completion of the cycle in 1931. Observant Jews then integrated the *Daf Yomi* program into their lives. In 1947, the rabbinate in the *Yishuv*, led by Rabbi Dr. Isaac Herzog and the Union of Orthodox Rabbis of the United States and Canada and the rabbinate of England, united to make the *Daf Yomi* a universal part of observant Jewish life. The Jews of Germany responded, too, but few had copies of the Talmud.[12]

When Baruch approached the military authorities for authorization and assistance to publish religious material his requests were denied. The function of the Army was not to play nursemaid to the DPs they claimed, but to keep order and serve as a buffer against Russian encroachment. Baruch was not deterred. He turned instead to those who had access to the Army warehouses. Since the military had an abundance of supplies—an assessment not shared by General Clay—Baruch thought he might be able to "barter" for his needs. Among his contacts was a Jewish girl working for the military and some non-Jewish quartermasters who were sympathetic and willing to provide paper and materials.

One of Baruch's contacts worked in the Army Post Exchange (PX) and purchased whiskey for him. A number of officers who didn't need their alcohol rations sold their rations to Baruch at a fraction of their worth. The same was true of others who had coffee and cigarette rations. Thus, coffee, whiskey and cigarettes were traded for paper, ink, printing and binding. Baruch and his associates found a photo-offset processing plant and went into the now financially viable business of publishing prayer books and other religious texts.

As soon as the books were printed and bound, they were sent to the DP camps and to leading rabbis and scholars throughout the world. Some people in Europe came to the Vaad office in Germany to collect their copies. Pincus Schoen asked that prominent donors and every Orthodox rabbi in the U. S. receive sets of these *seforim* to induce them to fund the project. Regrettably, there was no *quid pro quo*. Baruch never received any additional funds from the Vaad or anyone else who received copies of these special editions. If any money was generated from these activities, they went directly to the Vaad office in New York.[13]

To meet the demand for copies of the Talmud, Baruch printed and distributed 10,000 pocket-sized editions of individual *masechtas* (tractates). By the end of 1947, he had published some 240,000 religious texts and distributed them to camps and to the rest of the world Jewish community. These included "*siddurim, Tehillim, Hagaddahs* [sic], *Megillas Esther, Pirkei Avos, Mesillas Yeshorim, Or Israel, Shev Shmateso, Kesses Hasofer, Yiddish Leben, Kitzur Shulchan Aruch, Sha'agas Aryeh, Taharas Hamishpacha*, and the *Bible*." [14]

Shortly after the *seforim* arrived in the U.S., Baruch received requests for additional publications. Despite his many obligations, he complied. Pincus Schoen asked for 1,000 copies of *Pirkei Avos* (*Ethics of Our Fathers*) with the following inscription: "Dedicated to you and to all friends and supporters of Vaad Hatzala who in thick and thin realized their great moral obligation and responsibility and gave wholeheartedly to rescue their brethren and to rebuild their lives. May the Almighty bless you." The copies were shipped to America where they were sent to Vaad supporters with thank you letters enclosed. Schoen was so impressed with the response he received, he declared that the publications were "...worth their weight in gold and propaganda and public relations for the Vaad."[15]

On June 2, 1947, Pincus Schoen sent Baruch an additional request for 200 copies of books to include the inscription: "In grateful acknowledgement to Mr. Louis Clark and to all members of Congregation Agudas Achim Bnei Jacob for their generous contributions to Vaad Hatzala during the past several years."

On another occasion, the New York office requested that thousands of *Haggadahs* be printed for Passover. They later complained that the package was so bulky, they had problems with the U.S. Customs Service.[16]

Baruch also printed texts requested by Rabbi Issac Lewin, a member of the Agudath Israel in the United States who worked with the Vaad. One of these was *Avnei Hefetz*, a rabbinical work by the Rzeszow Rav, Rabbi Aaron Ben Nathan Lewin of Rzeszow, Poland. Rabbi Lewin was elected to the Polish Parliament (*Sejm*) in 1922. As a leader of the Agudath Israel, Rav Aaron succeeded his father as the rabbi of Rzeszow in 1926. When he attempted to flee to Lemberg after the Nazis took over his city, Rabbi Lewin was apprehended and killed. His manuscript was lost during the Holocaust and recovered after the war.

His son, Dr. Isaac Lewin, suggested that Baruch reprint *Avnei Hefetz* as part of a series of publications. Lewin offered to pay for an additional 1,000 copies so that he could send them to rabbis in the United States and abroad. He viewed the publication "as a great credit for the *She'erith Hapleitah* and personally will give me great satisfaction for my share in the Hatzala work."[17]

The publishing program was so successful that Baruch decided to dedicate a book of Psalms, with an English translation, to General Lucius D. Clay. Before proceeding, he asked Abraham Hyman, assistant Advisor on Jewish Affairs, to discuss the idea with William Haber. Haber agreed to the idea and said he would tell the general about the project at their next meeting. Haber also suggested that in the dedication it would be appropriate to mention what the general's "sympathetic policies have meant" to the Jewish DPs.

Hyman quickly pointed out that Haber did not want to "make much ado" about the dedication by bringing in the press and photographing the event because of an existing agreement—signed on Sept. 11, 1946 between the JDC and the Rabbinical Council U.S. Zone Germany—to publish 750 sets of a 19-volume Talmud. That edition was supposed to be distributed jointly by authorized representatives of the JDC and the Rabbinical Council.[18] The Theater Commander would receive a quantity for distribution to those he saw fit, educational institutions in the United States and Palestine would receive a finite number and the majority would be distributed to *yeshivos* and suitable libraries in the U.S. Zone of Occupation.[19]

The Army Talmud "would be of such importance that it will deserve special attention," Hyman pointed out. Though the Vaad's proposal had been "inspired by the best of intentions," Haber and Hyman felt "it would be imprudent to have the spotlight thrown on an occasion such as that one."[20]

Publishing the Talmud had been a major interest of Rabbi Samuel Snieg and his assistant, Rabbi Samuel Rose. Rabbi Philip S. Bernstein, a Reform rabbi and the Advisor on Jewish Affairs from May 1946 to August 1947, liked the idea and convinced General Clay to approve its publication. The JDC agreed to underwrite part of the production costs, and the Army guaranteed that the Germans would contribute the rest of the funds—up to 250,000 DMs. Each volume measured 11 by 16 inches, and was "modeled" after the *Vilna Shas*.

The Talmud was dedicated to the "United States Army for having played a major role in the rescue of the Jewish people from total annihilation, and after the defeat of Hitler bore the major burden of sustaining the DPs of the Jewish faith." It was proffered that "this special edition of the Talmud published in the very land, where, but a short time ago, everything Jewish and of Jewish inspiration was anathema," would "remain a symbol of the indestructibility

Title page from the Army Talmud
Courtesy of YIVO

DEDICATION

This edition of the Talmud is dedicated to the United States Army. This Army played a major role in the rescue of the Jewish people from total annihilation, and after the defeat of Hitler bore the major burden of sustaining the DPs of the Jewish faith. This special edition of the Talmud published in the very land where, but a short time ago, everything Jewish and of Jewish inspiration was anathema, will remain a symbol of the indestructibility of the Torah. The Jewish DPs will never forget the generous impulses and the unprecedented humanitarianism of the American forces, to whom they owe so much.

In the name of the Rabbinical Organization

RABBI SAMUEL A. SNIEG
Chairman and Chief Rabbi of the U. S. Zone

ב"ע'ה

ברוך שהחינו וקימנו והגיענו לזמן הזה — הדפסת הש"ס !

בחמדו הגדול ית"ש עלה בידינו לחוציא חש"ס הנדול עם רב אלפסי ז"ל כליל חיופו וחהידור.

אחרי החורבן הגורא, ימי האבדון וההשמדה שעברו עלינו, שעת ברה כמוה עוד לא נהיתה מהיות ישראל לגוי, משמם אחר היה לישראל וחורתו, כי חרשעים שהשמדו חרפו את יחודי איירופא, השחדלו גם כן כן שלא לחשאיר שום ספר עברי, רשיאה יחתדי נשרף כרוך בספר החורה.

עוד חקוק בזכרונגו חיסב אותו יום חמר, הופאת הפקודה בגימו, משלשום חרשע חנגים יס"ש, לאסוף את כל הספרים אל מקום אחר, בכדי לחניאם ולכלוחם, וסכנת מות היתה פפויה לות אשר יסתיר ספר אחד, איכבו החחכמו עלינו לא להשמיד אותנו בלבד אלא גם לחדיאכנו יותר כל עוד רוח חיים בקרבנו מצאו, כי נשילת הספר מעם חספר והו מצע עמוק בנשמת יש"ראל שאין מעלה ארוכה. כל ספרי ישראל נשלו לענבות ניר, לחשמש גזו'ו או נשרפו, שאיפשו של חזר חמשאיר היתה שמחת חלילה שם ישראל לא מבין חיים בלבד אלא גם סן הספר. ברמפיו חמרובים של חשי'ה חשאיר שארית פלישה, שרידי חרב שנצולו פידי חרשעים הארורים אך בלי ספר בידם.

בשנת חשי אחרי רוב השחדלות עלה בידינו לחדפיס מספכחות קודשי"נדרים ולהפצים בין שארית ישראל ישיבות וכתי מודרשים וליחידים הלומדים, אולם ש"ס שלם ביחד עדיין הוא יקר חמדי'את ואינו כמפט בנכסא אצלנו בלבד מסכחות בודדות שנמצאח פח ושם.

במשך חזמן שאמנו להוציא את חש"ס בשלמותו אבל לוח דרושת חוצאת מרובה מה שאינה ביכולתנו, לפיכך פנינו לשלמון הצבא האמריקאי כאשכנו שמה יאפשרו לנו את חוצאת חש"ס, וחצף ד' הצליח בידינו חודות לסיוע יעץ הצבא לעניני חיחודים בגרסני" ד"ר רבי ₱. ברנשטין נ"י ובקשחנו נחמלאת בעתי"ח ותינ הוא יום בשרוה לישראל.

כדאי להעיר, שכמאשי ימי נלות ישראל הארוך לא פעם נשרפו ספרי ישראל ע"י חשלשונות ואף אוח מהן לא הקימח אותם לגו, זהו חפעם חראשונה בדברי ימי ישראל שמחשלח חעוזר לחניאים את ספרי החלמוד אשר הם חיינו ואורך ימנו, צבאות ארצות הברית הצילו אותנו סמות לחיים והם חמניגים עלינו גם עחת בארץ זו, ובעזורחם מופיע החלמוד שוב באשכנז.

מלבד חנ"ל חשחחף בחואת ה,חוינים", אותה חברת חעזור חעונקית שעבודח חהצלח שלה מקפח את כל ענפי החיים שלנו, מלבד חפיכחח בחים חחוסריים, חופכת גם בין בחי חרוה חוצאת ספרים ועוד. חודות לחשחדלותם של פרופ. ו' פרום. ר' **שמואל ל. זר** מנחל צעגם. ארם. קאפ. והרב **שלמה שפירא** נ"י מנחל משרה חרחי יד חדוויגא, חפכים ח,חוינם" לחשתחף בחואאת זו לנגר'ל את מספר העקוסמפרים. בכדי שיספיק מעט לרוות את צמאונם של חלוסדים לספרי חחלמוד.

בשם חיהיוות החריית אנו מביעים את חודתנו חעמוקה לצבא ארצות חברית, ול,חוינים" בעד זה. זכות הקמת חתורה ינן עליהם.

לפרות חמורה וחסל ח"ב החנחה ועוד שחי" לנו בזה לא מגנין את עומנו מעברות קודש זו, בידינו את הצער וחכאב של צעירי ישראל בישיבות, והלומדים בגבוי, שש בחיקון ספרי החלמוד, מלבד חבטול חורה שיש בזה, והי רצון שחחף ד' יצליח בידינו וחזבנ חש"ס הברד על חמומד לנגר'ל חורה ולהאהירה, וגוכה בקרוב לחרמם קרן חחורה ולגאולה שלמה בביאת משיח צדקנו אמן.

כה דברי חמציאים לאור חמצפים לישועת ד'.

ועד אנודת הרבנים באזור האמריקאי

שמואל יעקב ראז   שמואל אבא סניעג
חבר ועד אנו"חר   יושב ראש ועד אנו"חר
סינגן   החוח"ק סינגן יע"א

סינגן, אסרו חנ סכות חש"ט

1948

Printed: Manul-Offset by Druckerei Carl Winter, Heidelberg (Germany)
under supervision of Procurement Division, European Quartermaster Depot, United States Army

Dedication page from the Army Talmud
Courtesy of YIVO

of the Torah." The Jewish DPs would "never forget the generous impulses and the unprecedented humanitarianism of the American forces, to whom they owe so much."[21]

The Army was proud that it had made publication of this edition possible, but only printed a limited number of copies. The original agreement had indicated an earlier publication date, but a number of obstacles in 1947 and 1948, including a shortage of paper, lack of appropriate printing equipment and a weak German economy forced a delay. The first volumes were bound in 1949, but it was not until 1951 that the work was delivered to prominent individuals and libraries in the U.S., Canada, Europe and Israel.[22]

Thus, despite all the claims about its importance and its mission of "sustaining the DPs of the Jewish faith," the Army Talmud served little purpose for the survivors who needed it most because by the time the volumes were available, the vast majority of them were no longer in Europe. Between May 1948 and the end of 1951 about 304,000 Jewish survivors from Central Europe had immigrated to Israel. Similarly, between July 1948 and 1952 about 58,000 Jews had left for the United States.[23]

As the Talmud project neared completion, Rabbi Solomon Shapiro, the JDC's Director of Religious Affairs, informed his New York office that when they first began working on the Talmud his staff in Paris knew very little about it: "You would be interested to know that there has been a great amount of reading of books about the Talmud among members of our staff as a result of our involvement in the project...Many people became involved in one way or another in the Transportation Department, in the Accounting Department, in the Budget Department, and in turn those who are in close relationship with these departments have been requesting material on the subject and we have not enough to go around."[24]

At a news conference on July 29, 1949, at JDC headquarters in New York, Rabbi Shapiro remarked that the printing of this new edition of the Talmud in Germany "represents a small measure of moral restitution to the Jewish people for all we have lost." He also noted "this is the first Hebrew

Picking up *seforim* in Pasing
Photos courtesy of Rabbi Nathan Baruch

Rabbi Aviezer Burstin distributing *seforim*
Photo courtesy of Rabbi Nathan Baruch

religious work to be printed in Germany since Hitler came to power."[25]

When Baruch presented his book of Psalms to General Clay on behalf of the Jewish DPs in July 1947, Clay remarked that he would "always cherish this book of Psalms among my most priceless possessions." Copies were also given to General Clarence Heubner, Deputy Commander in Chief of the European Command and Robert Murphy, political advisor to General Clay. When Baruch later sent General Clay a Bible, the general wrote that the Bible "will serve to remind me of the faith and courage of a people who refused to bow to the forces of evil which attempted their destruction."[26]

Among those who received books published by Baruch's makeshift publishing company were: American generals in Europe, the Far East and the United States; American admirals; U.S. Secretaries of War, Labor, Treasury; the Mayor of New York; the Secretary-General of the United Nations; U.S. Supreme Court Justices and a number of Jewish celebrities. After thanking Baruch for "remembering" him "with such a splendid gift," General Dwight D. Eisenhower—then the Chief of Staff of the War Department—said he would pass along his report on the Vaad "to the appropriate agency of the War Department staff for information and study."[27]

After they received Vaad publications, the Frankfurt Jewish GI Council made inquiries at several Jewish DP camps to determine their religious needs and submitted a list to the Vaad's Frankfurt office. The Council was established in June 1946 by David Bar-El (Schacter) and Eliezer Dembitz, American citizens whose families were living in Palestine, and by Chaplain Yosef Miller, a 26-year-old Orthodox rabbi assigned to Headquarters Command for the United States Forces in Frankfurt.

The Council proceeded to visit camps in Zeilsheim, Bensheim, Wetzlar, Ziegenhain, Babenhausen, Schwatzenborn, Lindenfels, Dieburg, Lampertheim and Kibbutz Buchenwald.[28] They permitted Baruch to make a presentation about Vaad activities so the Council could help. The Council also cosponsored a learning contest in the *yeshivos* during Passover, allocating $50 to purchase fountain pens and pencils to be awarded as prizes.[29]

Harry A. Goodman, Secretary of Agudah Israel World Organization, asked Baruch in early 1948 if the Vaad could supply the Agudah in London with copies of its publications. Goodman assured Baruch that the books would be distributed to institutions in England that "really need them," and that the Agudah would pay for the publications "if necessary."[30] Goodman had received parcels of books from Baruch less than a month before and was eager to obtain more.[31]

In addition to the thousands of *seforim* published by Baruch, the JDC also participated in delivering Hebrew books and other works that "were urgently needed" for schools, libraries and *yeshivos*. In 1946, UNRRA reprinted 7,000 copies of *Chaveri* by Ashman and Feller, Jewish authors in Palestine, without securing proper permission from the publishers. JDC distributed the books in September and reprinted another 5,000 copies in December. Most of the books were stamped "Not for sale—for use by She'erith Hapleitah." After learning of the copyright violation, The Union of Hebrew Book Publishers in Palestine sent a letter on April 28, 1947 inquiring about royalties on books JDC had printed in Germany.[32]

Leo Schwarz, JDC director for Germany from 1946 to 1947, initially believed that the Military Government in Germany had suspended the copyright laws and that royalties were not an issue since the books were not being sold.[33] George Weiss, the JDC General Counsel in Paris, was not as sanguine. While efforts were made to determine if JDC was liable for damages, additional books were printed. This was "unavoidable" as these books were already in print when the question was raised.[34]

The Offenbach Depot was another source JDC hoped would provide its need for books. After visiting Germany and Austria from August 3 to August 15, 1948, Judah Shapiro, JDC Director of Education, reported that the JDC was close to clearing the legal obstacles to obtain the material from the archive. "There is no channel at the present time" for JDC to obtain books from the depot, he lamented. "Haphazard attempts" to secure books and "improper distribution" of those that were inappropriately taken "has been most embarrassing to the AJDC," other Jewish organizations, depot officials and the military. Shapiro urged that the director of education be designated as the official JDC representative to receive and distribute these books.[35]

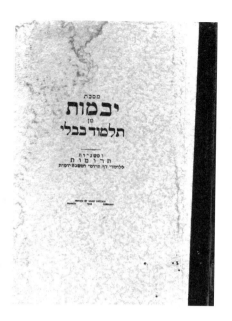

Tractate Yivamos published by the Vaad Hatzala
for use by those studying Daf Yomi
Courtesy of Beth Medrash Govoha, Lakewood, NJ

A presentation volume for
General George C. Marshall
Photo courtesy of Rabbi Nathan Baruch

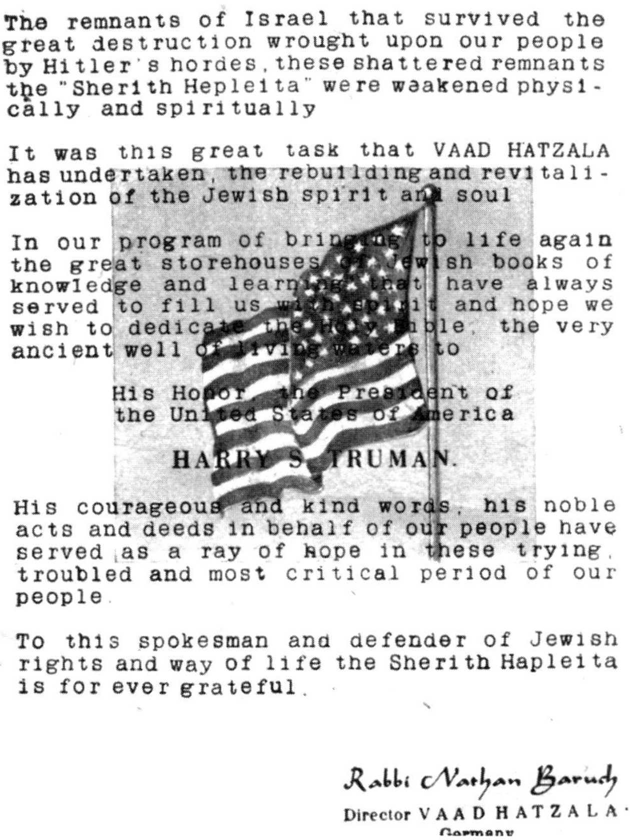

The remnants of Israel that survived the great destruction wrought upon our people by Hitler's hordes, these shattered remnants the "Sherith Hepleita" were weakened physically and spiritually

It was this great task that VAAD HATZALA has undertaken, the rebuilding and revitalization of the Jewish spirit and soul

In our program of bringing to life again the great storehouses of Jewish books of knowledge and learning that have always served to fill us with spirit and hope we wish to dedicate the Holy Bible, the very ancient well of living waters to

His Honor the President of the United States of America

HARRY S. TRUMAN.

His courageous and kind words, his noble acts and deeds in behalf of our people have served as a ray of hope in these trying, troubled and most critical period of our people

To this spokesman and defender of Jewish rights and way of life the Sherith Hapleita is for ever grateful.

Rabbi Nathan Baruch
Director VAAD HATZALA·
Germany

Dedication page of the Vaad's tribute Bible to President Harry S. Truman

Courtesy of Beth Medrash Govoha, Lakewood, NJ

Title page of the Vaad's tribute Bible dedicated to
President Harry S. Truman

Courtesy of Beth Medrash Govoha, Lakewood, NJ

Chapter 8

The Trials and Tribulations of Immigration: Stuttgart and Paris

One of the main functions of the Vaad was to facilitate the immigration of rabbis and yeshiva students under a special nonquota project recognized by the U.S. Department of State. This program enabled them to come to the United States under "4(d)" and "4(e)" regulations. To qualify under section 4(d), a rabbi had to have been practicing in the rabbinate for at least two consecutive years preceding admission to the U.S. and seeking entry to the U.S. to continue this vocation. Wives and unmarried children under 18 years of age could accompany or follow him if the Consul concluded that the rabbi could support them on the salary he was guaranteed in his contract. The contract had to be signed by the congregation employing the rabbi, with an attached notarized report verifying the congregation's ability to fulfill monetary requirements of the contract.

Legitimate students at least 15 years of age who wanted to study at an accredited academic or religious institution in the U. S. could be admitted under section 4(e). Since they were to be in the U.S. for a limited period, they had to prove that they had sufficient funds to sustain themselves. The students also had to prove that when their studies were completed, they would return to Europe or go to another country, but not remain in the U.S. Nonquota immigrants "were not subject to numerical limitations."[1]

In July 1946, Irving Bunim, Stephen Klein and Rabbi Joseph Baumel met with Dean Acheson, then-Under Secretary of State (1945-47), to obtain 4(d) visas for rabbis and yeshiva student refugees in Shanghai. After the meeting with Acheson, the State Department "borrowed help from the Consuls" to start processing 250 men, women and children.

In November 1946, Bunim announced that the Vaad had paid for part of their transportation to the U.S., and that they were still the Vaad's responsibility. Then 300 additional visas became available and Acheson promised that he would use the 4(d) visas for the rabbis and yeshiva students in Europe just as he had for the rabbis in Shanghai.[2]

After the meeting with Acheson, Bunim proclaimed he "became our best friend." The reason was clear: "Instructions went out to all the Consuls to process the rabbis and students. They have made concessions for us that are unknown and unheard of in the entire history of the U.S. They allow us entirely to certify that a man is a rabbi or student and they take our word for it without their own investigation. Furthermore, we investigate the synagogues, and if we say a synagogue is reliable and financially responsible, they ask no questions. They have given us a man here in New York, with instructions from Acheson, to proceed with this work. When he came to the Crown Heights Yeshiva (where Baumel was the principal) and saw all the work that was being done there, he put them down for three extra rabbis. When Torah Umesorah gave them a program and asked for 30 rabbis, he said they could use 50. They rushed down to us asking whether they should assume responsibility for 50 rabbis."[3]

Before this meeting it took a year and-a-half for rabbis to obtain a visa. It took between four to six months before they could see a Consul. Rabbis had to prove that they had *smicha* (rabbinic ordination), which then had to be approved by Washington. Then the synagogues offering them employment had to be investigated. But by working with the Vaad, the rabbis did not have to go through this process. When the cases went to Washington, they cabled the Consul who called the rabbis to come and pick up their visas. Dr. Isaac Lewin opened two consulates, one in Vienna and the other in Prague. His attempts to open consulates in Lodz and Warsaw, however, failed.[4]

When the Vaad completed its paperwork on a case, it was turned over to Acheson's representative in New York. Once he approved it, the Vaad received a letter from the State Department. If a student was married, his wife received a visa to allow her to accompany him to the U.S. When the State Department asked if they should send letters or cables to the consuls, the Vaad asked that cables be sent at Vaad expense to expedite the procedure. When the Vaad requested a visa for a woman teacher, the State Department wondered how a woman could be a rabbi. After the Vaad explained the importance of women teachers in Jewish education and in Jewish life, the State Department issued the permits.[5]

As of late October 1946, 148 visas were approved: 30 had been received, 200 were still pending in the Visa Division in Washington, bringing the total number to 378 cases. By early November, the number was closer to 500.[6]

All the visas Bunim mentioned were nonquota visas. "They do not take...any space reserved for another Jew. They come in over and above the quota."[7] The Vaad paid for the transportation because it feared that if it asked the JDC for financial assistance, "they might upset the whole works. In many instances, we can't tell the world," Bunim observed, and not just because of the JDC. There were always those who wanted to stop the Vaad. "We already have a letter from a congressman in Massachusetts who wants to know whom we are sponsoring," Bunim reported. "He is anti-immigration.

We gave him an answer! We told him we cannot get anybody out because of the Polish quota."[8]

Unfortunately while this procedure worked in the U.S., the American consuls in Europe continued to follow the frustrating and time-consuming procedures to discourage Baruch and others. Yet through the "4(d)" program, 40 rabbis immigrated to the U.S. by late 1947 and worked as pulpit rabbis and teachers around the country. Several hundred students were permitted to enter the U.S. for an extended period and continued their studies at *yeshivos* that provided for their welfare.[9]

When the Vaad reported that it had brought 1,100 families to the U.S. in 1947 through the nonquota program, in reality it had brought in between 3500-4500 Jews. In one case, a man from Hungary received a visa that covered himself, his wife and their 11 children. All these cases were outside the regular immigration quota. Without the Vaad's efforts, these people could not have entered the U.S., since they were from countries whose quotas had been exhausted for the next eight to ten years.

Stephen Klein noted that only Orthodox families were eligible to take advantage of the nonquota program. It was unfortunate, but there was no law that could be used to bring others to the U.S. at that time. Outside the restrictions on immigration, Klein was proud that the Vaad had assisted thousands who were not "yeshiva people and *b'nei Torah*." In particular, he mentioned the packages sent by the Vaad to Russia, where one package sustained a family, any Jewish family, observant or not, for a month.[10]

Baruch continued to receive many individual requests from Klein, Bunim and others, to help survivors immigrate to Palestine or the U.S. A typical request would state: "There are two children...from one of the finest families in Poland. They are in...[Bergen] Belsen. Perhaps you can arrange to have someone see them, and find out what their plans are...whether they want to go to Palestine or the United Sates. In that case transfer them to Paris, and from there, to one of our [Vaad] homes, and then perhaps we can arrange for them to come to the U.S. Perhaps you can suggest something else. Maybe they will fit in under the children program...."[11]

Baruch assisted in the immigration of a number of children to the U.S. He even facilitated the adoption of several of them.

The incessant delays frustrated survivors wanting to emigrate, and this took its toll on at least one member of the Vaad staff. Rivke, a woman in charge of the office in Frankfurt, had a warrant issued for her arrest after a bureaucrat at the American Embassy informed his superiors that she had offered him a bribe to expedite a visa application. Rivke went into hiding from the police and called Baruch in desperation.

Baruch went to the American consul and explained the psychological trauma facing the Jewish DPs who felt imprisoned in Germany. Rivke's foolish offer, he said, was not for her benefit; it was made to help tortured souls who needed to escape from the horror that was Germany. Baruch's pleas succeeded—the arrest was vacated and Rivke got off with a warning. The consul explained to both of them that everything had to be above board because American journalists were always interested in fomenting scandals.[12]

Corporate Affidavits

To preclude immigrants from becoming public charges, U.S. immigration policy stipulated that prospective immigrants needed affidavits from close relatives and/or American citizens who were financially secure, and would guarantee their support in the U.S. But those affidavits and letters did not always guarantee admittance. American consuls had the authority to accept or reject such assurances.

In 1938, Jewish organizations tried to organize a committee to provide financial assistance to immigrants, and discussed obtaining statements of support from welfare and other agencies. Nothing came of it. At the time, large and small refugee agencies around the country were asking the State Department to recognize their guarantees. These organizations realized the "friendship affidavits [would] be of very little value...unless they [were] backed by substantial evidence of the ability and intention of the affiant or of some strong group to carry out the obligation undertaken."[13]

In 1939, the National Refugee Service (NRS), the largest refugee assistance service in the U.S.—and the United Service for New Americans (USNA) that replaced it—was authorized to provide corporate affidavits for potential immigrants. "These affidavits committed the agency to assume full responsibility for a designated number of immigrants, otherwise eligible but unable to furnish acceptable affidavits from individuals, with the provision that the agency would not permit them to become public charges."[14]

In early February 1948, Klein informed Baruch that new arrangements were made with the State Department to allow the Vaad to bring rabbis to any American Jewish institution. He wrote: "Very strong interventions are going to the various Consuls that visas should be given these men which we designate. It will be necessary to move as many people as possible to Paris, because the Paris Consul is working very satisfactorily."[15]

Bunim credited this to a meeting he, Klein and Rabbi Kotler had with Undersecretary of State Robert Lovett, where they "received some new concessions from him about nonquota immigration."[16]

Klein began sending lists of individuals and copies of their contracts to Paris to prove that these Jews had no intention of staying in France. Klein also gave the names of DPs being blocked by the consul in Stuttgart to Herve J. L'Heureux, the State Department Visa Division Chief. L'Heureux promised to send a very strong letter to Stuttgart asking why these cases had not been expedited and why so many difficulties had been placed in their path.[17]

Several months later, Klein asked Baruch to alert the Vaad when individuals were issued their visas against the Vaad's corporate affidavit. That way they could alert relatives of their impending arrival and keep track of the immigrants for the Department of Justice. The Justice Department required an initial report on each person entering the country and biannual reports until there was proof of self-sufficiency.[18] These reports enabled the INS to determine whether further follow-up was necessary. Between October 30, 1948 and July 21, 1952 more than 400,000 immigrants came to the U.S. under the Displaced Persons Act. Sixteen percent of them were Jews. An INS report later concluded that without assistance from the Vaad and other relief agencies, this would not have been accomplished.[19]

But because the Vaad was so involved in this immigration process, Baruch and his overwhelmed small staff invariably had huge backlogs of paperwork that failed to get processed expeditiously. As a result, immigration officials began sending letters to the New York office to say it was neglecting its legal obligations.[20] Despite requests for help, none was forthcoming. The Vaad's interest was to get people out, not in the technicalities of accomplishing same.

In mid-July 1948, Klein, Tenzer and Bunim went to Washington to ask permission for 300 students to stay in the U.S under a provision of the Displaced Places Person Act of 1948. The law allowed 15,000 temporary visitors to apply for resident status. Under Communist rule, they explained, Orthodox Jews were oppressed because the Soviets opposed religious institutions and religious practice.[21]

Bunim observed that the Vaad was so successful with the nonquota visas program, that Catholic relief agencies were copying their approach, and sending people to Europe to sign up Catholic refugees as ministers and teachers. The Vaad also had Pinchas Schoen make regular trips to Canada to arrange contracts for immigrant rabbis and teachers who could then enter the country. Bunim believed the work could not be left to other Jewish relief agencies.[22]

As the Cold War began heating up and exigent political realities changed, in late 1948 the U.S. Department of Justice advised the Vaad that American Consular offices in Europe would no longer accept corporate affidavits.

Involvement of Vaad in Immigration

Some American Jews wanted to know why Klein and Bunim insisted that it was important for the Vaad to play a key role in immigration and why the JDC didn't assume that role.

Rabbi B. Orlansky, the former head of the yeshiva in Radin, and a refugee in Siberia, Poland and France, said that just as a person has a father and mother, so did the Orthodox Jewish community. The JDC was the father and the Vaad was the mother. Jews in Europe, including those who headed the relief agencies, did not ask these questions because the answer was obvious. They understood that a single agency could not respond to the needs of all the DPs and that the Vaad had experience in dealing with specific issues facing observant Jews.[24]

Rabbi Orlansky pointed to the success of the *Brichah*, the underground mass migration of Jews from Eastern Europe (between 1944 and 1948) to Palestine. About 250,000 Jews fled Eastern Europe through the *Brichah* or affiliated programs. It is estimated that 170,000 were from Poland, 35,000 from Romania and the rest mostly from Hungary and Czechoslovakia. Those Orthodox Jews who weren't willing to alter their traditional, distinctive appearance and dress, were not able to escape through the *Brichah* because they would endanger the mission.[25]

Another reason for this insistence became obvious during Rabbi Eliezer Silver's visit to Poland in July 1946. He was on a fact-finding mission for the Vaad, and came to offer financial support and inspiration to the *She'erith Hapleitah* and Jews in the Middle East (Holland, Belgium, France, Czechoslovakia, Poland, Germany, Austria, Switzerland, Italy, Egypt and Palestine). Somehow he convinced the Polish government to give him 10,000 visas for rabbis and yeshiva students unwilling to live under Communist rule.

At a meeting with Polish President Boleslaw Bierut on July 10th, Rabbi Silver said, "It is better for you [the Poles] to rid yourselves of these bothersome and stubborn Jews once and for all...Issue passports and exit permits to all Jews remaining in your land, and try to solve at the same time the problem of Polish citizens who were exiled in Siberia. My advice is that these exiles be returned to Poland on condition that they leave here as soon as possible. I promise you that the

Czechoslovakian government will open their border to the Polish Jews and allow them to pass through to Palestine."[26]

Those who were able to obtain the visas and leave Poland for Czechoslovakia discovered they could not stay in Prague very long because of rampant antisemitism. Rabbi Silver went to the Prague Hebrew Immigrant Society (HIAS) office to seek transportation to Paris for 400 Polish rabbis and yeshiva students and their families. The HIAS officials advised Rabbi Silver that before he asked HIAS for assistance, the refugees should contact relatives. If their relatives were not responsive, then HIAS would do what it could for them.

Rather than wait in Prague and risk physical harm, the religious Polish refugees managed to get to Paris, where they met with a representative of the Mizrachi who then went to the JDC. For "technical reasons," the JDC refused to help and the "entire matter was dropped." Rabbi Orlansky concluded that all of the 400 families who immigrated to the U.S. from the Yeshiva of Bailly, France came through efforts of the Vaad.[27]

Rabbi Michael Munk, the JDC representative who came from Berlin in mid-1948, noted that the JDC did provide the Orthodox community with prayer books, *tefillin*, matzoh and other religious items, but that it did not take care of the specific needs of *yeshivos*. The Vaad, on the other hand, provided tractates of *Gemoras* and other necessary basic and advanced texts. Wherever there were a few yeshiva students scattered around, the Vaad brought them together and started a yeshiva. The JDC could not be expected to do that.

Rabbi Munk was very concerned about the physical safety of the Jews remaining in Berlin, especially the 225 rabbis, yeshiva students and other Orthodox Jews who were "thought of last by other organizations." Based on the obstacles and delays he experienced trying to get out of Berlin as a Joint representative on an American passport, he understood the difficulties confronting the refugees. He believed the JDC did not want to bring Jews to Paris because of the added financial burden they would create. Rabbi Munk urged Vaad officials in New York to find a way to get the Polish refugees to Frankfurt or Munich. "He pleaded that this should not be left to other organizations...."[28]

Rabbi Eliezer Silver had serious reservations about allowing the JDC to assume responsibility for the immigration of Orthodox Jews. He did not trust the JDC to bring them to the U.S., because the JDC would have to support them. He believed the JDC did not care about *yeshivos* and did not "care particularly if there are some yeshiva people less or some rabbis less."[29]

Rav Aharon explained the essential differences between the Vaad and the JDC by explaining that, "*Yiddishkeit* and ministering to the religious needs is only one phase and a rather small one in a large and extensive program. It cannot be given the particular attention and service that it needs. The JDC will not initiate the establishment of *yeshivos*, kosher kitchens, *mikvehs* and other religious needs. It will only answer a specific request and only within the realms of their budget and other considerations. Not so with the Vaad Hatzala. The Vaad Hatzala was created to answer the specific religious needs of our people. Its record during the almost 10 years of its existence proves the fact. It built *yeshivos*, established kosher kitchens, Bais Yaacov Schools [for girls], and religious *kibbutzim* because this is an essential part of Jewish life. In fact, the Vaad believes that there can be no other Jewish life. The Vaad prevented *shmad* (conversion to another religion) in several countries by a monthly subsidy and by giving additional allotments so that the threat of assimilation could be removed...Whenever the Vaad curtailed its work, no one stepped in to take the job over."[30]

Paper Walls

Why were so many stumbling blocks erected to keep Jews out of the U.S.? Part of the problem was long-standing antagonism in the U.S. against providing refuge to the Jews of Europe. Three major factors in American life contributed to public resistance to immigration in the late 1930s and continued throughout the war: unemployment, nativistic nationalism and antisemitism. "Debate, generally centering on the first two elements, often carried overtones of the third." Separation was almost impossible. "For example, nativistic nationalism included a general dislike of aliens," that at times became overtly antisemitic. Many Americans "no more than a generation removed from being immigrants themselves, responded to several years of economic insecurity" by accepting the popular nativistic slogan, "America for the Americans."[31]

In May 1938, a poll about Jews was conducted in the States and when asked whether Jews had too much power in the U.S., 36 percent polled said yes. By 1945, 58 percent held this view. Another survey taken in February 1942 asked which "nationality, religious or racial groups" in the U.S. were a menace [threat] to Americans." Twenty-four percent of the respondents answered the Japanese, 18 percent identified the Germans and 15 percent chose the Jews. In June 1944, almost one year before the war ended, 24 percent of those surveyed identified the Jew as the greater threat; while 9 percent chose the Japanese and 6 percent identified the Germans.[32] A survey in *Fortune* magazine in November 1942 asked American high school students which groups of people—Swedes, Protestants, Catholics, Jews, Irish, Chinese and Negroes would be their last choice as a roommate. Seventy-eight percent responded Negro followed by Jew at 45 percent.[33]

A number of polls expressed widespread fear of foreigners, especially Communists. Since many Jews came from Eastern Europe, they were suspected of being Communists or having communist leanings. American soldiers in Europe felt the same way. In March 1948, a representative of the Jewish Agency for Palestine working in Germany complained that "Polish Jews were welcomed," by the American military, "while those fleeing from Communist-controlled countries are prejudged as [being] Soviet agents."[34]

In 1945, American soldiers were surveyed about allowing "persons from Europe to come to this country." Six percent were in favor of increased immigration of foreigners, while 38 percent wanted a reduction and 12 percent wanted to stop it altogether.

The hostility towards Jews was only partly inspired by bigotry. Much of it was generated by fear of mass immigration per se. Jews constituted the largest number of would-be immigrants throughout the prewar and war years, "so that the terms 'refugee' and 'Jewish refugee' may well have been almost synonymous to at least a substantial portion of the public...They were evidently not ready to risk possible sacrifice for persons they did not consider members of their own group. In the years that followed, more sympathy and desire to help were expressed toward refugees from Communist regimes than had ever been bestowed upon those who were seeking to escape the Nazi Holocaust."[35]

The lack of urgency in responding to the problems facing the DPs may have been the result of the "welter of confusion that characterized the months that followed the close of the Second World War. [T]he problem of displaced persons went virtually unnoticed in the United States."[36] Even "most congressmen knew little about the DPs, could not understand why they had not gone home after the war, and feared depression or scarcities if a large number of immigrants started coming to the United Sates. Many also shared their constituents' anti-immigrant and anti-Semitic feelings."[37] First Lady Eleanor Roosevelt revealed that "every representative in Congress with whom I talked has told me that the general feeling is that they wish to stop all immigration."[38]

American Jews were aware of this antipathy toward Jewish immigration to the U.S., but they also understood the unique problems facing the remnants of European Jewry. As a result of the contemporaneous reports from American Jewish chaplains, Jewish soldiers, newspaper correspondents, DPs and others, American Jewish leaders became alarmed by what they heard about the plight of the Jews of Europe.

In May 1945, Henry Morgenthau, Jr., Secretary of the Treasury, asked President Harry Truman to establish a cabinet-level committee to deal with the DPs because the Army was having difficulty handling them. After Truman rejected the proposal, Morgenthau approached the State Department to investigate the conditions in Europe. As a result, Earl G. Harrison, former U.S. Commissioner of Immigration and the

U.S. representative on the Intergovernmental Committee on Refugees was sent to Europe in early July 1945.[39]

For almost two months, Harrison visited 30 camps and displaced persons centers in Bavaria in the American Zone, Bergen-Belsen in the British Zone, and Jewish camps in Austria. Joseph J. Schwartz, Rabbi Abraham Klausner, and the other American Jews with extensive experience working with refugees, accompanied him. Harrison met survivors, military and UNNRA personnel. His preliminary report went to President Truman before August 3, 1945 and a final report was sent on August 24th. Harrison noted the unique problems facing the Jews, including their need to be reunited with their families, to receive separate status by being officially recognized by the American government and military, and their desire to leave Germany for Palestine immediately. In particular, he urged that the British allow 100,000 Jews to enter Palestine and that "reasonable numbers" of the Jewish DPs come to America "under existing American immigration laws." He was careful not to ask for any increase in the number of Jews permitted to immigrate to America.

But Jews could not resettle in Palestine because the British restricted the number allowed into the country. The British White Paper of May 17, 1939, allowed only 75,000 Jews to enter Palestine during the next five years and declared that all future immigration was dependent on the consent of the Arabs. Land purchased by Jews would be limited in over 90 percent of the area under the British mandate, and in 1949 an Arab-Palestinian State would be established.[40]

Truman sent a copy of Harrison's report to Clement R. Attlee, the newly elected Prime Minister of Great Britain. He urged the British to allow 100,000 survivors into Palestine. Attlee rejected the proposal and countered by demanding that an Anglo-American committee of inquiry investigate the problem of the Jewish DPs and suggest a solution. Truman agreed, and the committee was established in November 1945. The committee completed its report in April 1946, and unanimously recommended that Britain permit 100,000 Jews to immigrate to Palestine. Attlee refused to accept the report. All attempts by Truman to find a solution with the British failed. American Jews finally realized that something had to be done to resolve the DP problem.[41]

In 1946, the American Jewish Committee took a leading role in lobbying for liberalization of U.S. immigration laws. Until then, American Jews had been reluctant to attempt any change because the Zionists insisted on getting Jews to Palestine first. Non-Zionist Jews and non-Jewish organizations had hesitated "for fear of being denounced as anti-Semites and for fear of actual sabotage by the Zionists of any movement they might start."[42]

Why did the AJC finally try to liberalize American immigration law? In the fall of 1946, Judge Joseph M. Proskauer, the group's president, sensed that a few months before there had been a chance for the British to admit more Jews into Palestine, but then they changed their minds. Furthermore, "...the number of Jewish displaced persons in the [Western] occupation zones...has already grown to 200,000, and with continuing infiltration of refugees from Poland, is expected to reach a quarter of a million by the end of the year. In Hungary, Romania, and other Eastern European countries, there are additional hundreds of thousands of Jews on whom the pressure to emigrate is, and will probably continue, strong." Even if Palestine were opened at some point, other countries would still be needed to accommodate a "far larger number of European Jews than was anticipated." Proskauer saw no alternative but to approach the American government because "appeals to the nations of the world would have fallen on deaf ears, and it is now clear that unless the U.S. sets an example, no change in attitude can be expected."[43]

Irving M. Engel, chairman of the AJC's Immigration Committee, knew the DP issue had to be presented to Congress and the American people as a humanitarian effort affecting approximately one million DPs unable to return to their former homes. Engel and others emphasized that 80 percent of the DPs were Christians, and only 20 percent were Jews—a point generally not known in the U.S. A broad range of prominent individuals from the civic, religious, social welfare and business communities formed the Citizens Committee on Displaced

Persons (CCDP) in November 1946, to lobby for "the enactment of legislation which will permit the admission to the United States of its fair share of Europe's Displaced Persons." Its other goal was to show that the DP issue wasn't a solely Jewish one.[44]

The CCDP asked for the admission of 400,000 DPs. The word Jewish was never used in any of their campaigns. They sought the support of Catholic and Protestant church leaders, Congress and White House staff members. *The New York Times*, the *New York Herald-Tribune*, the *Washington D.C. Evening Star*, the *St. Louis Post-Dispatch* and the *Louisville Courier-Journal* were staunch supporters of the CCDP.[45] Among those who lent their names to the committee were Fiorello LaGuardia, director general of UNNRA; Eleanor Roosevelt; Edward R. Stettinus, the former Secretary of State; William Green of the American Federation of Labor, and Charles P. Taft, the brother of Robert A. Taft, senator from Ohio. Earl G. Harrison served as the chairman.[46]

Haber noted that by the time Congress enacted the Displaced Persons Act of June 1948, the Jewish DPs were convinced their "hope to migrate to the U.S. was illusionary, but it helped to crystallize the thinking of these Jews as to where they had to go." That place was the State of Israel, established in May 1948.[47]

The bill Congress finally passed, however, discriminated against Jews and limited the total number of all immigrants to 205,000. Nevertheless, the bill was helpful in several ways. Under the provisions of the Act, as of December 1950, 41,218 Jews were admitted to the U. S., which was 20.4 percent of the Jewish DP population in Austria and Germany.[48]

Altogether 100,000 Jews were allowed into the U.S. under the Truman Directive of December 22, 1945 (permitting voluntary agencies to provide for corporate affidavits), the DP Act of 1948 and the amended DP Act of June 1950, which increased the number of people permitted to enter the country by about 100,000.[49]

The DP Act was viewed by some "as a landmark in the history of American immigration. The bill broke precedent with existing legislation by mortgaging future quotas, and laid the groundwork for granting asylum to escapees from repressive governments. It was the principle of helping the politically dispossessed that allowed the U.S. to assist the Hungarian, Cuban, and Vietnamese refugees in the 1950s, '60s and '70s. It also provided, for the first time, a specific agency, the Displaced Persons Commission, to facilitate immigrants' entry into the United States."[50]

As Jews immigrated to Israel, the attitude toward them by the American military authorities "softened." Instead of criticizing them as they had in the past, the military took "an intense interest" in helping them leave Europe. When the IRO indicated that it would not help them leave for Israel, the Army stepped in and provided logistical support.

By the end of 1948, Haber reported that the number of DPs in all zones of Germany and Austria was 93,100. There were approximately 75,000 Jewish DPs in the U.S. Zone in Germany, another 9,700 in the U.S. Zone in Austria; about 6,500 in the British Zones in Germany and Austria; and about 1,600 in the French Zones of Germany and Austria. This did not include an additional 25,400 Jews living in Jewish communities in Germany and Austria. There were 10,500 in Vienna; 7,900 in Berlin; 3,000 in the American Zone; 3,500 in the British Zone and the remainder in Austria. A considerable number of them were DPs from Eastern European countries accepted as members of their new communities. In Vienna, for example, an estimated 2,000 of the 10,500 Jews were not Austrian.[51]

Implementing the DP Act of 1948 did not proceed smoothly or quickly for several reasons. The U.S. Displaced Persons Commission (DPC), responsible for processing the DPs in Europe and resettling them in America, began functioning only in August 1948. It took several months to organize offices in Washington and Europe and to "overcome the legalistic and functional rivalries." UNNRA and IRO personnel were hired to work in Europe because of their familiarity with the DPs.

Eligibility requirements were also an impediment. Forty percent of the visas had to be allocated to people from annexed territories and 30 percent to agricultural workers. Prospective immigrants also had to have been in the American Zones of Germany and Austria on or before December 22, 1945. This excluded most Jews who had fled from Poland and other Eastern European countries after outbreaks of antisemitism in 1946.

Finding qualified DPs in these categories took time and slowed the immigration process considerably. Only 19 percent were found from the annexed territories and 20 percent qualified as farmers. Proving an individual was in the American Zone of Occupation prior to December 22, 1945 was also difficult. Many people were unable or unwilling to provide the necessary documentation. Issuing visas was such a slow and tedious process, that DPC personnel feared they would not send 200,000 immigrants to the U.S. over the next two years and meet their stated goal. To ensure that the quotas would be filled, the commissioners pressured their staffs to interpret the law as liberally as possible. When that did not yield desired results, they instructed staff "to pass everything no matter how."[52]

In addition, American consular officials were unwilling to use the voluntary relief agencies with substantial experience in previous emigration programs. Haber claimed that these officials remembered that, "when the number of visas were scarce, the zealousness of our organizations, working with immigration, often got the best of them and some showed no reluctance in sponsoring people whose eligibility for migration was questionable." He singled out the Vaad Hatzala for having an "elastic conscience" for sponsoring rabbinical students and rabbis "who were neither." He said it "was a matter of common knowledge among American Consuls and when Mr. Ugo Carusi [Chairman of the DPC and a former commissioner of Immigration and Naturalization] was here [Germany] in 1947, he got an earful on this subject."[53]

Haber was disappointed that the voluntary agencies were prevented from helping to provide documentation for prospective immigrants. The American immigration commission relied solely on the IRO resettlement workers who were told not to work with them. The Jewish organizations were charged with having conspired with the DPs to file false documents with the American consulates in the American Zone "or at least not to have made any effort to distinguish the false from the true."

According to Haber, the Army allegedly told Mr. Carusi, "It would be a serious error to utilize the Jewish organizations in connection with any documentation for U.S. immigration." Haber urged the organizations involved in immigration to approach the DPC to correct this misconception. The National Catholic Welfare Council and the Jewish agencies lodged their own strong objections to these allegations.[54]

The situation was resolved when the DPC "welcomed the cooperation of the voluntary agencies,"[55] because the agencies did most of the work resettling the DPs. The DPC's responsibility was "to coordinate, expedite, streamline and give general guidance to the whole cooperative effort"—a time consuming and complicated process of its own.[56]

Stuttgart

In October 1947, Stephen Klein met Samuel Schmidt in New York to discuss sending someone to Germany to take responsibility for immigration work. Klein was convinced Baruch was "not interested" in this area "and that many hundreds of people" could "be brought out of Germany if the proper person" were in charge. Baruch sent Schmidt a separate report describing his work with the nonquota visa program,[57] but apparently Vaad leadership ignored him.

At that time, the American consulates in Munich and Frankfurt were overwhelmed with people trying to obtain visas. Vaad requests were so backlogged, it decided to use the consulate in Stuttgart, located in a villa on a hill on the outskirts of the city. Since there were no connecting flights to Stuttgart, and the Autobahn was under construction because of the damage caused by American bombers, the relative inaccessibility of the city and the villa probably contributed to its reduced traffic.

To expedite the work in Stuttgart, Isabel Jacobs, a young

Jewess from England, was hired to run the office. She processed the paper work and had to secure the documents to prove that applicants had contracts with *yeshivos*, synagogues, or institutions guaranteeing employment in America. But getting these documents was a difficult undertaking. Immigration guidelines required an exhaustive family history, often entailing an investigation by indigenous German personnel. Each application had to be accompanied by a fee (about $10.00), a birth certificate, ordination papers, or papers reflecting the applicant's student status.[58]

To further complicate matters, the consuls in Stuttgart were exceptionally difficult. Dell Topasky and Reed Robinson utilized every regulation and tactic possible to delay and reject applications. They were adherents of Breckinridge Long's antisemitic policies, and worked to make Baruch and his colleagues' miserable. When problems developed during an interview, Jacobs would invariably have to contact Baruch and tell him to come to Stuttgart.

Applicants were summoned to appear before the consuls for interrogation via an interpreter. Though these applicants had all the proper documents, Topasky and Robinson insisted on testing them on their knowledge of the Bible. Baruch asked the consuls to use one of the rabbis from a DP camp and a Jewish military chaplain to question an applicant and verify his religious knowledge, but they refused.

A typical Robinson response to a visa application for a Vaad applicant read: "Visas have been refused and the applications have been canceled because it did not appear that Rabbi...is a nonquota immigrant...The claimant had placed on file an offer of employment extended to him by Torah Umesorah under the terms of which he was to be employed as a rabbi and a religious teacher." An investigation [has] revealed that, "Torah Umesorah is not in itself an institution of learning or a religious congregation ...within the meaning of the immigration statute." Furthermore, the offer of employment extended to the rabbi expected him to act as "both a minister of religion and an instructor...The Rabbi's acceptance of such an agreement would seemingly prevent him from entering the U.S. solely for the purpose of carrying on the vocation of a minister of religion or solely for the purpose of carrying on the vocation of a professor."[59]

The two consuls loved to embarrass the Vaad, and deny their applications. When Rabbi Meyer Gruenwald, assistant head of Agudas Harabonim and a rabbi in Czechoslovakia before the war, filled out an application when he arrived in the American Zone, he unwittingly gave an erroneous home address in Munich. Though he was Rabbi Snieg's deputy, the consuls hired Germans to do a background check, and they found the building at the address he gave them was totally obliterated during the war.

They asked Baruch why the leaders of the Jewish people were such liars. He told them that in wartime, American officers and the OSS forged passports and documents and did everything they could to save lives. Given all that the Jewish survivors had experienced, they would do almost anything to leave Germany. The consuls disqualified Rabbi Gruenwald, despite his reputation. To circumvent them, Baruch applied to the Canadian consulate to get the rabbi a visa to Canada.

When the Spinker Rebbe presented his papers to the consulate, he was rejected on medical grounds when they determined he had tuberculosis. The rabbi was subsequently examined by a German professor who found no trace of the disease. With a set of x-rays and the medical report, Baruch presented the information to the consul who exclaimed, "And now you're a doctor, too?" Nevertheless, they finally granted the rabbi and his family a visa.[60]

Topasky once asked Baruch if he liked the idea of allowing Nazis into the U.S. to help counterbalance the threat of communism, by which he meant the influx of Jews into America. They also asked Baruch why he worked so diligently to get Jewish scholars and students to America, instead of sending them to Palestine to be leaders. They always wanted answers, and Baruch told them, again and again, that the DPs wanted to go to America where there was an established Jewish community. Once the State of Israel was formally declared, they would move and establish communities there.

Rabbi Elya Meir Bloch of the Telshe Yeshiva in Cleveland, Ohio, asked Baruch's help with a relative and her affianced. When Robinson saw that her fiancé had been offered a faculty position at Cleveland's Telshe Yeshiva, he asked him who had suffered the most in Jewish history. When he said "Moses," the consul disagreed with him, and Baruch had to break the impasse by coming to Stuttgart.

Robinson told Baruch that Job suffered the most, so the application was denied. Baruch explained how Moses came from a royal house and when he saw the suffering of the Hebrews he was so distressed he tried to help them. Subsequently, Moses suffered with each individual from the time of the Exodus from Egypt through the 40 years wandering in the desert, and therefore the rabbi was not wrong when he replied "Moses." Robinson retorted, "If Nat Baruch suffered the most, you would find some *Midrash* for that."[61] The couple eventually received their visas.

Though the procrastination and application denials came from the American consuls in Germany, the Vaad leadership nevertheless blamed Baruch for the constant delays. In a letter signed by Rabbi Kotler, Rabbi Reuven Grozovsky and Rabbi Menachem Mendel Zaks, they expressed their thanks for his dedicated work and reiterated the Vaad's mission to facilitate the transfer of rabbis and yeshiva students from Germany to France so they could immigrate to the U.S. Since the Vaad prepared the immigration documents, they assumed that getting people out of Germany would not be a problem, especially since the JDC provided transportation fees. But months and months passed and nothing was happening. The *b'nei Torah* had to flee from Germany, like one has to flee from a lion or other vicious animals. They blamed Baruch because the Vaad constantly received pleas for help and complaints. Rumors in the U.S. accused Baruch of thwarting immigration and that the JDC was not cooperating either. It was considered Baruch's fault that the Vaad's integrity was being attacked by its enemies who had succeeded in questioning its *raison d'etre*. They urged him to get the job done.[62]

Given Baruch's dedication and devotion, this missive hurt him deeply. The letter was written by people he admired and they were accusing him of malfeasance. He knew that before they would have put something like this in writing there would have been a formal meeting to discuss the issue. The letter made him realize that his efforts were being attacked and his reputation tarnished. Though greatly disheartened, Baruch reintensified his efforts.

One of his first responses was to have Isabel Jacobs arrange for him to meet with Dana Hutchins, the senior consul in the American Zone. After exchanging pleasantries with Hutchins at his office in Stuttgart, Dell Topasky and Reed Robinson joined them. One sat on each side of him, to Baruch's great discomfort.

Baruch blurted out that he came to "present charges that the consuls in Stuttgart are antisemites." Hutchins said, "Rabbi, it grieves me to hear that." Baruch responded that it pained him to have to make such a charge, but he had proof that they were obstructing and delaying the immigration process. When he finished his presentation, Hutchins assured him that if he had any complaints, he would personally review each and every case.

Before the Fourth of July, a jeep pulled up to Baruch's office in Munich and two MP's presented him with an invitation from Hutchins to a Fourth of July celebration in Stuttgart. Baruch had some reservations about going, but cocktail parties were a very important part of the social scene, and after his meeting with Hutchins he thought he had no choice but to accept. Baruch had never attended a party before, but Rabbi Snieg insisted that he go.

When he arrived in Stuttgart, Hutchins was standing in the receiving line and warmly greeted Baruch with both hands. "Rabbi," he said, "I am so happy you were able to come. We are all good Americans." A week later, Baruch received a copy of *Stars and Stripes* (the military newspaper) announcing that Consul Dana Hutchins had died of a stroke. Though Baruch had made an impression on the consul, nothing changed. He was gone and Baruch was back to square one with the problem of getting people into France.[63]

Paris

Samuel Schmidt ran the Vaad office in Paris. Affectionately known as Reb Shmuel, Baruch found him an experienced, professional social worker, a wonderful human being, a gentleman, well spoken, and dignified—a real father figure. But Baruch was disturbed that Schmidt did not have the fire of a fighter for the cause. Schmidt felt anything could be accomplished through negotiation. This did not work well given the Vaad's circumstances: One couldn't negotiate for months when there was one crisis after another.[64]

Schmidt was designated as the Vaad's first European director. Though he stayed in Paris intermittently—a few weeks or a few months at a time—he eventually had to return to America to tend to his business and family matters. Consequently, Baruch became responsible for the operation of the Paris office. Just before Schmidt left, Baruch was informed of his new responsibilities by the New York office. He explained that he could not run an operation in Paris given all his commitments in Munich and Frankfurt, but it was to no avail. Months later, Schmidt was induced to return to Paris, but, in the meantime, Baruch carried the burden.

The JDC

In 1946, the Vaad had difficulty getting people to France because of the JDC. Rabbi Philip Bernstein, the Advisor of Jewish Affairs, had a "clear understanding" with the JDC in Paris that 10,000 Jews with visas would go as quickly as possible to Paris to ease the pressure of thousands of Jews fleeing to the American Zone. It would also be viewed as a sign of good faith to the American Army. However, Bernstein soon discovered that the Jews had not been sent to Paris, and instead the JDC sent a group of more than a 1,000 people from Agudath Israel, who had permits to France, to the American Zone of Germany. The JDC did this, he believed, "in order to spare...expenses and care." Bernstein appreciated the JDC's difficulties, but maintained that, "this must be measured against the infinitely greater difficulties which JDC and Jewry would face if, as a result of non-cooperation, the [German] borders should be closed."[65]

The French authorities were also willing to consider a plan to settle 5,000 or more Polish refugees in camps in the French Zone. Because the JDC would not make a definite commitment to provide food for them, a "workable formula" never materialized. The French were interested in receiving dollar credits and might have provided the food themselves, but the JDC did not initiate any agreement. Bernstein knew the French were interested from Nahum Goldmann, cofounder of the World Jewish Congress, who was involved in negotiating German reparations for Holocaust survivors. Goldmann had spoken with Georges Bidault, president of the provisional government of France and later premier, who expressed sympathy for the DPs, but did not know how to feed them.[66]

Bernstein felt that since the attitude of the U.S. Army was "crucial to the welfare of the Jews in Central Europe," the JDC should cultivate a good relationship with the military. Instead, "those officers in USFET Headquarters who are closest to the DP problem do not have a particularly high regard for [the] JDC." He wrote: When the Army was told that accepting Jews from Poland was a "matter of life and death the constant refrain was, 'Where is the JDC? What is the JDC doing?' In these matters JDC is Jewry and, when all that JDC offers is not commitments, but excuses and rationalizations and a sanctimonious reaffirmation of established precedents, there is the inevitable tendency for the Army authorities to feel that the Jews are simply dumping the problem on the Army...It should be clear to New York JDC that, merely as strategy alone, it is necessary to undertake a vigorous and well-publicized program of cooperation with the Army in meeting this vast, difficult unprecedented problem of Polish evacuation."[67]

Vaad Office in Paris

France had a relatively open-door policy, the most liberal policy in the world for refugees. Anyone could come to France, go to a local prefect of police and declare his intent to be a temporary resident, thereby making it easier to immigrate to the U.S. On a typical day, 400 people would pass through the Vaad office at 7 Rue de la Paix in Vincennes, a suburb of Paris where Vaad staff would explain immigration procedures in 10 different languages.[68]

The Vaad had been fortunate to secure the services of Eleanor Bohne-Hene as its Liaison Officer in Paris. Because of her extensive contacts in the French Foreign Office, she was able to arrange for visas from Germany to France. Once Jews entered France, the Vaad helped them get visas to the U.S. and elsewhere.

Now in charge of the Vaad's Paris office, Baruch had to do whatever he could to keep the operation running—which was not helped by the constant requests originating from Vaad headquarters in New York.

In addition to the extensive paperwork required to prepare each immigrant, sleeping quarters had to be found, kosher food procured and children placed in Jewish schools. Although the Paris office obtained visas for rabbis and yeshiva students, staff member Maurice Ungar noted there was "hardly a human problem" that did not become the responsibility of the office. Children who became sick, pregnant women with special needs, people who required a dentist, all had to be attended to while their documents were being processed.

It generally took three months to process a rabbi to immigrate and six weeks for a student. Proper documents had to be obtained, and the refugees had to be taken to the appropriate consuls, to doctors, to the French police for fingerprinting and myriad places to file dozens of different papers.[69]

But problems invariably developed. As Pincus Schoen noted on April 21, 1947: "Recently we've had several discouraging experiences with…those arriving on non-quota visas. A few…have been called to Ellis Island for examination and…it became apparent that they have not oriented themselves with their own cases and don't know how or why they are coming in.

"To avoid aggravation and...prevent the collapse of our entire 4(d) and 4(e) program I would suggest that you or someone else go to Paris...to issue a circular preferably in Yiddish advising them of their exact status and under what provision of law they are [going] to the U.S. It would be even better if you could set aside a day or two to spend at the Yeshiva[s] center in Paris and interview each [person who has a visa] prior to their sailing. It will save them and us much trouble. We have a case under appeal now simply because the person...did not know that he came here under 4(d)."[70]

In early February 1948, he was notified that since France was more hospitable to the DPs than Germany, he should quickly arrange to move the yeshivos in Germany to France. As a result, one of the first to leave was the yeshiva in Windsheim.

From his first day, requests to Baruch made it impossible for him to stay within the parameters set by UNRRA. In one case, Rabbi Kotler and other *roshei yeshivos* asked Baruch to assist Rabbi Wolf Bejlis, a *rosh yeshiva* from the Makover Yeshiva in Poland, who lived in Wiesbaden. His documents as a professor of Talmud had been sent to Frankfurt months ago, but the consulate never responded. The rabbi had provisional approval from the U.S. Department of State, but could not leave Germany. If he could not secure a visa in Germany, the Vaad in New York would arrange for his documents to be presented to the American consul in Paris. Rabbi Kotler also asked Baruch to provide the *yeshivos* in Windsheim and Zeilsheim with "a goodly portion" of each month's subsidies since he took great interest in the welfare of these institutions.[71]

Similarly, Rabbi Shumel Pardes, the editor of *Hapardes*, asked Baruch in November 1947, to submit papers to the American consul in Stuttgart for a young man described in his application as a professor. Since he was clearly too young to be a professor, Baruch suggested that the papers be changed to read instructor. Unfortunately, they had been submitted to Washington. When he heard a new consul might come to Stuttgart, Rabbi Pardes asked Baruch to try again.

Rabbi Pardes and Baruch continued to correspond about other individual requests throughout his stay in Germany.[72]

Chaplain Irving Ganz, an American rabbi serving as Assistant Constabulary Chaplain, asked Baruch to intervene for a friend registered for a visa to the U.S. The process had taken so long that he had passed the eligible age limit, so another way had to be found to get him to France.[73] Less than a year later, Rabbi Ganz asked Baruch to help a rabbi with papers from the Vaad confirming his employment in New York. Rabbi Ganz had been working with this rabbi for some time, but needed help.[74]

Alexander Guttman, a professor of Talmud and Rabbinics at The Hebrew Union College in Cincinnati, contacted Samuel Schmidt to help bring his brother to the U.S., since he had been offered a position as a rabbi in St. Johnsbury, Vermont. The rabbi and his family had a military clearance, but the visas were being held up until the Vaad could prove that he had served as a rabbi in the DP camp from July 1946 to July 1948.[75]

Stephen Klein provided Baruch with a steady stream of requests and people, but rather than wait for an answer by mail, he would sometimes phone Baruch or send a telegram to find out about particular cases. In some situations he would say, "Whatever expense you may have in obtaining this [affidavit] is to be charged to me" or "spare no costs for this case." He had a sense of urgency in his requests because he was under pressure from relatives in the U.S. for quick results.

Another reason for resolving individual cases quickly was that while the Vaad had "no objection to sending as many people...as possible" to the U.S. through corporate affidavits, it was expensive. The Vaad requested the names of American relatives of Jews who immigrated to the U.S. to solicit them to recover some of the costs.[76]

Since there were many cases of DPs registered in New York and Germany still being processed, Klein and his committee asked, "that the emigration office...concentrate on...cases which have already been registered" with the New York office, "and which have been pending, in some instances, for two years before they accept others." Some might interpret this request "unsympathetic," but he assured Baruch that if he knew "what headaches were involved in trying to soothe impatient relatives, I would forgive him for some slight impatience."[77]

Most requests for assistance were sent by mail, but Baruch received a fair number of telegrams from people who expected him to drop other urgent appeals to attend to their crisis. The most unusual request came from Rebbetzin Rose Soloveitchik of Spring Valley, New York who came to Munich to ensure that her nephew, Judah Eidelman, received a visa to immigrate to the U.S. Frustrated with the American consuls procrastination, she persuaded Baruch to help her. As a result, her nephew arrived in the U.S. on February 18, 1947.[78]

Sometimes immigration issues could be resolved quickly, while others took much longer. But failure to appreciate the complexity of the problems caused significant tensions on both sides of the Atlantic. Rabbi Pinchas Teitz of Elizabeth, New Jersey, a member of the Executive Board of the Vaad— and through whose efforts the Vaad received "a substantial amount of money"—once requested help for a young man in Germany. The Vaad offices in Paris and Frankfurt arranged a French visa for him and even sent a cable to the boy's father in Elizabeth informing him that the visa had been secured. When the boy did not receive his visa as quickly as had been reported, he cabled his father that a visa had not been issued to him. The father informed Rabbi Teitz who called the Vaad office in New York. Baruch, of course, was blamed.

"Now, when such a situation develops," Schoen informed Baruch "it creates a deep mistrust of the Vaad Hatzala and definitely undermines our work...You understand the difficult situation which we face here in trying to uphold the prestige of the Vaad and secure the funds which will enable you in Germany and the other leaders in other countries in Europe to carry on."[79]

Fortunately, the Vaad's relations with Rabbi Teitz did not suffer. He continued to help the Vaad and to send requests to Baruch to help his people get out of Germany.[80]

Chapter 9

The Central Orthodox Committee (COC)

The constant divisiveness over providing relief to the survivors led the Mizrachi and Agudas Harabonim to explore an alternative approach. On February 12, 1947, the JDC, the Agudas Harabonim, Mizrachi and the CRC, officially the Central Relief Committee for the Relief of Jews Suffering Through the War, met to discuss a JDC proposal to establish "a central body or committee representative of all shades in American Orthodoxy." The group would "assume responsibility for the stimulation of orthodox life and institutions in the European countries."[1]

The JDC claimed it could not "assume responsibility for stimulating any one phase of Jewish life. It had always relied on local community agencies and local leadership to meet these responsibilities."[2] Given that most of the Orthodox leadership in these countries was no longer alive, the responsibility had to be assumed "by [the American] Agudas

Harabonim, or some other central body which represents the orthodox point of view."[3]

Representatives of the CRC were in attendance because as Rabbi Joseph H. Lookstein pointed out, following the First World War, the CRC was established in the U. S. to represent Orthodox Jewish interests. They and other Jewish organizations formed the JDC.[4]

Rabbi Lookstein, the rabbi of Congregation Kehilath Jeshurun in New York and an active leader in the Mizrachi movement, was upset that a number of organizations claiming a "special interest" in providing for the Orthodox community had caused confusion at home and abroad. He wanted an authoritative body recognized by the Orthodox community and the JDC to stimulate Orthodox Jewish life in Europe and provide access to the JDC's financial resources. JDC expenditures, he believed, far exceeded funds donated by the Vaad Hatzala, Agudath Israel, Mizrachi, Zeirei Agudas Israel and other Orthodox institutions.[5]

Rabbi Reuben Levovitz, representing Agudas Harabonim, also favored a central body, and wanted to reach an understanding with the JDC. Allocating a specific amount for the new organization would end multiple appeals, but he questioned whether the new agency could raise enough funds to cover its overhead.[6] The JDC could not cover administrative costs or guarantee a specific budget because that was against its policy and practice. It could, however, provide facilities and assistance for a new organization once in Europe, but all start-up organizational costs had to come from other sources.[7]

At the same time, *Hapardes* reported complaints against the JDC for not appropriating sufficient resources for the Lubavitcher Hasidim at Pocking. Funds were channeled through a central committee of irreligious Jews who did not care about *yeshivos*, *mikvehs* or their other religious needs.[8]

On April 22, 1947, the Union of Orthodox Rabbis and the CRC unanimously agreed to recognize the CRC "as an independent constituent body of the JDC vested with authority...to deal with matters of relief work pertaining to the stimulation and maintenance of Orthodox life and institutions in the various European countries."[9] A letter to this effect was sent to Moses A. Leavitt, Executive Vice-Chairman of the JDC and signed by Rabbis Eliezer Silver and Israel Rosenberg on April 23, 1947.[10]

The JDC emphasized that the agency, to be called the Jewish Central Orthodox Committee (COC), would be responsible for Orthodox Jews alone, as the World Union for Progressive Judaism represented the Reform and Liberal Jews, and the United Synagogue represented the Council of America for Conservative Jews. JDC leadership, however, was concerned about the Vaad's relationship with the Union of Orthodox Rabbis. They had learned from the Yiddish press that the Vaad was to be reorganized under the auspices of the Union, and would concentrate only on assisting *yeshivos* and the *b'nei Torah* to immigrate to the U.S.[11]

Since all *yeshivos* received some assistance from the JDC, the Vaad believed the real purpose of the agreement was to stop it from raising funds. Vaad leadership repudiated the accord with regard to the *yeshivos*, refused to be bound by it, and claimed it had never been implemented.[12]

Through its sponsorship of the Vaad, the Union was associating with a competing organization, which the JDC claimed, violated the agreement. In a telegram to Rabbis Silver and Rosenberg, the JDC recognized their "duty and obligation...in aiding" *yeshivos*, and had no objection to the Vaad's activities on behalf of *yeshivos* not supported by the JDC.[13]

The JDC also objected to the Vaad providing "emigration aid." It felt "strongly that within the spirit of the proposal [the Union] as well as their active leaders, should disassociate themselves from efforts which compete with the JDC, whether directly or through separate organizations, such as Rescue Children, Inc., set up by the Vaad Hatzala."[14]

On June 9, 1947, the JDC and members of the Vaad met to air their concerns. Rabbi Silver reiterated that the Agudas Harabonim had accepted the JDC proposal and would not support any competing campaign. The Vaad would continue to assist yeshiva students and rabbis because it was in a "better position to secure visas and emigration opportunities" for them. The JDC would continue arranging and paying for their transportation. Should the Vaad try to expand its activities beyond these areas, the Agudas Harabonim would speak out publicly against the Vaad so that the entire community would know of its opposition. Rabbi Levovitz did not criticize the Vaad's fundraising for *yeshivos* because if the agreement between the JDC and the Agudas Harabonim succeeded, the Vaad would "eventually go out of existence."[15]

Rescue Children, Inc.

By the end of the war, the Vaad had rescued more than 2,000 Jewish orphans and placed them in homes throughout Europe. Centers were established in France, Belgium, Sweden and Germany. Nine were in France.[16] The JDC worked closely with Rescue Children in registering the children with the Chief Rabbi's Council in France and in arranging for many of them to be sent to children's homes in Palestine. The JDC, in turn, viewed this as a "duplication" of its activities[17] and objected to the separate fundraising campaigns. When Rescue Children solicited funds from United Jewish Appeal (UJA) supporters, the umbrella organization through which the JDC received its money, this became "a source of continued confusion and irritation to local communities," Louis H. Sobel, assistant secretary of the JDC, complained.[18] Rabbi Lookstein wanted these campaigns to stop to "clear up a good deal of confusion" and increase "giving to the UJA."[19]

Before making a final decision, Herbert Tenzer went to Europe to see whether the program should be terminated. To continue, it would have to be administered from the U. S., with the Paris committee serving only in an honorary capacity. Rabbi Kotler would appoint a board to oversee the education issues. Until a decision could be reached, Mr. Bloch, the administrator, was instructed not to close any of the homes or turn over any of the children to the JDC. In the meantime, Stephen Klein sent $10,000 to fix up the home at Hannoville and one other that was just being established.[20]

In early 1948, Rescue Children, Inc. was taken over by the JDC. In March, Rabbi William Z. Novick, the director of Rescue Children, went to Europe to arrange for the four remaining children's homes to be absorbed by the JDC. Abraham Horowitz, executive director of the COC in New York, reflecting the animus of the COC toward the Vaad, bragged to Samuel Sar that the COC and he had "personally been instrumental in the negotiations" resulting in JDC control of Rescue Children, including the first ten homes established by the Vaad, two institutions in France and two more in Belgium.[21]

The COC'S Function

The Union of Orthodox Rabbis was authorized to establish the COC at its national conference held May 11-13, 1947. They and the JDC ratified the accord on July 29, 1947. Ostensibly, the COC was to "eliminate the confusion...of competitive appeals for support of... religious activities in Europe," and the JDC would have "the benefit of recognized Orthodox opinion in the conduct of its work...to the support of religious activities in the European countries...."[22]

The COC was an autonomous organization that invited leading Orthodox rabbis and laymen to serve as officers, directors and members of committees. It had authority to hire staff, but "consideration" had to be "given" to selecting individuals who would "work in harmony with...the JDC." The COC had to consult with the JDC, but the JDC did not have veto power over its hiring decisions.[23]

The COC's regional representatives were stationed in different places in Europe, with COC headquarters at the JDC's Paris headquarters. Representatives of the COC conducted a five-month fact-finding mission of Jewish communities in Europe to "stimulate, coordinate, and strengthen" Orthodox programs and institutions. They left in August 1947 and returned in December. The COC also "advised, recommended and negotiated" with the JDC about Orthodox religious and financial needs. The COC was the sole body that Orthodox rehabilitation problems were referred to after consulting with local Orthodox groups and JDC representatives.[24]

All financial aid recommended by the COC came from the general budget of the JDC for each country.

Administrative expenses were the responsibility of the COC, which would "have no functional responsibilities and that it[s] expenditures" would be "limited to its overhead requirements." The JDC agreed to advance the COC the net sum not exceeding $60,000 for overhead and expenses for the first year, and expected that within a reasonable time, the COC would fund its own operations and reimburse the JDC for the start up loan. To avoid fundraising conflicts, appeals made for the COC were cleared with the JDC, as well as with the local Jewish Welfare Funds.[25]

The Union agreed to disassociate itself from groups raising funds for Orthodox institutions involved in activities within the "purview" of the JDC/COC. It also agreed to discourage such appeals from other groups.[26] The Union further agreed that the Vaad would be limited "solely in assisting yeshivas abroad which received no subsidies from the...JDC, and to securing emigration opportunities for rabbis, yeshiva students and Torah scholars in Europe. Under no circumstances would "the Union of Orthodox Rabbis represent that the Vaad Hatzala campaign has the endorsement or approval of the Joint Distribution Committee."[27] Finally, the Union would inform the Orthodox communities about the agreement and urge their complete support for the JDC and the United Jewish Appeal.

Edward M. M. Warburg, chairman of the JDC, and Moses A. Leavitt, executive vice-chairman, signed for the JDC and Rabbis Eliezer Silver, Israel Rosenberg and Bernard Louis Levinthal, members of the presidium of the Union of Rabbis, signed for the Union on July 29, 1947.[28]

Baruch's Response

As the Vaad began to disintegrate, Baruch wondered why its leaders failed to see what was happening to the Orthodox community because of their organizational disunity. Despite the concentrated efforts of the left and secular or nonsectarian Jewish groups to thwart his work in Germany, he fervently believed the true Jewish soul yearned for the ancient teachings and aspired toward a religious life. Baruch waged his own war against these forces with one goal in mind: to bring about the spiritual reawakening of Jews and to reintroduce them to Jewish sacred texts and Torah way of life.[29] With this new arrangement, the heart could remain intact—the Vaad would take care of the *yeshivos* and the *b'nei Torah*—but a heart without a complete body in which to function was also worthless.

Baruch did not want be held accountable to the American Jewish community when it judged the actions of those who deserted the Vaad. On that day of reckoning when "the thousands, both young and old, who wished to be spiritually rehabilitated and were never afforded that opportunity" pointed their accusatory finger, the leaders of the Orthodox community would be held responsible for their lack of dedication.[30]

By late June and early July 1947, Baruch thought of asking Stephen Klein to find a replacement for him. Nevertheless, after his last conversation with Klein—who sounded very discouraged and disillusioned—Baruch decided to stay. He knew that if he left, he would be deserting the very people who needed him most. He did wonder, however, how he would bear up under the tremendous strain and pressure he faced daily, and whether or not the rabbis were going to fulfill the pledge to the Six Million martyrs by helping the surviving Jews return to a Torah way of life.[31]

Baruch received his answer on July 29, 1947, when the COC was formed.[32] Stephen Klein sent him a copy of the agreement and suggested that he obtain funds from them. He warned Baruch not to mention his name or Irving Bunim's in any discussions with the COC, since members of the committee "see 'red' when they hear the sound of it."[33]

Klein also informed Baruch that the Vaad was launching a campaign to solicit clothing and other items. Klein had just sent 180 packages and 100 pounds of hard candy from his office, and now that the weather was becoming cooler, he would also send chocolate candy. Klein commended Baruch on the "excellent job" he was doing and urged that he continue this "fine work" to preserve "whatever we already have succeeded to accomplish."[34]

Breaking with the Vaad

Stephen Klein and Irving Bunim tried to stop the creation of the COC and the agreement with the JDC, but there was nothing they could do. When Klein returned to the U.S., he learned that the Mizrachi was leaving the Vaad on March 28, 1947,[35] after their representatives in Germany accused the Vaad of discriminating against them. They alleged that when members of Mizrachi asked for food, clothing and other items, they were denied, while members of the Agudath Israel and non-Zionists were provided with ample supplies.[36] The Vaad office in New York had no information about the alleged discrimination since Mizrachi members were represented in all Vaad projects.[37] Klein asked Baruch to send him a report detailing its assistance to Mizrachi *kibbutzim*, schools and individuals,[38] and urged them to rejoin the Vaad.[39]

One newspaper complained that the split meant American Jews faced another relief campaign of $500,000 for the Mizrachi in addition to the general campaign to raise $170,000,000. "The duplication" deserves "the attention of those who give and those who administer," the paper declared. If the Orthodox Jews under Mizrachi supervision need more money, it should come from "the J.D.C...which already [supplies] funds for Orthodox relief needs...."[40] The paper continued that "...this was not the "time...to interfere in any manner...with the unity in...Jewish fundraising...It behooves our Orthodox leaders to work out their problem with the Vaad Hatzala and the J.D.C...to avoid harming the united campaign for overseas relief of which all groups, Orthodox, Conservative and Reform are the recipients."[41]

The break provided a pretext for people to withhold funds already pledged. Even those not associated with Mizrachi used this excuse not to give. Klein was optimistic that within a short time money would be raised from a campaign started in the *Jewish Morning Journal*. He also expected to receive "a bigger allocation" from Chicago after having made peace with the Union of Orthodox Rabbis.[42]

The constant fundraising fell to a small group of people, and even without the COC stumbling block, it was quite a burden. Irving Bunim confessed in mid-July 1947 that he was "pretty well fagged out with this *schnorring* [begging] and am beginning to feel that many of my clients and customers are beginning to feel likewise. However, we have to try to help."[43]

As the situation deteriorated, Klein, Bunim and several other members of the Vaad met with the Union of Orthodox Rabbis in March 1947 to find a way to resolve the conflict. At a meeting with representatives from Agudath Israel, Mizrachi, Agudas Harabonim and Vaad Hatzala, a committee of 10 people was established to address the problems. After a number of weeks, they agreed that the Vaad Hatzala would continue under the auspices of the Union of Orthodox Rabbis, and that the board of the Vaad would consist of six members from Mizrachi, six from Agudah, six from Agudas Harabonim and ten from the Vaad. Rabbi Israel Rosenberg would be the chairman, and Rabbi Eliezer Silver and Rabbi Jacob Levinson (a former president of the American Mizrachi and a prominent Brooklyn rabbi) the co-chairmen. They would appoint as many rabbis as they wanted to join the Vaad.[44]

The agreement stipulated that 33.3 percent of the Vaad budget would be given to *kibbutzim*, Agudath Israel and Mizrachi. The rest would be given to the Vaad. Since the Union of Orthodox Rabbis was holding its convention at Bradley Beach, New Jersey that weekend, the rabbis decided to announce the new agreement at the conference to add prestige to the Union. Members of the Vaad and Mizrachi were invited to attend the session where questions about the Vaad would be discussed.[45]

On the Monday before the convention, the JDC held a meeting at its offices with representatives of Agudah, Mizrachi and the Union of Orthodox Rabbis. When Klein heard the Vaad had not been invited, he contacted Rabbi Silver who agreed that he would insist that immigration remain with the Vaad. Klein's friends and Vaad supporters backed Rabbi Silver so the JDC acceded to their demands.

In a letter to the Sternbuchs, Stephen Klein expressed his utter disappointment with this turn of events: "I don't have to tell you how hard I worked to get the *balabatim* and

Rabbis interested in the work of the Vaad Hatzala—and now the Joint comes and asks that Immigration should be dissolved. I sent committee after committee to the Union of Orthodox Rabbis and nothing helped...." For his staunch defense of the Vaad, Klein came under personal attack that weakened him and his position.[46]

After the COC was established, Samuel Schmidt was pressured to resume his duties as European director of the Vaad.[47] He left for Europe in June 1947. Before accepting the position, he had been approached by the COC to be its European director.[48] Pincus Schoen assured Baruch that Schmidt's appointment was a positive development because "No one intends to interfere with you or hinder your work in any way."[49]

Bunim also assured Baruch the situation was not hopeless: "Do not lose faith or hope. This thing will ultimately work out. Some of the viciousness perpetrated against our program is already being regretted...and very soon we shall...get together and continue the work so urgent at the present time."[50] He told Baruch that when he met William Alpert, he told him of Baruch's many accomplishments: "He did not have to answer because I read it all over his face—with a smile reaching from his mouth to his ears. You have done a swell job and we are very proud of you. However, this means nothing compared to your inner satisfaction."[51]

When Rabbi Silver failed to be elected president of the Presidium of the Agudah, Klein used the opportunity to salvage their relationship, which at that point had become strained. At a private four-hour meeting they agreed that together they would oversee Schmidt and the work of the Vaad in Europe. All disagreements between them would be resolved at a regular meeting of the Vaad.[52]

Schmidt's Arrival in Paris

When Schmidt arrived in Paris, Klein asked that he and Baruch speak to the JDC representative in Germany about moving Jews to France. Klein didn't care if the JDC took credit for arranging transportation for the Vaad's people, but under no circumstances were Baruch and Schmidt to allow the JDC to handle Vaad visas with the American consul. Schmidt needed to move 500 applicants for nonquota visas out of Germany as soon as possible.[53]

He found that obtaining nonquota visas was a difficult and time-consuming process that continued to be an ongoing problem. During June, and up to July 20, 1948, for example, there were only five nonquota visas granted to the Vaad office in Paris. The Paris offices of the JDC and HIAS received none. Some of the delays were attributed to the lack of personnel, as well as to the inexperience of the new consuls handling the visas. The main reason was that consulates and embassies were strict in applying the laws and regulations to the 4(d) and 4(e) visas. This did not affect these people in the long run, except it did make it harder for the Vaad to establish refugee credentials and created problems with the JDC.[54]

Because the people assisted by the Vaad had to stay in Paris until granted a visa, the JDC wanted them treated as if they were not able to immigrate. The JDC claimed it had a limited budget for Paris and could not support Vaad people indefinitely. Those who could not immigrate immediately were given the opportunity to learn a trade. The JDC thus reduced their stipends by having them transferred to a different department.[55]

On July 9, 1948, Schmidt met with Laura Margolies, Director of the French Department in the JDC office in Paris, James Rice, assistant director of the JDC for France, A. Fink, director of the Comité Juive d'Action pour l'Assistance Sociale et la Reconstruction—popularly known as COSAJOR—the French organization through which the JDC administered its aid to refugees in France, and Samuel Sar, who was appointed European director of the COC when Schmidt declined the position. They agreed to screen all the refugees in France under the auspices of the Vaad to determine their eligibility as rabbis or yeshiva students. People in those categories would continue to receive JDC support as they had before.

The yeshiva in Bailly, France—including those students

who came from the Windsheim Yeshiva—was immediately placed in this category. Margolies asked Joseph Schwartz to see if the group could be handled directly through the JDC and not through COSAJOR. Sar also signed the recommendation.

Other Vaad immigration cases were to be treated on an individual basis and on their own merit. If the Vaad determined that a particular case was eligible, it sent a letter to the immigration department of the JDC recommending regular support for three months. If the immigration department considered the case to be eligible, COSAJOR would continue its support for another three months. At the end of those three months, if the visa had not been obtained, the case would be reconsidered.[56]

Samuel Sar

Samuel Sar was one of those members of the American Jewish Orthodox community who had rabbinical ordination, but preferred to be called Mr.[57] He had received *smicha* from the Telshe Yeshiva and as Dean of Students at Yeshiva University in New York, he served as Bernard Revel's main advisor and confidant. (Revel founded Yeshiva College and shaped the Rabbi Isaac Elchanan Theological Seminary.) The COC had been so intent on enlisting Sar, that they wrote to Dr. Samuel Belkin, president of Yeshiva University, asking that Sar be temporarily relieved from his university post to take up this "essential service to our destitute brethren."[58] Sar enthusiastically agreed: "Words fail me to describe the emotions I went through" upon receiving this call to serve.[59] Belkin reluctantly acceded, but was not happy about losing a key administrator while the university was experiencing enormous growth and his responsibilities had tripled.[60]

Sar also served as Vice-President of the Mizrachi Organization of America and was Chairman of its Executive Board.[61] He was no stranger to the DPs. In 1945, the American Jewish Conference had sent Sar and two other Jewish leaders on a fact-finding tour to the American Zone in Germany.[62]

Samuel Sar
Photo courtesy of Yeshiva University Archives

The COC also recruited Jacob Griffel as Sar's assistant because of his official connections to Agudath Israel and the Vaad Hatzala in Istanbul during the war. He understood the DPs and appreciated the urgency of religious rehabilitation. In explaining the choice of both men to the JDC, the COC leadership said they tried "to satisfy the two major Orthodox parties." Yet, in spite of their different organizational affiliations, Sar and Griffel "more than demonstrated that in their social work they have disregarded party lines."[63]

Financial and Other Impediments

Because of the COC, Vaad fundraising became more difficult than ever. By mid-September 1947, the Vaad's financial status was tenuous. The Vaad was at least $60,000 "in the hole" and no one knew when it would get better. Until more money became available, Baruch was forced to retrench.[64] Altogether, the Vaad sent about $30,000 from February-March 1947 to the beginning of October.[65] "If the Vaad was to continue," Schmidt said, "it will be because of us who refused to give up when rational thinking demanded that we should throw up[sic] the sponge."[66] He was convinced that during the last three months of 1947, the situation would be straightened out.[67]

Although Schmidt found it difficult to solicit funds, he threw "all personal considerations to the winds" to raise money. In early December, he and Rabbi Silver solicited at least $15,000 in Cincinnati. A trip to San Francisco yielded $1,600 with a promise of another $2,000 to come at a later date.

Working with Rabbi Silver was not always easy for Schmidt, yet he respected his "greatness in Torah" and his "devotion to the cause." He understood that Rabbi Silver appreciated what the Vaad was doing in Germany. "Besides," he said, Rabbi Silver "is the only one who really is worrying about the situation and he has no help from anyone."[68]

More disturbing to Schmidt was Rabbi Israel Rosenberg's apparent indifference to the future of the Vaad. Rabbi Rosenberg was "quite satisfied" with the arrangement with the COC, perhaps because he was now its chairman. When

Schmidt made a special trip to New York, Rabbi Rosenberg was in the Agudas Harabonim office and did come down to meet with him. Afterward, Schmidt wrote: "Some day the Rabbinate will wake up and realize the sins they are committing by their indifference to the situation of the remnants of our *B'nei Torah.*"[69]

By 1948, Vaad income was one-third of what it had been in 1947. During the first half of 1948, they had raised only 20 percent of the previous year's amount. Federation funds amounted to only 40 percent of what they were in 1947. Campaigns in major American cities, critical for meeting even drastically reduced budgets, did not reach expectations. Additionally, the Vaad had to deal with UJA fundraising campaigns that were all billed as "all inclusive."[70]

Confusion about the role of the COC and the Vaad was another problem. As Rabbi Alexander S. Rosenberg reported: "It is unfortunate that through misunderstanding and through errors of judgment, your work is in jeopardy. It is very difficult to raise funds for the Vaad Hatzala as most people are under the impression that its work has been taken over by the J.D.C. [sic], lock, stock, and barrel."[71]

As of January 1948, the monthly budgets were: France $7,500; Germany $5,000, and $2,000 a month for Prague and Katowice, Poland. Had this money been available, Samuel Schmidt claimed that the most significant parts of the Vaad program, including help for Jews still in Poland, could have been implemented. Considerably less than half this amount was actually provided, and even this "meager sum was obtained with great difficulty and heartache." Under the circumstances, Schmidt felt "it impossible to continue to work...."[72] This was in sharp contrast to the period from May 8, 1945 and mid-1946, when the Vaad sent one million pounds of food and $1,250,000 to the camps in Germany, France, Belgium, Hungary and China.[73]

By mid-June 1948, the Vaad faded further in the minds of its donors after the establishment of the State of Israel. All you heard was "*Eretz Yisrael* and rightfully so," Schoen observed. "The UJA has first call on all monies" in each community, and within the Jewish federations "which were a good source of income...." Rabbi Saul Lasher, one of Vaad's few fund-raisers, had been ill for some time, leaving fundraising at a "standstill," and the organization in arrears by approximately $30,000. Expecting that the crisis in Israel would "continue for some time," Schoen asked Schmidt and Baruch to "economize to the greatest extent [possible]."[74]

To make matters worse, the Vaad had to deal with "backstabbing and insidious propaganda of the JDC," which filtered through the COC[75] and had begun almost from the COC's inception. Schoen wanted to respond publicly to those who vilified the Vaad, but "the wiser and cooler heads" restrained him.[76] Rabbi Lasher did, however, ask Baruch to send him 200 picture books to document Vaad activities.[77] He knew "that the C.O.C. [sic] is doing nothing but talking, talking and again talking...."

The question of COC accomplishments, if any, was raised at a meeting of the Vaad with the members expressing support for Baruch, who was standing up to those who sought to malign the organization. Such talk about the COC was so sensitive that Lasher requested the letter be destroyed after Baruch read it.[78]

"The only way" the COC could "assume prominence in the field of religious rehabilitation is if they assume some of the work and the purposes which heretofore were a province of Vaad Hatzala" Schoen told Baruch in "strictest confidence." The goal was to deliberately undermine the Vaad by questioning its claims of helping the DPs,[79] and by asking the heads of *yeshivos* in France and Germany to put themselves under the auspices of the JDC.[80]

In a July 1948 report, Rabbi Solomon Shapiro, JDC director for religious affairs in Germany and Austria, complained that he could not verify the sums allegedly provided by the Vaad to certain *yeshivos*. The number of religious books and the costs of printing these volumes could not be verified either: "In general we have good reason to doubt the veracity of these claims," he said.[81]

Part of the difficulty in substantiating these numbers was the method used by the Vaad in dispensing aid. When an institution received supplies, food or funding, a photographer took pictures and the recipients were asked for a letter of appreciation. In many cases, the Vaad did not continue supporting the institutions for lack of funds. Once it established a kosher kitchen, for example, the JDC often had to assume ongoing responsibility for its operation.[82]

Another problem was the way Baruch calculated how funds were spent. For example, in a report covering January 1, 1947 to March 31, 1948, Baruch said he printed and distributed 265,000 religious books consisting of *siddurim, Tehillim, Haggadahs, Megilath Esther, Mesilas Yeshorim, Or Israel, Shav Shmatasa,* the Torah, *Kesses Hasofer, Yiddish Leben, Kitzur Shulchan Aruch, Shaagath Aryeh, Taharath Hamishpacha,* valued at $90,000. He also claimed receipt of 111,854 pounds of staple items valued at approximately $55,000, including soup mix, fats, coffee, rice, prunes, dehydrated milk, canned milk, raisins, tea, sugar, salmon, chocolate, cocoa, matzo, soap and candies forwarded to Vaad headquarters in Munich. Twelve tons of clothing for men, woman and children were also shipped during this period.

In turn, the Vaad supported 13 *yeshivos* with $40,095 and 665,000 DM; 61 Talmud Torahs and *yeshiva katanos* that received 2,538,000 DM; 21 kosher kitchens received 1,300,000 DM; four hospitals received 427,000 DM; seven Bais Yaakov Schools received $375 and 104,000 DM; aid to old age homes, schools for *shochtim* and assistance for weddings and similar functions was $8,400 and 322,000 DM. Vaad offices in Munich, Stuttgart and Frankfurt cost $10,000, $4,500 for various immigration services and aid for those going to Paris and the U.S., and for cables and telegrams.[83]

The total amount of aid provided in Germany during this period by Baruch was valued at $203,970. This did not mean that he actually paid $203,970 in cash to institutions, individuals and for administrative costs. He calculated the value of pots, pans, other utensils and items obtained from Dr. Philipp Auerbach to establish kosher kitchens, the food and clothes received from the U.S., purchases made on the black market and other sources available. He did not pay $90,000 to print his religious books. The $90,000 is what he estimated that the printing would have cost had he published the volumes in the U.S. Instead of exchanging dollars at the legal rate of four Marks per dollar, Baruch received 300 on the black market. The difference in rate enabled him to do a great deal on a very small budget. Given the Vaad's precarious financial situation, the amount of $203,790 seemed strange to those unfamiliar with Baruch's accounting practices. The staff and lay leadership of the Vaad, however, knew exactly how much money Baruch received each month, and were clearly aware of how he reached his numbers.[84]

Baruch claimed the Vaad supported a number of the *yeshivos*, but eight under the supervision of the Klausenberger Rebbe allegedly never received any help. The heads of one yeshiva told Shapiro they received an urgent telegram asking them to come to Munich, and to bring their official rubber stamps with them. When they met with Rabbi Aviezer Burstin, he asked them for letters to confirm that their funding came from the Vaad. When the rabbis refused because most of their assistance came from the JDC, they alleged that Burstin threatened that the Vaad would stop handling their immigration applications. Shapiro assured the yeshiva students who were registered with the Vaad, that the JDC "would not tolerate such tactics and that they need not worry." Should the Vaad "carry out its threat," the JDC would handle their applications for them. "In general these tactics characterize Vaad Hatzala operation [sic] in Germany," Shapiro observed.[85] He assured them that his operation had no connection with the Vaad whatsoever.[86] As of October 1947, the JDC claimed that it was responsible for the support and maintenance of the *yeshivos* in Germany.[87]

After the COC asked the heads of a number of yeshivas in Germany and France to affiliate with the JDC, Abraham Horowitz admitted to Schoen that the Vaad would be pushed out altogether. Schoen suggested that every institution the Vaad supported, including the Union of Rabbis in Germany, issue a letter stating the nature of Vaad assistance they received during the previous two years[88] so that the Vaad could refute the allegations leveled against it. [89] Schoen asked for a concise and detailed report about Vaad immigration work in Germany and its activities to transfer Jews to France, Palestine, Italy, the U.S. and other countries.[90]

In March 1948, Abraham Horowitz and Samuel Sar discussed the possibility of providing the 1,500 yeshiva students in Paris and vicinity with the equivalent of $1 a day if the *yeshivos* would dissociate themselves from the Vaad.[91] Horowitz was able to consider this plan because the American dollar was worth 300 francs while it had once brought only 120 francs. This competition became an ongoing battle that consumed a lot of time and energy and exacerbated relations.[92]

Sar was happy to advance the COC position even further at the expense of the Vaad. He complained to Joseph Schwartz that the Vaad was "becoming more aggressive and loud," by making claims that he knew "for a fact" were "not true," but Sar also admitted that he did not have the figures to prove it. He was especially suspicious of a Vaad claim that it had spent $203,970 plus 5,356,000 DM in Germany alone between January and September 1948. He also couldn't believe the Vaad was supporting 13 *yeshivos*, 21 kosher kitchens, four hospitals, seven Bais Yaakov schools, provided special aid to old age homes, schools for *shochtim*, assistance for weddings and "similar functions." He appreciated that Schwartz was a busy man, but implored his help: "I beg of you to be kind and send me a reply to this letter as soon as possible."[93]

Sar's letter was forwarded to JDC personnel, including Samuel Haber, the Zone director for the JDC. After consulting with Rabbi Shapiro, Haber concluded that, "it would be next to impossible to secure real information on any of the claims which Vaad Hatzala makes."[94]

Questions about the duplication of Vaad and JDC/COC activities prompted the Council of Jewish Federations and Welfare Funds to contact the New York JDC office to help verify Vaad claims. After receiving a Vaad report on April 22, 1948, listing institutions it supported, the Council asked the JDC whether the groups also received assistance from them, and if so, to what extent. If the Vaad and the JDC offered aid, what plans had they developed to maintain these institutions in the future?

They specifically wondered about expenditures made in 1947—the $11,700 grant Baruch claimed for the Windsheim Yeshiva, the Beth Josef Yeshiva which received $9,200 and the Lubavitcher group in Pocking that received $4,900— because these "amounts were so substantial that it would seem that the groups...should have required no further help from anyone...."[95]

Inquiries from other Federations also caused concern in the COC. They were especially disturbed that the Vaad had asked for greater allocations than before. The Federations had copies of the agreement with the JDC and questioned Vaad requests. In frustration, the COC informed Rabbi Silver, "These excessive demands create confusion in the minds of the people."[96]

There were so many questions from the Federations around America about the agreement between the JDC and the Union of Orthodox Rabbis, that the JDC found it necessary to send a letter of clarification to all of them. In answer to a query about how the agreement affected the Vaad, the JDC responded that "the Vaad Hahatzala will continue to be sponsored by the Union of Orthodox Rabbis without, however, the blessing or approval of the JDC." Furthermore, the Vaad had to "limit its activities to securing—not financing—emigration opportunities for rabbis, yeshiva students and Torah scholars in Europe and to assisting *yeshivoth* [sic] abroad which receive no subsidies from the Joint Distribution Committee."[97]

The Union of Orthodox Rabbis had specifically asked the JDC to accept this program for the Vaad because it had already committed itself to the Vaad for these limited activities. "In the interests of harmony and in the belief that this represented an important forward step towards an even better resolution of the problem, the JDC went along with the Union of Orthodox Rabbis on this request."[98]

As a result, one Federation continued to allocate funds to the Vaad, on the assumption that the Vaad was engaged in "specific relief activities" on behalf of European Orthodox Jews. It did ask, however, if the JDC had any information about the *yeshivos* that received no subsidies from the JDC, but would receive monetary support from the Vaad.

The JDC noted that the only "specific relief activities" on behalf of Orthodox Jewry "in which the Vaad is to have any role is…in helping *Yeshivoth* [sic] abroad which are not supported by the JDC. However, we must point out that the support of *Yeshivoth* [sic] and religious institutions has always been a traditional part of the JDC program. Within the limits of our financial means, we have not declined help to any Yeshiva which needs and merits aid. The JDC does not have any wish to imply that the Vaad is not extending some help to institutions here and there, but we have no specific data as to just what they are doing or what they plan to do in Europe within the understanding set forth in our agreement with the Union of Orthodox Rabbis."[99]

When asked why the JDC denied "endorsement or approval" of Vaad fundraising activities in support of *yeshivos*, it responded that it "does not, and can not, endorse or veto the fundraising efforts of other organizations. However, we have always felt that the need is for more money with which to carry on the program through existing organizations which are equipped to conduct the various relief and reconstruction activities abroad, and not for additional organizations which only serve to complicate the situation abroad and cause confusion and irritations to the contributing public here."[100]

With regard to the Vaad's claim of support of *yeshivos*, the JDC said it believed that the "contributing communities have a right to ask the Vaad for a budget as well as for a list of the institutions they are supporting in the European countries, and the extent of their financial assistance to each such institution." If the Council of Jewish Federations and Welfare Funds wanted to enlist the cooperation of the JDC to obtain this information, it would ask its European representatives to provide as much information as may be available to them.[101]

Fearful that the Vaad would infringe on its territory, the JDC monitored Vaad activities and those involved with the organization. When an announcement about Keren Aliyah U'Klitah (a fund for helping people go to Palestine) appeared in the *Jewish Morning Journal* with Rabbi Silver listed at its head, the JDC asked if this had violated the agreement between the JDC and the Union of Orthodox Rabbis. After all, the Union had agreed to dissociate itself from fundraising activities for organizations that fell under the purview of the JDC.[102]

As for the COC, it found it difficult to obtain funds from the Federations in 1947 as well, but for different reasons: (1) The applications for funds arrived too late in the year to be considered, and (2) the 1947 campaign had been devoted to the United Jewish Appeal, and it had not been a success.[103] A COC lay leader speculated that people were not giving more because of the high cost of living or perhaps they were suffering from donor fatigue.[104]

Henry Bernstein of the New York UJA told the COC that their campaign had not gone well, and what funds they raised were earmarked for the JDC, the Hebrew University in Jerusalem, United Service for refugees and one or two other institutions. No other organization could be considered. This was after the JDC had assured the leaders of the COC that they could expect $10,000 from the New York UJA. The JDC then suggested that the COC begin an immediate fundraising campaign in the New York City area on *Shabbos Chanukah.* The COC also thought of contacting rabbis in communities where the Federations had turned them down, to ask them to make a special appeal.[105] Given the urgent need to launch the campaign, it did not appear to be a realistic option. These were the same sources the Vaad had used.

As usual, the hostility between the JDC and the Vaad continued unabated. Samuel Schmidt believed the friction and misunderstanding in Germany reverberated in the U.S. and made "matters more difficult for everyone." This was caused in part by the outstanding success the Vaad had in religious rehabilitation, achievements that were quite noticeable and probably created "some feeling of rivalry" among some lower level officials of the JDC. Instead of ignoring these "petty rivalries," officials at the higher level of the JDC made "important issues out of them."[106]

Chapter 10

The Campaign to Undermine the Vaad

The campaign to undermine the Vaad came at a time when it was important for the Vaad to work together with the COC,[1] but this was not a simple task. The COC's arrangement with the JDC was not working, in part because the COC did not have its own budget. Decisions about how the money would be spent were made by the JDC, which meant that the COC functioned basically "as an advisory body."[2]

In 1948, Sar reported that the JDC expenditures for Passover had increased substantially over the previous year, as had their budgetary outlays for other religious needs.[3] The JDC tried to credit this increase to the COC, but Abraham Horowitz admitted that it was "not easy to point to the actual contribution of the COC, because we do not hand out funds or products to the needy...From the outset it had been quite clear that the function of the COC would be a moral one: serving as liaison between the JDC and the religious Jews in DP camps and in the revived open communities in Europe."[4]

Samuel Schmidt further put the COC claims in perspective when he noted that Passover items had been provided by the JDC in previous years, and the JDC did not need a COC delegation to ask for this increase in assistance. "I am convinced that Joseph Schwartz...never failed to recognize these needs and always did his very best to take care of them as much as possible,"[5] he said. But there were additional needs Sar ignored in what otherwise was an excellent report.[6]

Fact-Finding Tour

Sar left for Europe at the beginning of March 1948 to determine the needs of the observant Jews in Germany and Austria and did not finish his survey until mid-1948. Griffel returned from a fact-finding tour of Romania at about the same time. The COC then called a conference in Paris in late November 1948 to discuss rehabilitating Jewish life in Europe. Representatives from North and South Africa, Australia, Israel, Europe, the U.S. and the Jewish Agency were present. Only the Soviet Union was not represented.[7]

A number of the delegates complained that Orthodox religious needs were given too much attention, while Orthodox Jews in America accused the JDC of not doing enough. Joseph Schwartz assumed the JDC must have been providing the right amount, since both sides were displeased. By enlisting Rabbi Moses Beck, the Opsher Rav, to praise the COC as a "wonderful thing" and to say that Sar and Horowitz had "done magnificent work for our kind of people,"[8] Schwartz hoped to defuse some of this criticism.

When the leadership of the COC—Rabbi Ephraim Epstein of Chicago, Illinois, Rabbi Bezalel Cohen of Paterson, New Jersey, David L. Meckler and Abraham Horowitz conducted their five-month fact-finding mission (August through December 1947), they found the kosher kitchens in almost every camp were not large enough to satisfy the needs of the

DPs. In casual discussions with them, the DPs "established beyond doubt that all people, including members of the left-wing parties, would be happier if the public kitchen would give them kosher food instead of *treif* (non-kosher) meals." The group concluded that, "kosher food is apt to serve [as] one of the strongest morale builders of the despairing Jews in the camps."[9]

The situation in the homes for children, the sick and the aged was even worse. The COC found that "the matter of food [was] even in a more deplorable state. Despite the explanations that we were given," the group found "no justification for maintaining *treif* kitchens in homes ...supported by the JDC."[10]

One large JDC hostel in Prague, Czechoslovakia, served kosher food to the refugees waiting to leave for Palestine, but in other hostels rented by the JDC, the kitchens were *treif*. At one of these hostels, housing about 120 people, the rabbis witnessed a "painful" scene. Approximately half of the people were recently arrived Lubavitchers who could not find a hostel with other Lubavitchers already in the city. In this JDC hotel, they saw men, women and children eating a dinner meal prepared by the hotel. Next door to the dining room, they found men, women and children pacing around. They had never eaten non-kosher food in their lives, but having been "broken and crushed" by their recent experiences, they did not "have the strength to fight and demand kosher food." In one family, the husband ate dry food while the wife and children ate *treif*.[11]

Members of the COC were careful not to attack the JDC for failing to provide the groups with kosher food. "This is not due to the evil heart of the JDC people, for it should be known that all Orthodox Jews, rabbis and, especially so, Lubavitz [sic] Hassidm [sic], value greatly the attitude of the JDC towards them." The Orthodox "could not expect that the JDC should itself establish this (*kashrus*). In this respect we see the necessity of our committee."[12] Why the rabbis believed it was unreasonable to expect the JDC to provide kosher food instead of *treif* is not clear. The COC then had to prod the JDC to do so.

Classic examples of this took place on Passover for two consecutive years—in 1947 and 1948—when the JDC supplied *treif* Passover chickens to the DP camps in Austria. As already noted, Rabbi Joshua Aronson in Austria protested so vigorously that Sar wrote to Abraham Horowitz to complain. Horowitz believed that JDC headquarters in Paris or the office in Austria, or both, shared the blame, since no chickens had been sent from the U.S. Horowitz sent Rabbi Aronson's complaint to Joseph Schwartz along with a "painful protest" from the COC. The purpose in doing so, Horowitz said, was not to dwell on the "painful occurrence of the past," but to prevent it from happening again.[13]

In their final report, the group strongly recommended that "as a matter of principle" kosher food be provided in all institutions supported by the American Jewish community through the JDC. The JDC "must radically change its purchasing policy, so that it ships...only kosher canned food."[14] Although this urgent matter had been brought to the attention of the JDC in late September 1947, as of April 1948, the issue of kosher food in JDC installations was still under discussion with Joseph Schwartz, Moses Leavitt and other JDC functionaries.[15]

In May 1948, there were complaints from Italy that "despite numerous promises, JDC still distributes *treif* canned meat and observant Jews either remain without meat entirely, or are compelled to trade—on the black market—what they cannot eat and with the money realized from the deal, they may try to get kosher meat which, again, may hail from the black market at exorbitant prices."[16]

In December 1948, the JDC transient camps in Marseilles, where people stayed on their way to Israel were serving *treif,* leaving residents hungry and angry. And when the JDC Supply Officer ordered *treif* margarine for all of Europe it became clear that the JDC purchasing office needed an on-site *kashrus* consultant.[17]

True, non-kosher food was easier and cheaper to obtain, and while the JDC had a very limited budget, it is also true that kosher food was a fundamental, unquestionable necessity. It is surprising the JDC did not ask the Orthodox community for extra funds to help them cover the expense of kosher food. Now the COC was adamantly demanding that the JDC provide kosher food, as had the Vaad before it, and sent Sar to raise the issue with Joseph Schwartz again. As Horowitz noted: "We have made it clear more than once that the matter of *kashruth* is a principle around which the whole problem of religious rehabilitation revolves. It is true that kosher food is more expensive than *trefa* [sic], but the effect of kosher food is so strong in the matter of religious rehabilitation, that it should warrant the extra expense...."[18]

Other Religious Needs

In 1947, the JDC allotted $400 a month for religious books. In response to requests sent to the JDC and the COC, the COC began purchasing books and sending them to Germany, Austria, Greece, Italy and France beginning in December 1947. Not all requests could be fulfilled, either because the books were not available or the cost was prohibitive.[19] The JDC also corrected and reconditioned 363 Torah scrolls that were distributed to DP camps and communities in France, Hungary, Italy, Romania, Belgium, Yugoslavia, Greece and Holland. Thirty went to Germany.[20]

The COC also tried to cope with the paucity of religious items such as *tefillin* and *taleisim*. Members of the COC fact-finding mission "found practically none of these articles in the possession of the JDC regional offices," though the demand for them was "considerably great."[21] The COC urged the JDC to purchase and distribute religious articles to the camps through the local religious committees.

Horowitz announced in mid-May 1948 that he had sent 200 pairs of *tefillin* from Palestine to Sar, but many could not be used because the parchments were damaged. The scribes had been negligent, indifferent or the manufacturer had substituted reproductions for handwritten parchments. Several months earlier, the JDC ordered 10,000 pairs of *tefillin*—$6 per set in Paris—and 8,000 *mezzuzahs*, and they were still waiting for shipment. (At the time, a pair of *tefillin* written by a competent scribe cost approximately $80. The JDC knew a $6 pair would not be perfect, but wanted them to conform at least to the basic standards of Jewish law.[22])

Another sticking point for the Orthodox was that the JDC forced employees to violate the *Shabbos* and Jewish holy days at JDC offices. To them, it was another example of how the JDC was unable to grasp their needs. On October 1, 1947, a telegram from Austria was sent to Rabbi Israel Rosenberg complaining that the JDC was making religious Jews desecrate the *Shabbos* by "compelling religions [sic] people to work on Sukoth [sic] and each Sabath [sic] in all their offices. All interventions in vain."[23]

In June 1948, the JDC called a conference for its zone directors to take place on a Friday and Saturday in early June. Rabbi Snieg wrote to Samuel Haber asking the conference be postponed to another day of the week.[24]

It is not clear how the COC responded to the initial appeal from Austria, but from March 5, 1949 on, the offices of the JDC in Paris were closed on *Shabbos*. The offices in Munich were already following this procedure. The COC European director told Joseph Schwartz how "gratified" he felt "to discover that, without any suggestion from us, this step has been taken. I hope that it will remain a permanent arrangement of the AJDC administration."[25]

Samuel Sar Redux

In the meantime, Samuel Sar continued in his activities against the Vaad. Baruch could not understand Sar's determination to destroy the Vaad or how he could beg the JDC for information to incriminate the organization created by the greatest rabbis of the generation. Why would Sar engage in such tactics?

The answer may lie in Sar's *hashkafah* (religious philosophy). Although he received *smicha* from the Telshe Yeshiva in Lithuania, Sar was never accepted as an equal colleague by the Agudas Harabonim, or by the rabbis of the COC. Rabbis schooled in European *yeshivos* regarded

American rabbis as not having the same extensive background and rigorous training as they had. American and European rabbis were also divided on how to prevent assimilation. European rabbis wanted emphasis on Jewish education, *Shabbos* observance, *kashrus* supervision, marriage and divorce laws. The American Orthodox rabbinate, which "preached a synthesis of Jewish and American values," was perceived as a threat to the survival of Judaism by "seeking to wean East European Jews away from their traditional religious communities."[26]

Sar's close relationship with Rabbi Bernard Revel at Yeshiva University may also have influenced his attitude toward the Vaad. As Revel developed the university following secular American educational philosophies, the Agudas Harabonim became increasingly critical of their friend and colleague. Sar could not help but be disturbed by the ongoing rabbinical scrutiny and heightened criticism of Revel and the college.[27]

Baruch also could not understand why if there was still so much work to be done in Germany, Sar questioned the need of having a COC representative in Munich. After meeting with Rabbi Solomon Shapiro in late May 1948 at JDC offices in Munich, Sar observed: "Conditions in Germany are pretty well organized and Rabbi Shapiro is handling them very effectively. I seriously wonder wether [sic] opening here a bureau for the COC will accomplish much more than the Religious Department of the AJDC does at the present." The only reason for a COC representative to be in Munich would be to exert influence on the JDC if Shapiro had any difficulties. Nevertheless, Sar began negotiating with a candidate recommended to him by Rabbi Sneig because COC had to be represented to remain credible.[28]

Sar wrote letters complaining that for the COC "Germany was a problem in a problem." When he arrived in Munich on May 20, he met with Rabbi Snieg and representatives from the Agudah and Mizrachi. He understood immediately that the difficulties between these factions were based on jealousy "of each other," and "anything you do is judged by how much the party taking part in it will gain prestige and influence" among the DPs.[29]

At a meeting of the executive committee of the Agudas Harabonim, he outlined a plan to employ people who were idle by design—those who could not find suitable work or who were unwilling to participate in the rebuilding of the German economy. He also presented plans to ensure cooperation between the various groups, and explained the important role the rabbis could play in religious rehabilitation, particularly in the area of education.[30]

While Sar was pleased with the discussion, many of those present found his attitude patronizing. They were indignant that an American rabbi who had arrived in May 1948—three years or more after their liberation—had the audacity to tell them what they needed and how they should get it. Sar assumed he "had reached a full understanding" with them, but soon learned that there were no easy solutions in Germany.

Once, without consulting the Agudas Harabonim or the Vaad, the JDC Religious Department in Munich called a conference of all Talmud Torah teachers for June 8. Transportation, food and lodging were arranged for a 100 rabbis expected to attend, and Sar was scheduled to address them. Members of the Agudas Harabonim were subsequently informed of the event and were invited to speak to the participants. Since they had not initiated the conference, the rabbis sent telegrams urging the teachers not to attend. Sar claimed the teachers were prepared to defy the rabbis, but the JDC cancelled the sessions.[31]

The Agudas Harabonim wanted to demonstrate that it, not the JDC, was the authority on religious education. Though his past experience should have made him an adept politician, Sar was wrong not to confer with the Agudah or the Vaad before calling his conference. As a result, the teachers were urged not to participate "to prevent the undermining of the authority of the rabbinate which Mr. Sar's independent action" had threatened.

This episode highlighted the COC's problems. At a meeting with the rabbis in Munich on June 10, 1948, the rabbis stressed it was "undesirable under the existing set-up of the COC, to turn over any of the work of the Vaad Hatzala to the COC...The Vaad Hatzala is their organization, over which they have a definite rabbinical authority that is always recognized...and they are convinced that under the set-up of the COC they would have to relinquish that authority."[32]

Sar was deeply upset and his attempt to establish "harmonious co-operation in the country [so] paralyzed," he seriously considered leaving Europe immediately. He realized that the COC could not "execute a plan requiring the active support and assistance of the Joint [and at the same time] ally ourselves with the Rabbis who are fighting the Joint Religious Department."[33] In despair, Sar sent a telegram to Horowitz: "Survey and Observation in Germany Impress Me As The Most Difficult Country To Work In Disunity Partisanship ans [sic] Suspicion Prevalent...."[34]

Instead of leaving, Sar spent the weekend with Rabbi Sneig, who assured him they held COC in the highest regard, but would not work with them while they were under the auspices of the JDC. The only value the JDC had to the survivors was in dispensing aid and nothing more.[35]

Before Sar left Germany, Snieg agreed to meet with Rabbi Shapiro to iron out a working arrangement. Afterwards, a conference was called to discuss the plans submitted by the COC through S. Rapayke, a brother-in-law of Dr. Zalman Grinberg, the former president of the Central Committee of Liberated Jews in Bavaria. At the suggestion of Rabbi Sneig, Sar would hire Rapayke to represent the COC in areas of Jewish education. He had studied at the Slobodka Yeshiva and belonged to Mizrachi, but was not active enough in the movement to provoke opposition from the Agudah. Rabbi Snieg assured Sar that Rapayke would receive the full cooperation of the Agudas Harabonim and all the other parties. Sar wanted to proceed, but when he learned that "the Religious Department viewed "such activity as an infringement on their territory and Rabbi Shapiro...felt very unhappy with the plan," he realized that he could not engage Rapayke at a cost of $3,000 a year, without receiving approval from the JDC in New York.[36]

If Sar appeared naive and arrogant it was because he believed he could visit the DPs for a week or so and expect to correct problems that were years in the making. The survivors

COC representatives on European mission
Photo courtesy of JDC, New York Archives

were not people to order around. They wanted respect and dignity, and to have their opinions taken seriously. After years of degradation by the Nazis and suffering unspeakable horrors, no Jewish bureaucrat with his own personal agenda was going to push them around. Sar had not taken this into account. And, and in many cases, neither had the JDC. The individuals who worked most successfully with the survivors were those who understood their need to reassert themselves and encouraged them to take control of their own institutions and own destiny.

Rabbi Shapiro's response to Sar's proposal to hire Rapayke reflected the difficult situation facing the COC. The COC, an advisory group, could not make binding decisions on its own; it had to get approval from the JDC before implementing anything. Assuming that Sar had found the solution—and that was a big if—he still had to deal with JDC representatives in Munich who felt threatened by Rapayke's potential position. The JDC had to consider the extra cost of hiring a person who would be doing part of Rabbi Shapiro's job while trying to avoid alienating and embarrassing its own representative.

Before he came to Germany on March 30, 1948, Sar submitted requests for a 25 percent increase in the daily allowance for observant Jews in France to the French JDC offices. He was told that JDC European Headquarters had to approve the request, and that he would be informed when they received an answer. When Sar asked them to send money to Hapoel Hamizrachi to pay for a *bris*, he was advised that "these were expenditures that the Joint could not assume" since Hapoel Hamizrachi had money of its own, and given that Hapoel Hamizrachi had already "accepted this explanation," the JDC did not believe any "further action on our part... is required."[37]

When Sar asked for special allocations for religious teachers to instruct children in children's homes, the JDC claimed it had many such requests from organizations in France. It could not provide funds because in "attempting to meet the basic needs of the Jews in Europe, Joint has been unable to meet these requests and we do not see the possibility of doing so in the near future. We realize that such services are extremely important but cannot allocate funds for them when we are not able to provide sufficient money for food and lodging."[38]

Sar's failure to receive the 25 percent increase for observant Jews in France was further "evidence of the budgetary limitation" under which the JDC labored. As early as April 1947 it had to establish spending priorities that were to provide for the DPs, the children, the aged and for reconstruction services. "We have had to adopt the policy that Jewish communities in France should meet needs other than the priorities listed above, and have progressively reduced our subventions for religious and cultural activities."[39] The JDC tried to assure Sar that this did "not mean that we have in any way withdrawn our help from observant groups, but the help is limited to food, shelter, clothing and other essentials."[40] Eventually, this monetary problem did improve somewhat in late November 1948, and the COC reported that the JDC had substantially increased assistance to the 2,061 Orthodox functionaries in France.[41]

Sar never had the opportunity to follow through on resolving these problems and others he encountered on his mission. His health became seriously impaired while in Europe and he was on the verge of a nervous breakdown. He returned to New York in late August 1948 and was succeeded by Rabbi Dr. Manuel Laderman, a pulpit rabbi for 16 years from Denver, Colorado. A graduate of the Chicago Yeshiva with a Ph.D. from the University of Chicago, Laderman was a national vice-president of the Mizrachi Organization of America. Because of his rabbinical duties, Laderman could not leave for Europe until early November 1948. Until his arrival, Abraham Horowitz went to Paris to cover for him.[42]

Even after Sar returned to the U.S. and Yeshiva University, he monitored the activities of the COC. When the Vaad Hatzala held its conference in September 1948, Sar complained that members of the COC were involved with it. He could not understand how Rabbi Ephraim Epstein, a commissioner of the COC, had taken "a very prominent part in the deliberations" of the conference and had been "one of the prime movers" of the event. Sar was unhappy with Rabbi

Epstein's response, but decided to overlook the rabbi's participation because he was over 70 years old and Sar did not know what his own mental state would be at that age: "I might be out of my mind also at that time." He could not fathom why David L. Meckler had participated. Meckler, after all, was a "sensible man, an intelligent man, and not a Rabbi, and does not need the whole publicity connected with the conference of the Vaad Hatzala and yet he too was there at the conference, taking part in the deliberations."[43]

On September 29, 1948, Sar attended a meeting of representatives of the Vaad and the COC including Rabbis Eliezer Silver, Aharon Kotler, Jacob Karlinsky, Irving Bunim, Nathan Baruch and Reuben Levovitz. Sar listened with disbelief to Baruch, "their biggest gun," but did not respond. He was not "in a fighting mood that evening because" he would have been the "only one" to protest. The next day he sent a letter to Rabbi Shapiro urging that he send him official letters from *yeshivos* and the rabbis to refute Baruch's claims of supporting 6,000 children in Talmud Torahs and *yeshivos*, in addition to kosher kitchens and other institutions and projects. The Vaad was about to embark on a new appeal for funds and Sar wanted those involved in the UJA to have this material. The information was so vital he asked that it be sent by cable and telegram.[44]

Sar was critical of Baruch and others in the Vaad. He noted that Rabbi Silver had resigned from the COC in early 1948 ostensibly for its failure to live up to its agreements. This he opined "did not augur well for the unification of Orthodox Jewish life in America. Very soon I expect statements in the press lauding the accomplishments of the Vaad Hatzala, insinuating at the same time that the C.O.C. [sic] sold out its birthright to the J.D.C. [sic]...."[45]

Sar referred to Irving Bunim, one of the most revered members of the Orthodox Jewish community, as "His Lordship."[46] Then Sar claimed the Vaad had personally attacked him at the conference, as well as in a letter describing him as a nice man, but one who did nothing to help his fellow Jews. Rabbi Rosenberg took issue with this attempt to malign him, but Sar felt "it should be a source of delight...to know that the COC has been criticized by these people. I certainly...feel proud of the criticism so generously given and freely handed out at the conference."[47]

When asked to issue a statement in writing denying the Vaad's allegations against the JDC and COC, he said it "should be below the dignity of any decent fellow...to indulge in such methods...to fight an opponent."[48] Instead, he planned to prepare a positive statement describing the accomplishments of the COC during the six months it began operating in Paris.

Given the objectives of éach organization, the turf wars and the personalities involved, it is doubtful whether the COC and the JDC could have ever worked together with the Vaad in Germany. In a letter to Bunim in early 1949, Schmidt explained, "the C.O.C. [sic] is not considered highly by the JDC administration in Germany and...even Dr. Schwartz...is not fully convinced that the C.O.C. [sic] is an essential factor to them." The purpose of creating the COC was "apparently to undermine the Vaad Hatzala. There can be no doubt that in a considerable measure they have succeeded in that direction."

Although Schmidt knew the COC and JDC were responsible for failing to develop a productive relationship with the Vaad, he believed the Vaad could have acted differently. "As you know, it has always been my policy to work with the JDC" and, while there was no point in rehashing the past, "our policy in Germany, which was militant to the JDC, did not help the situation." He believed that the Vaad "must continue" and that "a cooperative *modus vivendi* could be worked out with the AJDC...We ought to try and approach the powers that be."[49]

Chapter 11

An Unexpected Ending

Nathan Baruch's first two years in Europe (1946-1947) were tumultuous, and 1948 was even more so. His daily workload increased under the weight of the bureaucracies he had to work with, but there were some good times as well. One of the more joyous occasions took place on February 2, 1948 at Philanthropy Hall in Frankfurt, when students and rabbis from the Vaad Hatzala rabbinical seminaries of Windsheim, Weisheim, Wetzlar, Bergen-Belsen, Leipheim, Ulm, Wasseralfingen, Pocking, Aschau, Feldafing, Bamberg, Heidenheim and Landsberg assembled to bid farewell to a hundred rabbis and students leaving Germany.

The guests of honor at this affair were Rabbi Snieg and Major General Miller G. White, U.S. Deputy Chief of Staff, who commended the Vaad on its accomplishments in reconstructing and rehabilitating the religious DPs and institutions. The General said that as much as it pleased him to see the rabbis go, he felt the group should be the last to leave Germany and not the first, so that they could continue to provide spiritual sustenance to the DPs who remained behind. Brigadier General Thomas L. Harrold delivered very warm greetings and cited the remarkable record of the Windsheim Yeshiva. William Haber expressed excitement about attending his first major event since assuming his new duties. Rabbi Zvi Thornheim, from Windsheim, delivered the closing address and thanked the American Army for its hospitality.

After greetings by other representatives and leaders, the rabbis and students sang Hebrew songs and danced. Beverages were served, and the traditional toast to life, "*L'chaim*," was offered. During dinner, two young Zeilsheim Yeshiva boys performed Hebrew songs, and a 13-year-old from the Wetzlar Yeshiva delivered a discourse on the Talmud. Afterward the Grace After Meals was recited and hundreds of yeshiva students continued to dance and sing, while others offered Talmudic discourses until the early hours of the morning.[1]

Parcels and a Passover Appeal

In July 1948, Pincus Schoen told Baruch that the Vaad would send parcels of food every several weeks for general distribution to the DPs. Other parcels would be specially marked for individuals. Schoen understood Baruch's limitations, but had no alternative.[2]

The Vaad Passover Food Package drive was launched in the New York newspapers and through a direct mail campaign in 1947. The Vaad hoped to show the public that the money raised went for actual food for the DPs.[3] An ad in *The New York Times* ran with the caption: "At Least Give The *Bread* Of Freedom." The blurb read: "Liberated in 1945, in 1948, Jewish D.P.'s must still look to you for food to celebrate the Festival of Freedom ...for food to nourish starved bodies still prisoners in concentration camps [sic]."[4]

Baruch wrote to his friends in the U.S.: "I wish you could sit at my desk with me, as did the great and beloved

(l-r) Rabbi Samuel A. Snieg, Chief Rabbi, U.S. Zone,
Major General Miller G. White, and Rabbi Nathan Baruch
at Windsheim Yeshiva dinner
Photo courtesy of Rabbi Nathan Baruch

(l-r) Professor William Haber, Advisor on Jewish Affairs, General Miller G. White, Deputy Chief of Staff Headquarters U.S. Ground and Service Forces, Europe, General Thomas L. Harrold, Rabbi Aviezer Burstin, Major Hyman and Rabbi Nathan Baruch. The youngster (center) was one of the performers at the Windsheim Yeshiva dinner
Photo courtesy of Rabbi Nathan Baruch

Rabbi Sneig, Chief Rabbi of Germany, and see the steady stream of D.P.'s [sic] who come to my office. Each man has a different need. Yet all stem from the same source: something that means Jewish living to him—some symbol of his former life. The cry is always: 'It is not enough to remain alive, I want to *remain* a *Jew!*' Now their great concern is, 'Will I be able to observe Passover as the *Haggada* [sic] directs?'

"Rabbi Snieg told me that the matzos being baked in Germany [would] be insufficient. The religious Jews in Germany, France and other European countries...all look to us to provide them again with Passover food packages. I know that you, who happily observe Passover in a free America, will not disappoint them—will want to show them that it is as important to you as it is to them that Judaism survives. Ten dollars feeds a D. P. for the week of Passover. It gives him the matzos, matzo meal, fats, tea, coffee and other foods that he requires to observe the Festival of Freedom—to nourish his starved body. I beg of you, do not let our people down. Invite one D.P. [sic] and more if you can afford it, to 'eat' with you this Passover" [sic]. [5]

By April 5, 1948, 325 parcels weighing approximately five-and-a-half tons were shipped to Europe.[6]

Vaad Projects: Yeshivos, Talmud Torahs and Kosher Kitchens

Rabbi Gershon Liebman of the Shearith Beth Joseph Yeshiva recalled that at the end of the war, when the camps were organized and camp committees were formed, the idea of establishing *yeshivos* had not occurred to anyone. But as of September 1948, there were 14 *yeshivos* in various camps in Germany supported by the Vaad Hatzala. Rabbis and teachers in many other camps also asked the Vaad to establish 12 additional *yeshivos*.[7]

Additionally, the Vaad also organized 69 Talmud Torah schools in the American Zone. At one point, they maintained six religious children's homes, but all were disbanded when the children were placed at the top of the Vaad's list of priorities and sent to the *Yishuv* in 1947 and the early part of 1948.[8]

By March 1948, when elections were held in the camps for the Congress of the Central Committee of Liberated Jews in Germany, the two Orthodox parties between them garnered almost 20 percent of the vote. Agudath Israel received 10 percent, Mizrachi, nine percent. At the same time, Labor, including leftist splinter groups like Hashomer Hatzair and Poalei Zion, received 30 percent, the left-of-center Mapai (Zionist-socialist Land of Israel Worker's Party) twenty percent and the Revisionists 21 percent.[9]

Before the various Vaad projects could be implemented, a number of serious obstacles had to be overcome. Baruch continually faced bitter opposition from irreligious forces in the camps, and sometimes from Jewish Agency representatives who simply did not understand the kind of work the Vaad was doing. There were also those bureaucrats who thought the Vaad infringed on their turf. Some of this negative response also exposed basic ignorance of their own Judaism in addition to their insensitivity to the survivors.

In the Landsberg DP Camp, the well-meaning director of the UNNRA team asked the JDC to provide two dozen pairs of soccer shoes to help the people nourish their souls. He explained that, "This is infinitely related with the spiritual rejuvenation of these people because they can create a kind of identity and give joy and release on their own terms, as people to people [sic]."[10]

With perseverance, the Vaad managed to establish or provide seed money for some religious activity or project in each of the DP camps. The problems faced in founding a Talmud Torah illustrate the obstacles that had to be overcome: The Vaad had to find a place to house the yeshiva when there was hardly any viable real estate available; it needed to secure approval from the IRO and the local camp committee to set it up; and it had to pay the teachers and supply the school with books and material. Then the Vaad had to recruit students from the nonreligious schools. From the Talmud Torah the students graduated to the *yeshivos katanos.* And every time the Vaad wanted to establish a new institution, it faced major battles.[11]

Establishing kosher kitchens also presented many challenges. The IRO and Jewish agencies imported millions of dollars worth of food and supplies, most of it non-kosher. The Vaad had to obtain facilities, subsidize the cost of kosher food and provide new cooking utensils and dishes. In the camps, where food was pooled and shared by the entire camp population, the Vaad organized committees to barter non-kosher meat and fats in their possession for kosher items. The Jewish community in Frankfurt-am-Main, with the largest kosher kitchen, served more than 500 people each day.[12]

Baruch's carefully cultivated cordial relations with the U.S. Military helped every phase of Vaad programming. Many of the top generals in the U.S. Army graciously appeared at the Vaad's ceremonies and events. Their presence provided a valuable morale boost to the survivors. The military men appreciated that the Vaad's programs were based on moral teachings stressing obedience, restraint and living according to the doctrines of the Torah. Major General Miller G. White was especially proud of the Vaad's work and said he truly appreciated spending many hours with yeshiva students.[13]

After Israel was declared a state on May 14, 1948, 25,526 Jewish DPs left the U.S. Zone in Germany. The exodus continued in 1949 when 31,290 left the U.S. Zone. By June 1950, most of the Jews in Germany, Austria and Italy who had planned to go to Israel had done so.[14] By 1950-51, two-thirds of the survivors had gone to Israel; the rest went to other countries.[15] Less than 100,000 refugees came to the U.S.[16] There might have been more, were it not for Patrick McCarren, the senior senator from Nevada. As chairman of the Senate Judiciary Committee, he delayed DP legislation for so long, that by the time the Senate ratified the DP law to allow Jews to enter the U.S., most were already in Israel or elsewhere. McCarren, an isolationist, did not like Jews and did not have a good relationship with President Truman, his fellow Democrat.[17]

277

Return Call

In late 1948, Baruch returned to the U.S. for a special conference to evaluate the Vaad's program for 1949 after the failure of the COC agreement. Baruch was billed as the guest speaker, and Irving Bunim would make the appeal. Gertrude Gould suggested that the press meet Baruch at LaGuardia Airport in New York to publicize his return. "Be sure to have a statement ready with some news angle," she suggested. "Of course if you have something to say about the growth of antisemitism in Germany since liberation, or any new angle on the attitude of the Jews, that would be news."[18]

Prior to his departure, Baruch's concerns about the conditions in Germany prompted a note from Rabbi Silver. In late November 1948, Rabbi Silver thanked Baruch for the "letters, protocols, books and other items," that enabled Silver to understand the issues Baruch confronted daily. "We are all in debt to you for your deeds," he said. "Your recent letters indicate a sense of despair...as well as a lack of confidence" in the future viability of the Vaad Hatzala. Rabbi Silver wanted him to know what was happening in order to "drive away the despair and strengthen" his "confidence" in the viability of the Vaad. He knew of Baruch's "travails," his suffering and the "correctness" of his complaints, and assured him he was not alone. The office in New York encountered "hardships" and difficulties, but did not surrender. Rabbi Silver hoped that from now on the Vaad would be able to provide him with "regular support."

Rabbi Silver asked Baruch whether he had heard "the false propaganda of the Mizrachi against us, the gossip, slander and libels that they publicized against the Vaad Hatzala, and its leadership in Europe. They came out with new propaganda against the refugees and Torah scholars." In order not "to defame God's name," the Vaad did not fight or quarrel with them.

To lessen its burden, therefore, Rabbi Silver said the Vaad approached the JDC to take over about half of its work in Europe, leaving them "with the task of assisting the Torah and its scholars." The Vaad would then be able "to organize the large and small *yeshivos,* assist rabbis and Torah scholars and their families scattered over many lands, and organize emigration...to the United States and Eretz Yisrael. There is much work left for the Vaad Hatzala. We are aware that many of the scholars suffered, because we abandoned them and assumed responsibilities on general matters that really were not in our domain, but in fact belonged to the JOINT'S domain. We set up a special committee to supervise the Joint's activities, and this was not easy to do. Therefore the Vaad Hatzala has suffered from every corner and sector."[19]

At a preliminary meeting to prepare for the September 15 Conference, there was an open discussion about the JDC and COC. At the end of July 1948, Pincus Schoen told Baruch: "Many of the DP's [sic] who have just come across [the ocean from Europe] have explained fully the necessity of the Vaad Hatzala and the evils of the JDC." Bunim and Rabbi Silver praised Baruch for his fine work in Europe and discussed their plans to announce publicly that the agreement with the JDC was "null and void." Schoen remarked that this was "quite a sharp statement coming from Silver."[20]

Rabbi Silver also testified that: "'Not one penny' was given by the Joint Distribution Committee to the Agudas Harabonim. 'Not one penny' was given by the J.D.C. [sic] to the Vaad Hatzala, 'not one penny' was given to the Committee of Rabbis that went to Europe to investigate the school situation for the J.D.C. [sic] The agreement was made for one year. Now that the year had expired, no agreement is in force. 'It is off,' said Rabbi Silver, 'and the Vaad Hatzala must bestir itself or all religious education will cease in Germany and elsewhere in Europe.'"[21]

Arrival in New York

When Baruch arrived at LaGuardia, the press was there to greet him. Though he presented a realistic analysis of events in Germany, it proved to be his undoing. Baruch allegedly criticized the American military and the IRO for being more concerned about rebuilding Germany and the German economy than about the plight of the Jewish DPs, which led to the DPs being ignored and/or treated with contempt by the military, while fostering antisemitism among American soldiers.

Baruch was disturbed by public service announcements in Germany encouraging American soldiers and their wives to volunteer time to the German Youth Administration. Americans were being asked to fraternize with the Germans in an effort to help instill democratic ideas and ideals into the German way of life. They were also urged to entertain German children. He noted that nothing was ever said about helping Jewish DP children. Every effort was made to make the Germans happy, but the average American soldier, who had not seen the concentration camps and the depravity of the German people, considered the DPs to be parasites and irritants.

Baruch cited *Stars and Stripes*, the military newspaper, as an example of how the military fostered this negative view of the Jews. It printed banner headlines about black-market activities in the camps, but rarely, if ever, published sympathetic stories about the DPs and the unprecedented brutalities the Jews had endured. When the Jewish DP camps were raided to search for black market contraband, Baruch saw MPs line up the DPs, frisk and search them, even make them take off their shoes, and talk to them as if they were criminals.[22]

Baruch had looked forward to coming back home, but did not anticipate the consequences of his 25 minute interview with the Associated Press. Repercussions from the interview continued for some time. Questions were raised about whether he could continue to serve effectively in his post in Germany. Baruch said that the press distorted his statement to make it appear that he had been critical of the Army. During the course of the interview he stated: "Because of the preoccupation of the Military Command with the political problems of Germany and especially because of the Berlin situation, it was not possible for the Military Command to give the DPs the attention which they had received heretofore." Baruch made it clear that he had only the highest praise for the cooperation and valuable assistance he received from the Army Command in carrying out his mission in Germany.

In an attempt to do some damage control, Pincus Schoen, the Union of Orthodox Rabbis and other supporters wrote to American political leaders and military authorities to set the record straight. This was especially important because when he returned to Germany, Baruch was *persona non grata* and told to leave.

Schoen asked Major General John H. Hilldring, then Assistant Secretary of State for Occupied Areas, to call General Lucius Clay to explain what had happened at the press conference and to urge Clay to keep Baruch at the Vaad. Hilldring had been involved with the Vaad during the latter part of 1945 by helping it arrange its first shipment of 180,000 pounds of food and religious items. Schoen also reminded the General that the Army had expressed its "deep satisfaction" with Baruch's work in raising the "spirits and morale of the DPs... which made the work of the Army easier...."[23]

Hilldring responded that since he was about to leave Washington, D.C. for Arizona, it would be better to turn the problem over to General G.L. Eberle, Chief of the Civil Affairs Division, who would pursue the case with sympathy and vigor. Hilldring expected there would be considerable trans-Atlantic cabling involved before the issue would be resolved. If Hilldring would carry on the correspondence from Arizona, there would be unavoidable delays in resolving the case promptly.[24]

Schoen wrote to Eberle on November 11 and followed up with a conversation on December 2. In the meantime, the Union of Orthodox Rabbis and the Vaad Hatzala sent two separate cables to General Clay. The first signed by Rabbi Eliezer Silver "most urgently request[ed] you permit continuation such program [Vaad Hatzala] in Germany under capable leadership of Rabbi Nathan Baruch."[25] The second missive from the Vaad Hatzala, signed by Rabbis Silver, Kotler and Yechiel Mordecai Gordon, the former *rosh yeshiva* of the Lomza Yeshiva, stated: "At an emergency conference participated by the Union of Orthodox Rabbinical Council of America, Mizrachi Organization of America, Young Israel Movement of America, leading rabbis of [the] country and representatives of many congregations [are] greatly disturbed at reported news that Rabbi Nathan Baruch might be compelled [to] leave post. In [the] name of participating organizations we respectfully request review entire matter and continuation of the Vaad Hatzala program so vital to the morale and spirit of the DPs and the continuation of Rabbi Baruch who with the assistance of the Army command was able to formulate and effectively carry out such program."[26]

The Union received a response to the attention of Rabbi Silver from General Clay that read: "The matter referred in your message [concerning Rabbi Baruch] has been reviewed with my Advisor on Jewish Affairs [William Haber] who informs me that Rabbi Baruch has tendered his resignation and will leave Command by 30 November. Urge that a suitable replacement be furnished to insure continuation of Vaad Hatzala's present highly desirable program."[27]

In a letter to Schoen on December 9, Eberle informed Schoen that he had received information from the European Theater that Baruch would be leaving the United States Zone of Germany "for certain reasons unrelated to his statement in the press. He was involved in certain activities which it is believed would reflect unfavorably upon both himself and Vaad Hatzala if adjudicated, as would be required if he should remain in Germany. William Haber felt that under the circumstances it was best that Rabbi Baruch should return home, and I understand that the theater commander concurred in this."[28] Eberle suggested that if the Vaad "so desires" Schoen should move quickly to assign Baruch's successor. If he wished to pursue the Baruch case further, Eberle suggested that Schoen contact Haber directly.[29]

It appears that Baruch left Germany under of a cloud of suspicion, and Baruch understood there was nothing that he could do to change the decision. But there were a number of reasons the Army was eager for him to leave Germany, and not just because of his remarks about the American military. Throughout Baruch's service in Germany, Baruch walked a fine line to stretch his funding to the maximum. Some people, in principle, refused to deal in the black market, but since Baruch had done so to help the survivors, he had no moral problem engaging in this activity. Abraham Hyman, the Assistant to the Advisor of Jewish Affairs and later the last advisor, understood Baruch's motives and protected him. But when the issue was brought to the authorities, they decided they could no longer turn a blind eye to this violation of the law.

In a letter to Samuel Sar, Abraham Horowitz mentioned a rumor that Baruch "had encountered trouble with the authorities in connection with cigarette dealings."[30] Baruch did not understand the reference to cigarettes since the Vaad was one of 10 relief organizations permitted by the Department of the Army to import tobacco into Germany.[31] In fact, after he had brought in a shipment from Belgium, and after Colonel Scithers ordered him to account for every cigarette, Baruch decided not to waste his time in this time-consuming project again. Baruch countered that it was possible that some DPs picked up by the military police for possession of contraband—whether cigarettes or other illegal items—claimed that they had gotten it from Baruch to divert blame from themselves.[32]

In the same letter to Sar, Horowitz reported "illicit dealings in merchandise which was brought to France ostensibly for the Vaad Hatzala. No doubt you are acquainted with that new chapter in the history of the Vaad Hatzala. I am told in connection with a certain fire that destroyed goods of the American Friendship Ship, a confession was made by a certain Kitiaitz in Paris that he received merchandise from Mr. Maurice Enright to be sold in the 'free' market, although it was shipped for Vaad Hatzala."[33] In the face of mounting irregularities, the die was cast. Rabbi Nathan Baruch's term as the Vaad Hatzala's representative in Germany was over.

Pincus Schoen was sent to Europe until the Vaad could

assess the future of the organization in Germany. At a meeting of the Vaad in New York on February 22, 1949, the executive committee decided to ask the IRO to renew its application for another year. Schoen advised them to do so at the suggestion of Harry Greenstein, the new Advisor on Jewish Affairs, who felt the Vaad should remain one more year because it was needed. The committee realized it would take that long to get the rabbis and yeshiva students out of Germany and into Israel.

The Vaad also agreed, at Rabbi Silver's urging, to maintain the rabbis and yeshiva students for three months once they arrived there because there were no services in the country to assist them. Rabbi Silver asked that a letter be sent to the Orthodox rabbis in the U.S. to ask them for funds, a portion of which would be sent to Israel.[34]

In March 1950, the Agudas Harabonim asked the Vaad to assume larger roles in specific areas. In Israel they were to provide assistance to the newly arrived rabbis and students and "help in their rehabilitation." In Europe they were to assist the *yeshivos* they helped to establish; to continue the immigration program for rabbis and yeshiva students; to assist children in Morocco who came from Orthodox backgrounds; to provide aid in other European countries with special emphasis on rabbis and students, and to solve the problem of intermarriage in Sweden.

In the U.S., the Vaad was asked to advise newly-arrived rabbis and students about job prospects, as they had done in Europe; to assist them to become American citizens, and to secure bonds for the release of those who might be detained at Ellis Island. A one million dollar budget was adopted to implement all these programs.[35]

In 1954, its post-war mission completed, the Vaad, at the request of the Chief Rabbinate in Israel, the *roshei yeshivos* and religious leaders fulfilled its last mission to raise funds to provide *seforim* for *yeshivos*, religious *kibbutzim* and *moshavim* (settlements) in Israel.[36]

The Vaad continued to work on a smaller scale and as the needs of the survivors decreased the organization eventually dissolved.

As for Baruch, after he returned to the U.S., he went into business with the assistance of William Alpert. He also continued to work with Rav Aharon to build Beis Medrash Gevoha in Lakewood, New Jersey, and assisted other religious institutions. He died in 2003.

Conclusion

In this volume, we have addressed three major issues: Whether the Vaad succeeded in achieving its objectives during the post-war era; the challenges it faced in trying to realize these goals, and the struggles within the Jewish community that thwarted its efforts.

That the Vaad succeeded in its mission can be seen by the number of people it helped send to North America and Israel; the number of religious institutions and children's homes it created and supported, and by the number of survivors who were personally helped. We will never know how many adults and children returned to a Torah way of life because of the Vaad, but we know that the Vaad helped thousands of Jews to do so.

In the weeks and months after the war, the DPs searched for ways to reconnect to the Jewish community, to reestablish their roots, to gain some stability in their lives. It was a period of transition, and some people opted out of Jewish observance, angry at a God who allowed their innocent loved ones to perish. There were also survivors who rebuilt Jewish life by establishing *yeshivos, mikvehs* and other religious institutions, and by once again eating kosher food. They studied Jewish texts and held regular *minyanim.* They started families and created social and political associations. The survivors took these initiatives by themselves despite the tribulations they had suffered because they were Jews, and that was a tribute to their determination to go on living a Jewish life. Religious life also provided an alternative for those unsure of what route to take with their lives.

With the arrival of the Vaad, observant survivors gravitated to its doors because they saw it as an organization that understood them. Baruch was their kindred spirit, one whose religious background and upbringing enabled him to understand and appreciate them. He spoke their language and was one of them. And most of all, because of his dedication, they trusted in his help as they waited on hated German soil until they could leave.

It was indeed fortunate for the Vaad that it had found a Nathan Baruch as its representative. Totally selfless, Baruch saw himself as the emissary of Rabbi Aharon Kotler, the driving spiritual and moral force behind the Vaad. Rav Aharon understood that in this transitional post-war period Jews needed to be immediately reconnected to Jewish tradition, Jewish learning and Jewish ritual for their spiritual healing. Without this urgent infusion of Orthodox Jewish life, Rabbi Kotler feared that the survivors would lose their faith. He threw the weight of his personality, scholarship and rabbinic authority behind the Vaad in spite of his lifelong connection to Agudath Israel in Europe and in the U. S. In the end, he saw the Vaad as the best vehicle to help the *She'erith Hapleitah.*[1]

Rav Aharon's insight into the religious needs of the survivors had a secondary effect as well. It played a vital and critical role in the revival of Orthodox Judaism in America in the post-war years. In this major undertaking—which continued long after Jews left Europe—Irving Bunim, Stephen Klein, William Alpert, Nathan Baruch and many others helped Rav Aharon.

In the post-war era the Orthodox community in the United States found the Vaad to be an organization it could turn to for help when it wanted to find relatives, to provide family members with funds and assist them to immigrate. By not using the regular European quotas to gain entry into the United States, the rabbis and yeshiva students did not compete with the other Jewish DPs for American visas. The Orthodox did not create the system—they worked it.

The Vaad had recognized that the demands of the survivors were so great that no Jewish or non-Jewish relief organizations working alone could possibly care for everyone. None of the other agencies had the understanding and appreciation for who the Orthodox were, the lives they had lived, and their commitment to Torah and observance of *mitzvos*. And so, with the Vaad in Europe, observant Jews had full-time advocates. Though a number of American Jewish chaplains and others had interceded on behalf of observant survivors, so much work had yet to be done that additional people were needed in Europe to make sure their needs were met.

Initially, the Vaad's aim was to assist the *b'nei Torah*, but it immediately became clear that they had to include any Jews who sought its aid. Though it was not in the Vaad's best interests to expand its mandate—because of limited resources and intrusion on areas deemed sacrosanct by the JDC and other agencies—the Vaad never turned anyone away. Some unknown Vaad writer summed it up:

> We do not compete with, nor do we duplicate the activities of any other agency or organization. No competition or duplication can be possible when we consider the tragedies of the many multitudes, their problems, their particular and specific needs. No one organization, no matter how authoritative its position, can assume the entire responsibility for solving this unprecedented catastrophe of our European Jewry. The Vaad Hatzala, by its methods and by its undaunted fiery spirit of stopping-at-

nothing, has blazed a trail for others to follow. This is a time for "Mesiras Nefesh [self-sacrifice]."[2]

Because of its willingness to stretch the rules, the Vaad Hatzala was able to accomplish a great deal more with limited funds than would have been otherwise possible.

Pressure to help other survivors also came from Vaad headquarters in New York. Lay leadership and donors continually demanded that Baruch help individuals who were not rabbis or yeshiva students thereby diffusing Baruch's efforts and resources. If Orthodox Jewish social workers, rabbis and other professionals had come to Europe from the United States to assist him, much more could have been done. Few, if any, volunteered and there was no concerted effort to recruit people because the Vaad did not have the money.

The Vaad writer continued:

> "If the Vaad Hatzala had had more funds during the past years, many more of our lost brothers would be alive today. While this must disturb our conscience and placidity of yesterday, it must and should serve as a moral lesson that we should not again be found with 'Too little and too late.'"[3]

With regard to the JDC, its leaders were correct that the work of aiding all the survivors fell within its purview, but the majority of the JDC's professional staff were secular Jews. As such, many of them saw no need to introduce Judaism into the DP camps because they did not expect religion to revitalize the Jews. Sports, theater, general education and vocational courses were offered, but Jewish learning was reserved for the few fervently Orthodox who were wedded to their old ways. This attitude in the rank and file of the JDC simply reflected the prevailing views of the time. Religion was passé; secularism was in vogue.

The JDC is also right when it says that it did not have

enough personnel or sufficient funds to respond to all of the needs of the survivors. American Jewry did not provide the money the JDC desperately required and repeatedly asked for in its appeals. Nor did enough American Jewish social workers go to Europe, despite the JDC's concerted efforts to enlist their help. Louis H. Sobel, assistant secretary of the JDC, complained that, "American Jewish social workers did not respond to the JDC's call for volunteers."[4]

In addition to the JDC's secular bias and lack of personnel, money was also a prime motivator. Sobel reported that the JDC "could not do a $60 million or a $75 million job with the $20 million made available in 1945, and it is beyond reasonable expectation to ask any organization to do that kind of job with the funds put at its disposal, and the responsibility for the frustration for that rests squarely upon the American Jewish community... American Jews were warned time and time again that the requirements and the needs were such that we needed untold millions more. The American Jews were told time and again that there were many things that were not being done for lack of funds."[5]

But this begs the question, if funds were at a premium, why did the JDC establish the COC as a separate organization that used community funds to assess the needs of the traditional Jews? Why couldn't JDC field representatives provide the information? Why didn't they just ask the survivors? Why did it take until mid-1948 for them to address these issues in a substantial way? Why didn't the JDC furnish people with this kind of help at the outset when Orthodox Jews began clamoring for these things after the liberation? If all of this had been addressed soon after the war, there would have been no need to set up the COC with personnel, a New York office, European headquarters and four regional field offices at a cost of $100,000 for 1947 and $150,000 for 1948.[6]

When the war ended, the JDC had the opportunity to hire American Jewish chaplains after they were discharged from the armed forces to help them with the DPs. This valuable human resource would have cost less than recruiting people in the United States. These chaplains were Reform,

Conservative and Orthodox rabbis already in Europe, who had been working with the survivors for many months. They understood their needs, had their respect and were eager to help. Since these men were already on site, the JDC did not have to pay for their transportation to Europe or provide them with any training. As Rabbi Alexander Rosenberg demonstrated, the JDC was quite capable of dealing with the needs of the observant DPs in a very significant way. Had the JDC enlisted the help of these equally knowledgeable workers to assist Rabbi Rosenberg, they could have obviated the need for the Vaad.

All the JDC had to do was ask, but it didn't accept most of those who did volunteer because the JDC wanted trained social workers with at least five years experience to work with the survivors. After working with JDC personnel, including the top professionals, Rabbi Abraham Klausner indicated that the JDC regarded the chaplains as "irritants" because only the JDC staff were experts and everyone else was viewed with contempt.[7]

Baruch's complaint was that the JDC wanted to be in charge of Jewish relief, but would not tolerate anyone or any institution that might upstage it. When the chaplains initiated a very successful package program, JDC officials tried to stop it, just as they tried to stop the Frankfurt Jewish GI Council from doing the same thing. Similarly, the Vaad Hatzala was considered an irritant to be neutralized or, failing that, destroyed. It had nothing to do with the Vaad being an Orthodox institution. The JDC did not discriminate, it wanted all Jewish relief organizations out of its way.

In the campaign to discredit the Vaad, the JDC found willing partners in the Mizrachi. The accusation that the Vaad favored the Agudah was never proven. It was just an excuse for Mizrachi to push its own agenda. As Irving Bunim observed: "It is regrettable that there is so much *sina'ath chinom* [baseless hatred] among our ranks...Were it not for the intercession of Satan, so much more could be done for our needy brethren. It seems that *Galuth* [the Diaspora] has severed us into little fragments and only those who see the light objectively and nobly can carry on."[8]

Hillel Lichtenstein, Rabbi of Krasna, confirmed the open nature of the Vaad in a letter to Baruch in August 1948. Just before he left Germany for France, he told Baruch he was deeply disturbed by the divisiveness within the Orthodox community because it hurt the survivors. The Vaad Hatzala, he wrote, is the only institution that "can...claim that from the day it was founded till now, that its sole purpose and all of its actions were only for the good of our brethren, the Torah observant children of Israel."

He went on to say that if American Jews were wise, they would understand and appreciate "the greatness" of the Vaad, which has "opened its doors to *every* [ed. emphasis mine] institution and every Torah observant individual." He continued his written statement with, "Surely everyone who valued the work of the Vaad would rush to be among its supporters...to glorify and elevate it."[9]

Rabbi Lichtenstein had never before favored or praised any institution or individual either in writing or verbally, yet here he insisted on strengthening the Vaad so it "should be in a position of authority and strength."[10]

If the JDC had been able to serve the needs of *all* the survivors, there would have been no need for the Vaad. But perhaps this was never really possible or realistic given the different priorities of these two organizations. The JDC had its mandate and within its financial, legal and personnel constraints and limitations, it did what its leadership considered feasible. And it should be very clear that without the JDC in Europe at the end of the war, there would have been much greater chaos and much greater suffering for the Jewish survivors.

The leadership of the Vaad was bound by *halacha* to help in the spiritual rehabilitation of the *She'erith Hapleitah*. Had they not done what they did, many more Jews would have severed their links with Judaism and perhaps with the Jewish people. Each organization had its own mission, its own priorities, and nothing could change that.

The proliferation of organizations in the American Jewish community during and after the war and in our present day reflects the diversity of the Jewish people and its diverse goals. It is the Jewish community's strength and at times its weakness. No more so was this evidenced than in post-Holocaust Germany.

INTRODUCTION - Endnotes

1. Yehuda Bauer, *Rethinking the Holocaust* (New Haven: Yale University Press, 2001): 246; Malcolm J. Proudfoot, *European Refugees* (London: Faber and Faber, 1957): 98-110.
2. Bauer: 246-247. Leo Schwarz, *The Root and Bough.* (New York: Rinehart and Company, 1949): 310; *Yiddisher Kempfer* 6.16.45; *Forward* 6.15. 45; *T'khias Hamesim.* 5.4.45, a newspaper published by the Jews in Buchenwald. World Jewish Congress Archives, New York: Drawer 272, No file number.
3. Bauer: 246; Lucjan Dobroszycki, "Restoring Jewish Life in Postwar Poland." *Soviet Jewish Affairs* London, 3 No. 1973: 58-60; Michael C. Steinlauf, *Bondage to the Dead: Poland and the Memory of the Holocaust* (Syracuse, New York: Syracuse University Press, 1997): 46-61.
4. Yisrael Gutman and Shumel Krakowski, *Unequal Victims: Poles and Jews During World War II.* (New York: Holocaust Library, 1986): 351-352
5. Gutman and Krakowski: 352.
6. Gutman and Krakowski: 352.
7. Gutman and Krakowski: 351-352.
8. Dorothy Rabinowitz, *New Lives: Survivors of the Holocaust Living in America* (New York: Alfred A. Knopf, 1976): 61; See

also Azriel Eisenberg. *Witness to the Holocaust* (New York: The Pilgrim Press, 1981): 504-523.

9. Gutman and Krakowski: 370-372.

10. Bauer: 246.

11. Gutman and Krakowski: 372-373.

12. Gutman and Krakowski: 372.

13. Michael J. Cohen, *Palestine Retreat from the Mandate* (New York: Holmes and Meier, 1978): 98-124; Morris Beckman, *The Jewish Brigade: An Army With Two Masters, 1944-45* (New York: Sarpedon Publishers, 1999).

14. Alex Grobman, *Rekindling the Flame: American Jewish Chaplains and the Remnants of European Jewry, 1944-1945* (Detroit, Michigan: Wayne State University Press, 1993): 2.

15. Yehuda Herzl Henkin, "Hagoen Yosef Eliyahu Henkin," in *HaDarom*, Chaim Dov, ed. Vol.50 Nissan (New York: Rabbinical Council of America, 1980):108-116.

16. Aaron Rakeffet-Rothkoff, *The Silver Era in American Jewish Orthodoxy: Rabbi Eliezer Silver and his Generation*, (New York: Yeshiva University Press and Feldheim Publishers, 1981): 155; "Agudat Israel" in the *Encyclopedia Judaica*. Jerusalem (Jerusalem: Keter Publishing House, 1972), vol: 22:422.

17. *Jewish Telegraphic Agency Daily News Bulletin* (J.T.A) 9.12.39:1,69. On September 17, 1939 the Soviet Union invaded Poland and on September 27, the Poles surrendered. On September 28, Germany and the Soviet Union signed the Molotov-Ribbentrop Non-Aggression Pact ceding eastern Poland to the Soviets, which became part of Belorussia and Ukraine. This area had been seized by the Soviets when the Germans invaded Poland. The area consisted of 75,675 square miles with a population of four to five million Poles including a Jewish population of 1.2 million. Dov Levin, *The Lesser of Two Evils: Eastern European Jewry Under Soviet Rule, 1939-1941* (Philadelphia, Pennsylvania: The Jewish Publication Society, 1995): 4-8.

18. Alex Grobman, "What Did They Know? The American Jewish Press and the Holocaust, 1 September 1939-17 December 1942," *American Jewish History*, March, 1979: 329.

19. Efraim Zuroff, *The Response of Orthodox Jewry in the United States to the Holocaust: The Activities of the Vaad ha-Hatzala Rescue Committee 1939-1945*, (New York: Yeshiva University Press and Hoboken, New Jersey: KTAV Publishing House, Inc., 2000): 26-27.

20. Zuroff: 24-25.

21. Yom Tov Porges, *Mirrer Yeshiva* (Bnei Brak: Mishor Publications, 2001): 390; Hillel Levine, *In Search for Sugihara* (New York: The Free Press, 1996): 195, 245-248, 256, 268; Zuroff: 25-26; David Kranzler interview and "The Grand Escape From Lithuania to Japan." *The Jewish Observer* June, 2000: 19-20; Efraim Zuroff, "Rescue Via The Far East: The Attempt To Save Polish Rabbis and Yeshivah Students, 1939-1941." *Simon Wiesenthal Center Annual* 1984 Volume 1: 153-162.

22. Jeffrey S. Gurock, "Resisters and Accomodators: Varieties of Orthodox Rabbis in America, 1886-1983," *American Jewish Archives* 1983:110,112-113; Aaron Rakeffet-Rothkoff, *Bernard Revel: Builder of American Jewish Orthodoxy* (New York: Feldheim Publisher, 1981): 14-15; Zuroff: 5.

23. Rakeffet-Rothkoff, *The Silver Era* 156-166; "Agudat Israel," 426; David Kranzler and Eliezer Gevirtz, *To Save A World.* (New York: CIS Publishers, 1991): 43-44.

24. Efraim Zuroff, "Va'ad Ha-Hatsala" (*Encyclopedia of the Holocaust* New York: Macmillan Library Reference 1990):1557-1558; Kranzler, "The Grand Escape From Lithuania to Japan" *The Jewish Observer* 19-20; Zuroff: "Rescue Via The Far East: The Attempt To Save Polish Rabbis and Yeshivah Students, 1939-1941," 153-162; David Kranzler, *Solomon Schonfeld: Holocaust Hero* (Jersey City, NJ: KTAV, 2004) 87,244.

25. Zuroff: "Va'ad Ha-Hatsala": 157-158.

26. Zuroff: "Va'ad Ha-Hatsala": 157-158.

27. Zuroff: 158.

28. Zuroff: 158.

29. Rakeffet-Rothkoff: 156; author interview with David Kranzler on February 13, 2001.

30. Rakeffet-Rothkoff: 156.

31. Rakeffet-Rothkoff: 161-162.

32. Arthur Hertzberg, ed. *The Zionist Idea: A Historical Analysis and Reader* (New York: Atheneum, 1969): 403, 399- 405, 434-435-439, 547-555.

33. Hertzberg: 402.

34. "Agudat Israel": 422; Hillel H. Ben-Sasson. *A History of the Jewish People* (Cambridge, Massachusetts: Harvard University Press, 1976): 901, 904, 906.

35. Rakeffet-Rothkoff: 163-166.

36. Rabbi Schnieerson (sic) to Dr. Cyrus Adler, February 2, 1927, Yeshiva University Archives Central Relief Committee (CRC), Box 102, Folder 4; CRC, Box 270, Folder 20; CRC, Box 269, Folder 7.

37. Maurice Eigen to Dr. Joseph J. Schwartz January 13, 1947 YIVO Archives Leo Schwarz Collection, Folder 244, Reel 22.

38. Leonard Dinnerstein, *America and the Survivors of the Holocaust*, (New York: Columbia University Press, 1982): 10.

39: Dinnerstein: 10.

40. Dinnerstein: 10-11.

41. Dinnerstein: 11-13; Proudfoot: 102-106; 133-140, 143-146.

42.Dinnerstein: 9-10.

43. Dinnerstein: 11-12.

44. Dinnerstein: 11-12.

45. Dinnerstein: 9.

46. Dinnerstein: 9.

47. Leo Schwarz, *The Root and the Bough* (New York: Rinehart and Company, 1949): 310.

48.Dinnerstein 13,28; Arieh J. Kochavi, *Post-Holocaust Politics: Britain, the United States and Jewish Refugees, 1945-1945* (Chapel Hill, North Carolina: North Carolina University Press, 2001): 276.

49. Dinnerstein: 13.

50. Author interviews with Rabbi Abraham Klausner, Dr. Marvin Linick, a Jewish GI and Ann Borden, a JDC representative in Germany. Oral History Division of the Institute of Contemporary Jewry, Hebrew University, Jerusalem.

51. Yehuda Bauer, *My Brother's Keeper: A History of the American Jewish Joint Distribution Committee 1929-1939* (Philadelphia, Pennsylvania: The Jewish Publication Society of America, 1974): 3, 6.

52. Naomi W. Cohen, *Not Free To Desist: A History of the American Jewish Committee 1906-1966* (Philadelphia, Pennsylvania: The Jewish Publication of America, 1972): 85.

53. Bauer: 3.

54. Bauer: 5.

55. Bauer: 4-5.

56. Bauer: 3.

57. Cohen: 85; Bauer: 6-7.

58. Cohen: 85.

59. Arthur Hertzberg, *The Jews in America: Four Centuries of an Uneasy Encounter* (New York: Simon and Schuster, 1989): 226; Cohen: 23-24.

60. Bauer: 5.

61. Bauer: 5.

62. Bauer: 5-6.

63. Cohen: 219, 221-222; Bauer 248.

64. Grobman: 39, 42-43, 65-67,72-77,106-108, 121.

65. Grobman: 20.

66. Abraham Klausner to author, November 24, 1989 (Author's file).

67. Report from Abraham J. Klausner, March 20, 1947 Abraham Hyman Archives.

68. Leo Schwartz to Joseph Schwartz, November 15, 1946, She'erith Hapleitah-Germany, YIVO, File 162.

69. Ephraim Zuroff: *The Response of Orthodox Jewry in the United States to the Holocaust: The Activities of the Vaad ha-Hatzala Rescue Committee 1939-1945* xxiii.

70. Zuroff: 52.

71. Zuroff: 52.

72. Dinnerstein: 201.

73. Dinnerstein: 202.

74. Michael Berenbaum to Professor Harry Reichler February 22, 2000, (Author's file).

75. Berenbaum.

76. Robert Reeve Brenner, *The Faith and Doubt of Holocaust Survivors* (New York: Free Press, 1980): 28, 38

77. Brenner: 37.

78. *Hapardes*, May 1945, Vol.19, No. 2: 9.

79. Rabbi Yekusiel Halberstam, *Shefa Chaim-Yar'each HaEitanim.* (Kiryat Sanz, Netanya): 239.

80. Author interview with Stanley Abramovitz, April 2003.

81.Rabbi Mozes Ruttner to American Jewish Joint Distribution Committee, July 21, 1947, JDC-NY Archives, JDC Collection 45164 File No. 3190.

CHAPTER 1 - Endnotes

1. Author interview with Nathan Baruch, June 25, 2000.

2. Author interview with Nathan Baruch, June 25, 2000.

3. M. Altshuler, "The Jewish Antifascist Committee in the USSR in the Light of New Documentation." *Studies in Contemporary Jewry,*1 (1984): 253-291. See also Shimon Redlich, *Propaganda and Nationalism Wartime Russia: The Jewish Antifascist Committee in the USSR, 1941-1948* (Boulder, Colorado: Eastern European Monographs, 1982); Yehuda Bauer, *"American Jewry and the Holocaust: The American Jewish Joint Distribution Committee, 1939-1945"* (Detroit, Michigan: Wayne State University Press, 1981): 297-298; William Korey, *The Soviet Cage: Anti-Semitism*

In Russia (New York: Viking Press, 1973): 34, 73; Joshua Rubenstein and Vladimir P. Naumov eds. *Stalin's Secret Pogrom: The Postwar Inquisition of the Jewish Anti-Fascist Committee* (New Haven, Connecticut: Yale University Press, 2001). The Jewish Anti-Fascist Committee, founded in April 1942, was one of several anti-fascist committees connected to the Soviet Propaganda Office. It was established to encourage the support of Jews throughout the world to aid the Soviet regime in its fight against the Nazis.

4. Author interview with Nathan Baruch, June 30,2000. For the reluctance of American Jewry to accept the authenticity of atrocity reports see Alex Grobman, "What Did They Know? The American Jewish Press and the Holocaust, 1 September 1939-December 1942." *American Jewish History* (March, 1979): 333. See also: Deborah Lipstadt, *Beyond Belief: The American Press and the Coming of the Holocaust 1933-1945* (New York: The Free Press, 1986); Yehuda Bauer, "When Did They Know?" *Midstream* 14 (1968): 51-57; Haskel Lookstein, *Were We Our Brother's Keepers?: The Public Response of American Jews to the Holocaust, 1938-1944* (New York: Vantage Books, 1985); David S. Wyman, *The Abandonment of the Jews: America and the Holocaust* (New York: Pantheon, 1984); Robert W. Ross, *So It Was True: The American Protestant Press and the Nazi Persecution of the Jews, 1933-1945* (Minneapolis, Minnesota: University of Minnesota Press, 1980); Marie Syrkin, "What American Jews Did During the Holocaust," *Midstream*, (October 1982) 6-12; Bernard Wasserstein, "The Myth of Jewish Silence." *Midstream* August/September (1980): 10-16.

5. David Kranzler, *Thy Brother's Blood: The Orthodox Jewish Response During the Holocaust*. (Brooklyn, New York: Mesorah Publications, 1967): 144.

6. Author interview with Nathan Baruch, June 25, 2000.

7. Rabbi Zvi Rotberg, director of Mishnas Rebbi Aaron Publications, to author May 13, 2003; Alter Pekier, *From Kletzk To Siberia: A yeshiva bachur's wanderings during the Holocaust* (Brooklyn, New York: Mesorah Publications, 1985): 48-52.

8. Rabbi Zvi Rotberg to author May 13, 2003; Holocaust Archives Beth Medrash Gevoha (BMG), File 9;

9. Rabbi Aharon Kotler to Rabbi Silver July 7, 1940 BMG File 11. See also Rakeffet-Rothkoff, *The Silver Era in American Jewish Orthodoxy*, 195.

10. Pekier: 48-52

11. David Kranzler, *Japanese, Nazis and Jews: The Jewish*

Refugee Community of Shanghai (New York: Yeshiva University, 1976) 144-145; Zuroff, *Response of Orthodox Jewry in the United States to the Holocaust: Vaad ha-Hatzala Rescue Committee*:136-137; Rakeffet-Rothkoff:204.

12. Author interview with Nathan Baruch, June 25, 2000.

13. Kranzler, *Thy Brother's Blood*: 144.

14. Author interview with Nathan Baruch, June 25, 2000.

15. Rakeffet-Rothkoff. *The Silver Era.* Author interview with Nathan Baruch, June 25, 2000.

16. Author interview with Nathan Baruch, June 25, 2000.

17. Louis Rapoport: *Shake Heaven and Earth: Peter Bergson And The Struggle To Rescue The Jews of Europe,* (Jerusalem: Gefen Publishing House, 1999): 109; Wyman: 153.

18. David S. Wyman and Rafael Medoff, *A Race Against Death: Peter Bergson, America, and the Holocaust* (New York: The New Press, 2002) p. 11.

19. Wyman: 341-343.

20. Author interview with Professor David Kranzler, Nov. 15, 2000; Henry L. Feingold, "Did American Jewry Do Enough During the Holocaust?" Syracuse University: The B.G. Rudolph Lectures in Judaic Studies, (April) 1985:14.

21. Kranzler: 71; Zuroff: 137.

22. Author interview with Nathan Baruch, June 25, 2000

23. Wyman, 152-153.Rakeffet-Rothkoff: 219-220.

24. Rapoport: 9; Henry L. Feingold, "Did American Jewry Do Enough During the Holocaust?": 15.

25. Wyman: 345-346.

26. David Wyman and Rafael Medoff, *A Race Against Death: Peter Bergson, America, and the Holocaust* (New York: The New Press, 2002):178; Rafael Medoff, *Militant Zionism in America* (Tuscaloosa and London: The University of Alabama Press, 2002.): 86-87.

27. David Wyman and Rafael Medoff, *A Race Against Death*: 144-145.

28. Saul S. Friedman, *No Have for the Oppressed: United States Policy Toward Jewish Refugees, 1938-1945* (Detroit, Michigan: Wayne State University Press, 1973): 148.

29. Wyman, *The Abandonment of the Jews*: 152.

30. Haskel Lookstein, *Were We Our Brother's Keepers?: The Public Response of American Jews to the Holocaust, 1938-1944* (New York: Vantage Books, 1985): 165-166; Rakeffet-Rothkoff, 219.

31. Congressional Record: Proceedings and Debates of the 78th Congress, First session, October 6, 1943, No. 147:11.

32. Rabbi Rotberg to author September 14, 2003
33. BMG, Holocaust File 10. All translations have been edited for clarity.
34. Congressional Record: 10.
35. Congressional Record: 7.
36. Congressional Record: 7.
37. Congressional Record: 9.
38. Congressional Record: 10.
39. Congressional Record: 9.
40. Congressional Record: 9.
41. Rapoport: 114. Medoff, *Militant Zionism in America*:106.
42. David S. Wyman and Rafael Medoff, *A Race Against Death: Peter Bergson, America, and the Holocaust*, p. 11.
43. Wyman and Medoff: 11-13.
44. Wyman and Medoff: 12, 48-55.
45. Wyman, *Abandonment of the Jews*: 178-192.
46. Rapoport: 112-113.
47. Rapoport: footnote 31, 245.
48. Wyman, *Abandonment of the Jews*: 347.

CHAPTER 2 – Endnotes

1. Henry Feingold "Did American Jewry Do Enough During the Holocaust?": 11.
2. The World Jewish Congress, for example, established the Institute of Jewish Affairs (IJA) in February 1941 under Jacob N. Robinson (director from 1941–1947), to assess the legal, political, and economic condition of world Jewry between 1916 and 1941, and to create a post-war policy to protect Jewish rights throughout the world. Also established in 1941 were the American Jewish Committee's Research Institute on Peace and Post-War Problems under Dr. Max Gottschalk, the Research Institute for Jewish Post-War Problems of the Jewish Labor Committee, and A Research Institute of the War Problems on Torah Jewry of the American branch of the Agudath Israel. Professor Salo W. Baron established Jewish Cultural Reconstruction, Inc. to identify, preserve and dispose of Jewish religious and ritual objects, libraries stolen by the Nazis. *The American Jewish Yearbook* (Philadelphia, Pennsylvania: The Jewish Publication Society) Vol.43 1941-1942): 736-751; *Contemporary Jewish Record*, April, 1941:110-125; *Congress Weekly*, 2.7.41: 4, 2.21.41:5-6; *The Jewish Spectator* March,

1941:6; *NYT,* 6.24.41:13, 12. 17.41:17; *Jewish Frontier,* March 1941:21-22; Naomi W. Cohen, *Not Free To Desist: The American Jewish Committee 1906-1966* (Philadelphia, Pennsylvania: The Jewish Publication Society, 1972): 265-266; Nathan Schachner, *The Price of Liberty: A History of the American Jewish Committee* (New York: American Jewish Committee, 1948):133-135.

3. David Kranzler, *Thy Brother's Blood:* 67. Wyman, *Paper Walls:* 137-154.

4. Varian Fry. *Surrender on Demand* (Boulder, Colorado: Johnson Books, 1997): xii; Andy Mario, *A Quiet American: The Secret War of Varian Fry* (New York: St. Martin's Press, 1999): 53-55. Kranzler: 67.

5. Wyman, *Paper Walls:* 141; Kranzler: 67;Yehuda Bauer. "Rescue Operations through Vilna," *Yad Vashem Studies* IX, 1973: 215; Efraim Zuroff "Rescue Priority and Fund Raising as Issues During the Holocaust: A Case Study of the Relations between the Vaad Ha-Hatzala and the Joint, 1939-1941" *American Jewish History,* March, 1979 Volume LXVIII, Number 3: 312-313. The exact number of rabbis, their families and yeshiva students in need of visas is not clear. David Kranzler states that there were approximately 2,800. Yehuda Bauer and Efraim Zuroff put this number at 2,440 yeshiva students and 171 rabbis. They also disagree about the number of *yeshivos* involved. Kranzler claims there were thirty *yeshivos*; Zuroff says there were twenty.

6. Kranzler: 67.

7. Kranzler: 67- 68.

8. Zuroff, "Rescue Priority and Fund Raising as Issues During the Holocaust": 312.

9. Bauer, "Rescue Operations through Vilna": 222.

10. Kranzler: *Thy Brother's Blood:* 69.

11. Brody, David, "American Jewry, The Refugees and Immigration Restriction 1932-1942," *American Jewish Historical Quarterly* (June 1956): 343-347. Kranzler: 69; David Kranzler: "Stephen S. Wise and the Holocaust." in *Reverence, Righteousness and Rahamanut.* Jacob J. Schacter, ed. (Northvale, New Jersey: Jason Aronson Inc., 1992): 158; See also Naomi S. Cohen, *Encounter With Emancipation: The German Jews in the United States 1830-1914* (Philadelphia: Jewish Publication Society, 1984): 110-114 and Moses Rischin, *The Promised City: New York's Jews, 1870-1914* (Cambridge, Massachusetts: Harvard University Press, 1977).

12. Brody: 220-227; Zosa Szajkowski, "The Attitude of American

Jews to Refugees from Germany in the 1930's," *American Jewish Historical Quarterly,* LXI. December, (1971); Feingold, "Did American Jewry Do Enough During the Holocaust?": 23-24.

13. Zosa Szajkowski, "The Attitude of American Jews to Refugees from Germany in the 1930's," *American Jewish Historical Quarterly,* LXI. December, (1971): 105.

14. Szajkowski: 105.

15. Szajkowski: 105.

16. Szajkowski: 106-107.

17. Szajkowski: 109-11.

18. Carl Hermann Voss, ed., *Stephen S. Wise: Servant of the People.* (Philadelphia, Pennsylvania: The Jewish Publication Society of America, 1969): 242.

19. Zuroff, "Rescue Priority and Fund Raising as Issues During the Holocaust": 313.

20. Kranzler: "Stephen S. Wise": 169.

21. Kranzler: 169.

22. Kranzler: 169.

23. Kranzler: 169.

24. Deborah Dash Moore, *At Home in America.* cited in David Kranzler: "Stephen S. Wise and the Holocaust," 170.

25. Kranzler: "Stephen S. Wise": 171.

26. Kranzler: 170.

27. Kranzler: 171.

28. Morris B. Abram, About UN Watch; www.unwatch.org/level2/mb.html.

29. Kranzler: "Stephen S. Wise and the Holocaust": 171.

30. The Resolution of the Agudath Harabonim Convention, no date, but from the text it is clear that it was written in 1939 (November), Yeshiva University Archives, Vaad Hatzala Collection, Box No. 216, Folder No.16; Shmuel Safrai "The Era of the Mishnah and Talmud (70-640)" in *A History of the Jewish People.* ed., H.H. Ben-Sasson (Cambridge, Massachusetts: Harvard University Press, 1976): 312.

31. Zuroff, *Rescue Priority and Fund Raising as Issues During the Holocaust:"* 308.

32. Kranzler, *Thy Brother's Blood*: 84-85.

33. Kranzler: 85.

34. Kranzler: 85.

35. Kranzler: 86.

36. Kranzler: 8; Rakeffet-Rothkoff: 173.

37. Kranzler: 87.

38. Kranzler: 87.
39. Kranzler: 87.
40. Kranzler: 87.
41. Kranzler: 88.
42. Henry Feingold: 7, 11.
43. Kranzler, *Stephen S. Wise and the Holocaust*: 181-182.
44. Kranzler: 181-182.
45. Kranzler: 181-183.
46. Bat-Ami Zucker, *In Search of Refuge: Jews and US Consuls in Nazi Germany 1933-1941*. (Portland, Oregon and London: Vallentine and Mitchell, 2001): 56-58.
47. Wyman, *Paper Walls*.
48. Henry L. Feingold. *The Politics of Rescue: The Roosevelt Administration and the Holocaust* (New Brunswick: Rutgers University Press, 1970): 142; Henry L. Feingold, "Who Shall Bear Guilt for the Holocaust: 266.
49. Zucker: 58.
50. Zucker: 59.
51. Zucker: 60.
52. Fred L. Israel, *The War Diary of Breckinridge Long: Selections from the Years 1939-1944*. (Lincoln, Nebraska: University of Nebraska Press, 1996): January 11, 1944 entry.
53. Interview with Rabbi Nathan Baruch: June 2000. Interview with Rabbi Zvi Rotberg.
54. Interview with Rabbi Nathan Baruch: September 2000.
55. Interview with Rabbi Nathan Baruch: September 2000.
56. Interview with Rabbi Zvi Rotberg June 22, 2003. *Numbers Rabbah* 16:1.
57. *Numbers Rabbah* 16:1. See also: Amos Bunim. *A Fire In His Soul: The Man and His Impact on American Orthodox Jewry*. (New York: Feldheim Publishers, 1989): 100-101.

CHAPTER 3 – Endnotes

1. Edward N. Peterson, *The American Occupation of Germany: Retreat to Victory*. (Detroit, Michigan: Wayne State University Press, 1977): 54-55.
2. William Hardy McNeill, *Survey of International Affairs 1939-1946* (New York: Oxford University Press, 1953): 582.
3. Peterson: 54.
4. Peterson: 86-87.
5. Alex Grobman, *In Defense of the Survivors: The Letters and*

Documents of Oscar A. Mintzer, AJDC Legal Advisor, Germany, 1945-46 (Berkeley, California: Judah L. Magnes Museum, 1999): 4-5; Alex Grobman, *Rekindling the Flame: American Jewish Chaplains and the Survivors of European Jewry, 1944-1948* (Detroit, Michigan: Wayne State University Press, 1993): 43-44.

6. Grobman, *In Defense of the Survivors*: 4-5; Grobman, *Rekindling the Flame*: 43-44 Leonard Dinnerstein, *America and the Survivors of the Holocaust* (New York: Columbia University Press, 1982): 13; Abraham Klausner, "A Detailed Report on the Liberated Jew as He Now Suffers His Period of Liberation Under the Discipline of the Armed Forces of the United States," June 24, 1945, (Author's file).

7. Grobman, *Rekindling the Flame*: 43-44; Dinnerstein, *America and the Survivors of the Holocaust*: 14; Peterson: 114-115.

8. W. Stawwell for F.E. Morgan to Rabbi Solomon Wohlgelernter, May 1, 1946. (RNB file).

9. James Brunot to Rabbi Abraham Kalmanowitz, no date (RNB file).

10. Brunot.

11. Brunot.

12. Brunot.

13. Brunot.

14. Rakeffet-Rothkoff, *The Silver Era:* 189-190; Zuroff, *Response of Orthodox Jewry in the United States to the Holocaust*: 53.

15. Rakeffet-Rothkoff: 226, 246.

16. Rakefett-Rothkoff: 225-226; Baruch interviews September 2000; Rabbi Nathan Baruch to William Alpert September 3, 1946. (Author's file). On May 8, 1945, Rabbi Silver said: "Messengers must be sent to uncover what actually transpired. The survivors must be encouraged to once again live in accordance with the dictates of the Torah. *Rabanim,* teachers and *shohatim* must be appointed for them. Comfort and aid must be generously extended since all is destroyed and uprooted. Even the cemeteries were not left intact. We must also redeem those children who sought refuge in the Christian institutions. We must prepare to extend remuneration, pray for success, and even be ready to fight for our rights" (Rakefett-Rothkoff: 225-226).

17. Rabbi Nathan Baruch to William Alpert, September 3, 1946. (Author's file)

18. Rabbi Nathan Baruch to William Alpert, September 3, 1946. (Author's file)

19. Rabbi Nathan Baruch to William Alpert, September 3, 1946. (Author's file)

20. Interviews with Rabbi Nathan Baruch, September 2000.

21. Rabbi Nathan Baruch to William Alpert, September 15, 1946 (Author's file).

22. Interviews with Rabbi Nathan Baruch, September 2000.

23. Interviews with Rabbi Nathan Baruch, September 2000.

24. Rabbi Nathan Baruch to William Alpert, September 15, 1946. (Author's file)

25. Rabbi Nathan Baruch to William Alpert, September 15, 1946. (Author's file)

26. Rabbi Nathan Baruch to William Alpert, September 15, 1946. (Author's file)

27. Rabbi Nathan Baruch to William Alpert September 15, 1946. Alpert responded to the letter on October 4, 1946 to assure him that he would send all the items Baruch had requested. (Author's file).

28. Rabbi Nathan Baruch to Irving Bunim, November 3, 1946. (RNB file).

29. Rabbi Nathan Baruch to Irving Bunim, November 3, 1946.

30. Rabbi Nathan Baruch to Irving Bunim, November 3, 1946.

31. Rabbi Nathan Baruch to Irving Bunim, November 3, 1946.

32. Rabbi Nathan Baruch to Irving Bunim, November 3, 1946; H.V. Lerner to Rabbi Nathan Baruch September 21, 1946 (RNB file).

33. Rabbi Nathan Baruch to Irving Bunim November 3, 1946.

34. Judith Arond to Rabbi Nathan Baruch, May 21, 1947 (RNB file).

35. Rabbi Nathan Baruch to Irving Bunim, November 3, 1946

36. Rabbi Nathan Baruch to Irving Bunim, November 3, 1946. Mr. Mannes Zytnicki, a member of the Presidium of the Agudath Israel central office in Salzburg, Austria and a leading activist, made many of these same observations. See Joseph Friedenson and David Kranzler *Heroine of Rescue: The Incredible Story of Recha Sternbuch Who Saved Thousands From the Holocaust* (New York: Mesorah Publications, Ltd, 1984): 182-184.

37. Rabbi Nathan Baruch to Irving Bunim, November 3, 1946.

38. Rabbi Nathan Baruch to Irving Bunim, November 3, 1946.

39. Rabbi Nathan Baruch to Irving Bunim, November 3, 1946.

40. Rabbi Nathan Baruch to Irving Bunim, November 3, 1946.

41. Rabbi Nathan Baruch to Irving Bunim, November 3, 1946.

42. Rabbi Nathan Baruch to Irving Bunim, November 3, 1946.

43. Rabbi Nathan Baruch to Irving Bunim November 3, 1946.

44. Rabbi Nathan Baruch to Irving M. Bunim, December 9, 1946 (RNB file).

45. Rabbi Nathan Baruch to Irving M. Bunim, December 9, 1946.

46. Rabbi Nathan Baruch to Irving M. Bunim, December 9, 1946.

47. Supper Meeting of the Plan and Scope Committee November 6, 1946; Jonathan Helfand, editor. *Archives of the Holocaust: An International Collection of Selected Documents,* Volume 18. Yeshiva University, New York, February 5, 1947 [15 Shevat 5707] (New York and London, Garland Publishing, Inc., 1991): 227.

48. Alex Grobman. *Rekindling the Flame: American Jewish Chaplains and the Survivors of European Jewry, 1944*-1948, (Detroit: Wayne State University Press, 1993): 123-129.

49. "Oscar M. Lifschutz to Agudah Israel," Agudah Israel Archives, London, March 26, 1946.

50. Ronald Webster, "American Relief and Jews in Germany, 1945-1960" (New York: Leo Baeck Institute, 1993): 295.

51. Judith Baumel, "The Politics of Spiritual Rehabilitation in the DP Camps." *Simon Wiesenthal Center Annual,* Vol. 6, 1989: 5.

52. Interviews with Rabbi Nathan Baruch, September 2000.

53. Koppel S. Pinson, General Directives For Educational Program AJDC in Germany and Austria, April 15, 1946. (Author's file)

54. Pinson, General Directives.

55. Pinson, General Directives.

56. Pinson, General Directives.

57. Pinson, General Directives.

58. Pinson, General Directives.

59. Pinson, General Directives.

60. Pinson, General Directives.

61. "Report of Education Survey-American Zone Third Army Are Germany," December 26, 1945-January 5, 1946, Yeshiva University Archives, Vaad Hatzala Collection, Box No. 214, Folder No. 4. For the past eight years Joslow served as chairman of the Board of Education of the United Hebrew Schools in Springfield, Massachusetts. "Minutes of the Cultural Committee, October 15, 1945," JDC-NY, JDC Collection 45164, File No.3391.

62. Report of Education Survey.

CHAPTER 4 - Endnotes

1. Minutes of meeting held at McAlpin Hotel, March 6, 1946, Jonathan Helfand: editor, *Archives of the Holocaust*: 187-188.
2. Helfand: 188.
3. Helfand: 188.
4. Helfand: 188.
5. Helfand: 189.
6. Helfand: 190.
7. Helfand: 191.
8. Rabbi Jacob Rosenheim to Irving Bunim, March 21, 1946; Helfand: 192.
9. Helfand: 192.
10. Irving Bunim to Rabbi Jacob Rosenheim, July 2, 1946; Helfand: 203.
11. Irving M. Bunim to Mr. I. Sternbuch July 31, 1946; Helfand: 214.
12. Irving Bunim to Agudath Israel of America August 20, 1946; Helfand: 216.
13. Helfand: 216.
14. Supper Meeting of the Plan and Scope Committee, November 6, 1946: Helfand: 228.
15. Helfand: 229.
16. Helfand: 229.
17. Menachem Glickman-Porush, *Ish Ha'halacha V'hamaseh: Rabbi Eliezer Silver, Shlita,* Jerusalem: Sapira 1946-1947.
18. Executive Meeting of the Vaad Hatzala November 26, 1946; Helfand: 231.
19. Helfand: 231; *Vaad Hatazla Bulletin*, June 12 and June 28, 1946 (RNB file).
20. Excerpt from Certificate of Incorporation of Rescue Children, Inc., July 24, 1946. (Author's file).
21. Helfand: 232.
22. Helfand: 232.
23. Helfand: 232.
24. Helfand: 234.
25. Helfand: 233.
26. Pincus Schoen to Helen Lavalle, October 1, 1946, Yeshiva University Archives Vaad Hatzala Collection, Box No. 3, File 16.
27. Helen Lavalle to Pincus Schoen, September 13, 1946 Yeshiva University Archives Vaad Hatzala Collection, Box No. 3, File 16.

28. Interview with his son, George Klein, January 12, 2001.
29. Invitation signed by Irving Bunim to Vaad Hatzala supporters September 13, 1946.Yeshiva University Archives, Vaad Hatzala Collection, Box No. 13, File 1.
30. Pincus Schoen to Stephen Klein, October 25, 1946, Yeshiva University Archives Vaad Hatzala Collection, Box No. 13, Folder No. 1.
31. Schoen to Klein.
32. Schoen to Klein.
33. Schoen to Klein.
34. Stephen Klein to Benjamin Pechman, December 13, 1946, Yeshiva University Archives, Vaad Hatzala Collection, Box No. 13, File 1.
35. Klein to Benjamin Pechman.
36. Klein to Benjamin Pechman
37. Klein to Benjamin Pechman.
38. Klein to Vaad Hatzala, December 21, 1946.
39. Stephen Klein to Pincus Schoen, November 17, 1946, Yeshiva University Archives, Vaad Hatzala Collection, Box No.13, Folder 1.
40. Klein to Benjamin Pechman.
41. Copies of cables sent by Stephen Klein, no date. Yeshiva University Archives, Vaad Hatzala Collection, Box No.13, Folder 1. We know that this is when Klein began sending these telegrams because he wrote to Irving Bunim on December 13, 1946 and mailed on the 15th that he had started "to send out telegrams and letters to our friends for funds and supplies. The first letter I sent out was to Benny Pechman for food. If his delivery of these supplies will be rightly [sic] organized a big part of the Vaad Hatzala program should be done with supplies." Stephen Klein to Irving Bunim, December 15, 1946, Yeshiva University Archives, Vaad Hatzala Collection, Box No. 13, File 1.
42. Copies of cables sent by Stephen Klein.
43. Copies of cables sent by Stephen Klein.
44. Copies of cables sent by Stephen Klein.
45. Stephen Klein to Vaad Hatzala, December 21, 1946, Yeshiva University Archives, Vaad Hatzala Collection, Box No.13, Folder 1.
46. Proposed talk of Mr. Stephen Klein: 4.
47. Klein to Vaad Hatzala, December 21, 1946.
48. Klein to Vaad Hatzala, December 21, 1946.
49. Klein to Irving Bunim, December 15, 1946.
50. Irving Bunim to Stephen Klein, November 15, 1946, Vaad Hatzala supporters September 13, 1946. Yeshiva University Archives, Vaad Hatzala Collection, Box No. 13, File 1.

51. Bunim to Klein, November 15, 1946.
52. Bunim to Klein, November 15, 1946.
53. Dinnerstein, *America and the Survivors*:11.
54. Klein to Bunim, December 15, 1946.
55. Klein to Schoen, November 17, 1946.
56. Klein to Irving Bunim, December 15, 1946, dictated December 13, 1946.
57. Klein to Vaad Hatzala, December 21, 1946.
58. Klein to Schoen, November 17, 1946.
59. Klein to Bunim,December 15, 1946.
60. Klein to Vaad Hatzala, December 21, 1946.
61. Klein to Vaad Hatzala, December 21, 1946.
62. Klein to Vaad Hatzala, December 21, 1946.
63. Klein to Vaad Hatzala, December 21, 1946.
64. Irving Bunim to Stephen Klein, November 8, 1946, Yeshiva University Archives, Vaad Hatzala Collection, Box No. 13, File 1. Interview with Rabbi Nathan Baruch.
65. Klein to Vaad Hatzala, December 21, 1946.
66. Klein to Vaad Hatzala, December 21, 1946
67. Klein to Vaad Hatzala, December 21, 1946.
68. Klein to Vaad Hatzala, December 21, 1946.
69. Samuel L. Sar to Rabbi Alexander Rosenberg, August 8, 1946, YIVO Archives, Leo Schwarz Collection, Folder 247, Reel 22.
70. Klein to Vaad Hatzala, December 21, 1946.
71. Stephen Klein to Vaad Hatzala, December 25, 1946, Yeshiva University Archives, Vaad Hatzala Collection, Box No.13, Folder 1.
72. Pincus Schoen to Stephen Klein, December 5, 1946, Yeshiva University Archives, Vaad Hatzala Collection, Box No. 13, File 1; Pincus Schoen to Stephen Klein, December 23, 1946, Yeshiva University Archives, Vaad Hatzala Collection, Box No. 13, File 1; Pincus Schoen to Stephen Klein, December 31, 1946, Yeshiva University Archives, Vaad Hatzala Collection, Box No. 13, File 1; Pincus Schoen to Stephen Klein, January 8, 1947, Yeshiva University Archives, Vaad Hatzala Collection, Box No. 13, File1.
73. Rabbi Jacob Karlinsky to Stephen Klein, December 4, 1946, Yeshiva University Archives, Vaad Hatzala Collection, Box No. 13, File 1.
74. Rabbi Jacob Karlinsky to Stephen Klein, November 27, 1946, Yeshiva University Archives, Vaad Hatzala Collection, Box No. 13, File 1.
75. Pincus Schoen to Stephen Klein, January 24,1947 Yeshiva University Archives, Vaad Hatzala Collection, Box no, 13, File 1.

76. Stephen Klein to Irving Bunim, December 15, 1946, dictated December 13, 1946, Yeshiva University Archives, Vaad Hatzala Collection, Box No. 13, File 1.
77. Klein to Schoen, November 17, 1946.
78. Stephen Klein to Herbert Tenzer, no date, Yeshiva University Archives, Vaad Hatzala Collection, Box No. 13, File 1.
79. Reported conversation between Irving M. Bunim and Stephen Klein, December 9, 1946, Yeshiva University Archives, Vaad Hatzala Collection, Box No. 13, File 1.
80. Irving Bunim to Stephen Klein, December 5, 1946, Yeshiva University Archives, Vaad Hatzala Collection, Box No. 13, File 1.
81. Pincus Schoen to Stephen Klein, December 5, 1946, Yeshiva University Archives, Vaad Hatzala Collection, Box No. 13, File 1.
82. Irving Bunim to Stephen Klein, December 11, 1946, Yeshiva University Archives, Vaad Hatzala Collection, Box No. 13, File 1.; Rakeffet-Rothkoff: 252.
83. Irving Bunim to Stephen Klein, January 3, 1947, Yeshiva University Archives, Vaad Hatzala Collection, Box No. 13, File 1.
84. Stephen Klein to Irving Bunim, December 15, 1946, dictated December 13, 1946, Yeshiva University Archives, Vaad Hatzala Collection, Box No. 13, File 1.
85. Stephen Klein to Irving Bunim, December 15, 1946, dictated December 13, 1946. Yeshiva University Archives, Vaad Hatzala Collection, Box No. 13, File 1.
86. Rabbi Nathan Baruch to William Alpert January 28, 1947, (RNB file).
87. Rabbi Jacob Karlinsky to Stephen Klein August 6, 1946, Yeshiva University Archives, Vaad Hatzala Collection, Box No. 13. File 1.
88. Rabbi Saul Lasher to Stephen Klein May 31, 1946, Yeshiva University Archives, Vaad Hatzala Collection, Box No. 13, File 1.
89. Gertrude H. Gould to Stephen Klein, May 1, 1946, Yeshiva University Archives Vaad Hatzala Collection, Box No. 13, File 1.
90. Proposed talk of Mr. Stephen Klein on Chana Spector's Program WEVD, Yeshiva University Archives, Vaad Hatzala Collection, Box No.3, folder 16, 1-2.
91. Proposed talk of Mr. Stephen Klein, 4.
92. Proposed talk of Mr. Stephen Klein, 3.

93. Helfand: 256.
94. Helfand: 256.
95. Helfand: 256.
96. Helfand: 256.
97. Helfand: 256.
98. Helfand: 260.
99. Helfand: 260.
100. Helfand: 260.
101. Helfand: 260.
102. Helfand: 260.
103. Helfand: 260.
104. Helfand: 260.
105. Helfand: 260.
106. Helfand: 263.
107. Helfand: 263.
108. Helfand: 265.
109. Helfand: 265.
110. Helfand: 265.
111. Helfand: 265.

Chapter 5 - Endnotes

1. Interview with Rabbi Nathan Baruch, June 25 and June 30, 2000.
2. Interview with Rabbi Nathan Baruch, June 25 and June 30, 2000.
3. Abraham Hyman, *The Undefeated* (Jerusalem, Gefen, 1993): 290-291.
4. Interviews with Rabbi Nathan Baruch, June 25 and June 30, 2000.
5. Pincus Schoen to Rabbi Nathan Baruch, February 6, 1948 (RNB file).
6. Interviews with Rabbi Nathan Baruch.
7. Lee Stein to Rabbi Nathan Baruch April 17, 1947. RNB file; Pincus Schoen to Rabbi Nathan Baruch, May 13, 1947 (RNB file); Pincus Schoen to Rabbi Nathan Baruch, January 8, 1948 (RNB file); Pincus Schoen to Rabbi Nathan Baruch, July 6, 1948 (RNB file); Irving M. Bunim to Rabbi Nathan Baruch, March 8, 1948 (RNB file).
8. Rabbi Tuvia (Tobias) Geffen to Rabbi Nathan Baruch, August 13, 1947; Rabbi Tuvia (Tobias) Geffen to Rabbi Nathan Baruch, November 20, 1947 (RNB file); Irving Bunim to Rabbi Nathan

Baruch, October 31, 1947 ((RNB file); Gertrude Gould to Rabbi Nathan Baruch, January 14, 1947 (RNB file); Irving Bunim to Rabbi Nathan Baruch, January 23, 1947, (RNB file); Congressman Frank Karsten to Rabbi Nathan Baruch, January 24, 1947. (RNB file); Gertrude Gould to Rabbi Nathan Baruch, February 11, 1947 (RNB file); Rabbi Jacob Karlinsky to Rabbi Nathan Baruch, February 24, 1947, (RNB file); Gertrude Gould to Rabbi Nathan Baruch, April 22, 1947 (RNB file); Gertrude Gould to Rabbi Nathan Baruch, May 5, 1947, (RNB file); Rabbi Jacob Karlinsky to Rabbi Nathan Baruch, July 8,1947 (RNB file); Rabbi Jacob Karlinsky to Rabbi Nathan Baruch, August 1, 1947, (RNB file); Samuel Schmidt to Rabbi Nathan Baruch, September 4, 1947 (RNB file); Pincus Schoen to Rabbi Nathan Baruch, September 22, 1947 (RNB file); Rabbi S. Pardes to Rabbi Nathan Baruch, November 28, 1947 (RNB file); Rabbi Samuel Chill to Rabbi Nathan Baruch, January 21, 1948 (RNB file); Irving Bunim to Rabbi Nathan Baruch, March 8, 1948 (RNB file); Rabbi L. Seltzer to Rabbi Nathan Baruch, April 22, 1948 (RNB file); Rabbi Philip Harris Singer to Rabbi Nathan Baruch, June 17, 1948 (RNB file); Pincus Schoen to Rabbi Nathan Baruch, August 11, 1948 (RNB file).
9. Pincus Schoen to Rabbi Nathan Baruch, August 25, 1947 (RNB file).
10. Pincus Schoen to Rabbi Nathan Baruch, February 10, 1948 (RNB file); Pincus Schoen to Rabbi Nathan Baruch, January 8, 1948 (RNB file).
11. Pincus Schoen to Rabbi Nathan Baruch, January 8, 1948 (RNB file).
12. Pincus Schoen to Rabbi Nathan Baruch, April 9, 1948 (RNB file).
13. Schoen to Rabbi Baruch, April 9, 1948 (RNB file); Pincus Schoen to Rabbi Nathan Baruch, January 9, 1947, (RNB file); Rabbi Maurice Lyons to Rabbi Nathan Baruch, August 28, 1947;Rabbi Jacob Karlinsky to Rabbi Nathan Baruch, June 16, 1947. (RNB file); Rabbi Maurice Lyons to Rabbi Nathan Baruch, March 23, 1948 (RNB file); Telegram 053 from Rabbi Jacob Karlinsky to Rabbi Nathan Baruch, no date (RNB file); Telegram 09 from Rabbi Eliezer Silver and Dr. Samuel Schmidt to Rabbi Nathan Baruch, no date, (RNB file). Telegram 022 from Rabbi Eliezer Silver and Dr. Samuel Schmidt to Rabbi Nathan Baruch, no date, (RNB file); Telegram 041 from Dr. Samuel Schmidt to Rabbi Nathan Baruch no date, (RNB file); Telegram 098 from Eleanor Bohne for Schmidt to Rabbi Nathan Baruch, no date,

(RNB file); Bernard Bergman to Rabbi Nathan Baruch March 29, 1948. (RNB file); Gertrude Gould to Rabbi Nathan Baruch, June 18, 1948 (RNB file); Lee Stein to Rabbi Nathan Baruch, July 26, 1948 (RNB file).

14. Samuel Schmidt to Rabbi Nathan Baruch, November 10, 1947 (RNB file); Samuel Schmidt to Rabbi Nathan Baruch, October 14, 1947 (RNB file).

15. Lee C. Dowling to Messrs. Tenzer, Greenblatt, Fallon and Kaplan August 21, 1946 Rescue Children Inc., Collection Yeshiva University Archives Box 13 folder No.20; Certificate of Incorporation of Rescue Children, Collection Yeshiva University Archives Box13 folder No. 20;Alizah Zinberg, Barbara Martin and Rodger Kohn. Inventory to the Rescue Children, Inc. Collection 1946-1985. Yeshiva University Archives: 17; Vaad Hatzalah Bulletin June 28, 1946. In June 1946, Herbert Tenzer formed Rescue Children, Inc. as an independent organization and received a charter incorporating it as a New York organization in October 1946.

16. Inventory: 19.

17. D. R. Bittan to Dr. Nathan Baruch, August 18, 1947, (RNB file).

18. Esther Donner to Rabbi Nathan Baruch, June 17, 1947, (RNB file).

19. Gertrude Schoenhof to Rabbi Nathan Baruch, June 20, 1947 (RNB file); William Z. Novick to Rabbi Nathan Baruch, July 9, 1947 (RNB file); William Z. Novick to Rabbi Nathan Baruch, June 6, 1947 (RNB file).

20. Hyman: 290-291.

21. Report of Rabbi Nathan Baruch to the Board of the Vaad Hatzala, September 1948:1 (RNB file).

22. Baruch to the Board of the Vaad Hatzala: 2.

23. Baruch to the Board of the Vaad Hatzala: 3.

24. Report of Rabbi Nathan Baruch to the Board of the Vaad Hatzala, September 1948:3 (RNB file).

25. *Hapardes*, June 1947:325.

26. Baruch interview, September 2000.

27. Baruch, September 2000.

28. Baruch, September 2000.

29. Baruch, September 2000. David Kranzler and Eliezer Gevirtz, *To Save A World*. (New York: CIS, 1991, 1995); Nathan Baruch to Vaad Hatzalah, October 1946, Yeshiva University Collection, Box 4, Folder No.35. Members of the committee included such prominent *roshei yeshiva* as Rabbis Yechezkel Sarna, Eliezer

Yehuda Finkel of the Mir Yeshiva, Isser Zalman Meltzer, Chezkiah and Yosef Mishkowsky.

30. Kranzler and Gevirtz: 196.

31. Kranzler and Gevirtz, 198; David Kranzler, *The Man Who Stopped The Trains to Auschwitz: George Mantello, El Salvador and Switzerland's Finest Hour* (Syracuse, New York: Syracuse University Press, 2000): 231-232. Griffel also worked with Rabbi Avigdor Vorhand of Prague and the Skulener Rebbe to help Jews leave Poland and other countries under Communist control. He managed to acquire 1,000 blank Salvadoran citizenship papers from George Mantello, a Jewish diplomat in El Salvador's Consulate in Geneva, Switzerland. An entire family could use each document, so approximately 5,000 to 6,000 people could be helped. Griffel brought the Salvadoran papers to Prague where Rabbi Vorhand used his influence in the Czech government to assist thousands of Jews to enter the city. From Prague they were helped to immigrate to other countries in the West. These papers were especially valuable because the British did not view them as an illegal means for Jews to go to Palestine. Italian visas, on the other hand, were suspect since they knew Jews could make their way from Italy to *Eretz Israel*.

32. Report of Philip S. Bernstein, Advisor on Jewish Affairs U.S. Zones, Europe: May 1946 to August 1947: 4 (Author's file).

33. Michael Brenner, *After The Holocaust: Rebuilding Jewish Lives In Postwar Germany* (Princeton, New Jersey: Princeton University Press, 1995): 52-53; William Haber to the American Jewish Committee, American Jewish Conference, American Jewish Distribution Committee, Jewish Agency for Palestine and World Jewish Congress December 20, 1948: 21.

34. Brenner: 54.

35. Brenner: 54-5.

36. Brenner: 55.

37. William Haber to American Jewish Committee, Jewish Agency for Palestine, American Jewish Distribution Committee, American Jewish Committee and World Jewish Congress, June 10, 1948: 11. (Author's file).

38. Haber: 11-12 (Author's file).

39. Haber: 11-12 (Author's file).

40. William Haber to the American Jewish Committee, American Jewish Conference, American Jewish Distribution Committee, Jewish Agency for Palestine and World Jewish Congress, December 20, 1948: 21.

41. Haber:21.

42. Haber: 21.

43. Haber: 21-22.

44. "U.S. Military Admits Guilt of Soldiers Who Assaulted Jewish DPs," American Jewish Outlook, May 2, 1947; "American Military Police Attack Munich Agudist Conference. Rabbis Injured," *The Jewish Weekly* May 2,1947; "MPs in Germany Assault Rabbis at Meeting," *Trends of Events*, May 2, 1947.

45. Interview Rabbi Nathan Baruch.

46. Interview with Rabbi Nathan Baruch.

47. Haber, June 10, 1948: 7. (Author's file); William Haber to the American Jewish Committee, American Jewish Conference, American Jewish Distribution Committee, Jewish Agency for Palestine and World Jewish Congress, February 24, 1948: 3-4.

48. Haber, June 10, 1948: 7. (Author's file); Haber, February 24, 1948: 3-4.

49. Haber, December 20, 1948: 8.

50. Haber, December 20, 1948: 8.

51. Mark Wyman, *DP: Europe's Displaced Persons: 1945-1951* (Ithaca, New York: Cornell University Press, 1989), 173-174. Abraham Hyman knew of many examples of "personal acts of kindness...almost to the point of saintliness" on the part of American GIs. This was especially true with soldiers assigned to work with the DPs. They were, however, a small percentage of those who had contact with the DPs. "In the main," he noted, the American soldiers "were hostile. Won over to the Germans. There was hardly any fraternization between soldiers and DPs." If the "army is to be criticized for anything," it was its lack of imagination in dealing with the Jews. "Without sacrificing either efficiency or moral position," they could have acted with more understanding and empathy. In some dealing with the DPs, the army did not take into account the background of these people. The raids on the camps hurt the Jews, but also the army's mission by showing the Germans that their views of the Jews were correct. They failed to show the Germans "that Jews are part of humanity." Statement by Abraham Hyman, nd. (Abraham Hyman Archives).

52. Haber, June 10, 1948: 7-8.

53. Statement by Lieutenant-Colonel Jerry M. Sage, United States Army, Headquarters of European Command, Frankfurt, Germany, Before the House and Subcommittee on Immigration and Naturalization, July 2. 1947, 6. (Author's file).

54. Statement by Lieutenant-Colonel Jerry M. Sage.

55. Hyman: 290-291.

56. Haber: June 10, 1948: 13.
57. Haber: June 10, 1948: 13.
58. Hyman: 293.
59. Hyman: 294.
60. Interview with Rabbi Nathan Baruch, September 2000.
61. Abraham Klausner, "Jewish Displaced Persons in the American Occupied Zone of Germany" to American Jewish Conference, May 1948: 2. (Author's file).
62. Edward N. Peterson, *The American Occupation of Germany: Retreat to Victory* (Detroit: Wayne State University Press, 1977) 91-92.
63. Peterson: 91.
64. Peterson: 91.
65. Rabbi Nathan Baruch to Pincus Schoen, June 10, 1947 (RNB file.)
66. Daniel Adelson to Rabbi Nathan Baruch May 21,1948 (RNB file). See also John C. Parker, To Whom It May Concern, October 23, 1947 (RNB file).
67. Stephen Klein to Rabbi Nathan Baruch. March 12, 24, 28, 1947; April 8, 14, 1947; May 5, 6, 23, 1947; June 30, 1947; March 31, 1948; July 30, 1948. (Author's file); Pincus Schoen to Rabbi Nathan Baruch May 16, 1947, July 23, 1947, April 14, 1948, July 9, 1948; Irving Bunim to Rabbi Nathan Baruch, April 18, 1947 (RNB file).
68. Amos Bunim, *Fire In His Soul: Irving Bunim 1901-1980*: 348-349, footnote 30. In adhering to this philosophy, Alpert followed in his father's tradition by sending $500.00 before Passover and other holidays to the Chief Rabbi of Jerusalem, Rabbi Zvi Pesach Frank. This was meant for distribution to individuals. Baruch discovered this altruism years later when he visited Rabbi Frank in Israel. Though William Alpert was a mainstay of the Vaad during the war, he continued his support of its institutions (i.e., Rabbi Kotler's Lakewood Yeshiva) for many years thereafter.
69. Irving Bunim to Rabbi Nathan Baruch, March 16, 1947 (RNB file).
70. Gertrude Gould to Rabbi Nathan Baruch, February 25, 1947 (RNB file).
71. Gertrude Gould to Rabbi Nathan Baruch, April 3, 1947 (RNB file).
72. Gould, April 3, 1947. Gertrude Gould to Rabbi Nathan Baruch, June 20, 1947; Gertrude Gould to Rabbi Nathan Baruch, April 16, 1947; Gertrude Gould to Rabbi Nathan

Baruch, February 11, 1947 (RNB file). See also Yiddish newspapers like *Der Tog* (July 9, 1948, July 15, 1948, September 16, 1948), the *Morgen Journal* (May 1, 1947, May 9, 1947; February 27, 1948; July 9, 1948; August 12, 1948; September 14, 1948; September 15, 1948; September 16, 1948; September 17, 1948; September 30, 1948) *Der Americaner* ("*Yiddishe News Fun Der Ganza Veld*," May 2, 1947), *Der Wochenzietung* (*Jewish Weekly*, February 27, 1948), *Yiddishe Stimme* and the *Yiddisher Zeitung* carried articles and pictures about the Vaad's work as did the Anglo-Jewish press. Articles, for example, appeared in *Hapardes* (November, 1947), *The B'nei Brith Messenger of Los Angeles* (April 4, 1947), *Every Friday* in Cincinnati ("286 Yeshiva Boys," March 4, 1947; "On The Way From Frankfurt To Paris," March 5, 1947; "A Holy Cause," December 10, 1948); the *Hebrew Journal of Toronto* (September 20, 1948). The Vaad also had articles in the DP press, including *Unzer Weg*, a Yiddish weekly sponsored by the Central Committee of Liberated Jews in Germany. In Europe, articles appeared in the *Israelitisches Wocheblatt* in Zurich, Switzerland (April 4, 1948). On January 10, 1947, *PM*, a liberal New York newspaper, printed a full page pictorial about the Jewish DPs under the heading "Doomed To A Life of Wandering" (January 10, 1947; 13). On April 7, 1947 *PM* also published a picture of the Vaad distributing Passover food packages. The *New York Post* published a picture of Baruch giving a child his first piece of candy ("The First Gift," *New York Post*, March 12, 1947), another with a group of girls at the Vaad home in Ulm showing how they knit ("Something to Do," *New York Post*, March 12, 1947), and a third picture of a group of young Jewish DP orphan girls lying on their bunks in a dormitory with the caption "No Pillows for Their Heads" (March 15, 1947). *Stars and Stripes*, the Army newspaper, also carried pictures and stories about Vaad activities ("DP Rabbis Receive Menorahs," *Stars and Stripes*, December 16, 1947).

73. Rabbi Nathan Baruch, "Report to the Vaad," October 20, 1947 (RNB file).

74. Malcolm J. Proudfoot. *European Refugees: 1939-52: A Study in Forced Population Movement* London: Faber and Faber, 1957:406-409.

75. Proudfoot: 409-411.

76. Rabbi Nathan Baruch to Daniel Adelson, December 14, 1947: 1 (RNB file).

77. Rabbi Nathan Baruch to Daniel Adelson: 2-3.

78. Don Adelson to Rabbi Nathan Baruch, February 8, 1947, (RNB file).

79. W.S. Boe to Rabbi Nathan Baruch, July 7, 1947 (RNB file).

80. Rabbi Nathan Baruch to W.S. Boe, Chief, Voluntary Agencies Division, PCIRO Sub-Zone Hq., Pasing-Munich, APO, 407, July 8, 1947,1. (Author's file); Rabbi Nathan Baruch to Mr. J.M. Gadras, Chief Field Operations, Area Team 1022, May 17, 1947 (RNB file).

81. Paul B. Edwards to Director, UNNRA Area Team 1022, Frankfurt, May 20, 1947 (RNB file).

82. J.M. Gadras to Rabbi Nathan Baruch, May 16, 1947 (RNB file).

83. J.M. Gadras to Rabbi Nathan Baruch.

84. W.S. Boe to Rabbi Nathan Baruch, June 26, 1947 (RNB file).

85. Rabbi Nathan Baruch to W.S. Boe, July 8, 1947: 2.

86. Rabbi Nathan Baruch to W.S. Boe, July 8, 1947: 2.

87. Robert J. Corkery to Rabbi Nathan Baruch, April 12, 1948, (RNB file).

88. Corkery.

89. Vaad Hatzala Bulletin, September 7, 1948, 1, (RNB file).

90. W.S. Boe to Rabbi Nathan Baruch, September 16, 1948 (RNB file).

91. H.S.D. MacNeal to Department Area Director, PCIRO HQ Area 2, Nellingen—Air Filed, August 24, 1948 (RNB file).

92. Vera W. Owen to W.S. Boe, September 17, 1948 (RNB file).

93. Rabbi Aviezer Burstin to W.S. Boe, September 20, 1948 (RNB file).

94. Interview with Rabbi Nathan Baruch, September 2000.

95. Rabbi Nathan Baruch, "Report to the Vaad, October 20, 1947 (RNB file).

96. Hyman: 160-162.

97. Hyman: 161-162.

98. Hyman: 162.

99. Baruch, October 20, 1947 (RNB file).

100. *Kol Israel in the Diaspora*, Munich, 23 *Av*, (1946): 6-7.

Chapter 6 - Endnotes

1. Kosher Meat Project, Rabbi Alexander S. Rosenberg, March 7, 1946, YIVO Archives, Leo Schwarz Collection, Folder 249, Reel 22.

2. Israel Upbin to Joint Distribution Committee, August 24,

1945, JDC-NY, JDC Collection 45164, File No. 4353; Rabbi Herbert S. Goldstein to Joseph Hyman. September 26, 1945, JDC-NY, JDC Collection 45164, File No. 4353.

3. Sol Firestone to Dr. Samson Weiss, August 15, 1945, JDC-NY, JDC Collection 45164, File No. 4353.

4. J.C. Hyman to Rabbi Herbert S. Goldstein, October 1, 1945, JDC-NY, JDC Collection 45164, File No. 4353; Louis H. Sobel to Israel Upbin September 6, 1945.

5. Hyman to Rabbi Herbert S. Goldstein.

6. Louis H. Sobel to Israel Upbin; Moses A. Leavitt to Israel Weisberger, August 31, 1945; JDC-NY, JDC Collection 45164, File No. 4353.

7. Lightman to Jointdisco New York, December 12, 1945, JDC-NY, JDC Collection 45164, File No. 4353.

8. Kosher Meat Project.

9. Kosher Meat Project.

10. Jacob L. Trobe to General S.R. Michelson, December 20, 1945, JDC-NY, JDC Collection 45164, File No. 4353; Jointdisco to Jacob Trobe, December 16, 1945, JDC-NY, JDC Collection 45164, File No. 4353; Jointdisco to Jointfund Paris, January 5, 1946, JDC-NY, JDC Collection 45164, File No. 4353.

11. Kosher Meat Project.

12. Kosher Meat Project.

13. Kosher Meat Project.

14. Kosher Meat Project.

15. Kosher Meat Project.

16. Grobman, *Rekindling the Flame*: 97.

17. Kosher Meat Project.

18. Kosher Meat Project.

19. Alexander S. Rosenberg to Leo W. Schwarz, July 22, 1946, YIVO Archives, Leo Schwarz Collection, Folder 247, Reel 22.

20. Rosenberg to Schwarz.

21. Rosenberg to Schwarz.

22. Emanuel Rackman to Rabbi Alexander Rosenberg, July 23, 1946, YIVO Archives, Leo Schwarz Collection, Folder 247, Reel 22.

23. Rabbi Abraham Klausner to National Jewish Welfare Board, April 19, 1947, YIVO Archives, Leo Schwarz Collection, Mk 488 Folder 104–116, Reel 13.

24. Klausner, April 19, 1947.

25. Klausner.

26. Klausner.

27. Rabbi Joshua Aronson to AJDC, NY, July 7, 1947, JDC-

NY, JDC Collection 45164, File No. 4353
28. Kranzler, *To Save A World*: 197.
29. Kranzler: 198.
30. Rabbi Joseph I. Schneersohn to American Joint Distribution Committee, June 23, 1945, JDC-NY, JDC Collection 45164, File No. 4353.
31. M. Jacob Joslow to Rabbi I. Schneersohn, June 30, 1947, JDC-NY, JDC Collection 45164, File No. 4353.
32. Usher Brandstater to AJDC director in Rome, October 27, 1947, JDC-NY, JDC Collection 45164, File No. 4353.
33. Melvin Goldstein to JDC, New York June 18, 1947, JDC-NY, JDC Collection 45164, File No. 4353; "JDC Sends Orthodox DP's To Dublin To Prepare Million Pounds of Meat Offered By Eire For Relief OF Jewish Displaced Persons," Joint Distribution Committee, October 23, 1947, JDC-NY, JDC Collection 45164, File No. 4353; Joseph J. Schwartz to AJDC New York, July 18, 1948, JDC-NY, JDC Collection 45164, File No. 4353; JDC newsletter October, 1948, JDC-NY, JDC Collection 45164, File No. 4353; "JDC sends 27 Rabbis To Dublin To Supervise Preparation of Million Pounds of Meat Given To DP's By Eire," Joint Distribution Committee, September 4, 1947, JDC-NY, JDC Collection 45164, File No. 4353.
34. Rabbi Nathan Baruch to Daniel Adelson, Deputy Voluntary Agencies Liaison Officer, PCIRI Sub-Zone Hq., December 8, 1947; Report of Rabbi Nathan Baruch to the Board of the Vaad Hatzalah September, 1948: 4-5.
35. Ronald Webster, "American Relief and Jews in Germany, 1945-1960: Diverging Perspectives," *Leo Baeck Institute YearBook XXXVIII* (London: Secker and Warburg, 1993): 312-313.
36. Baruch interview, September, 2000.
37. Webster: 312.

Chapter 7 - Endnotes

1. "Offenbach Archival Depot—Antithesis To Nazi Plunder," United States Holocaust Memorial Museum, Online Interview with Colonel Seymour J. Pomrenze November 30, 1998. Martin Dean, "Cultural Looting: the seizure of archives and libraries by Einsatzstab Reichsleiter Rosenberg, 1940-45," www.ushmm.org/intro.html,United States Holocaust Memorial Museum. Abraham S. Hyman, who became the legal consultant

to the Advisor on Jewish Affairs in August, 1946 says that the Offenbach Archival Depot contained "a sufficient number of copies of the Talmud to meet the requirements of *yeshivot* which sprang up in the Jewish DP camps in Germany immediately after the war. Therefore, from a practical viewpoint, it would have been hard to justify the publication of additional copies of the Talmud...." Abraham S. Hyman, *The Jerusalem Post*, Letter to the Editor, n.d. JDC Archives-NY JDC Collection 45164, File No.1268. This was not correct. The survivors asked for copies of the Talmud because there were not enough available.

2. Estelle Gilson. "The Fate of the Roman Jewish Libraries, " in *October 16, 1943: Eight* Jews. by Giacomo Debenedetti (South Bend, Indiana: University of Notre Dame Press, 2001): 91-100.

3. Dean; Kopel S. Pinson, "Report on the Remains of the Sturmer Jewish Library in Nuremberg," July 9, 1946, Yeshiva University Archives, COC Collection, Box No.2, folder No.8.

4. Dean.

5. Pomrenze.

6. Pinson, "Report on the Remains of the Stürmer Jewish Library in Nuremberg."

7. Pomrenze. See also Dawidowicz, Lucy S. ed. *What is the Use Of Jewish History* (New York: Schocken, 1992): 36-37.

8. Nathan Reich, "Overseas Aid" *American Jewish Year Book* Philadelphia: The Jewish Publication Society, 1947: 236. The report also states the JDC provided 1,000 sets of Talmud to students studying in yeshivas in various DP camps. This seems to contradict other reports that the JDC Talmud had not yet been printed due to technical problems.

9. Gerd Korman, "Survivors' Talmud and the U.S. Army," *American Jewish History*, Vol. 73, March 1984: 262-263.

10. Korman: 261; Charles E. Saltzman to Rabbi Abraham Kalmanowitz, November 15, 1947 (RNB file).

11. Korman: 261-262.

12. Interview with Rabbi Nathan Baruch; "Meir Shapira" in *Encyclopaedia Judaica* (Jerusalem, Israel: Keter Publishing House Jerusalem Ltd, 1972) Vol. 14:1299.

13. Interview with Rabbi Nathan Baruch; Pincus Schoen to Rabbi Nathan Baruch, March 5, 1947; March 20, 1947 (RNB file).

14. Rabbi Nathan Baruch, "American Vaad Hatzala Emergency Committee, Munich: Amount Extended To Our Institutions During The Year 1947." n.d. Yeshiva University Archives, Vaad Hatzala Collection, Box No. 13, File No.4.

15. Interview with Rabbi Nathan Baruch; Pincus Schoen to Rabbi Nathan Baruch, March 5, 1947; March 20, 1947 (RNB file).

16. Pincus Schoen to Rabbi Nathan Baruch, June 2, 1947 (RNB file).

17. Isaac Lewin to Rabbi Nathan Baruch, October 30, 1947; Isaac Lewin to Rabbi Nathan Baruch, December 17, 1947; May 6, 1948 (RNB file).

18. Abraham S. Hyman to Rabbi Nathan Baruch, July 20, 1948 (RNB file).

19. Rabbi Samuel A. Snieg and Leo Schwarz Agreement Between The American Joint Distribution Committee And The Rabbinical Council, U.S. Zone Germany, Regarding The Printing Of The New Edition Of The Talmud, September 11, 1946, YIVO Archives, Leo Schwarz Collection, Folder 245, Reel 22.

20. Hyman to Rabbi Nathan Baruch.

21. Herbert A. Friedman, *Roots of the Future* (New York: Gefen Publishing House, 1999): 100.

22. Friedman: 99. On October 21, 1949 Judah Shapiro reported that only four volumes had been printed to date because of paper shortages, but that this was no longer an obstacle. The one remaining problem was binding. Judah J. Shapiro to S. Tarashansky, October 21, 1949, JDC-NY Archives, Collection 45164, File No.1268.

On November 3, 1949, Samuel L. Haber told Judah Shapiro that the first eight volumes of 650 copies had been printed, and that one and a half to two volumes would be printed per month for the remaining volumes. Haber would print 650 volumes of each set, but only bind 500 of them in order to stay within the budget allocated for the project. He urged Shapiro to come to Germany within the next few weeks to discuss the remaining financial issues concerning the Talmud, and questions of where it should be stored and how it was to be distributed. Samuel L. Haber to Judah Shapiro, November 3, 1949, JDC-NY Archives, Collection 45164, File No.1268.

23. Korman: 273-274. Dinnerstein, *America and the Survivors of the Holocaust*: 251.

24. Korman: 272-273.

25. JDC Religious Director For Germany Describing Printing of New "Talmud of Shearith Hapletah," July 14, 1949, JDC-NY Archives, Collection 45164, file No.1268.

26. Lucius D. Clay to Rabbi Nathan Baruch, July 16, 1947 (RNB file).

27. Dwight D. Eisenhower to Rabbi Nathan Baruch, July 22, 1947 (RNB file).

28.Alex Grobman, "Jewish GIs and Holocaust Survivors," *Jewish Spectator* Spring, 1979: 49-52.

29. David I. Lippert to Rabbi Nathan Baruch, April 7, 1948 (RNB file).

30. H.A.Goodman to Rabbi Nathan Baruch, January 4,1948 (RNB file).

31. H.A.Goodman to Rabbi Nathan Baruch, February 8, 1948 (RNB file).

32. Melvin S. Goldstein to AJDC New York, Printing Books in Germany, June 30, 1947, JDC Jerusalem, Germany and Cultural File.

33. Melvin S. Goldstein.

34.George Weiss, Paris, Office of the General Counsel to AJDC New York, November 10, 1947, Palestine JDC Jerusalem, Palestine File.

35. Judah J. Shapiro, Report on Visit to Germany and Austria, August 3 to 15, 1948, JDC Jerusalem, File C47.803.

CHAPTER 8 – Endnotes

1. Bat-Ami Zucker, *In Search of Refuge: Jews and US Consuls in Nazi Germany 1933-1941* (London: Valentine and Mitchell, 2001): 38-40, 114,118-119.

2. Supper Meeting of the Plan and Scope Committee held on November 6, 1946. Jonathan Helfand, *Archives of the Holocaust*: 226.

3. Helfand: 227.

4. Helfand: 227.

5. Helfand: 227.

6. Helfand: 227.

7. Helfand: 227.

8. Helfand: 227.

9. "Continuation of Vaad Program and future plans of operation," Rabbi Nathan Baruch to W.S. Boe, Chief Voluntary Agencies Division, PICO Sub- Zone Hq., Pasing-Munich, APO 407, October 20,1947 (RNB file).

10. Minutes. Special Meeting of the Vaad Hazala Held At Hotel Astoria, July 27, 1948: 1-2 (RNB file).

11. Stephen Klein to Rabbi Nathan Baruch, February 23, 1948 (RNB file).

12. Interviews with Rabbi Nathan Baruch, September 2000.

13. Zosa Szajkowski. "The Attitude of American Jews to Refugees from Germany in the 1930's," *American Jewish Historical Quarterly*, vol. 61, December, 1971: 112-114; Joseph Savoretti to Stephen Klein, April 24, 1946 (RNB file).

14. Szajkowski: 115.

15. Stephen Klein to Rabbi Nathan Baruch, March 31, 1948 (RNB file).

16. Irving Bunim to Rabbi Nathan Baruch, March 8, 1948 (RNB file).

17. Stephen Klein to Rabbi Nathan Baruch, March 31, 1948 (RNB file).

18. Stephen Klein to Rabbi Nathan Baruch, May 13, 1948 (RNB file).

19. Lee Stein to Rabbi Nathan Baruch, July 30, 1948 (RNB file).

20. Klein to Rabbi Nathan Baruch, May 13, 1948 (RNB file).

21. Minutes, Special Meeting.

22. Minutes, Special Meeting.

23. Lee Stein to Stephen Klein, November 3, 1948, Yeshiva University Archives, Vaad Hatzala Collection, Box No. 13, File 1.

24. Minutes: 3.

25. Yehuda Bauer, *Flight and Rescue: Brichah* (New York: Random House, 1970). See also: Alex Grobman, *In Defense of the Survivors: The Letters and Documents of Oscar A. Mintzer, AJDC Legal Advisor, Germany, 1945-46*: 412.

26. Aaron Rakeffet-Rothkoff, *The Silver Era*: 237-239.

27. Minutes, Special Meeting of the Vaad Hazala Held at Hotel Astoria. Aaron Rakeffet-Rothkoff, *The Silver Era*: 3.

28. Minutes: 4.

29. Minutes: 4.

30. Minutes: 3.

31. David S. Wyman, *Paper Walls: America and the Refugee Crisis 1938-1941* (Amherst, Massachusetts: University of Massachusetts Press, 1968) 3; Leonard Dinnerstein, *Antisemitism in America* (New York: Oxford University Press, 1994): 128-149.

32. Dinnerstein: 131. See also: Charles H. Stember et al. *Jews in the Mind of America* (New York: Basic Books, 1966): 136-170.

33. Dinnerstein: 131.

34. "Minutes of a Meeting in the Office of the Jewish Advisor on Monday 15, 1948": 3 (RNB file); Joseph W. Bendersky, *The "Jewish Threat": Anti-Semitic Politics of the U.S. Army* (New York: Basic Books, 2000): 349-387.

35. Charles H. Stember, *Jews in the Mind of America* (New York: Basic Books, 1996): 148, 153-154.

36. Robert A. Divine, *American Immigration Policy, 1924-1952* (New Haven: Yale University Press, 1957): 112 quoted in Leonard Dinnerstein, "Anti-Semitism in the Eightieth Congress: The Displaced Persons Act of 1948," *Capitol Studies* (1973) vol.6, No. 2. Fall: 11.

37. Dinnerstein, "Anti-Semitism in the Eightieth Congress: The Displaced Persons Act of 1948": 17

38. Dinnerstein: 17.

39. Grobman, *Rekindling The Flame*: 71-73.

40. *Rekindling The Flame*: 71-73; Abraham S. Hyman, *The Undefeated*: 46-63.

41. Dinnerstein, "Anti-Semitism in the Eightieth Congress: The Displaced Persons Act of 1948: 12-13.

42. Dinnerstein: 12-13.

43. Dinnerstein: 13-14.

44. Haim Genizi, *America's Fair Share: The Admission and Resettlement of Displaced Persons, 1945-1952* (Detroit: Wayne State University Press, 1993): 70.

45. Dinnerstein, *Antisemitism in America*: 70-72; Dinnerstein, "Anti-Semitism in the Eightieth Congress": 16.

46. Dinnerstein, "Anti-Semitism in the Eightieth Congress": 15.

47. Dr. Haber's Final Report, December 20, 1948: 2.

48. Genizi: 85.

49. Genizi: 67-68, 111.

50. Dinnerstein, "Anti-Semitism in the Eightieth Congress": 23-25.

51. Haber: 2-4.

52. Genizi, 114-115.

53. Haber: 18.

54. Haber: 19.

55. Genizi: 119.

56. Genizi: 119.

57. Samuel Schmidt to Rabbi Nathan Baruch, October 15, 1947. (RNB file).

58. Rabbi Nathan Baruch, Interview, October 2000.

59. Reed P. Robinson to Mr. Nathan Baruch, November 29, 1948. (RNB file).

60. Rabbi Nathan Baruch, Interview, October 2000.

61. Rabbi Nathan Baruch, Interview, October 2000.

62. Rabbi Nathan Baruch, Interview, October 2000.

63. Rabbi Nathan Baruch, Interview, October 2000.

64. Rabbi Nathan Baruch, Interview, October 2000.

65. Philip S. Bernstein to Joseph C. Hyman, September 8, 1946: 3 (Author's file).

66. Bernstein: 3, 5.

67. Bernstein: 4.

68. Rabbi Nathan Baruch, Interview, October 2000.

69. Vaad Hatzala Bulletin, June 28, 1948 (RNB file).

70. Pincus Schoen to Anne Goldman, April 21, 1947, Yeshiva University Archives, Vaad Hatzala Collection, Box No. 13, Folder No. 2. Anne Goldman, an experienced administrative aid, headed the administrative staff of the Vaad Hatzala office in New York.

71. Pincus Schoen to Rabbi Nathan Baruch, January 5, 1948 (RNB file); Pincus Schoen to Rabbi Nathan Baruch, December 8,1947 (RNB file).

72. Rabbi S.A. Pardes to Rabbi Nathan Baruch, November 18, 1947 (RNB file); Pincus Schoen to Rabbi Nathan Baruch, December 8, 1948 (RNB file).

73. Irving Ganz to Rabbi Nathan Baruch, February 5, 1946 (RNB file).

74. Irving Ganz to Rabbi Nathan Baruch, June 23, 1947 (RNB file).

75. Alexander Guttman to Samuel Schmidt, September 10, 1948 (RNB file).

76. Lee Stein to Rabbi Nathan Baruch, July 30, 1948; Zosa Szajkowski, "The Attitude of American Jews to Refugees from Germany in the 1930's,": 112-114.

77. Stein.

78. Rose Soloveitchik to Rabbi Nathan Baruch, February 25, 1947 (RNB file); Rabbi J. Soloveitchik, 2 *Tamuz, Taf shin zayin* (RNB file). Upon her return to the US, Mrs. Soloveitchik called Baruch's mother to convey his regards. She also wrote him a thank you note in which she said, "I feel specifically grateful for the exit permit which made it possible for me to depart from that country peacefully and even comfortably." She enclosed a check for $110.

79. Pincus Schoen to Rabbi Nathan Baruch, May 6, 1948 (RNB file).

80. Pincus Schoen to Rabbi Nathan Baruch, July 6, 1948 (RNB file).

CHAPTER 9—Endnotes

1. Henrietta K. Buchman, "Notes On Meeting With Representatives of Agudas Harabonim and Central Relief

Committee," February 12, 1947, Yeshiva University Archives, COC Box No.1, Folder No.4.

2. Buchman, Notes On Meeting.

3. Buchman, Notes On Meeting.

4.Yehuda Bauer, *My Brother's Keeper: A History of the American Jewish Joint Distribution Committee 1929-1939* (Philadelphia: Jewish Publication Society, 1974): 6-7.

5. Buchman, Notes On Meeting;

6. Buchman, Notes On Meeting.

7. Buchman, Notes On Meeting.

8. *Hapardes*, September 1947, Vol. 21, number 12:8-9.

9. Rabbi Eliezer Silver and Rabbi Israel Rosenberg to Moses A. Leavitt, April 23, 1947, Yeshiva University Archives, COC Box No. 1, Folder No. 4.

10. Henrietta K. Buchman, Minutes: A meeting with representatives of the Union of Orthodox Rabbis, June 9, 1947, Yeshiva University Archives, COC Box No. 1, Folder No. 2.

11. Louis Sobel to Rabbi Israel Rosenberg, May 28, 1947, Yeshiva University Archives, COC Box No. 1, Folder No. 3.

12. Gertrude Gould to Rabbi Nathan Baruch, February 26, 1948 (RNB file). In a letter to Moses A. Leavitt, Executive Vice-Chairman of the JDC on July 22, 1947, H.L.Lurie, Executive of the JDC, wrote: "There is considerable question in my mind as to whether the Vaad Hahatzala now has any valid program in view of the establishment of the Central Orthodox Committee. According to the draft, the Vaad Hahatzala may continue to support yeshivoth which do not receive subsidies from the JDC and will continue to seek emigration opportunities for yeshiva students and Torah scholars in Europe. As I understand the JDC's program, there are really no yeshivas which would be ineligible for JDC support and therefore the Vaad would not seem to have a valid function in this field." H.L.Lurie to Moses A. Leavitt, July 22, 1947, JDC-NY Collection 45164, File No. 3384.

13. Sobel to Rosenberg, Yeshiva University Archives, COC, Box No. 1, Folder No. 1.Louis H. Sobel to Rabbis Rosenberg and Silver, May 13, 1947, Yeshiva University Archives, COC, Box No. 1, Folder No. 1.

14. Sobel to Rosenberg, May 28, 1947.

15. Buchman. Minutes: A meeting with representatives of the Union of Orthodox Rabbis, June 9, 1947. In a letter from H.L.Lurie to Moses A. Leavitt on July 22, 1947, about immigration, Lurie said, "As for the immigration problem, I

should like to see this handled by the Central Orthodox Committee rather than by Vaad Hahatzala. Our survey of USNA [United Service for New Americans, a major sectarian relief agency] has revealed very clearly the great need for coordinated thinking and planning by the Orthodox community in this field. One of the great problems has been the lack of unity and responsibility among various Orthodox groups in planning for immigration. The Central Orthodox Committee while not an operating agency, still affords a natural opportunity for coordinated policy-making. The actual operations such as the technical immigration work and transportation would, I assume, be handled by JDC.

"I fully realize the difficulty of liquidating Vaad Hahatzala, but still it is essential to the success of any agreement that the Vaad be controlled. Perhaps a compromise might be arranged whereby the Vaad would continue to function as the agent in immigration matters, but obtain its policy directives from the Central Orthodox Committee and also be respon-sible to that committee and to the JDC. In that case, I would strongly suggest that the Vaad obtain its funds from the Central Orthodox Committee rather than through an inde-pendent campaign. It would be most unfortunate to have two Orthodox agencies making appeals to the communities, especially if they can both claim the approval of JDC."- H.L.Lurie to Moses A. Leavitt, July 22, 1947.

16. Alizah Zinberg: Barbara Martin and Roger Kohn, *Inventory to the Rescue Children, Inc. Collection 1946-1985,* Yeshiva University Archives: 18, Between July 24, 1946 and June 30, 1947, Rescue Children, Inc received $235,860.45 from contributions; $217,161.88 of it from the adoption program. Between July 1946 and June 1947, the monthly cost per child was $25 a month in France. From July 1947 through November 1947, it cost $33. Following this period, Rescue Children sought funds from Jewish Federations and Welfare Funds to supplement money raised from the Adopt-a-Child Program.

17. Zinberg: 19.

18. Zinberg: 19

19. Zinberg: 19.

20. Stephen Klein to Rabbi Nathan Baruch, September 3, 1947, (RNB file): 4.

21. Abraham Horowitz to Samuel L. Sar, March 23, 1948, Yeshiva University Archives, COC Collection, Box 5, Folder No. 2.

22. Agreement Between the American Jewish Joint Distribution

Committee and the Union of Orthodox Rabbis of the U.S.A. and Canada, July 29, 1947, 1. (RNB file): Louis H. Sobel to Rabbi Israel Rosenberg, May 9, 1947, Yeshiva University Archives COC Box No. 1, Folder No.1.

23. Agreement: 2.

24. Agreement: 1.

25. Agreement: 2.

26. Agreement: 3.

27. Agreement: 3; Leavitt to Rosenberg.

28. Agreement: 3.

29. Rabbi Nathan Baruch to Rabbi Israel Rosenberg, Eliezer Silver and Leviton July 7, 1947, 1. (RNB file).

30. Rabbi Nathan Baruch to Rabbi Israel Rosenberg, Eliezer Silver and Leviton July 7, 1947, 1.

31. Rabbi Nathan Baruch to Pincus Schoen, June 10, 1947. (RNB file).

32. Rabbi Nathan Baruch to Rabbi Israel Rosenberg, Eliezer Silver and Leviton, 2.

33.Stephen Klein to Rabbi Nathan Baruch, September 3, 1947, 1. (RNB file).

34.Stephen Klein to Rabbi Nathan Baruch, September 3, 1947, 2.

35. Stephen Klein to Mr. and Mrs. Sternbuch, June 20, 1947, 1. (RNB file).

36. "Vaad Hatzalah and Mizrachi Break," *Jewish Press* (Omaha Nebraska), March 28, 1947.

37. JTA dispatch in the *Jewish Floridian*, March 28, 1947.

38. Stephen Klein to Rabbi Nathan Baruch, No date. (RNB file).

39. JTA dispatch in the *Jewish Floridian*, March 28, 1947.

40. *Jewish Press*, March 28, 1947.

41. *Jewish Press*, March 28, 1947.

42. Stephen Klein to Mr. and Mrs. Sternbuch, 1, 4.

43. Irving Bunim to Rabbi Nathan Baruch, July 7, 1947 (RNB file). See also Vaad HaHatzala: 3, JDC-NY Archives, JDC Collection 45164, File No. 3375

44. Stephen Klein to Rabbi Nathan Baruch, September 3, 1947, 2.

45. Stephen Klein to Rabbi Nathan Baruch, September 3, 1947, 2.

46. Klein to Sternbuch, 2.

47. Molly Flynn, Special Assistant to the Deputy Director General Bureau of Services [UNNRA] to Rabbi I. Rosenberg, Rabbi Eliezer

Silver, Rabbi J. Levinson, June 17, 1947. (RNB file).

48. Samuel Schmidt to Rabbi Nathan Baruch, October 14, 1947 (RNB file).

49. Pincus Schoen to Rabbi Nathan Baruch, June 18, 1947 (RNB file).

50. Irving Bunim to Rabbi Nathan Baruch, July 7, 1947 (RNB file).

51. Bunim, July 7, 1947.

52. Stephen Klein to Mr. and Mrs. Sternbuch, June 20, 1947, 3 (RNB file)

53. Stephen Klein to Dr. Samuel Schmidt, June 30, 1947 (RNB file).

54. Samuel M. Schmidt, Present Situation and Recommendations, August 2, 1948: 1 (RNB file).

55.Schmidt: 1.

56. Schmidt, 1.

57.Aaron Rakeffet-Rothkoff, *Bernard Revel: Builder of American Orthodoxy* (New York: Feldheim, 2000): 58.

58. Rabbi Israel Rosenberg to Rabbi Dr. Samuel Belkin, January 20, 1948 Yeshiva University Archives, COC Collection, Box 5, Folder No.1.

59. Samuel L. Sar to Rabbi Israel Rosenberg, January 22, 1948, Yeshiva University Archives, COC Collection, Box 5, Folder No.1.

60. Samuel Belkin to Rabbi Israel Rosenberg, January 22, 1948, Yeshiva University Archives, COC Collection, Box 5, Folder No.1.

61. Abraham Horowitz to Moses A. Leavitt, January 27, 1948, Yeshiva University Archives, COC Collection, Box 5, Folder No.1; Moses A. Leavitt to Abraham Horowitz. February 4, 1948, Yeshiva University Archives, COC Collection, Box 5, Folder No.1.

62. *The Record*, October 1945; *Bulletin of Activities and Digest of The Press* (American Jewish Committee), October 2, 1945; American Jewish Conference representatives in American Zone of Germany, interim report, December 13, 1945, Harry S. Truman Library and American Jewish Archives; Samuel L. Sar, "Supplementary Report to the American Jewish Conference," February 4, 1946 (RNB file).

63. Abraham Horowitz to Joseph J. Schwartz, February 24, 1948, Yeshiva University Archives, COC Collection, Box 5, Folder No. 1.

64. Samuel Schmidt to Rabbi Nathan Baruch, September 19, 1947 (RNB file).

65. Samuel Schmidt to Rabbi Nathan Baruch, October 2, 1947 (RNB file).

66. Samuel Schmidt to Rabbi Nathan Baruch, September 19, 1947 (RNB file).

67. Schmidt, October 2, 1947.

68. Schmidt to Rabbi Nathan Baruch (RNB file).

69. Schmidt to Rabbi Nathan Baruch.

70. Pincus Schoen to Rabbi Nathan Baruch, July 13, 1948 (RNB file).

71. Rabbi Alexander Rosenberg to Rabbi Nathan Baruch, June 30, 1948 (RNB file).

72. Pincus Schoen to Rabbi Nathan Baruch, June 1, 1948 (RNB file).

73. "Vaad Hatzala," *American Jewish Year Book*, Vol. 48, 1946-1947: 217.

74. Pincus Schoen to Rabbi Nathan Baruch, June 1, 1948 (RNB file).

75. Pincus Schoen to Rabbi Nathan Baruch, July 13, 1948 (RNB file).

76. Pincus Schoen to Rabbi Nathan Baruch, July 13, 1948 (RNB file).

77. Pincus Schoen to Rabbi Nathan Baruch, December 22, 1947 (RNB file).

78. Rabbi Saul Lasher to Rabbi Nathan Baruch, May 25, 1948 (RNB file).

79. Pincus Schoen to Rabbi Nathan Baruch, April 14, 1948 (RNB file).

80. Pincus Schoen to Rabbi Nathan Baruch, August 17, 1948 (RNB file).

81. Rabbi Solomon Shapiro to AJDC Paris, July 8, 1948 (RNB file).

82. Rabbi Solomon Shapiro to AJDC Paris, July 8, 1948 (RNB file).

83. Data and Statistics on Vaad Hatzala, August 2, 1948 (RNB file).

84. Data and Statistics

85. Rabbi Solomon Shapiro to AJDC Paris, July 8, 1948 (RNB file).

86. Shapiro to AJDC.

87. Shapiro to AJDC. The JDC even maintained and supported the Agudas Harabonim with a special budget. *Mohalim* and *shochtim* were also on the JDC payroll and received their religious supplies through them. The JDC provided a regular supply of *siddurim, machzorim, tefillin, taleisim, shofroth, megiloth, lulavim, esrogim* and candles and whatever religious items were needed. Teachers who taught in a Talmud Torah or *cheder* also received their compensation from the JDC. Each yeshiva received a special ration to sustain the needs of the institution. The JDC also agreed that each yeshiva should be headed by one *rosh yeshiva* and

have a teacher for every 15 students. In July 1947, there were 13 yeshivas with 585 students and a faculty of 43. This soon dropped to 10 when the Windsheim Yeshiva and its 75 students left for Paris and the Bensheim and Leipheim Yeshivas disbanded.

88. Pincus Schoen to Rabbi Nathan Baruch, April 14, 1948 (RNB file).

89. Pincus Schoen to Rabbi Nathan Baruch, August 17, 1948 (RNB file)

90. Shapiro to AJDC.

91. Abraham Horowitz to Samuel L. Sar, March 26, 1948, Yeshiva University Archives, COC Collection, Box 5, Folder No. 2.

92.Abraham Horowitz to Abraham Kolko, February 12, 1948, Yeshiva University Archives, COC Collection, Box 4, Folder No. 2.; Abraham Horowitz to Samuel Sar June 9, 1948, Yeshiva University Archives, COC Collection, Box 5, Folder No. 3; Abraham Horowitz to Henrietta K. Buchman, July 30, 1948, Yeshiva University Archives, COC Collection, Box 2, Folder No. 9.

93. Samuel L. Sar to Dr. Joseph Schwartz, September 29, 1948, Vaad Hatzala file in German Zone, AJDC Givat Joint Archives, AJDC Geneva, C45.097, 1948-1949.

94. Samuel L. Haber to M. Beckelman, November 4, 1948,Vaad Hatzala file in German Zone, AJDC Givat Joint Archives, AJDC Geneva C45.097, 1948-1949. See also Blanche Bernstein to Dean Samuel L. Sar, October 19, 1948, Vaad Hatzala file in German Zone, AJDC Givat Joint Archives, AJDC Geneva C45.097, 1948-1949; M.W. Beckelman to Samuel L. Haber, October 18, 1948 Vaad Hatzala file in German Zone, AJDC Givat Joint Archives, AJDC Geneva C45.097, 1948-1949; Blanche Bernstein to M.W. Beckelman, October 18, 1948 Vaad Hatzala file in German Zone, AJDC Givat Joint Archives, AJDC Geneva, C45.097, 1948-1949.

95. Melvin S. Goldstein to AJDC Munich June 25, 1948, Vaad Hatzala file in German Zone, AJDC Givat Joint Archives, AJDC Geneva, C45.097, 1948-1949.

96. David Winograd to Abraham Horowitz, November 19, 1947, Yeshiva University Archives, COC Collection, Box 3, Folder No. 8; David Winograd to Rabbi Eliezer Silver, October 10, 1947, Yeshiva University Archives, COC Collection, Box 3, Folder No. 8.

97. Harry M, Rosen, "Some Questions And Answers Concerning the Agreement Between the JDC and the Union of Orthodox Rabbis With Specific Reference to Status of Vaad Hahatzala,"

August 21, 1947, JDC-NY Archives JDC Collection, 45/64 File No. 4070.

98. Rosen, "Some Questions And Answers Concerning the Agreement Between the JDC and the Union of Orthodox Rabbis With Specific Reference to Status of Vaad Hahatzala."

99. Rosen, "Some Questions And Answers Concerning the Agreement Between the JDC and the Union of Orthodox Rabbis With Specific Reference to Status of Vaad Hahatzala."

100. Rosen, "Some Questions And Answers Concerning the Agreement Between the JDC and the Union of Orthodox Rabbis With Specific Reference to Status of Vaad Hahatzala."

101. Rosen, "Some Questions And Answers Concerning the Agreement Between the JDC and the Union of Orthodox Rabbis With Specific Reference to Status of Vaad Hahatzala."

102. Winograd to Rabbi Silver.

103. David Winograd to Abraham Horowitz, November 16, 1947, Yeshiva University Archives, COC Collection, Box 3, Folder No. 8.

104. David Winograd to Abraham Horowitz, November 19, 1947, Yeshiva University Archives, COC Collection, Box 3, Folder No. 8; David Winograd to Rabbi Silver, October 10, 1947.

105. David Winograd to Abraham Horowitz, November 19, 1947; Winograd to Rabbi Silver.

106. Statement by Samuel M. Schmidt, July 23, 1948.

Chapter 10 - Endnotes

1. Data and Statistics on Vaad Hatzala, August 2, 1948 (RNB file).

2. Data and Statistics.

3. Aid For the Religious Needs of Europe's Surviving Jews: A Special Report Submitted By Dean Samuel L. Saar, 1948 (RNB file). Sar reported that in the U.S. Zone of Germany one million pounds of matzoh were prepared at two JDC-maintained bakeries in Frankfurt and Munich. Provisions were also made for those who wanted *shmura* matzoh products. One thousand pounds of kosher for Passover margarine was manufactured for the JDC for distribution as well. Every person over the age of 13 received five pounds of matzoh, two pounds of matzoh meal and wine. Religious articles were also distributed, including 10,000 *Haggadahs*.

4. Abraham Horowitz to Dr. Samuel M. Schmidt, August 12, 1948, 2 (RNB file).

5. Samuel M. Schmidt to Abraham Horowitz, August 2, 1948,

Yeshiva University Archives, COC Collection, Box 3, Folder No. 3.

6. Schmidt to Abraham Horowitz.

7. Abraham Horowitz to Rabbi B. Cohen, July 1, 1948, Yeshiva University Archives, COC Collection, Box 3, Folder No. 10; Dr. Manuel Laderman to Rabbi Israel Rosenberg, December 1, 1948, Yeshiva University Archives, COC Collection, Box 2, Folder No. 2.

8. Laderman to Rosenberg.

9. Report and Recommendations by the Fact-Finding Commission of the Central Orthodox Committee On Their Five Month Survey of Jewish Displaced Persons Centers And Jewish Communities In Europe August thru December 1947," Yeshiva University Archives, COC Collection, Box 1, Folder No. 4.

10. "Report and Recommendations by the Fact-Finding Commission."

11. Bezalel Cohen and David L. Meckler to Rabbis Israel Rosenberg and Eliezer Silver, September 23, 1947, Yeshiva University Archives, COC Collection, Box 1, Folder No. 4.

12. Bezalel Cohen and David L. Meckler to Rabbis Israel Rosenberg and Eliezer Silver.

13. Abraham Horowitz to Samuel L. Sar, May 13, 1948, Yeshiva University Archives, COC Collection, Box 5, Folder No. 3.

14. Report and Recommendations by the Fact-Finding Commission.

15. Samuel L. Sar to Abraham Horowitz, April 7, 1948, Yeshiva University Archives, COC Collection, Box 5, Folder No. 2.

16. Abraham Horowitz to Samuel L. Sar, May 13, 1948.

17. Dr. Manuel Laderman to Rabbi Israel Rosenberg, December 1, 1948, Yeshiva University Archives, COC Collection, Box 2, Folder No. 2.

18. Abraham Horowitz to Samuel L. Sar, May 13, 1948.

19. Abraham Horowitz to Samuel L. Sar, May 14, 1948, Yeshiva University Archives, COC Collection, Box 5, Folder No. 3.

20. Abraham Horowitz to Samuel L. Sar, May 17, 1948, Yeshiva University Archives, COC Collection, Box 5, Folder No. 3.

21. Report and Recommendations by the Fact-Finding Commission.

22. Abraham Horowitz to Samuel L. Sar, May 14, 1948.

23. Isak Sternhell, Schwerer and Hermann to Grand Rabbi Rosenberg Israel, October 1, 1947, Yeshiva University Archives, COC Collection, Box 2, Folder No. 8.

24. Harav S.A. Sneig to Samuel Haber, May 31, 1948, YIVO Archives, Leo Schwarz Collection, Folder 244, Reel 22.

25. Dr. Manuel Laderman to Dr. Joseph Schwartz, March 4,

1949, Yeshiva University Archives, COC Collection, Box 2, Folder No. 9.

26. Jeffrey Gurock, "Resisters and Accommodators: Varieties of Orthodox Rabbis in America 1886-1983," *American Jewish Archives*, xxxv, No. 2 (November 1983): 110-112.

27. Rakeffet-Rothkoff, *Bernard Revel*: 135-157.

28. Samuel L. Sar to Abraham Horowitz, May 26, 1948, Yeshiva University Archives, COC Collection, Box 5, Folder No. 3; Abraham Horowitz to Samuel L. Sar, May 21, 1948, Yeshiva University Archives, COC Collection, Box 5, Folder No. 3.

29. Samuel L. Sar to Abraham Horowitz, June 17, 1948 Yeshiva University Archives, COC Collection, Box 5, Folder No. 4.

30. Sar to Horowitz, June 17, 1948.

31. Sar to Horowitz, June 17, 1948.

32. Samuel Schmidt to Vaad Hatzala Emergency Committee June 11, 1948 Yeshiva University Archives, Vaad Hatzala Collection, Box No. 30 Folder No. 79.

33. Sar to Horowitz, June 17, 1948.

34. Sar, June 16, 1948 Yeshiva University Archives, COC Collection, Box 5, Folder No. 35; Sar to Horowitz, June 17, 1948.

35. Sar to Horowitz, June 17, 1948.

36. Sar to Horowitz, June 17, 1948.

37. Lena P. Eisler to Samuel Sar, April 5, 1948, Yeshiva University Archives, COC Collection, Box 2, Folder No. 8.

38. Eisler to Sar.

39. Eisler to Sar.

40. Eisler to Sar.

41. Laderman to Rosenberg.

42. Samuel L. Sar to Abraham Horowitz, June 28, 1948, Yeshiva University Archives, COC Collection, Box 5, Folder No. 4; Abraham Horowitz to Samuel L. Sar, August 6, 1948, Yeshiva University Archives, COC Collection, Box 5, Folder No. 4; Abraham Horowitz to Joseph Schwartz, September 1, 1948, Yeshiva University Archives, COC Collection, Box 2, Folder No. 9.

43. Samuel L. Sar to Abraham Horowitz, September 17, 1948, Yeshiva University Archives, COC Collection Box 5, Folder No. 6.

44. YIVO Archives, Leo Schwarz Collection, Samuel L.Sar to Rabbi S. Shapiro, September 30, 1948, Folder 255, Reel 2.

45. Samuel L. Sar to Abraham Horowitz, May 10, 1948, Yeshiva University Archives, COC Collection, Box 5, Folder No. 3.

46. Sar to Horowitz, September 17, 1948.
47. Sar to Horowitz, September 17, 1948.
48. Sar to Horowitz, September 17, 1948.
49. Samuel Schmidt to Irving M. Bunim, February 1, 1949. Yeshiva University Archives, Vaad Hatzala Collection, Box No. 30, Folder No. 79.

Chapter 11 - Endnotes

1. Rabbi Nathan Baruch interview, September 2000.
2. Pincus Schoen to Rabbi Nathan Baruch, July 19, 1948 (RNB file).
3. Gertrude Gould to Rabbi Nathan Baruch, February 25, 1947 (RNB file).
4. *NYT*, February 17, 1948.
5. Rabbi Nathan Baruch to all our American friends, February 10, 1948 (RNB file).
6. Pincus Schoen to Rabbi Nathan Baruch, April 5, 1948 (RNB file).
7. Report of Rabbi Nathan Baruch to the Board of the Vaad Hatzala, September 1948. (RNB file): 1.
8. Rabbi Nathan Baruch to the Board of the Vaad Hatzala: 2.
9. Rabbi Nathan Baruch to the Board of the Vaad Hatzala: 3.
10. Rabbi Nathan Baruch to the Board of the Vaad Hatzala: 3.
11. Rabbi Nathan Baruch to the Board of the Vaad Hatzala: 4.
12. Rabbi Nathan Baruch to the Board of the Vaad Hatzala: 4-5.
13. Rabbi Nathan Baruch to the Board of the Vaad Hatzala: 5.
14. Abraham Hyman, *The Undefeated*: 435.
15. Yehuda Bauer, *A History of the Holocaust* (New York: Franklin Watts, 1982): 348.
16. Dinnerstein, *America and the Survivors of the Holocaust*: 251.
17. Dinnerstein: 217-253.
18. Gertrude Gould to Rabbi Nathan Baruch, February 26, 1948 (RNB file).
19. Rabbi Eliezer Silver to Rabbi Nathan Baruch, Fall 1948 (RNB file).
20. Pincus Schoen to Rabbi Nathan Baruch, July 29, 1948 (RNB file).
21. *Vaad Hatzala Bulletin*, September 7, 1948:4 (RNB file).
22. "Says GIs in Reich Breed Anti-Semitism,"*New York Post*, September 15, 1948, 48. Also reported "Rabbi Says U.S. Is Losing in German DPs," *New York Herald Tribune*, September 15, 1948;

"U.S. Officials Put Reich Plight Above DPs, Says Rabbi" *New York Post*, September 11, 1948; "Today the National Conference of the Vaad Hatzala" *Forward*, September 15, 1948.
23. Pincus Schoen to John Hilldring, November 11, 1948 (RNB file).
24. John Hilldring to Pincus Schoen, November 19, 1948 (RNB file).
25. Union of Orthodox Rabbis of the United States and Canada, November 19, 1948 (RNB file).
26. Rabbis Eliezer Silver, Aron Kotler and Yechiel Mordecai Gordon to General Lucius Clay, November 22, 1948 (RNB file).
27. G.P. Lynch to Union of Orthodox Rabbis of the United States and Canada with attention Rabbi Silver, November 29, 1948 (RNB file).
28. G.L. Eberle to Pincus Schoen, December 9, 1948 (RNB file).
29. Eberle to Schoen.
30. Abraham Horowitz to Samuel Sar, March 26, 1948, Yeshiva University Archives, COC Collection, Box No. 5, File No. 2.
31. John C. Parker, "To Whom It May Concern," October 23, 1947 (RNB file).
32. Interview with Rabbi Nathan Baruch.
33. Horowitz to Sar, March 26, 1948.
34. Minutes of the Executive Committee Meeting of the Vaad Hatzala, February 22, 1949 Helfand: 280-281.
35. Rabbi Israel Rosenberg "To Chairman of Allocations Committee," No date, Helfand: 285.
36. Rabbi Eliezer Silver, "To Conference of Jewish Material Claims Against Germany," August 25, 1954, Helfand: 286-287.

CONCLUSION—Endnotes

1. Interview with Dr. David Kranzler, June 18, 2001.
2. Activities and Budget of Vaad Hatzala, n.d., Yeshiva University Archives, Vaad Hatzala Collection, Box No. 5, Folder No. 39.
3. Activities and Budget of Vaad Hatzala, Box No. 5, Folder No. 39.
4. Grobman, *Rekindling the Flame*: 127.
5. Grobman, *Rekindling the Flame*: 127.
6. Jewish Central Committee Estimated Budget Jewish Calendar Year 5708, September 1947 to September 1948, Yeshiva University Archives, COC Collection, Box 8, Folder No. 1; Laderman to Rosenberg.

7. Grobman, *Rekindling the Flame*: 126.

8. Irving Bunim to Rabbi Nathan Baruch, April 18, 1947 (RNB file).

9. Hillel Lichtenstein letter to Rabbi Nathan Baruch, *Hapardes* Menachem Av 5708 (1948): 98.

10. Hillel Lichtenstein letter to Rabbi Nathan Baruch, *Hapardes* Menachem Av 5708 (1948): 98.

BIBLIOGRAPHY

Abella, Irving, and Harold Troper. *None is Too Many: Canada and the Jews of Europe, 1933-1948.* New York: Random House, 1983.

Acheson, Dean. *Present at the Creation: My Years at the State Department.* New York: W.W. Norton, Inc., 1969.

Adler, Cyrus, and Aaron M. Margalith. *With Firmness in the Right: American Diplomatic Action Affecting Jews, 1840-1945.* New York: Arno Press, 1977.

Agar, Herbert. *The Saving Remnant.* London: Hupert-Hart-Davis, 1960.

American Commission on the Holocaust. *American Jewry During the Holocaust.* New York, 1984.

Avriel, Ehud. *Open the Gates: A Personal Story of "Illegal" Immigration to Israel.* New York: Atheneum, 1975.

Backer, John H. *Priming the German Economy: American Occupation Policies, 1945-1948.* Durham, North Carolina: Duke University Press, 1971.

_____. *Winds of History: The German Years of Lucius Dubignon Clay.* New York: Van Nostrand Reinhold Company, Inc., 1983.

_____. *The Decision to Divide Germany: American Policy in Transition.* Durham, North Carolina: Duke University Press, 1978.

Balabkins, Nicholas. *Germany Under Direct Controls: Economic Aspects of Industrial Disarmament, 1945-1948.* New Brunswick, New Jersey: Rutgers University Press, 1964.

_____. *West German Reparations to Israel.* New Brunswick, New Jersey: Rutgers University Press, 1971.

Baldwin, Neil. *Henry Ford and the Jews: The Production of Hate.* New York: Public Affairs, 2001.

Bauer, Yehuda. *From Diplomacy to Resistance: A History of Jewish Palestine, 1939-1945.* Philadelphia, Pennsylvania: Jewish Publication Society of America, 1970.

_____. *Flight and Rescue: Brichah.* New York: Random House, 1970.

_____. *My Brother's Keeper: A History of the American Jewish Joint Distribution Committee, 1929-1939.* Philadelphia, Pennsylvania: Jewish Publication Society, 1974.

_____. *The Holocaust in Historical Perspective.* Seattle, Washington: University of Washington Press, 1978.

_____. *The Jewish Emergence from Powerlessness.* Toronto: University of Toronto Press, 1979.

_____. *American Jewry and the Holocaust: The American Jewish Joint Distribution Committee, 1939-1945.* Detroit, Michigan: Wayne State University Press, 1981.

_____. *A History of the Holocaust.* New York: Franklin Watts, 1982.

_____. *Out of The Ashes: The Impact of American Jews on Post-Holocaust European Jewry.* New York: Pergamon, 1989.

_____. *Jews for Sale? Nazi-Jewish Negotiations, 1933-1945.* New Haven, Connecticut: Yale University Press, 1994.

_____. *Rethinking the Holocaust.* New Haven, Connecticut: Yale University Press, 2001.

Baumel, Judith Tydor. *Unfulfilled Promise: Rescue and Resettlement of Jewish Refugee Children in the United States, 1934-1945.* Juneau, Alaska: Denali Press, 1990.

_____. *Kibbutz Buchenwald: Survivors and Pioneers.* New Brunswick, New Jersey: Rutgers University Press, 1997.

Beckman, Morris. *The Jewish Brigade: An Army With Two Masters, 1944-45.* New York: Da Capo Press, 1999.

Ben-Ami, Yitshaq. *Years Of Wrath, Days Of Glory: Memoirs from the Irgun.* New York: Robert Speller and Sons, 1982.

Bendersky, Joseph W. *The "Jewish Threat": Anti-Semitic Politics of the U.S. Army.* New York: Basic Books, 2000.

Ben-Sasson, Hillel H. *A History of the Jewish People.* Cambridge,Massachusetts: Harvard University Press, 1976.

Bentwich, Norman. *They Found Refuge.* London: Cresset, 1956.

Berenbaum, Michael, ed. *The Holocaust and History: The Known, the Unknown, the Disputed, and the Reexamined.* Bloomington, Indiana: Indiana University Press, 1998.

Berenbaum, Michael, and Abraham Peck. *The Holocaust and History.* United States Holocaust Museum: Washington, D.C.: University of Indiana Press, 1998.

Berman, Aaron. *Nazism, the Jews, and American Zionism, 1933-1948.* Detroit, Michigan: Wayne State University Press, 1992.

Bernard, William S., ed. *American Immigration Policy: A Reappraisal.* New York: Harper, 1950.

Bernstein, Philip. *Rabbis At War.* Waltham, Massachusetts: American-Jewish Historical Society, 1971.

Benson, Michael T. *Harry S. Truman and the Founding of Israel.* Westport, Connecticut: Praeger Publishers, 1997.

Bird, Kai. *The Chairman John J. McCloy: The Making of the American Establishment.* New York: Simon and Schuster, 1992.

Birnbaum, Meyer, and Yonason Rosenblum. *Lieutenant Birnbaum: A Soldier's Story — Growing up Jewish in America, Liberating the D.P. Camps, and a New Home in Jerusalem.* New York: Artscroll Mesorah Publications, Ltd., 1993.

Bloch, Sam E., ed. *Holocaust and Rebirth: Bergen-Belsen 1945-1965.* New York: Bergen-Belsen Memorial Press, 1965.

Blum, Howard. *The Brigade: An Epic Story of Vengeance, Salvation, and World War II.* New York: HarperCollins, 2001.

Blumenson, Martin, ed. *The Patton Papers: 1940-1945.* Boston, Massachusetts: Houghton-Mifflin, 1974.

Bolchover, Richard. *British Jewry and the Holocaust.* New York: Cambridge University Press, 1993.

Botting, Douglas. *From the Ruins of the Reich.* New York: Crown Publishers, Inc., 1985.

Bower, Tom. *The Pledge Betrayed: America and Britain and the Denazification of Postwar Germany.* Garden City, New York: Doubleday, 1982.

Brenner, Michael. *After The Holocaust: Rebuilding Jewish Lives In Postwar Germany.* Princeton, New Jersey: Princeton University Press, 1995.

Brenner, Reeve Robert. *The Faith and Doubt of Holocaust Survivors.* New York: Free Press, 1980.

Breitman, Richard. *Official Secrets: What the Nazis Planned, What the British and Americans Knew.* New York: Hill and Wang, 1998.

Breitman, Richard, and Alan M. Kraut. *American Refugee Policy and European Jewry, 1933-1945.* Bloomington, Indiana: University of Indiana Press, 1987.

Bridgman, Jon. *The End of the Holocaust: The Liberation of the Camps.* Portland, Oregon: Areopagitica Press, 1990.

Brinkley, Alan. *Voices of Protest: Huey Long, Father Coughlin, and the Great Depression.* New York: Vintage Books, 1983.

Bronner, Stephen Eric. *A Rumor about the Jews: Reflections on Antisemitism and the Protocols of the Learned Elders of Zion.* New York: St. Martin's Press, 2000.

Bullock, Alan. *Ernest Bevin, Foreign Secretary, 1945-1951.* New York: W.W. Norton & Company, 1983.

Bunim, Amos. *A Fire in His Soul: Irving Bunim 1901-1980: The Man and His Impact on American Orthodox Jewry.* New York: Feldheim Publishers, 1989.

Burstein, Samuel. *Rabbi with Wings: Story of a Pilot.* New York: Herzl Press, 1965.

Chamberlain, Brewster, and Marcia Feldman, eds. *The Liberation of the Nazi Concentration Camps, 1945.* Washington, D.C.: United States Holocaust Memorial Council, 1987.

Clay, Lucius D. *Decision in Germany: A Personal Report on the Four Crucial Years That Set the Course of Future World History.* New York: Doubleday, 1950.

Cohen, Michael J. *Palestine: Retreat from the Mandate.* New

York: Holmes and Meier, 1978.

_____. *Palestine and the Great Powers, 1945-1948.* Princeton, New Jersey: Princeton University Press, 1982.

_____. ed. *The Rise of Israel — The Holocaust and Illegal Immigration, 1939-1947.* New York: Garland Publishing, 1987.

Cohen, Naomi W. *Not Free to Desist: The American Jewish Committee, 1906-1966.* Philadelphia, Pennsylvania: Jewish Publication Society, 1972.

_____. *Encounter with Emancipation: The German Jews in the United States, 1830-1914.* Philadelphia, Pennsylvania: Jewish Publication Society, 1984.

_____. *Jacob H. Schiff: A Study in American Jewish Leadership.* Hanover, New Hampshire: Brandeis University Press; University Press of New England, 1999.

Cohen, Rich. *The Avengers: A Jewish War Story.* New York: Alfred A. Knopf, 2000.

Crossman, Richard. *Palestine Mission: A Personal Record.* New York: Harper and Row, 1947.

Crum, Bartley C. *Behind the Silken Curtain.* New York: Simon and Schuster, 1947.

Davies, J.E. *Mission to Moscow.* New York: Simon and Schuster, 1941.

Dawidowicz, Lucy. *From That Place and Time.* New York: Dimensions, 1989.

_____. *On Equal Terms: Jews in America 1881-1981.* New York: Holt, Rinehart and Winston, 1982.

Debenedetti, Giacomo. *October 16, 1943: Eight Jews.* South Bend, Indiana: University of Notre Dame University Press, 2001.

Deighton, Anne. *The Impossible Peace: Britain, the Division of Germany, and the Origins of the Cold War.* Oxford: Clarendon Press, 1990.

Dekel, Ephraim. *B'riha: Flight to the Homeland.* New York: Herzl, 1973.

Des Pres, Terrence. *The Survivor: An Anatomy of Life in the Death Camps.* New York: Oxford University Press, 1976.

Diner, Hasia R. *Lower East Side Memories: A Jewish Place in America.* Princeton, New Jersey: Princeton University Press, 2000.

Diner, Hasia R., and Henry L. Feingold, eds. *Time for Gathering:*

The Second Migration, 1820-1880. Baltimore,
Maryland: Johns Hopkins University Press, 1992.

Dinnerstein, Leonard. *America and the Survivors of the
Holocaust.* New York: Columbia University Press, 1982.

_____. *Uneasy at Home: Antisemitism and the American
Jewish Experience.* New York: Columbia University
Press, 1987.

_____. *Anti-Semitism in America.* New York: Oxford
University Press, 1994.

Divine, Robert A. *American Immigration Policy, 1924-1952.* New
Haven, Connecticut: Yale University Press, 1957.

Dobkowski, Michael N., ed. *The Politics of Indifference: A
Documentary History of Holocaust Victims in America.*
Washington, D.C.: University Press of America, 1982.

Dobroszycki, Lucjan. *Survivors of the Holocaust in Poland: A
Portrait Based on Jewish Community Records, 1944-
1947.* Armonk, New York: M.E. Sharpe, 1994.

Druks, Herbert. *Failure to Rescue.* New York: Speller and Sons,
1977.

_____. *Bearing Witness: How America and its Jews
Responded to the Holocaust.* Syracuse, New York:
Syracuse University Press, 1995.

Edelheit, Abraham. *The Yishuv in the Shadow of the Holocaust.*
Boulder, Colorado: Westview Press, 1996.

Eisenberg, Azriel. *Witness to the Holocaust.* New York: The
Pilgrim Press, 1981.

Eliach, Yaffa, and Brana Gurewitsch, eds. *The Liberators:
Eyewitness Accounts of the Liberation of the
Concentration Camps.* Vol. 1. New York: Center for
Holocaust Studies Documentation and Research,
1981.

Feingold, Henry L. *The Politics of Rescue: The Roosevelt
Administration and the Holocaust.* New Brunswick, New
Jersey: Rutgers University Press, 1970.

_____. *Zion In America: The Jewish Experience from
Colonial Times to the Present.* New York: Hippocrene
Books, Inc., 1974.

_____. *A Time for Searching: Entering the Mainstream,
1920-1945.* Baltimore, Maryland: Johns Hopkins
University Press, 1992.

_____. *Bearing Witness: How America and Its Jews
Responded to the Holocaust.* Syracuse, New York:
University of Syracuse Press, 1995.

Feldman, Egal. *Dual Destinies: The Jewish Encounter with Protestant America.* Urbana, Illinois: University of Illinois Press, 1990.

Finger, Seymour Maxwell, ed. *American Jewry During the Holocaust.* New York: Holmes and Meier, 1984.

Frederiksen, Oliver J. *The American Military Occupation of Germany: 1945-1953.* Frankfurt am Main, Germany: U.S. Army, 1953.

Friedenson, Joseph, and David Kranzler. *Heroine of Rescue: The Incredible Story of Recha Sternbuch, Who Saved Thousands from the Holocaust.* Brooklyn, New York: Mesorah Publications, Ltd., 1984.

_____. *Dateline: Istanbul: Dr. Jacob Griffel's Lone Odyssey through a Sea of Indifference.* Brooklyn, New York: Mesorah Publications, Ltd., 1993.

Friedlander, Henry, and Sybil Milton, gen. eds., Jonathan Helfand, ed. *Archives of the Holocaust: An International Collection of Selected Holocaust Documents.* Volume 18. New York: Garland Publishing, Inc., 1991.

Friedman. Herbert A. *Roots of the Future.* New York: Gefen Publishing House, 1999.

Friedman, Saul S. *No Haven for the Oppressed: United States Policy toward Jewish Refugees, 1938-1945.* Detroit, Michigan: Wayne State University Press, 1973.

Fry, Varian. *Surrender on Demand.* Boulder, Colorado: Johnson Books, 1997.

Fuchs, Abraham. *The Unheeded Cry: The Gripping Story of Rabbi Weissmandl, the Valiant Holocaust Leader Who Battled Both Allied Indifference and Nazi Hatred.* Brooklyn, New York: Mesorah Publications, Ltd., 1984.

Ganin, Zvi. *Truman, American Jewry, and Israel, 1945-1948.* New York: Holmes and Meier, 1979.

Gay, Ruth. *The Jews of Germany: A Historical Portrait.* New Haven, Connecticut: Yale University Press, 1992.

_____. *Safe among the Germans: Liberated Jews after World War II.* New Haven, Connecticut: Yale University Press, 2002.

Genizi, Haim. *American Apathy: The Plight of Christian Refugees From Nazism.* Jerusalem: Bar-Ilan University Press, 1983.

_____. *America's Fair Share: The Admission and Resettlement of Displaced Persons, 1945-1952.* Detroit, Michigan: Wayne State University Press, 1993.

Giere, Jacqueline, and Rachel Salamander. *Ein Leben aufs neu: das Robinson-Album: DP-Lager, Juden auf deutschem Boden 1945-1948*. Vienna: Christian Brandstätter, 1995.

Gimbel, John. *The American Occupation of Germany: Politics and the Military, 1945-1949*. Palo Alto, California: Stanford University Press, 1968.

Gottschalk, Max, and Abraham G. Duker. *Jews in the Post-War World*. New York: The Dryden Press, 1945.

Garcia-Granados, Jorge. *The Birth of Israel: The Drama As I Saw It*. New York: Alfred A. Knopf, 1948.

Greenbaum, Masha. *The Jews of Lithuania — A History of a Remarkable Community, 1316-1945*. Jerusalem: Gefen Publishing House, Ltd., 1997.

Grinberg, Zalman. *Schuchrarnu MeDachau*. Herzilya, Israel: Massada, 1948.

Grobman, Alex. *Rekindling the Flame: American Jewish Chaplains and the Survivors of European Jewry, 1944-1948*. Detroit, Michigan: Wayne State University Press, 1993.

_____. *In Defense of the Survivors: The Letters and Documents of Oscar A. Mintzer, AJDC Legal Advisor, Germany, 1945-46*. Berkeley, California: Judah L. Magnes Museum, 1999.

Gross, Jan T. *Neighbors: The Destruction of the Jewish Community in Jedwabne, Poland*. Princeton, New Jersey: Princeton University Press, 2001.

Grossman, Kurt R. *The Jewish D.P. Problem, and Its Origins and Liquidation*. New York: Institute of Jewish Affairs, World Jewish Congress, 1951.

Gutman, Yisrael, and Efraim Zuroff, eds. *Rescue Attempts During the Holocaust*. Jerusalem: Yad Vashem, 1977.

Gutman, Yisrael, and Shmuel Krakowski. *Unequal Victims: Poles and Jews During World War II*. New York: Holocaust Library, 1986.

Gutman, Yisrael, and A. Saf. *She'erit Hapleitah, 1944-1948: Rehabilitation and Political Struggle*. Jerusalem: Yad Vashem, 1990.

Halperin, Samuel. *The Political World Of American Zionism*. Detroit, Michigan: Wayne State University Press, 1961.

Halpern, Ben. *The Idea of the Jewish State*. Cambridge, Massachusetts: Harvard University Press, 1969.

_____. *A Clash of Heroes: Brandeis, Weizmann, and*

American Zionism. New York: Oxford University Press, 1987.

Handlin, Oscar A. *Continuing Task: The American Jewish Joint Distribution Committee, 1914-1964*. New York: Random House, 1964.

Hecht, Ben. *A Child of the Century*. New York: Simon and Schuster, 1954.

_____. *Perfidy*. New York: Julian Messner, Inc., 1961.

Heilbut, Anthony. *Exiled in Paradise: German Refugee Artists andIntellectuals in America, from the 1930's to the Present*. New York: Viking Press, 1983.

Helmreich, William B. *The World of The Yeshiva: An Intimate Portrait of Orthodox Jewry*. Hoboken, New Jersey: KTAV, 2000.

Hemmendinger, Judith, and Robert Krell. *The Children of Buchenwald*. Jerusalem: Gefen Publishing House, 2000.

Hertzberg, Arthur. *The Zionist Idea: A Historical Analysis and Reader*. New York: Atheneum, 1969.

_____. *The Jews in America: Four Centuries of an Uneasy Encounter: A History*. New York: Columbia University Press, 1998.

Higham, John. *Strangers in the Land: Patterns of American Nativism, 1860-1925*. New Brunswick, New Jersey: Rutgers University Press, 1988.

Hilliard, Robert L. *Surviving the Americans: The Continued Struggle of the Jews afterLiberation*. New York: Seven Stories Press, 1997.

Hirschmann, Ira. *The Embers Still Burn*. New York: Simon and Schuster, 1949.

_____. *Life Line to a Promised Land*. New York: Vanguard Press, 1946.

Hochstein, Joseph M., and Murray Greenfield. *The Jews' Secret Fleet*. New York: Gefen Publishing House, 1993.

Holborn, Louise W. *The International Refugee Organization*. London: Oxford University Press, 1956.

Howe, Irving. *World of Our Fathers: The Journey of the East European Jews to America and the Life They Found and Made*. New York: Harcourt Brace Jovanovich, 1976.

Howley, Frank. *Berlin Command*. New York: G.P. Putnam's Sons, 1950.

Hyman, Abraham S. *The Undefeated: The Story of the Jewish*

Displaced Persons. New York: Gefen Publishing House, 1993.

Isenberg, Sheila. *A Hero of Our Own: The Story of Varian Fry.* New York: Random House, 2001.

Israel, Fred L. *The War Diaries of Breckinridge Long.* Lincoln, Nebraska: University of Nebraska Press, 1965.

Kaufman, Menahem. *An Ambiguous Partnership: Non-Zionists and Zionists in America, 1939-1948.* Jerusalem: Magnes Press, 1991.

Kertzer, Morris N. *With an H on My Dog Tag.* New York: Behrman House, 1947.

Kimche, Jon and David. *The Secret Roads: The "Illegal" Migration of a People, 1938- 1948.* Garden City, New York: Farrar, Strauss, and Cudahy, 1955.

Klein, Isaac. *The Anguish and the Ecstasy of a Jewish Chaplain.* New York: Vantage Press, 1974.

Kluger, Ruth, and Peggy Mann. *The Last Escape: The Launching of the Largest Secret Rescue Movement of All Time.* Garden City, New York: Doubleday, 1973.

Kochavi, Arieh J. *Post-Holocaust Politics: Britain, the United States, and Jewish Refugees, 1945-1948.* Chapel Hill, North Carolina: University of North Carolina Press, 2001.

_____. *Prelude to Nuremberg: Allied War Crimes Policy and the Question of Punishment.* Chapel Hill, North Carolina: University of North Carolina Press, 1998.

Kranzler, David. *Holocaust Hero: Solomon Schonfeld* (Jersey City, NJ: KTAV,2004)

_____. *Japanese, Nazis and Jews: The Jewish Refugee Community of Shanghai, 1938-45.* New York: Yeshiva University Press, 1976.

_____. *Thy Brother's Blood: The Orthodox Jewish Response During the Holocaust.* Brooklyn, New York: Mesorah Publications, Ltd., 1987.

_____. *The Man who Stopped the Trains to Auschwitz: George Mantello, El Salvador, and Switzerland's Finest Hour.* Syracuse, New York: Syracuse University Press, 2000.

Kuklick, Bruce. *American Policy and the Division of Germany: The Clash with Russia over Reparations.* Ithaca, New York: Cornell University Press, 1972.

Laqueur, Walter. *The Terrible Secret: Suppression of the Truth About Hitler's 'Final Solution.'* Boston, MA: Little,

Brown and Company, 1980.

_____. *Generation Exodus: The Fate of Young Refugees from Nazi Germany.* Hanover, New Hampshire: Brandeis University Press, 2001.

Laqueur, Walter, and Richard Breitman. *Breaking the Silence.* New York: Simon and Schuster, 1986.

Lavsky, Hagit. *New Beginnings: Holocaust Survivors in Bergen-Belsen and the British Zone in Germany, 1945-1950.* Detroit, Michigan: Wayne State University Press, 2002.

Levin, Dov. *The Lesser of Two Evils: Eastern European Jewry Under Soviet Rule, 1939-1941.* Philadelphia, PA: The Jewish Publication Society, 1995.

Levin, Meyer. *In Search.* New York: Horizon, 1950.

Levine, Hillel. *In Search of Sugihara: The Elusive Japanese Diplomat Who Risked His Life to Rescue 10,000 Jews from the Holocaust.* New York: The Free Press, 1996.

Lipstadt, Deborah H. *Beyond Belief: The American Press and the Coming of the Holocaust, 1933-1945.* New York: The Free Press, 1986.

Loftus, John, and Mark Aarons. *The Secret War Against the Jews: How Western Espionage Betrayed the Jewish People.* New York: St. Martin's Press, 1994.

Lookstein, Haskel. *Were We Our Brothers' Keepers: The Public Response of American Jews to the Holocaust, 1938-1944.* New York: Vintage Press, 1985.

Lowenstein, Sharon R. *Token Refuge: The Story of the Jewish Refugee Shelter at Oswego, 1944-1946.* Bloomington, Indiana: Indiana University Press, 1986.

Mankowitz, Zeev W. *Life between Memory and Hope: The Survivors of the Holocaust in Occupied Germany.* Cambridge: Cambridge University Press, 2002.

Marcus, Jacob Rader, and Abraham J. Peck, eds. *Among the Survivors of the Holocaust, 1945: The Landsberg DP Camp Letters of Major Irving Heymont, United States Army.* Cincinnati, Ohio: American Jewish Archives, 1982.

Mario, Andy. *A Quiet American: The Secret War of Varian Fry.* New York: St. Martin's Press, 1999.

Marrus, Michael R. *The Unwanted: European Refugees in the Twentieth Century.* New York: Oxford University Press, 1985.

McNeill, W.H. *Survey of International Affairs 1939-1946.* London: Oxford University Press, 1953.

Medoff, Rafael. *The Deafening Silence: American Jewish Leaders and the Holocaust.* New York: Shapolsky, 1987.

_____. *Militant Zionism in America: The Rise and Impact of the Jabotinsky Movement in the United States, 1926-1948.* Tuscaloosa, Alabama: The University of Alabama Press, 2002.

Merritt, Anna J., and Richard L. Merritt, eds. *Public Opinion In Occupied Germany: The OMGUS Surveys, 1945-1949.* Champaign-Urbana, Illinois: University of Illinois Press, 1970.

Merritt, Richard L. *Democracy Imposed: U.S. Occupation Policy and the German Public, 1945-1949.* New Haven, Connecticut: Yale University Press, 1995.

Morrison, David. *Heroes, Antiheroes, and the Holocaust: American Jewry and Historical Choice.* New London, New Hampshire: Milah Press, 1995.

Nadich, Judah. *Eisenhower and the Jews.* New York: Twayne, 1953.

Neuringer, Sheldon Morris. *American Jewry and the United States Immigration Policy, 1881-1953.* New York: Ayer Company Publishers, 1981.

Newton, Verne W., ed. *FDR and the Holocaust.* New York: St. Martin's Press, 1996.

O'Brien, Conner Cruise. *The Siege: The Saga of Israel and Zionism.* New York: Simon and Schuster, 1986.

Ofer, Dalia. *Escaping the Holocaust: Illegal Immigration to the Land of Israel: 1939-1944.* New York: Oxford University Press, 1990.

Patton, George. *Patton Papers, 1940-1945.* New York: Da Capo Press, 1996.

Pekier, Alter. *From Kletzk To Siberia: A Yeshivah Bachur's Wanderings During the Holocaust.* Brooklyn, New York: Mesorah Publications, 1985.

Penkower, Monty Noam. *The Jews Were Expendable: Free World Diplomacy and the Holocaust.* Urbana, Illinois: University of Illinois Press, 1983.

_____. *The Holocaust and Israel Reborn.* Urbana, Illinois: University of Illinois Press, 1994.

_____. *Decision on Palestine Deferred: America, Britain, and Wartime Diplomacy, 1939-1945.* London: Frank Cass Publishers, 2002.

Peterson, Edward N. *The American Occupation of Germany: Retreat to Victory.* Detroit, Michigan: Wayne State

University Press, 1977.

Persico, Joseph E. *Roosevelt's Secret War: FDR and World War II Espionage*. New York: Random House, 2001.

Porges, Yom Tov. *Mirrer Yeshiva*. B'nei Brak: Mishor Publications, 2001.

Porush, Menachem Glickman. *Ish Hahalacha V'hamaseh*. Jerusalem: Sapira, 1946-1947.

Pritte, Terence. *Germany Divided: The Legacy of the Nazi Era*. Boston, Massachusetts: Little, Brown and Company, 1960.

Proudfoot, Malcolm J. *European Refugees, 1939-52*. London: Faber and Faber, 1957.

Rakeffet-Rothkoff, Aaron. *Bernard Revel: Builder of American Jewish Orthodoxy*. Nanuet, New York: Feldheim, 1981.

_____. *The Silver Era in American Jewish Orthodoxy: Eliezer Silver and His Generation*. New York: Yeshiva University Press; Feldheim, 2000.

Raphael, Marc Lee. *Abba Hillel Silver: A Profile in American Judaism*. New York: Holmes & Meier Publishing, Inc., 1989.

Rapoport, Louis. *Shake Heaven and Earth: Peter Bergson and the Struggle to Rescue the Jews of Europe*. Jerusalem: Gefen Publishing House, 1999.

Redlich, Shimon. *War, Holocaust, and Stalinism: A Documented Study of the Jewish Anti-Fascist Committee in the USSR*. Luxembourg: Harwood Academic Publishers, 1995.

Reznikoff, Charles, ed. *Louis Marshall, Champion of Liberty*. Philadelphia, Pennsylvania: Jewish Publication Society, 1957.

Rosenblum, Yonason. *They Called Him Mike: Reb Elemelech Tress, His Era, Hatzalah, and the Building of an American Orthodoxy*. Brooklyn, New York: Mesorah Publications, Ltd., 1995.

Rosensaft, Menachem Z., ed., *Life Reborn: Jewish Displaced Persons, 1945-1951*. Washington, D.C.: United States Holocaust Memorial Museum, 2001.

Ross, Robert W. *So It Was True: The American Protestant Press and the Nazi Persecution of the Jews, 1933-1945*. Minneapolis, Minnesota: University of Minnesota Press, 1980.

Rubenstein, Joshua, and Vladimir P. Naumov, eds. *Stalin's Secret Pogrom: The Postwar Inquisition of the Jewish Anti-Fascist Committee*. New Haven, Connecticut: Yale

University Press, 2001.

Rubenstein, William D. *The Myth of Rescue: Why the Democracies Could Not Have Saved More Jews from the Nazis.* New York: Routledge, 1997.

Sakamoto, Pamela Rotner. *Japanese Diplomats and Jewish Refugees: A World War II Dilemma.* Westport, Connecticut: Greenwood Publishing Company, 1998.

Schachner, Nathan. *The Price of Liberty: A History of the American Jewish Committee.* New York: American Jewish Committee, 1948.

Schechtman, Joseph. *Postwar Population Transfers in Europe 1945-1955.* Philadelphia, Pennsylvania: University of Pennsylvania Press, 1962.

Schwartz, Leo. *The Root and the Bough.* New York: Farrar, Strauss and Young, 1949.

_____. *The Redeemers: The Saga of the Years 1945-1952.* New York: Farrar, Strauss and Young, 1953.

Segev, Tom. *The Seventh Million: The Israelis and the Holocaust.* New York: Hill and Wang, 1993.

Shachtman, Tom. *I Seek My Brethren: Ralph Goldman and "The Joint": Rescue, Relief, and Reconstruction—The Work of the American Jewish Joint Distribution Committee.* New York: Newmarket Press, 2001.

Shafir, Shlomo. *Ambiguous Relations: The American Jewish Community and Germany Since 1945.* Detroit, Michigan: Wayne State University Press, 1999.

Sharf, Andrew. *The British Press and Jews Under Nazi Rule.* New York: Oxford University Press, 1964.

Sharp, Tony. *The Wartime Alliance and the Zonal Division of Germany.* New York: Oxford University Press, 1975.

Sherman, Andrew J. *Island Refuge: Britain and Refugees from the Third Reich, 1933-1939.* Berkeley, California: University of California Press, 1973.

Shimoni, Gideon. *The Zionist Ideology.* Lebanon, New Hampshire: Brandeis University Press; University Press of New England, 1995.

Shlaim, Avi. *The United States and the Berlin Blockade, 1948-1949: A Study in Crisis Decision-Making.* Berkeley, California: University of California Press, 1989.

Shpiro, David H. *From Philanthropy To Activism: The Political Transformation of American Zionism in the Holocaust Years, 1933-1945.* New York: Pergamon Press, 1994.

Smyser, W.R. *From Yalta to Berlin: The Cold War Struggle over*

Germany. New York: St. Martin's Press, 1999.

Stember, Charles H., ed. *Jews in the Mind of America*. New York: Basic Books, 1966.

Stern, Frank. *The Whitewashing of the Yellow Badge: Antisemitism and Philosemitism in Postwar Germany*. New York: Oxford University Press, 1991.

Stevens, Richard P. *American Zionism and U.S. Foreign Policy, 1942-1947*. New York: Pageant Press, 1962.

Stewart, Barbara McDonald. *United States Government Policy on Refugees from Nazism, 1933-1940*. New York: Garland, 1982.

Stone, Isidor F. *Underground to Palestine*. New York: Boni and Gaer, 1946.

Strauss, Herbert A. *Jewish Immigrants of the Nazi Period in the U.S.A.* Vol. 3 of *Classified Lists of Articles Concerning Immigration in Germany*. New York: K.G. Saur, 1982.

Tartakower, Arieh, and Kurt R. Grossman. *The Jewish Refugee*. New York: Institute of Jewish Affairs, 1944.

Tobias, Sigmund. *Strange Haven: A Jewish Childhood in Wartime Shanghai*. Urbana, Illinois: University of Illinois Press, 1999.

Truman, Harry S. *Memoirs: Years of Decision*. New York: Doubleday, 1955.

Touster, Saul, ed. *A Survivors' Haggadah*. Philadelphia, Pennsylvania: The Jewish Publication Society, 2000.

Tsamriyon, Tsemah. *The Press of the Holocaust Survivors in Germany as Expression of Their Problems*. Tel-Aviv: Organization of Holocaust Survivors from the British Zone, 1970.

Urofsky, Melvin I. *A Voice that Spoke for Justice: The Life and Times of Stephen S. Wise*. Albany, New York: State University of New York Press, 1982.

U.S. Department of the Army. *Fraternization with the Germans in World War II*. Frankfurt am Main: Department of the Army, 1947.

U.S. Seventh Army Staff, Michael W. Perry, ed. *Dachau Liberated: The Official Report*. Seattle, Washington: Inkling Books, 2000.

Vida, George. *From Doomed to Dawn: A Jewish Chaplain's Story of Displaced Persons*. New York: Jonathan David, 1967.

Voss, Carl Hermann, ed. *Stephen S. Wise: Servant of the People*. Philadelphia, Pennsylvania: The Jewish Publication Society of America, 1969.

Wall, Irwin M. *The United States and the Making of Postwar France, 1945-1954.* New York: Cambridge University Press, 1991.

Warhaftig, Zorach. *Relief and Rehabilitation: Implications of the UNRRA Program for Jewish Needs.* New York: Institute of Jewish Affairs, 1944.

_____. *Uprooted: Jewish Refugees and Displaced Persons After Liberation.* New York: Institute of Jewish Affairs, 1946.

Wasserstein, Bernard. *Britain and the Jews of Europe, 1939-1945.* London: Clarendon Press, 1979.

_____. *Vanishing Diaspora: The Jews in Europe Since 1945.* Cambridge, Massachusetts: Harvard University Press, 1996.

Wischnitzer, Mark. *To Dwell in Safety: The Story of Jewish Migration Since 1800.* Philadelphia, Pennsylvania: JewishPublication Society of America, 1948.

_____. *Visas to Freedom: The History of HIAS.* New York: World, 1956.

Wistrich, Robert S. *Antisemitism: The Longest Hatred.* New York: Schocken Books, 1991.

Woodridge, George. *UNRRA.* 3 vols. New York: Columbia University Press, 1950.

Wyman, David S. *Paper Walls: America and the Refugee Crisis, 1938-1941.* Amherst, Massachusetts: University of Massachusetts Press, 1968.

_____. *The Abandonment of the Jews: America and the Holocaust.* New York: Pantheon, 1984.

_____. Wyman, David S., and Rafael Medoff. *A Race against Death: Peter Bergson, America, and the Holocaust.* New York: The New Press, 2002.

Wyman, Mark. *DP: Europe's Displaced Persons, 1945-1951.* Philadelphia, Pennsylvania: Cornell University Press, 1989.

Zaar, Isaac. *Rescue and Liberation.* New York: Bloch, 1954.

Zertal, Idith. *From Catastrophe to Power: Holocaust Survivors and the Emergence of Israel.* Berkeley, California: University of California Press, 1998.

Ziemke, Earl F. *The U.S. Army in the Occupation of Germany, 1944-46.* Washington, D.C.: Center of Military History, 1975.

Zinberg, Alizah, Barbara Martin, and Roger Kohn. *Inventory to the Rescue Children, Inc., Collection 1946-1985.* New

York: Yeshiva University Archives.

Zink, Harold. *American Military Government in Germany.* New York: Macmillan, 1947.

_____. *The United States in Germany, 1945-1955.* Princeton, New Jersey: D. Van Nostrand, 1957.

Zucker, Bat-Ami. *In Search of Refuge: Jews and U.S. Consuls in Nazi Germany.* Portland, Oregon: Vallentine Mitchell, 2000.

Zuroff, Efraim. *Response of Orthodox Jewry in the United States to the Holocaust: Vaad ha-Hatzala Rescue Committee, 1939-1945.* Hoboken, New Jersey: KTAV Publishing House, Inc., 2000.

Articles

Albrich, Thomas. "Way Station of Exodus: Jewish Displaced Persons and the Refugees in Post-War Austria." *The Holocaust and History: The Known, the Unknown, the Disputed, and the Reexamined.* Ed. Michael Berenbaum and Abraham J. Peck. Bloomington, Indiana: University of Indiana Press, 1998.

Alpert, Carl. "We Don't Know the Meaning of Sacrifice." *Jewish Spectator* (June 1946).

Altman, Avraham, and Irene Eber. "Flight to Shanghai, 1938-1940: The Larger Setting." *Yad Vashem Studies* 28 (2000).

Altshuler, Mordecai. "The Jewish Antifascist Committee in the USSR in the Light Of New Documentation." *Studies in Contemporary Jewry* 1 (1984).

Arad, Yitzhak. "Concentration of Refugees in Vilna." *Yad Vashem Studies* 9 (1973).

Arendt, Hannah. "The Stateless People." *Contemporary Jewish Record* (April 1945).

Auerbach, Jerold S. "Joseph M. Proskauer: American Court Jew." *American Jewish History* (September 1979).

Baron, Salo. "The Spiritual Reconstruction of European Jewry." *Commentary* (November 1945).

Barzel, Neima. "The Attitude of Jews of German Origin in Israel to Germany and Germans after the Holocaust, 1945-1952." *Leo Baeck Institute Year Book* 39 (1994).

Bauer, Yehuda. "When Did They Know?" *Midstream* (April 1968).

_____. "The Initial Organization of the Holocaust

n Bavaria." *Yad Vashem Studies* 8 (1970).
ue Operations Through Vilna." *Yad Vashem*
1973).
Holocaust and American Jewry." *The*
n *Historical Perspective.* Seattle, Washington:
ɔf Washington Press, 1978.
Goldberg Report." *Midstream* (February

ʻdor. "The Politics of Spiritual Rehabilitation
ʼamps." *Simon Wiesenthal Center Annual* 6

ɔutz Buchenwald and Kibbutz Hafetz
ʻo Experiments in the Rehabilitation of
ʻivors in Germany." *Holocaust and Genocide*
(1995).
ɔutz Buchenwald: The Establishment of the
First *Hachsharah.*" *YIVO Annual of Jewish Social
Science* 23 (1996).
Becher, Frank W. "David Wyman and the Historiography of
America's Response to the Holocaust: Counter
Considerations." *Holocaust and Genocide Studies* 5.4
(1990).
Benz, Wolfgang. "Germans, Jews, and Anti-Semitism in
Germany after 1945." *Journal of Politics and History*
41.1 (1995).
Bernard, William S., and Abraham G. Duker. "Who Killed Cock
Robin? — The DP Act Discussed." *The Day* [New York]
29 Aug. 1948.
Bernstein, Philip S. "Jewish Chaplains in World War II."
American Jewish Year Book 47 (1945-1946).
_____. "Displaced Persons." *American Jewish Year Book*
49 (1947-1948).
Brody, David. "American Jewry: The Refugees and Immigration
Restriction, 1932-1942." *American Jewish Historical
Quarterly* (June 1956).
Carlebach, Julius. "Flight into Action as a Method of
Repression: American Military Rabbis and the Problem
of Jewish DPs." *Jewish Studies Quarterly* 2.1 (1995).
Cohen, Henry. "Life in a DP Camp." *Congress Weekly* (January
3, 1947).
_____. "The 'Jewish' Displaced Persons." *Jewish
Frontier* (March 1947).
_____. "The International Refugee Organization."

Jewish Frontier (May 1947).

Cohen, Naomi. "Anti-Semitism in the Gilded Age: The Jewish View." *Jewish Social Studies* (Summer/Fall 1979).

Dawidowicz, Lucy S. "Indicting American Jews." *Commentary* (September 1983).

_____. "Could America Have Rescued Europe's Jews?" *What is The Use of Jewish History?* Ed. Neal Kozodoy. New York: Schocken Books, 1992.

Dinnerstein, Leonard. "Anti-Semitism in the Eightieth Congress: The Displaced Persons Act of 1948." *Capitol Studies* 6.2 (Fall 1973).

_____. "The U.S. Army and the DP's Policies toward the Displaced Persons after World War II." *American Jewish History* 68.3 (March 1979).

Dobroszycki, Lucjan. "Restoring Jewish Life in Postwar Poland." *Soviet Jewish Affairs* [London] 3 (1973).

Duker, Abraham G. "Admitting Pogromists and Excluding Their Victims." *Reconstructionist* (October 1, 1948).

Dunner, Joseph. "The Jews That Remain." *Nation* (July 6, 1946).

Dushkin, Alexander M. "The Educational Activities of the JDC in European Countries." *Jewish Social Studies Quarterly* (June 1949).

"Executive Director Details HIAS Services." *Rescue* (February-March 1947).

Fay, Sidney B. "Displaced Persons in Europe." *Current History* (March 1946).

Feingold, Henry L. "Roosevelt and the Holocaust: Reflections on the New Deal Humanitarianism." *Judaism* (Summer 1969).

_____. "Who Shall Bear the Guilt for the Holocaust: The Human Dilemma." *American Jewish History* (March 1979).

_____. "Stephen Wise and the Holocaust." *Midstream* (January 1983).

_____. "'Courage First and Intelligence Second': The American Jewish Secular Elite, Roosevelt, and the Failure to Resist." *American Jewish History* (June 1983).

_____. "Did American Jewry Do Enough During the Holocaust?" The B.G. Rudolph Lectures in Judaic Studies. Syracuse University, Syracuse, New York. April 1985.

Flowerman, Samuel H., and Marie Jahoda. "Polls on Anti-Semitism." *Commentary* (April 1946).

Foster, Arnold, W. "Displaced Persons in Germany: UNRRA's Cooperation with the Armies." *Army Quarterly* (January 1946).

Friedman, Philip. "The Road Back for the DPs." *Commentary* (December 1948).

Genêt. "Letter from Aschaffenburg." *The New Yorker* 24 (October Bibliography 30, 1948).

Genizi, Haim. "New York is Big — America is Bigger: The Resettlement of Refugees from Nazism, 1936-1945." *Jewish Social Studies* 46 (Winter 1984).

_____. "Philip S. Bernstein: Advisor on Jewish Affairs, 1946-1947." *Simon Wiesenthal Center Annual* 3 (1986).

Giere, Jacqueline D. "We're on Our Way, but Not in the Wilderness." *The Holocaust and History: The Known, the Unknown, the Disputed, and the Reexamined.* Ed. Michael Berenbaum and Abraham J. Peck. Bloomington, Indiana: University of Indiana Press (1998).

Goldfeder, Pinchas. "A Practical Scheme To Settle the DP's." *Commentary* (August 1948).

Gilson, Estelle. "The Fate of the Roman Jewish Libraries. " *October 16, 1943: Eight Jews.* Giacomo Debenedetti. South Bend, Indiana: University of Notre Dame Press, 2001.

Greenberg, Gershon. "From *Hurban* to Redemption: Orthodox Jewish Thought in the Munich Area, 1945-1948." *Simon Wiesenthal Center Annual* 6 (1989).

_____. "Yehuda Leib Gerst's Religious 'Ascent' Through the Holocaust." *Holocaust and Genocide Studies* (Spring 1999).

Gringauz, Samuel. "Jewish Destiny as the DP's See It." *Commentary* (December 1947).

_____. Our New German Policy and the DP's." *Commentary* (June 1948).

Grobman, Alex. "Jewish GI's and Holocaust Survivors." *Jewish Spectator* (Spring 1978).

_____. "What Did They Know?' The American Jewish Press and the Holocaust." *American Jewish History* 68 (March 1979).

Gruss, Emanuel. "In a Camp For Displaced Jews." *Congress Weekly* (June 29, 1945).

Gurock, Jeffrey S. "Resisters and Accommodators: Varieties of Orthodox Rabbis in America, 1886-1983. " *American*

Jewish Archives 35 (November 1983).

Hadarom Hapardes (1939-1947).

Harrison, Earl G. "Hospitality with Limits: Displaced Persons Act of 1948." *Survey Graphics* (November 1948).

———. "The Harrison Report." *The Department of State Bulletin* 13 (September 30, 1945).

Henkin, Yehuda Herzl. "Hagoen Yosef Eliyahu Henkin." *Hadarom* 50 (May 2000).

Hyman, Abraham S. "Displaced Persons." *American Jewish Year Book* 50 (1948-1949).

Kagan, Shaul. "Reb Aharon Kotler: Ten Years After His Passing." *Jewish Observer* (May 1973).

———. "From Kletzk to Lakewood." *The Torah World: A Treasury of Biographical Sketches*. Ed. Nisson Wolpin. New York: Mesorah Publications, 1982.

Katz, Shlomo. "No Hope Except Exodus." *Commentary* (April 1946).

———. "The Jewish 'Displaced Persons.'" *Jewish Frontier* (July 1946).

Knox, Israel. "Is America Exile or Home?" *Commentary* (November 1946).

Kochavi, Arieh J. "The Displaced Persons' Problem and the Formulation of British Policy in Palestine." *Studies of Zionism* 10 (1989).

———. "British Policy Toward East European Refugees in Germany and Austria, 1945-1947." *Simon Wiesenthal Center Annual* 7 (1990).

———. "Anglo-American Discord: Jewish Refugees and the United Nations Relief and Rehabilitation Administration Policy, 1945-1947." *Diplomatic History* 14 (Fall 1990).

Kol Yisroel Bagolah [Munich] 1-20 (1947-1948).

Korman, Gerd. "Survivors' Talmud and the U.S. Army." *American Jewish History* 73 (March 1984).

Kranzler, David. "Stephen S. Wise and the Holocaust." *Reverence, Righteousness, and Rahamanut*. Ed. Jacob J. Schacter. Northvale, New Jersey: Jason Aronson, Inc., 1992.

———. "The Grand Escape from Lithuania to Japan. *The Jewish Observer* (June 2000).

Liebman, Charles S. "Orthodoxy in Nineteenth Century America." *Tradition* 6 (Spring-Summer 1964).

Mankowitz, Ze'ev. "The Affirmation of Life in *She'erith Hapleita*."

Holocaust and Genocide Studies 5 (1990).

_____. "The Formation of *She'erit Hapleita*: November 1944-July 1945." *Yad Vashem Studies* 20 (1990).

Margolis, Laura. "Race against Time in Shanghai." *Jewish Spectator* 9 (May 1944).

Penkower, Monty Noam. "In Dramatic Dissent: The Bergson Boys." *American Jewish History* 70.3 (March 1981).

_____. "Ben-Gurion, Silver, and UPA National Conference for Palestine: A Turning Point in American Zionist History." *American Jewish History* (September 1979).

_____. "American Jewry and the Holocaust: From Biltmore to the American Jewish Conference." *Jewish Social Studies* 67 (Spring 1985).

Neuburger, Gottfried. "An Orthodox G.I. Fights a War." *Commentary* (March 1949).

Peck, Abraham J. "The Displaced." *Dimensions* 9 (1995).

Pinsky, Edward. "American Jewish Unity during the Holocaust — The Joint Emergency Committee, 1943." *American Jewish History* 72.4 (June 1983).

Pinson, Koppel S. "Jewish Life in Liberated Germany." *Jewish Social Studies* 9 (1947).

Reich, Nathan. "Overseas Aid." *American Jewish Year Book* 49 (1947-1948).

Rifkind, Simon H. "The Disinherited Jews of Europe Must Be Saved." *American Jewish Conference* (April 2, 1946).

Rothkoff, Aaron. "The 1924 Visit of the Rabbinical Delegation to the United States of America." *Masmid* (1959).

Safrai, Shumel. "The Era of the Mishnah and Talmud (70-640)." *A History of the Jewish People.* Ed. Hillel H. Ben-Sasson. Cambridge, Massachusetts: Harvard University Press, 1976.

Schwartz, Leo W. "The DP's: Fiction and Fact." *American Zionist* 43.15 (June 1953).

_____."Summary Analysis of AJDC Program in the U.S. Zone of Occupation, Germany." *Menorah* (Spring 1947).

_____. "When Liberation Came." *Congress Weekly* (May 24, 1965).

Shalitan, Lavi. "To the American G.I." Trans. Abraham J. Klausner. *Menorah Journal* 35 (1947).

Spiegel, Yisroel. "Who Did the Rescuing During the Holocaust? Part I." *Yated Ne'eman* [Israeli ed.] (May 4, 2001).

_____. "Who Did the Rescuing During the Holocaust?

Part II." *Yated Ne'eman* [Israeli ed.] (May 11, 2001).

Srole, Leo. "Landsberg: A Vibrant Community Emerges from Rubble." *Hadassah Magazine* (December 1946).

_____. "Why the DP's Can't Wait." *Commentary* (January 1947).

Starr, Joshua. "Jewish Cultural Property under Nazi Control." *Jewish Social Studies* 12 (January 1950).

Syrkin, Marie. " I Met A Black Marketeer." *Jewish Frontier* (August 1947).

_____. "Two DP Children." *Pioneer Woman* (October 1947).

_____. "DP Schools." *Jewish Frontier* (March 19, 1948).

_____. "My DP Students." *Jewish Frontier* (June 1965).

_____. "Reaction to News of the Holocaust." *Midstream* (May 1968).

_____. "What American Jews Did during the Holocaust." *Midstream* (October 1982).

Szajkowski, Zosa. "Letter from Europe." *Jewish Frontier* (October 1945).

_____. "Jewish Relief in Eastern Europe, 1914-1917." *Leo Baeck Institute Year Book* 10 (1965).

_____. "Disunity in the Distribution of American Jewish Overseas Relief, 1919-1939." *American Jewish Historical Quarterly* 58.3 (March 1969).

_____. "Concord and Discord in American Overseas Relief, 1914-1924." *YIVO Annual of Jewish Social Science* 14 (1969).

_____. "The Attitude of American Jews to Refugees from Germany in the 1930's." *American Jewish Historical Quarterly* 61 (December 1971).

Tartakower, Aryeh. "UNRRA and the Jewish Case." *Jewish Frontier* (December 1943).

_____. "The Critical Task Ahead." *Congress Weekly* (June 30, 1944).

_____. "The UNRRA Program and Jewish Needs." *Congress Weekly* (September 15, 1944).

_____. "The Future of the Jew in Europe." *Congress Weekly* (December 29, 1944).

_____. "Jews in 'New Europe'." *Jewish Frontier* (July 1945).

_____. "The Displaced and Destitute." *Jewish Frontier* (January 1946).

_____. "The Less-Than-DPs." *Jewish Frontier* (August 1947).

_____. "The Stratton Bill." *Jewish Frontier* (August 1947).

Taylor, Maurice. "Jewish Community Organization and Jewish Community Life." *YIVO Annual of Jewish Social Science* 9 (1954).

Tuck, W. H. "UNRRA Polls: Displaced Jews on Migration Plans; First Vote Shows Palestine is Favored." *JTA Daily News Bulletin* (February 3, 1946).

_____. "Year of Decision of the DP's." *Rescue* (January 1948).

Unsdorfor, S. B. "Vignettes from the DP Camps." *Congress Weekly* (October 25, 1946).

Urofsky, Melvin I. "Stephen Wise and the Holocaust." *American Zionist* (May 1974).

_____. *Midstream* "American Jewry and the Holocaust: Stephen Wise and His Critics," *Jewish Frontier* (October 1981).

Warren, Helen."Jottings from Germany." *Jewish Frontier* (November 1945;March-April 1946).

Wasserstein, Bernard. "The JDC During the Holocaust." *Midstream* (February 1985).

_____. "The Myth of 'Jewish Silence'." *Midstream* (August-September 1980).

Webster, Ronald. "American Relief and Jews in Germany, 1945-1960: Diverging Perspectives." *Leo Baeck Institute Year Book* 38 (1993).

_____. "Why They Returned, How They Fared: Jews in Germany After 1945." *YIVO Annual of Jewish Social Science* (1993).

Werner, Alfred. "Defeat by Anti-Semitism." *Congress Weekly* (October 8, 1943).

_____. "When Will the DP's Be Admitted?" *Commonweal* (February 6, 1948).

Wise, Jonah B., and James O. Heller. "One Million Jews." *National Jewish Monthly* (June 1945).

Wyman, David. "Letters to the Editor." *New York Times Magazine* (May 23, 1982).

Yahil, Haim. "The Activities of the Palestine Mission for *She'erit Hapleitah*, 1945-1949." *Yalkut Moreshet* 30 (November 1980, April 1981).

"Yoman Exodus." *Yalkut Moreshet* (March 1968).

Ziv-Av, Yitchak. "The JDC Must Explain." *Congress Weekly* (November 23, 1945).

Zuroff, Efraim. "Attempts to Obtain Shanghai Permits in 1941: A Case of Rescue Priority During the Holocaust." *Yad Vashem Studies* 12 (1979).

_____. "Rabbis Relief and Rescue: A Case Study of the Activities of the Vaad ha-Hatzala of the American Orthodox Rabbis, 1942-1943." *Simon Wiesenthal Center Annual* 3 (1986).

_____. "Rescue Priorities and Fundraising as Issues during the Holocaust: A Case Study of the Relations between the Vaad ha-Hatzalah and the Joint, 1939-1941." *American Jewish Historical Quarterly* 68 (March 1979).

_____. "Rescue Via the Far East: The Attempt to Save Polish Rabbis and Yeshivah Students, 1939-1941." *Simon Wiesenthal Center Annual* 1 (1984).

Zweig, Ronald. "Restitution and the Problem of Jewish Displaced Persons in Anglo-American Relations, 1944-1948." *American Jewish History* 78 (1988).

Index

About the author

Alex Grobman is a historian with an MA and Ph.D. in contemporary Jewish history from the Hebrew University in Jerusalem. He is president of the Institute for Contemporary Jewish Life and the Brenn Institute, think tanks dealing with historical and contemporary issues that affect the Jewish community. He is a member of the academic board of the David S. Wyman Institute for Holocaust Studies and a contributing editor of *Together*, the publication of the American Gathering of Jewish Holocaust Survivors, Inc.

He served as the director of the first Federation-funded Holocaust center in the U.S., in St. Louis, Missouri, and later as a director of the Simon Wiesenthal Center in Los Angeles—where he was founding editor-in chief of the Simon Wiesenthal Annual, the first scholarly series in the United States focusing on the Holocaust. Grobman co-edited *Genocide: Critical Issues of the Holocaust*, a companion to the Center's Academy Award-winning film.

Rekindling the Flame: American Jewish Chaplains and the Survivors of European Jewry, 1944-1948 was published in 1993. Grobman edited *In Defense of the Survivors: The Letters and Documents of Oscar A. Mintzer AJDC Legal Advisor, Germany, 1945-46*. His last book, in 2000, was co-authored with Michael Shermer and titled *Denying History: Who Says the Holocaust Never Happened, and Why Do They Say It?* It was published by University of California Press in Berkeley. He has also edited three teaching tools: *Anne Frank in Historical Perspective*; *Those Who Dared: Rescuers and Rescued*, and *A Guide to Schindler's List*.

Grobman is currently working on a book on responses to Arab propaganda and is training a number of Jewish students to combat Arab propaganda on American college campuses.

Grobman lives in Northern New Jersey with his wife Marlene. Their three sons and families live in Jerusalem.